CITIZENSHIP, ALIENAGE AND THE MODERN CONSTITUTIONAL STATE

To have a nationality is a human right. But between the nineteenth and mid-twentieth centuries, virtually every country in the world adopted laws that stripped citizenship from women who married foreign men. Despite the resulting hardships and even statelessness experienced by married women, it took until 1957 for the international community to condemn the practice, with the adoption of the United Nations Convention on the Nationality of Married Women. *Citizenship, Alienage, and the Modern Constitutional State* tells the important yet neglected story of marital denaturalisation from a comparative perspective. Examining denaturalisation laws and their impact on women around the world, with a focus on Australia, Britain, Canada, Ireland, New Zealand and the United States, it advances a concept of citizenship as profoundly personal and existential. In doing so, it sheds light on both a specific chapter of legal history and the theory of citizenship in general.

HELEN IRVING is Professor of Law in the Faculty of Law at The University of Sydney and a Fellow of the Academy of Social Sciences in Australia, and of the Australian Academy of Law. She has published widely on constitutional law, history, and citizenship, most recently with a particular focus on gender. Her 2008 book, *Gender and the Constitution*, was published by Cambridge University Press.

CITIZENSHIP, ALIENAGE AND THE MODERN CONSTITUTIONAL STATE

A Gendered History

HELEN IRVING

CAMBRIDGE
UNIVERSITY PRESS

CAMBRIDGE
UNIVERSITY PRESS

University Printing House, Cambridge CB2 8BS, United Kingdom

Cambridge University Press is part of the University of Cambridge.

It furthers the University's mission by disseminating knowledge in the pursuit of education, learning and research at the highest international levels of excellence.

www.cambridge.org
Information on this title: www.cambridge.org/9781107065109

First published 2016

A catalogue record for this publication is available from the British Library

Library of Congress Cataloging in Publication data
Irving, Helen, author.
Citizenship, alienage, and the modern constitutional state : a gendered history / Helen Irving.
New York : Cambridge University Press, 2016.
LCCN 2015039218 ISBN 9781107065109 (hardback)
LCSH: Married women – Nationality. Citizenship. Women's rights.
Women – Legal status, laws, etc. BISAC: LAW / Constitutional.
LCC K3230.W6 I78 2016
DDC 342.08/3082 – dc23
LC record available at http://lccn.loc.gov/2015039218

ISBN 978-1-107-06510-9 Hardback

CONTENTS

Acknowledgements *page* vi
Preface vii

Introduction 1

1 The emergence of modern citizenship 30

2 Naturalisation 48

3 The impact of marital denaturalisation 73

4 Marital citizenship and war 115

5 Marital denaturalisation begins to unravel 150

6 The international response 193

7 What is a citizen? 237

Bibliography 275
Index 282

ACKNOWLEDGEMENTS

I have many acknowledgements to make and much gratitude to express. I was the fortunate recipient of an Australian Research Council Discovery Grant, which funded this research, including for travel to the national archives of a number of countries. At the project's beginning Katherine Fallah provided valuable research assistance. Kristin Macintosh then spent the following three years as my research assistant. I cannot imagine how the project would have progressed without Kristin's engagement, resourcefulness and energetic interest. As the project developed, I benefitted greatly from invitations to present my ideas in talks and seminars: at Colby College, at Indiana University Law School, Toronto Law School and Sydney Law School. For these invitations, I very warmly thank Professors Sandy Maisel, Susan Williams, Ran Hirschl and Kevin Walton. I have enjoyed and profited from discussions about the history, theory and law of citizenship and its loss with many people, including Elisa Arcioni, John Bannon, Linda Cardinal, Estelle Irving, Ian Lee, Megan McKenzie, Steve Ross, Rayner Thwaites, Anne Twomey, and John Williams. I thank Sydney Law School, and in particular the Research Office, for support and assistance. I also thank the constitutional and public law teaching team and my other colleagues on Level Six at Sydney Law School for their friendship, generosity and enjoyable lunches. I am, once again, enormously grateful to John Berger, Senior Editor at Cambridge University Press, and to Cambridge University Press, for their commitment to the book. My husband, Stephen Gaukroger, and our children, Cressida and Hugh, deserve, as ever, my deepest gratitude.

Finally, if it is possible posthumously to thank someone whom one has never met, I want to acknowledge Chrystal Macmillan (1872–1937), politician, barrister, mathematician, writer and activist, whose dedication to the goal of women's citizenship equality and remarkable life should be better known.

PREFACE

When virtually every country in the world does the same thing in the same era – something that requires political will and legislative action in each case and that reverses a long-standing legal practice or assumption – some explanation is needed. This study was driven by a single question: why, between the early-to-mid-nineteenth century and the interwar period or later in the twentieth century, did almost every country – countries with radically different legal systems, traditions and concepts of citizenship – have laws that made women's citizenship conditional upon the citizenship of their husband, and that reversed the historical principle of women's independent nationality? Why, in particular, did they strip citizenship from women who married foreign men? Why did this happen in an era when, in the developed world at least, democratic rights generally and women's rights specifically were beginning to emerge or expand? Why (as it turned out) did it take so long to reverse, even decades after the international community had recognised the problems to which it gave rise?

The evolution of modern citizenship has attracted numerous histories, but women's status as legal citizens seldom features, and even where it does, the specific status of married women's citizenship is rarely acknowledged. The loss of women's citizenship through marriage – a striking, puzzling, and, as it turns out, revealing phenomenon – has been astonishingly neglected. So, too, has the history of automatic marital naturalisation of alien wives. In working through this history, I have (for reasons that are explained in the Introduction) focused particularly on the first.

The question – *why did all countries strip citizenship from women who married foreign men, and why did this happen around the same time?* – would most convincingly be answered by a comprehensive account of the particular circumstances of each country at the relevant moment. Comparative country studies that attempt to explain commonalities, while remaining sensitive to differences, are, however, fiendishly difficult, and where the numbers are great, they are simply not feasible. The numbers, here, are formidable. In 1900 (to take the more-or-less temporal midpoint of our history), there were eighty or so sovereign states in the world; all practised conditional marital nationality, and virtually all had specific marital denaturalisation laws. To give another relevant datum, in 1930, at a time when married women's nationality had become the subject of heightened international attention, there were fifty-eight member states of the League of Nations.[1] Most still practised marital denaturalisation, and virtually none was entirely neutral as to marriage in determining a woman's nationality. Keeping this world scene in view, I have focused on a smaller, but explanatorily powerful, number of states that offer both case studies and windows onto the larger landscape. My research has drawn on the histories of conditional marital citizenship in Australia, Britain, Canada, Ireland, New Zealand and the United States, as revealed primarily in government records (many previously unopened). The archives of these countries, however, do not exclusively record their own legal and administrative histories. Many discussions of and copies of records from other countries are included. One also finds detailed materials arising from international inquiries into married women's nationality, in particular on the part of League of Nations, which on several occasions in the interwar period requested reports from all member countries about their laws and policies governing women's citizenship, as well as reports on the progress of women's equality as measured in multiple other ways.

The accounts and publications of many contemporary international law organisations also include wide-ranging and comparative overviews of numerous countries' laws and practices. To these sources, I have added other primary material (relevant legislation, international instruments, contemporary scholarship, judicial decisions, expert commentary, newspaper reports) from my case study countries and a range of others.

I have also drawn on the insights and findings of those few outstanding historians who have taken women's marital citizenship in individual countries as their subject (see the Introduction). What I do differently, in recognising the subject as a worldwide practice, is to move beyond the specific national reasons for its adoption and apply a comparative focal lens to it. In the final chapter of this book, I turn to secondary sources – recent citizenship theories – to explain my own theory about the foundation and quality of citizenship, as revealed by the 'gendered history'.

[1] We must also count the United States, which did not join the League, but played a significant part in its story, including, as we will see, the vital Hague Nationality Convention of 1930.

In telling the story of the rise and fall of conditional marital citizenship, I do several things. I explain a particular history, I situate this history in a broader context – the emergence and evolution of modern international relations – and, through this, I explore our current dominant conceptualisations of citizenship. I then challenge these conceptualisations, drawing on the accounts of women who experienced, in particular, marital denaturalisation, as a means of understanding what I refer to as the 'existential' nature of citizenship. I offer an alternative conceptualisation: citizenship as a relationship of protection on the part of the state to the citizen.

When I first began thinking about citizenship, it was in 'cosmopolitan' terms, defending the view that state borders should be as open as functionally possible, and that legal citizenship should be de-emphasised with regard to territorial rights. Indeed, I gave relatively little weight to citizenship as a value in itself. In the course of further studying the history of citizenship law, I came to understand that citizenship and territorial abode are conceptually and legally interdependent.[2] I did not, at that point, think of citizenship as a particular quality in itself, as *existential.* It was the historical voices that revealed it in this light.

I still believe that state borders should be as open as possible, and that rights, benefits and all that constitutes the good in a person's life should not be arbitrarily distributed according to whether or not the recipient is a citizen. There is, however, one powerful exception: the right that citizenship brings to a territorial home. That this right gives foundational, existential meaning to citizenship became apparent in studying its historical denial to married women. Factoring in the mostly untold history of the law governing women's citizenship gave a new perspective on what it means to be a citizen. I have, as a consequence, become a defender of citizenship as a legal status, and of the right not to be excluded from a particular territory as legitimately belonging to the citizen and not the alien. This conclusion, I emphasise, does not, and need not, devalue aliens or imply that they are disentitled to equality with citizens in any other respect. It is, rather, a conclusion that arises from recognising the special (territorially protective) character of citizenship as a human need, indeed, a human right. (These conclusions are explained in the final chapter.)

Settling on useful and accurate terminology has been difficult. The broad modern practice in legal discourse is to speak of persons as 'citizens'

[2] Helen Irving, 'Still Call Australia Home: Citizenship and the Right of Abode' (2008) 30 *Sydney Law Review* 133.

in reference to their legal status within a state, and 'nationals' from the perspective of international law. There are, however, many other distinctions. We may add the specific use of 'citizen' to distinguish legal members of a republic from 'subjects', the term used in the past for members of a monarchy (such as Britain). We should also note, however, that British law in the past also commonly referred to British subjects as 'nationals'.[3] Even this is an over-simplification, as the following summary alone indicates. Regarding British Nationality Law, in the 1950s, Mervyn Jones explained that the word 'nationals' was used in modern treaties as equivalent to the French word *ressortissants*, a usage, at that time, 'fairly established'. The British word 'nationals', he wrote, comprehended British subjects as defined by the law in force in any part of the British Dominions, including British protected persons and corporations incorporated under the relevant law. 'Ressortissants' comprehended 'all those who look to the [French] State for protection, and are identified with it for the purpose of its external relations'. This included: 'citoyens', 'sujets français' (natives of certain colonial territories who do not possess full civil rights in metropolitan France) and 'protégés' (all persons who normally received French protection).[4] The relevant terms used in other national languages would, of course, greatly expand this list.

Some countries also distinguish specifically between 'nationals' (those who hold the legal status) and 'citizens' (those who hold the legal status and also enjoy political rights). This distinction, too, may be made in federal systems, where 'nationality' is or was used to refer to the legal status of a person in his or her relationship to the (national) state, and 'citizenship' to 'that part of the federation in which [the person] resides and performs the ordinary civic duties'.[5]

To apply the technical or linguistically correct term on each occasion would run the risk of cluttering the text and possibly confusing the narrative. I have, therefore, employed 'citizen', 'subject' and 'national' as appropriate and/or comfortable to the discussion, using 'citizenship' generically and loosely, but applying more precise terms where these are needed to

[3] Hudson notes that the distinction is generally 'immaterial' in international law, except where the state creates a class of nationals without rights and obligations, as the German Jews were classified under Reich citizenship law of 1935. Manley O. Hudson, *Report on Nationality, Including Statelessness* (International Law Commission, Yearbook, 1952, Vol II) 6–7.

[4] J. Mervyn Jones, *British Nationality Law* (Oxford, Clarendon Press, 1956) 5.

[5] Richard W. Flournoy, 'The New British Imperial Law of Nationality' (1915) 9 *The American Journal of International Law* 870, 873.

distinguish the national legal status under discussion from 'citizenship' in the technical sense. As my study is concerned with the acquisition, retention and loss of the legal status governing a person's membership of a territorial state, I have employed the term 'constitutional citizenship', where relevant, specifically to convey the quality of citizenship as legal status, rather than as entitlement to political participation (or 'political citizenship').

But, what term to use to describe the loss or deprivation of citizenship? As already indicated, I have adopted the term 'denaturalisation', and specifically 'marital denaturalisation', for citizenship deprivation arising from marriage. Several alternative candidates are in circulation. 'Expatriation' is common, but this, I think, most readily evokes expulsion from one's native country or country of former citizenship, or alternatively, the condition of being an 'expatriate' (living away from one's native country), whereas the majority of reported problems caused by loss of citizenship through marriage were experienced by women who remained (post-maritally reclassified as aliens) in their native country, having made it their conjugal home.

Another common alternative is 'denationalisation'. Audrey Macklin explains that '[d]enaturalization refers to the non-consensual deprivation of citizenship acquired by naturalization, while denationalization encompasses deprivation of citizenship, however acquired'.[6] In Patrick Weil's words, denationalisation 'denotes a loss of citizenship, whereas, in theory, a *denaturalized* person has never been a citizen'.[7] The distinction, however, is excessively technical and I find 'denationalisation' awkward as applied to people, in particular as it suffers from having a political homonym (common at least in British history) meaning the privatisation of national industry.

In recent discussions of citizenship-stripping, the alternative terms 'revocation' and 'deprivation' have become common. 'Revocation', however, tends to suggest the confiscation or reversal of something that has been granted, and seems more suited to citizenship acquired by

[6] Macklin adds: 'The classification only matters where the rules for citizenship revocation differ as between naturalized and birthright citizens'. Audrey Macklin, 'Citizenship Revocation, the Privilege to Have Rights and the Production of the Alien' (2014) 40 *Queen's Law Journal* 2, fn 4. If this is correct, the choice of 'martial denaturalisation' to describe my subject is comfortable, as in most cases, the laws that stripped citizenship from women who married foreign men did not distinguish between naturalised and 'natural' citizens.

[7] Patrick Weil, *The Sovereign Citizen: Denaturalization and the Origins of the American Republic* (University of Pennsylvania Press, 2013) 2 (emphasis added).

naturalisation than by birth (which is the primary subject of this study). 'Deprivation' is a multi-purpose term, but it suffers from imprecision without the preposition and noun ('of citizenship') and 'marital deprivation' is a confusing expression, without more. The expression 'marital denaturalisation' describes both a policy and a process, and has the additional advantage of mirroring the uncontroversial term 'marital naturalisation' – the companion legal practice whereby foreign women who married citizen men were automatically treated as naturalised citizens of their husband's country. So, 'marital denaturalisation' and 'marital naturalisation' it is.

Finding a smooth, but useful noun to describe the subject or target of such practices was harder. I have tended to avoid such a noun, but where needed I have referred to the women affected as 'maritally denaturalised women' or 'maritally naturalised women'. Candice Bredbenner uses 'marital-expatriates' in reference to American women stripped of their citizenship for marrying foreign men (the subject of her exceptional history).[8] This is a very succinct and economical term, but it only works if one also refers to the practice of marital denaturalisation as 'expatriation'. Another neat alternative is 'statutory alien'. This, however, is insufficiently precise, since it may cover any case of legislative deprivation of citizenship; its companion, 'statutory citizen', is even broader, clearly embracing all those who are naturalised under the law. Since a significant part of my argument rests upon the difference between citizenship acquired by (ordinary) naturalisation and citizenship acquired by marital naturalisation, with the companion distinction between these two avenues of citizenship loss or denaturalisation, I have retained the more precise, albeit clunky, adjectival noun. These choices, I hope – notwithstanding what the foregoing may suggest – will help smooth the telling of a very complicated history (the complexity of which is, however, essential to the story).

A further terminological point. The general concept attached to the policy of tying women's citizenship to their marital status is commonly referred to in the literature (such as it is) as 'derivative marital nationality', and this was the term with which I first worked. However, it became clear (and important) that loss of citizenship applied, in most cases (at least until the 1930s), regardless of whether or not the woman acquired her foreign husband's nationality; that is to say, her citizenship was not necessarily 'derived' from his, although governments often assumed it to

[8] Candice Bredbenner, *A Nationality of Her Own: Women, Marriage, and the Law of Citizenship* (University of California Press, 1999).

be. To capture this important distinction, I have used the term 'conditional marital nationality': a woman's citizenship or lack of citizenship was conditioned upon whether and whom she married, regardless of other legal consequences.

A final decision needs to be explained. The archival records of governments contain numerous details about the circumstances of women who were affected by conditional marital nationality laws. Many of these identify the women by name; many of the details, indeed, are given by the women themselves in their letters or other entreaties to officials. These women did not intend their plight or their appeals to be made public. I have therefore chosen to identify them only by their first name and the first initial of their surname. Women who campaigned publicly, or whose circumstances were reported in open forums – in the courts, in parliamentary debate or in the press – can be assumed to have known that their identity was public, and in these cases, I have given the woman's full name. Since marital denaturalisation laws operated in many countries until the late 1940s, many women who were affected may still be alive, and certainly many were until recently (although this fact is not necessarily relevant to the protection of privacy), as was demonstrated in the Canadian 'war brides' controversy in the first decade of the twenty-first century (considered later in the book).[9]

There is another, vastly important dimension to the history of married women's citizenship – the ability to transmit citizenship to children. Historically (with a few exceptions), there was a single transmission rule: in a marriage, the husband's citizenship alone determined the citizenship of the children. This rule of paternal citizenship was in force in most countries in the past, and endured longer than conditional marital citizenship for wives. It is still practised in some countries, but has been displaced in many. The citizenship of both the father and the mother, whether married or not, can now commonly be transmitted to their children. This shift to gender-neutral transmission embraced principles of gender equality, but it also required the surmounting of certain complex legal hurdles, in particular, the long-standing objection on the part of the international community to dual nationality (which arises, among other ways, if the different nationalities of both parents are transmitted). It also required rules for special situations, for example, where the parents have different nationalities and are unmarried and/or live in different countries. But,

[9] Sidney Eve Matrix, 'Mediated Citizenship and Contested Belongings: Canadian War Brides and the Fictions of Naturalization' (2007) no. 17 *Topia* 68.

at its foundation, the transmission rule shift could not have occurred without the abandonment of the view that a married woman could not hold citizenship in her own right.

This book is a study of that once-intractable view and its ultimate relinquishment. It is an exploration of citizenship through the history of conditional marital nationality, of how it happened, and why.

Introduction

There was a time, in the not-distant past, when marriage turned women into aliens in their own country. For the simple act of marrying a foreign man their citizenship was stripped from them. Often it was replaced with another (that of the husband), although sometimes with none at all. This history is little known, and the laws that performed its strange alchemy are even less understood. The story's end lies in the United Nations Convention on the Nationality of Married Women.[1] The Convention, which was adopted in 1957 and entered into force in 1958, is, undeniably, one of the lesser known of the international rights-bearing treaties, overshadowed by the mighty UN Conventions that were ratified in the following decades, giving expression to the rights of disadvantaged groups and peoples, including women. Yet, in its day, the 1957 Convention was a great milestone in the protection of rights. It addressed a century-old (or older) practice that had caused hardship in the lives of countless individuals and at the heart of which lay what we recognise today as a profound denial of rights.

The Convention was overtaken by the 1979 Convention on the Elimination of All Forms of Discrimination Against Women (CEDAW) (among the reasons, perhaps, for the first Convention's relative obscurity). Its history, however, is directly relevant to public policy today. Indeed, it addresses a subject – citizenship-stripping – that governments around the world are increasingly contemplating in response, specifically, to the rise of terrorism by non-state actors (including 'home-grown' citizens) that has marked the first decades of the twenty-first century, throwing up

[1] This is not to say that gender discrimination in nationality law no longer exists. Many instances of discrimination (both direct and indirect) in laws and procedures governing naturalisation, transmission of citizenship to children, and diplomatic protection, among others, still operate around the world. Karen Knop and Christine Chinkin, 'Remembering Chrystal Macmillan: Women's Equality and Nationality in International Law' (2001) 22 *Michigan Journal of International Law* 523.

profound and troubling questions about the demands of citizenship and the conditions of its conferral.

The opening words of the Convention on the Nationality of Married Women (impervious to the irony of the masculine pronoun) include an affirmation of Article 15 of the United Nations Universal Declaration of Human Rights of 1948: 'everyone has the right to a nationality' and 'no one shall be arbitrarily deprived of his nationality nor denied the right to change his nationality'. The Convention continues:

> [N]either the celebration nor the dissolution of marriage between one of [a member State's] nationals and an alien nor the change of nationality by the husband during marriage shall affect the nationality of the wife.

It then adds that a woman should not be prevented from retaining her nationality by the change of her husband's nationality, and affirms that privileged arrangements for naturalisation (subject to national security and public policy limitations) should be available to alien wives, at their request.

Why, then, if nationality is a human right, already affirmed as such by the international community,[2] was a specific Convention on women's nationality and marriage needed? What, to use the lawyer's expression, was the 'mischief'? The Convention was a response to the long, almost-universal history of laws that had governed the nationality of married women between the early-to-mid nineteenth century and the mid-twentieth century. Such laws made a woman's citizenship dependent on whether and whom she married. A woman who did not marry was subject only to the general citizenship laws that applied in her country. Her native 'birthright' citizenship, all else being equal, was secure. A woman who married a fellow citizen was similarly secure. But the status of a woman who married a foreign man – a man whose citizenship was other

[2] The contrast between the 1948 United Nations Declaration and the 1930 League of Nations Hague Nationality Convention ('Convention on Certain Questions Relating to the Conflict of Nationality Laws') illustrates the evolution in thinking about nationality as a human right. The Convention's preamble states: 'it is in the general interest of the international community to secure that all its members should recognize that every person should have a nationality'. This is not to suggest that nationality was never thought of as a human right at that time. In 1930, Conservative British Member of Parliament, Victor Cazalet spoke in support of the (unsuccessful) UK Nationality of Married Women Bill, which sought to confer citizenship equality on British women, as a measure 'strongly on the side of human rights'; Labour MP, Edith Picton-Turbervill, added, concerning marital naturalisation, that '[t]o compel nationality upon any human being is surely a denial of human rights'. United Kingdom, House of Commons, *Debates*, 28 November 1930, 1683, 1716.

than her own – was fundamentally different. Simultaneously with her marriage, under the law of virtually all countries, she was automatically deprived of her native citizenship (a process that, for reasons explained in the Preface, I refer to as 'marital denaturalisation'). The marriage vow transformed her not only into a wife, but also into an alien in her own country. At the same time, more often than not (by 'marital naturalisation') she simultaneously became a citizen of her husband's country. Along with her husband's name,[3] his citizenship was transferred to her. With this change of status, the woman lost any rights and entitlements she had enjoyed as a citizen of her (former) country, and in most cases, acquired such rights as were afforded to married women in her husband's country.

Practically, the effects of both marital denaturalisation and marital naturalisation were often minor. In many cases, the latter was in practice beneficial, allowing a woman to gain the citizenship of her husband's country without undertaking the indeterminate process of applying for naturalisation and satisfying the eligibility criteria under that country's law, thus guaranteeing her the right to live securely in his country. In many other cases, however, the practical consequences were severe, even drastic. Women lost the protection of their former state, including the right to the particular diplomatic representation abroad that they had previously enjoyed; they lost the right to live or travel freely in what had been their home country (that of their pre-marital citizenship) or, if they remained in that country, they did so now as aliens, subject to the many legal limitations that applied to the alien.

The practical effects, whether negative or positive, were, however, far from the whole picture. Even where the functional consequences were minimal, women who experienced marital denaturalisation found themselves psychologically affected. Many described this experience in terms of injury: the loss of 'home', exposure or vulnerability, the stripping-away

[3] The history of taking the husband's surname varies greatly around the world. In some countries it was (and is) mandated under legislation; in others, it was a 'rule' of common law, and in others, merely a cultural practice. In France and Quebec, it was/is prohibited under law. In some (Japan and Switzerland) the old rule specifying the husband's surname has been replaced with the requirement of a single family name; the choice is almost always that of the husband. Heather MacClintock, 'Sexism, Surnames, and Social Progress: The Conflict of Individual Autonomy and Government Preferences in Laws Regarding Name Changes at Marriage' (2010) 24 *Temple International Law and Comparative Law Journal* 277. The arguments in favour of the rule of marital name-change resemble those regarding marital citizenship change: maintaining family unity, facilitating administration and identification. They are, equally, rebuttable.

of part of their personal identity, becoming alienated. A sense of inferiority or subordination often accompanied this experience. A married woman's vulnerability to citizenship deprivation, combined with the practical impact, created a particular, perhaps unique, existential effect. Even those who happily embraced their husband's citizenship had a sense of this. These characterisations of loss were expressed, again and again, by the women affected and by those who campaigned for reform or repeal of the particular laws.

Both the loss of one citizenship and the acquisition of another happened without any action on the woman's part. Her consent was neither sought nor required. She had no opportunity to decline; she did not even necessarily know what was to happen. Frequently, indeed, she did not. But, even if she did, there was no chance of negotiating an alternative arrangement, or of keeping her original citizenship while acquiring her husband's. The transformation occurred as a non-negotiable result of nothing more than the act of marriage.

A woman who married a foreign man was no longer a (legal) member of her pre-marital constitutional community. She was assumed to have become a member of her husband's. She could not be both. Until well after the Second World War, the international community, supported by the great majority of countries, opposed dual nationality. Although it was understood that the condition occurred, unavoidably and regrettably, in certain, limited circumstances (see Chapter 6), the consensus was clear: dual nationality was anathema, a condition to be eliminated as far as possible. *Forsaking all others*, in law as in love, one citizenship alone was permitted, and that was determined, not by the woman or her own country, but by the law of her husband's state.

The underlying assumption in the policy of conditional marital nationality was that the woman who married 'out' was automatically absorbed into her alien husband's community, and her allegiance was accordingly transferred. Allegiance was thus subjective and contingent, but only for women. Although, in a couple of limited cases, marriage to a citizen woman led to the naturalisation of the alien husband[4] or allowed him to acquire his wife's citizenship,[5] the circumstances in which this occurred

4 Under the Brazilian Constitution of 1891, the definition of Brazilian citizens included: 'Foreigners, residents of Brazil, who hold real estate in Brazil and who are married to Brazilian women or have Brazilian children, unless they have declared their intention to retain their original nationality'. Brazilian women who married foreigners were not denaturalised, and foreign women who married Brazilians were not naturalised.

5 Japanese law of 1899 included the extraordinary provision that an alien man acquired Japanese nationality if (among other things) he became the 'nyufu' of a Japanese woman,

were extraordinary and they involved both a voluntary act and a secondary criterion – property ownership or elite family status. The acquisition of a new citizenship, that is, did not follow from the act of marriage alone. More significantly, no country stripped a man of his citizenship for marrying an alien woman.

In a tiny number of early examples, the woman lost her citizenship only in cases where she acquired, in fact, the citizenship of her husband's country as a consequence of her marriage,[6] and her allegiance was thus considered to have been 'objectively' transferred (in the manner of ordinary naturalisation). This policy – no loss without gain – was, as we shall see, ultimately adopted in the 1930s by the international community and subsequently followed in many countries. It was, however, very rare in the nineteenth century when conditional marital nationality laws were spreading, and in the early twentieth century, when they were at their peak. Even widely adopted, as it came to be, it did not satisfy the demands of citizenship equality campaigners.

The simple proposition, as noted, was that a woman's citizenship (and allegiance) was changed, if she married 'out'. The simple reality was that foreign marriage led to the loss of her citizenship and, frequently, the acquisition of her husband's. Expressed in these terms, this arrangement sounds symmetrical and straightforward. In practice, however, it was anything but. To begin with, the loss of citizenship under the law of the woman's country, and the acquisition of citizenship under the law of her husband's country, were provided for in different legal instruments: those of the countries respectively involved. Consequently, marital denaturalisation and marital naturalisation did not automatically occur, either simultaneously or necessarily, at the same time. No state had a part in shaping or passing the legislation of another sovereign country. The 'reciprocity' between one country and another – depriving its own women of citizenship on the understanding that the other country (the husband's)

that is to say, the husband of 'the female head of a family and [if he] becomes a member thereof'. Richard W. Flournoy and Manley O. Hudson (eds) *A Collection of Nationality Laws of Various Countries as Contained in Constitutions, Statutes, and Treaties* (Oxford University Press, New York, 1929) 382.

6 The French Civil Code was amended in 1889 so that a French woman would preserve her citizenship upon marriage to an alien unless she acquired his nationality. The Venezuelan Civil Code of 1904 similarly provided that a Venezuelan woman did not lose her citizenship unless she acquired that of her husband, and the 1904 Venezuelan Constitution had the same provision. The Venezuelan Civil Code of 1922 elaborated further: 'A Venezuelan woman who marries a foreigner is considered a foreigner with respect to the personal rights of Venezuelans while she continues married, provided that through the marriage she acquires the nationality of her husband'.

would confer citizenship upon in-marrying women – was not, and could not be, synchronised.

There were, additionally, significant periods of time in which some countries automatically naturalised foreign wives but did not yet denaturalise their own citizen women, and vice versa. Furthermore, while all countries that denaturalised women who married foreign men did so without exception, there were also countries where, under their particular naturalisation law, certain classes of foreign wives (those who were racially ineligible for naturalisation, for example, as in the United States[7]) were denied marital naturalisation, despite their having lost citizenship under their own countries' laws. In such cases, the woman became stateless. Indeed, one of the most dramatic effects of marital denaturalisation, in particular after the First World War, was statelessness among married women.

Although marital denaturalisation applied, in practice, only to women who married foreign men, it remained significant for all women. For the unmarried woman, whether she knew it or not, it was a constant lingering factor in the lottery of the heart: the citizenship of the man with whom she fell in love (something she was unlikely to control) had profound consequences. In the case of marriage to a fellow citizen the impact was unnoticeable; the woman shared her husband's citizenship, the same citizenship she (already) held. But, even in such circumstances, marriage brought vulnerability. A woman's citizenship was only as secure as that of her husband. If the husband changed nationality by naturalisation, his wife – now married to a foreign man – automatically lost her citizenship, whether or not it had been acquired by her marriage to him. In many cases, the man's naturalisation also automatically led to his wife's naturalisation, again without requiring her consent or even knowledge. If it did not, she became stateless. If a man became stateless, his wife joined in him in his statelessness.

World practice

The adoption of the Convention on the Nationality of Married Women signalled that the international community had ultimately come to

[7] Section 2 of the United States Act of February 10, 1855 ('Naturalization Act') stated: 'Any woman who is now or may hereafter be married to a citizen of the United States, and who might herself be lawfully naturalized, shall be deemed a citizen'. Naturalisation was available only to 'white' persons.

recognise for married women what it had recognised for people generally: that vulnerability in nationality was the equivalent of vulnerability in the human community. It also revealed that conditional marital nationality had been a worldwide and long-standing policy.

The policy first appeared in a statutory instrument in the French (Napoleonic) Civil Code of 1804. The Code's Book I ('Of Persons') included a provision governing the nationality of married women: *L'étrangère qui aura épousé un Français suivra la condition de son mari* and *Une femme française qui épousera un étranger suivra la condition de son mari*: that is, a foreign woman who married a Frenchman took the citizenship of her husband, as did a Frenchwoman who married a foreign man. The principle of conditional marital nationality captured in the Code applied across Napoleonic Europe, and by the mid-nineteenth century was followed in most of the world. The British, who otherwise claimed to distinguish their nationality laws 'fundamentally' from those of continental Europe, also adopted the practice.[8]

There is something curious, and also revealing, in the formula expressed in the Code. The loss of a woman's citizenship is stated conversely. That is to say, rather than stating that a woman married to a foreign man lost her citizenship, the law declared that the woman acquired another person's citizenship. Many other countries followed this formula. The United Kingdom's Naturalization Act of 1870 (which first introduced marital denaturalisation for British women) stated: 'A married woman shall be deemed to be a subject of the state of which her husband is for the time being a subject'. The United States Act of March 2, 1907 (the 'Expatriation Act') stated: 'That any American woman who marries a foreigner shall take the nationality of her husband'.

In practice, the formula meant, as was intended, that the woman was automatically stripped of her pre-marital citizenship. It was a paradoxical and (as we shall see) erroneous way of expressing the law, but it captured a fundamental principle. Given the rule against dual nationality, in most countries, the acquisition of a foreign citizenship meant the forfeiture of

[8] In the course of a 1923 parliamentary committee review of the policy of conditional marital nationality, the Chairman (Viscount Chelmsford) pointed out that the first British 'Nationality' Act, in 1870 'did not bring the British law of nationality into entire accord with the Continental Law. As is well known, the fundamental principles of these laws are different. In most European countries a man takes his nationality from his parents. In the British Empire he takes it from the soil on which he is born, whatever nationality his parents may belong to'. *Report of the Select Committee on The Nationality of Married Women*, United Kingdom, House of Commons, July 1923, 66.

a prior citizenship. The result of declaring or 'deeming' that a married woman took her husband's citizenship was therefore denaturalisation for women who entered into a foreign marriage. The formula applied, however, regardless of whether or not a woman actually acquired her husband's citizenship. It was, in effect, and again as intended, a statement of expulsion from the woman's pre-marital constitutional community, rather than a positive statement about the woman's change of status.

By the late nineteenth century, in 'the [world's] systems of law the general rule [was] that the wife takes the nationality of the husband, whether it be that which he had at the time of marriage or that which he may acquire afterwards'.[9] In 1914, the British government, defending its law of marital denaturalisation, called it 'the practice of the whole civilised world'.[10] This was an understatement – democracies, authoritarian regimes and 'undeveloped' countries (sometimes through the imposition of colonial laws) adopted it.[11] So did countries with different degrees or intensities of nationalism. France and Germany (the first historically 'state-centred and assimilationist' in its understanding of nationhood, and the second '*Volk*-centred and differentialist'[12]) both practised marital denaturalisation in and after the nineteenth century. So did Meiji and post-Meiji Japan.[13] The United States, with its apparent constitutional protection of birthright citizenship under the Fourteenth Amendment of 1868 also

[9] G. G. Phillimore, 'Nationality of Married Women' (1917) *Journal of the Society of Comparative Legislation* 165, 167.

[10] United Kingdom, House of Commons, *Parliamentary Debates*, 20 July 1914, 1466. (Lewis Harcourt, Secretary of State for the Colonies.)

[11] The fact that British women acquired the nationality even of 'uncivilized' countries was sometimes recorded as an objection to the practice of conditional marital nationality; in parliamentary debate on the law, the fact that it was also 'Hindu' law, and the prospect that a British-born woman whose husband naturalised as a Turkish citizen would herself become Turkish were raised (albeit unsuccessfully) as reasons for opposing the British practice. United Kingdom, House of Commons, *Debates*, 19 July 1918, 1351, 1363.

[12] Rogers Brubaker, *Citizenship and Nationhood in France and Germany* (Harvard University Press, 1992) 1.

[13] Japanese law, up until 1898, provided that an alien woman who married a Japanese subject automatically acquired Japanese nationality and a Japanese woman who married an alien was deemed to have acquired his, and thus lost her own. The Law of July 9, 1898 retained the policy of unconditional marital naturalisation of alien wives of Japanese citizens, including those who acquired citizenship by naturalisation, but modified the denaturalisation rule: Article 18 specified that 'A Japanese who, on becoming the wife of an alien, has acquired her husband's nationality, loses Japanese nationality'. Japan thus became one of the first states in the world to protect women from statelessness through marriage. However, a Japanese female head of household required the permission of the Minister of the Interior to marry an alien.

practised it. To give a handful of other examples, in a 1917 overview of women's nationality laws, conditional marital nationality is illustrated, specifically (but far from exhaustively), by reference to the laws of Britain and the Dominions, the Congo, Mexico, Japan, Holland, Hungary, Portugal, France, Sweden, the United States, Switzerland and Serbia.[14] In 1929, a comprehensive survey found marital denaturalisation laws still operating in – to take just the first three letters of the alphabet – Afghanistan, Albania, Australia, Austria, Belgium, Bolivia, Britain and the British Empire, Bulgaria, Canada, China, Costa Rica, Cuba and the Czechoslovak Republic. In multiple other countries between the letters D and Z, as the survey records, the practice was also maintained.[15]

By the late 1920s, although significant variations had begun to appear in the practice, and some countries (the United States, the Soviet Union) had recently repealed their conditional marital nationality laws, the majority of countries still adhered to the policy. Variations in the details, including conditions under which denaturalised women might regain their original citizenship or the effect of a husband's naturalisation on a wife's citizenship, had begun to multiply. Nevertheless, in 1937, a survey of seventy countries[16] found that only fourteen allowed the wife of an alien to retain her own citizenship without qualification. The remaining countries still provided for deprivation of a woman's nationality upon marriage to an alien man. Of these, at least fifteen made the loss 'absolute and unqualified'. Around forty made the loss 'dependent upon certain conditions attendant to the marriage': the woman's consent (eight states); the acquisition of her husband's nationality (twenty-five states); and the acquisition of her husband's nationality along with the establishment of her domicile in another country (six states).[17] The laws governing the citizenship status of alien women upon marriage to a citizen also varied, although less so: around fifty-seven states conferred citizenship unconditionally, and eleven conferred it 'under conditions, principally of option or domicile'.[18] Only eight no longer automatically naturalised the alien wife upon marriage to a citizen. There were, in short, probably no cases where marital naturalisation was never practised and almost none where marital denaturalisation was never practised.[19]

[14] Phillimore, 'Nationality of Married Women', 165.

[15] Flournoy and Hudson, *A Collection of Nationality Laws.*

[16] Waldo Emerson Waltz, *The Nationality of Married Women: A Study of Domestic Policies and International Legislation* (The University of Illinois Press, Urbana, 1937) 72.

[17] Waltz, ibid, 72–73. [18] Waltz, ibid, 83.

[19] Chile provides an exception: the 19th century Chilean Constitutions defined citizenship but did not refer to the effect of marriage upon nationality. The 1925 Constitution provided

This demands explanation. Why was marital denaturalisation practised so widely, for so long? Why was it considered necessary? What harm could there have been in a marriage between a citizen and a foreigner? Why, if there was demonstrable harm, did marital denaturalisation not also apply to the men who entered into foreign marriages? Why, instead, did most countries grant automatic naturalisation to foreign wives, whether they wanted it or not?

Gender and citizenship law

Few studies have treated citizenship law as a matter of gender. As Jennifer Ngaire Heuer writes in her outstanding history of gender in post-revolutionary France, 'most big theories about nationality and national citizenship . . . have rarely taken into account the person as a gendered category'.[20] Even fewer have looked at the history of conditional marital

for loss of citizenship by naturalisation in a foreign country, which may have applied to citizen women married to foreign men, but did not otherwise provide for loss upon marriage. Brazil and Argentina provide partial exceptions. Brazil's law of 1860 provided that an alien woman married to a Brazilian followed the condition of her husband, as did a Brazilian woman married to a foreigner, although the word 'condition' was not interpreted as applying to nationality, while a decree of 1865 paradoxically provided for the recovery of Brazilian nationality by widows. Flournoy and Hudson, *A Collection of Nationality Laws*, 47. Additionally, the 1891 Constitution provided for the loss of Brazilian citizenship through 'naturalization in a foreign country' which would have applied to Brazilian women with foreign husbands, the country of which automatically naturalised foreign wives of citizens. Bills proposing legislation for marital denaturalisation were presented in 1860 and 1899, but were opposed as unconstitutional. Bertha Lutz, 'Nationality of Married Women in the American Republics', *Bulletin of the Pan American Union*, April 1926. Argentina, having no provision in its Civil Code regarding the effect of marriage upon a woman's citizenship may also appear as an exception. However, as Kif Augustine-Adams has shown, the Supreme Court of Argentina interpreted a married woman's domicile and nationality as following her husband's, and with some exceptions, depending on the case, a married woman's citizenship as dependent on her husband's. Foreign married women could, however, naturalise under the Civil Code, but required authorisation from the husband. Kif Augustine-Adams, '"She Consents Implicitly": Women's Citizenship, Marriage and Liberal Political Theory in Late-Nineteenth and Early-Twentieth Century Argentina' (2002) 13 *Journal of Women's History* 8, 13. In 1926, the Civil Code was reformed, giving Argentinian women civil rights, with the effect of protecting the woman's independent citizenship, including for jurisdictional purposes.

20 Jennifer Ngaire Heuer, *The Family and the Nation: Gender and Citizenship in Revolutionary France, 1789–1830* (Cornell University Press, 2007) 7. Laura Tabili is blunter. Her study, she writes, reveals 'how unimaginative and flawed remain the apparently objective, gender-blind categories through which scholars have conceived of and categorised the formation of citizenship and nationality in modern Europe'. Laura Tabili, 'Outsiders in the Land of Their Birth: Exogamy, Citizenship, Identity in War and Peace' (2005) 44 *Journal of British Studies* 796, 814. Regarding Canada's history, Philip Girard writes: 'Achievement of a citizenship

nationality or recognised its significance. It is revealing, if dismaying, to find that the author of one of the rare exceptions – a study of conditional marital nationality in Canada – has described his subject as 'obscure' and conceded that '[t]he law of married women's nationality may seem an arcane topic, even for devotees of legal history'.[21]

It is even more striking to find that a vast study of how American society was shaped in the nineteenth century by the regulation of immigration and aliens (with, ironically, its cover depicting a woman nursing her infant as she waits in a crowded American Immigration Landing Depot) pays almost no attention to the fate of immigrant women, let alone to the policies that turned countless American women into aliens, and countless alien women into American citizens.[22] A study of the evolution of French and German concepts of nationhood, despite recognising that France effectively 'invented' the modern concept of citizenship, includes no discussion of the effect of marriage on Frenchwomen's citizenship nor of the fact that the Napoleonic Code introduced the policy and practice of conditional marital nationality to Europe and the world.[23] These are only two examples of many other works whose subject invites, but does not include, a recognition of the gendered dimension of citizenship laws.

Among the small number of scholars to discuss the history of conditional marital nationality, almost all have focused on their country's individual story, finding an explanation in the histories or practices particular to that country and offering domestic accounts. Page Baldwin's valuable research on the policy (and women's campaigns to overthrow it) in Britain acknowledges the international context, but explains Britain's response in the imperial context.[24] Ann Dummett and Andrew Nicol,

status independent of marriage has never been part of the canon of female "firsts" or feminist victories, and has received virtually no attention by historians of Canadian women'. Philip Girard, '"If two ride a horse, one must ride in front": Married Women's Nationality and the Law in Canada 1880–1950' (2013) 94 *The Canadian Historical Review* 28, 29.

21 Girard, ibid, 52.

22 Aristide R. Zolberg, *A Nation by Design: Immigration Policy in the Fashioning of America* (Harvard University Press, 2006).

23 Brubaker, *Citizenship and Nationhood*, 35.

24 M. Page Baldwin, 'Subject to Empire: Married Women and the British Nationality and Status of Aliens Act' (2001) 40 *The Journal of British Studies* 522. An unpublished study of British women's campaign to repeal conditional marital nationality laws in the UK, based on exceptional primary source research, similarly focuses on the imperial impasse. Dorothy Page, '"A Married Woman, or a Minor, Lunatic, or Idiot": The Struggle of British Women Against Disability in Nationality, 1914–1933', PhD thesis, University of Otago, 1984.

also writing about British history, note the international context, but treat marital denaturalisation under the UK Naturalization Act of 1870, effectively, as a puzzle in British law.[25] (We shall see that the puzzle can be accounted for.) Barbara Todd explains it principally as a type of corrective to the 'great inconvenience' caused by the fact that alien husbands previously could not take common law title to their British wives' real estate; the Act, she writes, 'resolved that problem', permitting aliens to hold property, and allowing alien husbands to have a 'proper' role in the system of coverture, as well as removing the main deterrent to women's relinquishing of their British allegiance.[26] Laura Tabili focuses on the effect of conditional marital nationality laws on wives of foreign men in the British Tyne port of South Shields; her study contextualises Britain's Naturalization Act of 1870 in international developments, but accounts for the British law principally in terms of nation-building.[27] Daniel Gorman's study of British 'imperial citizenship' briefly acknowledges the conditional marital nationality provisions of the British nationality laws of 1870 and 1914 and locates these in an international 'pattern', following the general European and United States trend and reflecting 'the uneasiness legislators felt concerning large-scale immigration'.[28] Regarding the wider world of the British Empire, Philip Girard explains Canada's practice as 'always intertwined with ideas about Canada's future as a white settler nation, and the possible threat to that future represented by large-scale immigration . . . [prompted by] a version of "ethnic nationalism"' based on a British Canadian identity.[29]

Melissa Feinberg's study of gender and citizenship in the Czechoslovak Republic, 1918–50, is exceptional in directly locating her subject in the international community. She explains the Czechoslovak law of conditional marital nationality both as a response to international trends, and in its own terms: for the latter, the history of Czech nationalism, and a rigid cultural commitment to the doctrine of family unity in nationality, which meant that, regarding women's nationality, by the end of the 1930s,

[25] Ann Dummett and Andrew Nicol, *Subjects, Citizens, Aliens and Others* (Weidenfeld and Nicolson, 1990).

[26] Barbara J. Todd, 'Written in Her Heart: Married Women's Separate Allegiance in English Law', in Tim Stretton and Krista J. Kesselring (eds) *Married Women and the Law: Coverture in England and the Common Law World* (McGill-Queen's University Press, 2013) 163–4.

[27] Tabili, 'Outsiders in the Land of Their Birth'.

[28] Daniel Gorman, *Imperial Citizenship: Empire and the Question of Belonging* (Manchester University Press, 2006) 20.

[29] Girard, '"If two ride a horse"', 40.

'the Czech government publicly set itself against Western democracies'.[30] Brigitte Studer also explores the history of marital denaturalisation in one particular country, Switzerland, including with a discussion of the international context.[31] She chronicles the increasing strictness of the Swiss practice in the inter-war period, and the growing discourse of "Swissness" attached to it. Her main focus, however, like that of Feinberg, is the nationalism and sense of exceptionalism in her subject country, an important part of the story, but which leaves to be explained why the practice also applied in countries with weaker levels of nationalism.

The majority of the studies of conditional marital nationality are American. American law, indeed, appears to need special explanation. The Fourteenth Amendment of the United States Constitution opens with the declaration that 'All persons born . . . in the United States . . . are citizens of the United States'. It might be assumed to have protected the citizenship of American-born women. It did not. The 1907 Expatriation Act – a federal Act dealing otherwise with naturalisation – mandated denaturalisation for American-born women who married foreign men. This legislative interpretation of what was at stake, treating the marriage of an American woman as a matter for the law applying to foreigners, has led American scholars to explain marital denaturalisation as a tool of immigration control, and through this, in Nancy Cott's words, a means of 'sculpt[ing] the body politic',[32] akin to prohibitions on interracial marriage in the some of the US States. Martha Gardner also explores America's '[c]ontinued anxieties over immigration', to which 'deep-seated fears of racial heterogeneity' were added, as central to the shaping of American women's citizenship laws.[33]

30 Melissa Feinberg, *Elusive Equality: Gender, Citizenship, and the Limits of Democracy in Czechoslovakia, 1918–1950* (University of Pittsburgh Press, 2006) 97.

31 Brigitte Studer, 'Citizenship as Contingent National Belonging' (2001) 13 *Gender and History* 622.

32 Nancy F. Cott, 'Marriage and Women's Citizenship in the United States, 1830–1934' (1998) 103 *American Historical Review* 1443. Also, Cott, *Public Vows: A History of Marriage and the Nation* (Harvard University Press, 2000).

33 Martha Gardner, *The Qualities of a Citizen: Women, Immigration and Citizenship, 1870–1965* (Princeton University Press, 2005) 121. Evelyn Nakano Glenn advances a 'relational' account of citizenship that focuses on the historically interlocking structures of race and gender; it mentions the racial exclusions in the US married women's nationality laws: *Unequal Freedom: How Race and Gender Shaped American Citizenship and Labor* (Harvard University Press, 2002). Linda Kerber discusses citizenship primarily in terms of civil obligations, rather than as a legal status: *No Constitutional Right to be Ladies: Women and the Obligations of Citizenship* (Hill & Wang, 1998). Kerry Abrams's study of the law of derivative domicile (as it operated in the United States), and the conceptualisation of

When the United States reversed its derivative marital nationality laws with the passage of the 'Cable Act' (the Married Women's Independent Nationality Act) in 1922, the new law applied only partially, as scholars have noted: American-born women of Asian race, or whose husbands were of Asian race or origin, could not take advantage of independent citizenship until 1931. Candice Bredbenner who has done exhaustive archival research on marital denaturalisation in the United States, suggests that the history is paradoxical, that the general cultural distrust of foreigners and aliens in the nineteenth century had been 'checked' in the marital naturalisation law of 1855, which automatically conferred the 'gift' of citizenship upon foreign women who married American citizen men.[34]

There is no reason to doubt these accounts. However, immigration control and race relations do not explain, or only insubstantially explain, the fact that identical policies were in place in numerous other countries (a fact that formed the focus of official discussions concerning the desirability of marital nationality laws in the United States). The US Expatriation Act was chronologically coincident with the rise of mass immigration, but this does not explain why American women, citizens by birth, were alienated by foreign marriage and accorded the status of immigrants, including in cases where the husband was a 'desirable' foreigner (of British 'race', for example), or was already an assimilated resident of the United States.

We have noted that conditional marital nationality laws were found in countries with vastly different legal traditions and systems of government. We can add to this observation that marital denaturalisation was practised in countries that welcomed immigrants, as in countries that did not, as in those with selective immigration policies that welcomed some types of immigrant and repelled others. Marital *naturalisation* was also practised in countries with racial exclusions in general naturalisation or immigration laws. Consider, for example, Australia's Naturalization Act of 1903. Section 5 excluded from naturalisation any 'aboriginal native of Asia, Africa, or the Islands of the Pacific, excepting New Zealand' (exclusions that mirrored the Immigration Restriction Act of 1901). At the same time, with no reference to race, section 9 of the Act stated that:

'marriage as citizenship' deserves mention. While its focus is not on conditional marital nationality, it is a significant contribution to understanding the historical epistemology of citizenship: 'Citizen Spouse' (2013) 101 *California Law Review* 407.

34 Bredbenner, *A Nationality of Her Own*, 4.

> A woman who, not being a British subject, marries a British subject, shall in the Commonwealth [of Australia] be deemed to be thereby naturalized, and have the same rights powers and privileges, and be subject to the same obligations, as a person who has obtained a certificate of naturalization.

Australia also followed British law and applied marital denaturalisation to its own women, regardless of whether or not their racial status (or that of their husband) was 'desirable'. Again, Australia's history of racial exclusions is an important part of the story, but it leaves unexplained why other countries, with or without similar attitudes both to foreigners and their own citizens, treated married women in identical ways.

The histories and nation-building trajectories of individual countries are important, but they are specific versions of a much wider story. In short, while they enrich the story, they do not explain it. Kif Augustine-Adams offers an important alternative account, 'peeling back' the fiction of implied consent to the transfer of nationality in a woman's act of marrying a foreigner; she draws upon historical legal treatises and case law to identify an underling discourse of social contract liberalism in the enforcement of marital nationality laws.[35] Although my explanation of the rise of conditional marital nationality is different, hers is an unusual and theoretically rich epistemological account of the phenomenon. It does not, however, go beyond United States legal history. As with the other histories, her focus on the local leaves unanswered our question: why was the practice in force all around the world at broadly the same time? Why did the international community ultimately take it up as a subject of concern, indeed, as a matter of urgency?

Gender and political citizenship

In contrast to the paucity of studies of married women's citizenship, the slow and Herculean campaign for equal political rights for women has attracted numerous citizenship histories. The concept of citizenship is, indeed, often conflated with political rights, and in particular the right to vote and stand for public office. However, the distinction between citizens as such (those holding the status under law) – constitutional citizens – and citizens as bearers of political rights – political citizens – needs to be made.

[35] Kif Augustine-Adams, '"With Notice of the Consequences": Liberal Political Theory, Marriage, and Women's Citizenship in the United States' (2002) 6 *Citizenship Studies* 5.

In most cases, there was little historical correlation between laws conferring or abolishing conditional marital nationality and laws conferring women's right to vote. As Ruth Rubio Marin has noted, the achievement of women's suffrage has historically been associated with cultural factors and political developments in different countries, and in Europe has followed an 'inverted' pathway from that described in the conventional histories, in which political rights followed civil rights.[36] Women gained political rights well after – and in some cases, long after – they gained the legal status of citizen; '[i]n many European countries the modern legal order in fact came to deprive women of the suffrage rights they had [previously] enjoyed' under the *Ancien Régime*.[37]

To uncover inversions and paradoxical *décalages* in the story of the achievement of rights is a common experience, especially in researching histories that take account of the whole human population, and not merely its dominant sectors. The history of citizenship law provides a further and, I suggest, even more fundamental inversion: as we have seen, women in (virtually) all countries lost the right to retain independent citizenship, regardless of whether they were otherwise able to enjoy civil or social or political rights. In many countries, women were subject to marital denaturalisation after, and sometimes long after, the passage of laws that allowed married women to hold property in their own right. In certain European countries, and in some others, the right to vote came even later, sometimes after the repeal of marital denaturalisation, or after the repeal of its automatic imposition.[38] In other cases, the reverse occurred: in New Zealand, women were nationally enfranchised in 1893; in Australia, 1902; in Canada, 1918; in Britain, 1918 (for women aged thirty and over) and 1928 (for all adult women). Yet in all of these cases, marital denaturalisation was maintained until after the Second World War.

In the United States the developments were more or less simultaneous, at least with respect to marital denaturalisation. Women's federal suffrage was achieved in 1920. Marital denaturalisation, enacted in 1907, was

[36] Ruth Rubio Marin, 'The Achievement of Female Suffrage in Europe: On Women's Citizenship' (2013) 12 *International Journal of Constitutional Law* 4.

[37] Rubio Marin, ibid, 8.

[38] In France, marital denaturalisation was introduced in 1804, then modified in 1889 and 1927 giving French women a choice of nationality upon foreign marriage. Full gender equality in nationality law was achieved in 1973. Women's right to vote was granted in 1944.

overturned in 1922 (subject to a race test until 1931).[39] Marital naturalisation, however, which was simultaneously repealed in 1922, had been in place in American legislation since 1855. But the vote and the right to citizenship status were interwoven in America's equality discourse. In 1915 (as we see in Chapter 3), an unsuccessful constitutional challenge[40] to the Expatriation Act was prompted by the denial of a maritally denaturalised woman's application for registration as an eligible voter in California, and contemporary reporting of her case focused on this issue. The woman was herself an active women's suffrage campaigner.

It is also notable that the opening words of Cable Act of 1922, which achieved the (partial) repeal of conditional marital citizenship in the United States, echoed the language of the Nineteenth Amendment: '. . . the right of any woman to become a naturalised citizen of the United States shall not be denied or abridged because of her sex or because she is a married woman'.[41] In Congressional debate over the Cable Bill, speakers emphasised that the recently ratified Amendment demonstrated that a woman's citizenship, like a man's, 'should be preserved as her most priceless possession', since '[s]he is now in name, as well as in fact, an equal partner in the business of conducting the American Government'.[42] In the eyes of Massachusetts Congressman, John Rogers, the new constitutional protection of women's right to vote was indicative of both national and world trends towards 'extending the rights of women'. The Congressman received applause for his declaration that, at the moment when women were given 'civil equality' with men, 'the doctrine of dependent or derived citizenship became as archaic as the doctrine of ordeal by fire'.[43]

Notwithstanding the warm reception, the Congressman's sketch of international trends was, at best, exaggerated. Although, broadly, married women had gained equal legal rights with men, the right to vote still lagged behind the equalisation of citizenship rights in a number of countries.

39 Bredbenner argues that America's Congress was more willing to repeal marital denaturalisation once American women were constitutionally guaranteed the right to vote (following the ratification of the Nineteenth Amendment in 1920), and the connection between the two featured significantly in Congressional debate on the repeal. Bredbenner, *A Nationality of Her Own*, 7.

40 *Mackenzie* v. *Hare* 239 U.S. 299 (1915).

41 The first sentence of the Nineteenth Amendment reads: 'The right of citizens of the United States to vote shall not be denied or abridged by the United States or by any State on account of sex'.

42 United States, House of Representatives, *Congressional Record*, 20 June 1922, 9041.

43 United States, House of Representatives, *Congressional Record*, 20 June 1922, 9047.

A long history of democracy and universal suffrage is not a guide as to whether a country was likely to permit women, under law, to retain their own citizenship upon marriage, or to when the law was likely to have been repealed, or indeed, to whether women were likely to regard the vote as the focus of citizenship equality campaigns.[44] This is not to say that the two developments were unrelated. The campaign for citizenship equality was waged by some feminist organisations together with the campaign for political rights,[45] and, as in the United States, the fact that women had attained the franchise either in the campaigners' own or other countries was a rhetorically powerful tool for the repeal of conditional marital nationality.

The reasoning worked in more than one direction, however. The enfranchisement of women was said to demonstrate both their capacity and their right to be independent 'citizens', but (at least in some countries where female citizens had been enfranchised) it also invited the complaint that undeserving alien wives of citizens were, by their automatic marital naturalisation, acquiring a treasured political right denied to native citizen women who had lost their citizenship merely by marriage.[46] There were risks in conjoining the campaigns. As Bredbenner writes, before American women were enfranchised, suffragists realised that the fact that undesirable maritally naturalised foreign women would acquire the vote along with American-born women, if it were granted, was 'fuel for the anti-suffrage' campaign.[47] The argument against the franchise and the argument for maintaining the principle that a married woman could not hold independent citizenship overlapped in other ways, too. The often-asserted proposition that political participation would distract a woman

[44] A British Home Office memo in 1931 noted that the right to vote was important, but that many women's groups 'base[d] their claim for a change in the law rather on the importance of the recognition of the principle of equality between the sexes than upon any practical disadvantages which result from the existing law'. UK National Archives, HO 45/15147: 'Nationality of Married Women', 'Hague Conference' 23 December 1931.

[45] Carol Miller, '"Geneva – the Key to Equality": Inter-war Feminists and the League of Nations' (1994) 3 *Women's History Review* 219. Baldwin, 'Subject to Empire'.

[46] This was a significant theme in the United States campaign for the repeal of conditional marital nationality laws. Canadian women, it appears, were also more concerned by the automatic naturalisation of foreign women, in particular through their husbands' naturalisation as British subjects in Canada, than by the denaturalisation of Canadian women through marriage. See Girard, '"If two ride a horse"'. To this observation I would add, however, that marital denaturalisation became a major concern both for Canadian campaigners and the Canadian government in the 1930s.

[47] Bredbenner, *A Nationality of Her Own*, 60.

from her duties to her family found an analogue in the view that independent citizenship would disrupt family unity.

The reasons for denying or granting the vote to women and the reasons for maintaining or repealing conditional marital nationality were, in most cases, only tenuously connected. Worldwide, the stronger and most persistent objection to repeal was the anticipation of difficulties in international relations. Countries' recognition of each other's citizens was an international issue, in which (as we shall see) married women's citizenship was a constant theme. Conflicts of law and diplomatic inconveniences or embarrassment, it was believed, would follow if married women were to hold independent citizenship. The representatives of one country might, for example, be required to extend protection to a wife in a foreign country against the country of her husband. The grant or denial of women's suffrage in any one country made no difference at all to these issues. The franchise was entirely a national, domestic matter, and of no concern internationally. In contrast, the terms on which a married woman held, lost, or acquired citizenship were of primary concern to other countries. Ultimately, they would become the concern of the whole international community.

Coverture

The history of women's legal status offers other paradoxes. The doctrine of 'coverture' applied to married women throughout the nineteenth century, and sometimes later (and the expression was used well into the twentieth, to refer generally to the condition of being a married woman). Coverture meant that a woman's legal identity – her right to hold property, enter into a contract, and assume legal obligations – was subsumed under her husband's. She had, in effect, no independent legal capacity. As William Blackstone described it in 1765:

> By marriage, the husband and wife are one person in law: that is, the very being or legal existence of the woman is suspended during the marriage, or at least is incorporated and consolidated into that of the husband, under whose wing, protection and *cover*, she performs everything.[48]

However, the specific legal consequences of coverture had begun to diminish by the mid-nineteenth century. The first United States Married

[48] William Blackstone, *Commentaries on the Laws of England* Vol 1 (1765) (University of Chicago Press 1979) 430.

Women's Property Act was passed in 1839 (in Mississippi), and in the United Kingdom, in 1870, with completion of property rights in 1882 and 1884.[49] Incrementally, thereafter, married women gained independent legal rights, and, subsequently women generally gained political rights.

Strikingly, these developments occurred at the very time when laws of conditional marital nationality were being adopted in many countries. The date of the first British Married Women's Property Act is particularly notable. Like passing ships, it and the Act that introduced marital denaturalisation for British-born women with foreign husbands, were enacted in the same year. Previously, notwithstanding coverture, British-born women had enjoyed security in their nationality; indeed, as Linda Kerber has observed, 'women's national citizenship contained deep within it an implicit challenge to coverture'.[50] Until the nineteenth century, women's status was undisturbed by marriage. In common with men, they were British subjects, and subject status was perpetual and inalienable. This rule applied at least around the common law world. The law of marital denaturalisation displaced the rule, and was maintained in many cases over the years of progressive equalisation of women's rights.[51] In Britain, the law was even maintained for more than twenty-five years after the passage of the Sex Disqualification Act of 1919, with its progressive command:

> a person shall not be disqualified by sex or marriage from the exercise of any public function or from being appointed to or holding any civil or judicial office or post or from entering or assuming or carrying on any civil profession or vocation or from admission to any incorporated Society . . . and a person shall not be exempted by sex or marriage from the liability to serve on a jury.

[49] The 1870 Act provided that wages and property earned through a wife's own work were to be her property, separately from that of her husband. The 1882 and 1884 Acts extended this protection to all of the wife's property, regardless of its source or when it was acquired. A 1893 Act equalised the property rights of married and unmarried women.

[50] Linda Kerber, 'The Paradox of Women's Citizenship in the Early Republic: The Case of *Martin vs. Massachusetts*, 1805', (1992) 97 *American Historical Review* 351. See also Barbara J Todd, 'Written in Her Heart'.

[51] This did not go unnoticed, even in 1870. Debating the UK Naturalization Bill, one Member of the House of Commons (Mr Kinnaird) objected to the marital denaturalisation provision, specifically with regard to the impact it would have on a woman separated from her foreign husband and 'forced against her will to become the subject of she knew not what power'; he added that he was 'surprised that, at a time when the rights of women were advocated so loudly, the House should seem determined thus to curtail them'. United Kingdom, House of Commons, *Debates*, 25 April 1870, 1740.

Coverture must certainly be taken into account among the background assumptions that nourished the policy of conditional marital nationality, but so must the fact that it had receded by the time the latter was at its height. As Bredbenner observes, the marital denaturalisation provision in the United States Expatriation Act 'represented a stunning setback in women's progression towards full citizenship rights'.[52] This apparent paradox of overlapping rights emancipation and citizenship subordination can be resolved, but only through situating the citizenship of married women in its international context. What is revealed in the fact that marital denaturalisation began and expanded around the world in an era when women were otherwise inching towards independent legal capacity, is that a countervailing, common interest was at work. Nationality, as we shall see, only makes sense as a matter of international relations, in a system of reciprocal recognition of other states' citizens. States, prepared to liberate their women legally, even politically, became willingly locked into this system. It was a system that, at the particular stage in the development of international relations and in the logic of constitutional sovereignty, required the sacrifice of married women's former independent citizenship.

The right to a nationality

The Universal Declaration of Human Rights, adopted a decade before the Convention on the Nationality of Married Women, was a response to the terrible sufferings inflicted by governments on their own minorities, and experienced by many others in the course of the conflicts that followed. It set out the rights that the world agreed belonged inalienably to all persons and that compelled protection. It is not hard to understand why nationality was included. The twentieth century had witnessed great demographic dislocations, mass homelessness, statelessness and the emergence of large populations of refugees. The world wars had been their appalling catalysts.

Hannah Arendt wrote graphically of the 'millions of people . . . who had lost and could not regain' their communities of citizenship, and of 'the loss of home and political status . . . identical with expulsion from humanity altogether'.[53] To have no nationality, Arendt affirmed, was to be stripped of the most basic of human rights. What was lost was more profound than legal or political rights. For both the stateless person and

[52] Bredbenner, *A Nationality of Her Own*, 5.

[53] Hannah Arendt, *The Origins of Totalitarianism* [1951] (Harcourt, 1976) 297.

the refugee, she wrote, '[s]omething more fundamental than freedom and justice . . . is at stake when belonging to the community into which one is born is no longer a matter of course and not belonging is no longer a matter of choice'.[54] In this statement (although Arendt did not address this) we find a further answer to our question about why the Convention on the Nationality of Married Women was needed.

To lose one's nationality, and to have no other (as a stateless person) or to be alienated (as an exile) from one's home, were regular risks for women who married. As the twentieth century unfolded, and conflicts of nationality and marriage law increasingly occurred, these experiences became more common. Even when statelessness did not follow, when parallel national laws resulted in the automatic conferral of the husband's citizenship upon the foreign wife, maritally denaturalised women found themselves, effectively, and sometimes literally, banished from the community into which they were born. Belonging, for such women was, to apply Arendt's words, 'no longer a matter of choice'.

Of course, as Arendt's analysis indicated, citizenship deprivation was not unique to married women. By the time of her writing, it had become a mass phenomenon of conflict and post-conflict situations. But the practice had long operated. Once citizenship by naturalisation became generally available under the laws of individual countries (from around the early-to-mid nineteenth century), legal rules were also established for its forfeiture. Some countries stripped citizenship from naturalised persons who returned to and resided in their country of former citizenship (or another country) for more than a specified number of years. Citizenship by naturalisation could also be lost (as it can today) for the commission of criminal offences, character misrepresentation and acts of disloyalty. Probably most countries withdrew citizenship by naturalisation obtained by fraud. Deprivation of primary or 'birthright' citizenship also occurred in almost all countries; a common reason was a person's naturalisation in the citizenship of another country. Many countries also stripped birthright citizenship from individuals as a penalty, most commonly for entry into the service of a foreign government, for enrolment in the armed forces of a foreign government, or evasion of military obligations.[55]

Patrick Weil has listed the expanding number of categories of person for whom citizenship had become conditional by the mid-twentieth century, and in doing so, noted the 'increasingly precarious' status of

[54] Arendt, ibid, 296. [55] United Nations, *A Study in Statelessness*, New York, August 1949.

women's nationality as ideas of citizenship evolved in the nineteenth century. Those susceptible to denaturalisation included 'women marrying foreigners, naturalised citizens, native citizens recruited into foreign armies or civil services, or those who voted in foreign elections, [or] were naturalised in foreign countries or deserted in time of war'.[56] This is an important acknowledgement of the historically non-consensual character of citizenship law, against claims that citizenship entailed a relationship of consent between the individual and the state. What it overlooks, however, in treating marital denaturalisation as one example among others, are both the vast numerical differences between denaturalised married women and the other categories of denaturalised person, and the conceptual distinction between marrying and performing the other acts that led to forfeiture of citizenship. What distinguished these latter cases from loss of citizenship through marriage was, first, the numbers and breadth of the latter – virtually all countries practised it and, in the countries that did, all women married to foreign men experienced it. Secondly, the individual action that led to loss of citizenship upon foreign marriage was unrelated to, or was detached from, citizenship itself; that is to say, the act of marrying, unlike service in a foreign country's armed forces, had nothing to do with the qualities or duties associated with citizenship. Further, where denaturalisation (for other reasons) was styled as a penalty for certain forms of conduct, opportunities for legal appeal often existed. No such opportunities were available for maritally denaturalised women.

Marriage to a foreigner was perhaps most closely analogous to foreign naturalisation; indeed, as noted, marital denaturalisation was (at least until the 1920s) frequently accompanied by automatic naturalisation by the alien husband's state. Denaturalisation was commonly justified on the ground that foreign marriage was comparable to foreign naturalisation, or was actually such an act. But, again, the difference is important: unlike naturalisation, marriage and the motives for marrying were (and remain) conceptually distinct from the qualities or duties of citizenship. Unlike with naturalisation, no test applied, or could logically have applied, as to whether the woman, in marrying, intended to alter her citizenship status. Indeed, marriages entered into for the sole purpose of acquiring the citizenship of the husband's country were (and remain) legally invalid.

56 Patrick Weil, 'From Conditional to Secured and Sovereign: The New Strategic Link between the Citizen and the Nation-state in a Globalized World' (2011) 9 *International Journal of Constitutional Law* 615, 626.

The numbers

How many women were affected? Marriages between fellow-citizens were more numerically common, but the number of marriages between citizens and foreigners was anything but small. Official records, the literature produced by citizenship equality campaigners, and contemporary press reports, speak consistently of many hundreds or many thousands of women at any one time whose native citizenship, in a particular country, had been lost as a consequence of marriage. Statistical records specifically of such marriages are difficult to locate, but estimates are possible. One source finds that '[s]ome 250,000 Americans were living permanently in Canada in 1933, hundreds if not thousands of whom were men married to Canadian women, not to mention the large numbers of such women living in the United States with their husbands'.[57] In 1927, a Canadian Member of Parliament, responding to a proposal for the repeal of conditional marital nationality laws, pointed out that 'in this country, where we have 3,000 miles of an international boundary with two peoples of the same race and the same language living along this border, . . . hundreds and thousands of United States citizens are coming to Canada, and hundreds and thousands of Canadians are going over to the United States'.[58] There were numerous Canadian marriages with non-Americans, too: 'Between 1940 and 1947 the [Canadian] government paid for and orchestrated the safe ocean passage of almost 50,000 war brides to Canada, most of them British, all of them engaged or married to Canadian servicemen during overseas tours'.[59] In France, according to one source, 120,000 French women had become foreigners through marriage between 1914 and 1927;[60] in the 1920s, there were around 150,000 women residents who were French born, but had been transformed into aliens by marriage.[61] The largest numbers of stateless persons living in the United States in the interwar years were maritally denaturalised women.[62]

57 Girard, '"If two ride a horse"' 45. (Girard's source is Bredbenner, *A Nationality of Her Own*, 225.) The year, 1933, as we shall see, marked an important milestone in British law governing the status of married women.

58 Dominion of Canada, House of Commons, *Debates*, 6 April 1927, 1987 (Mr J. S. Woodsworth).

59 Matrix, 'Mediated Citizenship', 68.

60 Christophe Bertossi, 'Country Report: France' (EUDO Citizenship Observatory, 2010).

61 Patrick Weil, *How to be French: Nationality in the Making Since 1789* (Duke University Press, 2008) 6.

62 Linda Kerber, 'Toward a History of Statelessness in America' (2005) 57 *American Quarterly* 735.

Indirect statistics are also revealing. From the outbreak of the First World War until after the Second World War, aliens living in Britain were required to register at local police stations, giving details, among others, of their place of birth. Women born in Britain (and thus originally British subjects) who registered as aliens had in almost all cases lost their British citizenship through foreign marriage. In debate in the UK parliament in 1918, one Member estimated that 3,000 British-born women at that time, in Britain, were married to German husbands.[63] In 1922, an estimated 30,000 (more than 20 per cent) of the 139,000 alien women living in Britain were British-born.[64] In Australia, in 1936, an amendment of the nationality law allowed maritally denaturalised women, former British subjects, who were living in Australia to apply for the restoration of their political rights (see Chapter 5); in anticipation of such applications, 3,000 copies of the relevant form were printed for the Department of the Interior.[65] The estimated number of applicants was, of course, a subset (albeit, as we shall see, an eager one) of the total number of maritally denaturalised alien women in Australia at that time.

Such samples concern only maritally denaturalised women living in their country of origin at a particular historical moment. The numbers must be significantly multiplied, if we factor in women who lived in their husbands' country (or a third country). Additionally, the wives of men who changed citizenship by naturalisation were, in most cases, also affected. In the first decade of the twentieth century, an estimated 100,000 men were naturalised in the United States each year. We can assume that a good many of these men were married; their wives were automatically naturalised as a consequence. Taking further account of the number of countries in which conditional marital nationality laws operated, and the period over which they operated (in most cases, for several decades, if not longer), the numbers affected must have amounted to millions. The British Empire, to take one example, had a population of more than 420 million in the early years of the twentieth century; marital denaturalisation was practised across the Empire for close to eighty years (and marital naturalisation for over 100 years). Even a small percentage

63 United Kingdom, House of Commons, *Parliamentary Debates*, 12 July 1918, 661 (Charles Roberts).

64 Tabili, 'Outsiders in the Land of Their Birth'.

65 National Archives of Australia, Series A367 (A367/1) A1 1937/6737.

of foreign marriages in any year would have added up, over time, to a vast number.[66]

Arendt observed that, until the rise of totalitarianism, the international commonality of interests restrained the character of national citizenship laws. She commented: 'One is almost tempted to measure the degree of totalitarian infection by the extent to which the concerned governments use their sovereign right of denationalization'. By the interwar period, 'there was hardly a country left on the Continent that did not pass . . . some new legislation' allowing it to 'get[] rid of a great number of its inhabitants at any opportune moment'. Arendt continued: 'Prior to the last war, only totalitarian or half-totalitarian dictatorships resorted to the weapon of denaturalization with regard to those who were citizens by birth'.[67] Astonishingly, this great observer of statelessness and of the condition of refugees did not notice that policies of marital denaturalisation had, in large numbers over many decades, produced the condition she described: the loss of the legal community into which persons had been born. Furthermore, as we shall see, this effect was the very result of an international commonality of interests.

By the time Arendt was writing, marital denaturalisation had been abandoned in much of the world. Some countries still practised it for decades after the adoption of the Convention on the Nationality of

[66] In a discussion of Britain's post-9/11 citizenship-deprivation laws which includes details about the 1870 Naturalization Act and the 1914 British Nationality and Status of Aliens Act, Matthew Gibney makes a claim about the history of denaturalisation, offering it as a reason for the neglect of the subject: 'Relatively small numbers of people have lost citizenship in this way [involuntarily]. Since 1914, when [UK citizenship-deprivation] legislation first appears, only about 200 individuals have lost their British citizenship, most in the period before 1971'. He pertinently adds, however: 'Yet if deprivation provisions have affected only a small number of individuals directly, the consequences for those concerned have been weighty'. Gibney, '"A Very Transcendental Power": Denaturalisation and the Liberalisation of Citizenship in the United Kingdom' (2013) 61 *Political Studies* 637, 638. On the non-British record, Gibney explains that 'around 2 million political opponents of the communist regime' were denaturalised by Russia following the Soviet Revolution, and Germany withdrew citizenship 'from political opponents' in the 1920s. These are, he writes, 'archetypes of involuntary loss of state membership'. He then lists 'less noted' examples: 'many liberal states also had denaturalisation provisions during much of the twentieth century for those deemed disloyal, lacking commitment to the nation or convicted of crimes'. No reference is made to involuntary loss of citizenship by marital denaturalisation, even among the 'less noted' examples Gibney identifies in the history of non-British countries.

[67] Arendt, *The Origins of Totalitarianism*, 279.

Married Women,[68] and the practice has not entirely vanished,[69] but, notwithstanding the persistence of many instances of gender inequality in the laws governing marriage and divorce in many countries, the shift from virtual unanimity on the necessity for marital denaturalisation to its global rejection in a relatively short period is remarkable.

Conclusion

The policy of conditional marital nationality was once believed to be irreversible. Unravelling it – either allowing a wife to choose whether to adopt her husband's citizenship or keep her own, or simply allowing a wife and husband to have separate nationalities – was considered both impossibly complex and normatively objectionable. Citizenship equality campaigners challenged these conclusions, but governments and other defenders of the practice continued to protest that diplomatic embarrassments (or worse), family breakdown and international quarrels would follow its repeal. By 1957, the world had changed its mind: independent citizenship for married women was not only feasible (even if complications followed), but was normatively compelling. It was now a human right.[70]

[68] For example, the Philippines until 1994, when the *Republic Act* no. 8171 provided for the repatriation of, among others, Filipino women who had lost their citizenship by marriage to aliens. Repatriation is effected by taking an oath of allegiance and registration.

[69] Among other gender inequalities in Palestinian law (at the time of writing), a Palestinian woman loses her nationality if she marries a non-Palestinian, unless she submits a written application to the Minister of Interior within a year after her marriage. Suheir Azzouni, 'Palestine: Palestinian Authority and Israeli-Occupied Territories', in Sanja Kelly and Julia Breslin (eds) *Women's Rights in the Middle East and North Africa: Progress Amid Resistance* (Rowman & Littlefield, 2010).

[70] The 'Women's Convention', CEDAW, elaborates on this principle. Art 9, para 1, provides that: 'States parties shall grant women equal rights to men to acquire, change or retain their nationality. They shall ensure in particular that neither marriage to an alien nor change of nationality by the husband during marriage shall automatically change the nationality of the wife, render her stateless or force upon her the nationality of the husband'. The European Convention on Nationality, 1997, also includes parallel provisions protecting married women's independent nationality, including Section 4 d: 'neither marriage nor the dissolution of a marriage between a national of a State Party and an alien, nor the change of nationality by one of the spouses during marriage, shall automatically affect the nationality of the other spouse'. There are additional regional instruments, including the Protocol to the African Charter on Human and People's Rights on the Rights of Women in Africa, which provides that 'a woman shall have the right to retain her nationality or to acquire the nationality of her husband'. Radha Govil and Alice Edwards, 'Women,

The following chapters offer an overview of how, and why, conditional marital nationality laws came to be a routine part of the regime of modern citizenship law. The experience of women who were affected by the law is integrated into the larger picture, that of the transnational imperatives to which it was a response. This account, as noted in the Preface, focuses on the history and experience of marital denaturalisation more than that of marital naturalisation, since the effect of conditional citizenship was more powerfully felt, and is thus more readily understood, in the loss than in the gain. Citizenship-stripping allows us to understand more clearly, as a window onto a larger landscape, the existential nature of citizenship, in its own right. We can understand this, even now, after the practice (at least as applied to married women) has mostly ended. The protective character offered by the legal status of (secure) citizenship is, as we shall see (in Chapter 7) most powerfully illustrated in its association with the loss of 'home'. This is poignantly illustrated through the impact of denaturalisation on women.

My argument is not that women, as such, are in greater need of protection (and thus security of citizenship) than men, although the reality is that women experience greater vulnerability across their lifetimes than men. It is, rather, that the neglect of this part of women's history has distorted our understanding of citizenship. It has encouraged a focus on allegiance as a core marker of citizenship and has diminished the value of protection as its conceptual companion. It has overlooked the existential injury associated with its loss, including in the tragedy of statelessness. In the stories of women's experience, we can recognise the importance of protection for all who are vulnerable, whether temporarily or permanently. We can recognise, too, the significance, both practical and existential, of the home that is offered by non-contingent citizenship.

These claims may appear to validate the privileged lives of those whose citizenship is acquired by the unearned accident of birth in wealthy countries, and to suggest that the less-favoured must simply accept what the 'birthright lottery', as Ayelet Shachar has so powerfully called it, has delivered to them.[71] Shachar (as discussed in Chapter 7) has argued that that all persons, regardless of legal citizenship, should be entitled to the benefits that are conferred on the citizens of prosperous countries. An alternative,

Nationality and Statelessness' in Alice Edwards and Laura van Waas (eds) *Nationality and Statelessness under International Law* (Cambridge University Press, 2014).

[71] Ayelet Shachar, *The Birthright Lottery: Citizenship and Global Inequality* (Harvard University Press, 2009).

but foundationally related claim, made by advocates of 'cosmopolitan' citizenship, is that all persons should be free to move across national borders, to seek asylum or employment, or simply a new life, regardless of their passport status. These claims are, essentially, for social justice (more than citizenship), for the entitlement of all to the basic good in life, and for opportunities to flourish as human beings.

My argument about the relationship between citizenship and 'home' does not undercut these claims. The home offered by the country of one's citizenship – protection, shelter and existential comfort – can be offered equally to few or many. The practicalities of capacity (administrative and material) are a different subject. The claim I make is that we should not abandon citizenship as a good in itself, simply because the other goods enjoyed by citizens are contingent and unequal. Citizenship is more than instrumental. It means more than the material advantages or entitlements that may come with it. The loss of citizenship creates its own iniquities. The history of marital denaturalisation shows us this reality. The adoption in 1957 of the Convention on the Nationality of Married Women affirms it.

1

The emergence of modern citizenship

People today think of themselves *as* citizens of a particular country, as if this was a personal quality, part of themselves. They describe themselves as such (as they do their marital status, age or sex) when they fill out forms that record their legal identity. Probably most people do not realise how historically recent it is to do this, how modern it is for citizenship to be treated as a marker, or type of identity.

Modern citizenship is paradoxical. It is determined by formal criteria that are colourless and impersonal, outside individual control or subjectivity, and yet at the same time it is *identic.* It is pragmatic, but it is also existential. To explain what this means requires going back to the emergence of modern citizenship law, exploring what is distinctive about being a citizen (or national) and about what this signifies in the relationship between the person and the state. The development of citizenship law was not, as might be thought, primarily a matter of states deciding to classify the members of their population by passing appropriate legislation and issuing documents permitting individuals to be recognised as members of that state by and in other countries. The relationship of states with other states was, rather, at the core of the development.

The story of modern citizenship is the story of international arrangements. It is the story of a legal status, the primary application and significance of which lay, initially at least, outside the state. Modern citizenship law was initiated in the revolutions of the late eighteenth century, but its evolution mostly followed, rather than preceded, the formalisation of modern international relations. The early steps in the process of identifying citizens as a class began with (or were inextricably tied up with) a state's determining who did not belong to that class. Most states classified non-citizens before they systematically classified their own. The incidents of what we now consider markers of citizenship came much later. Passports (as we know them) were a twentieth century innovation,[1] adopted long after laws governing nationality and citizenship status had been regularised among states. Only much later, after the mid-twentieth century, did citizenship become conceptualised (at least in some important contexts) as belonging to the citizen, rather than the state.

What, then, has gender got to do with this history? Gender is both the key and the missing referent. Citizenship law – that is, the law governing the acquisition and loss of citizenship as a legal status – was different for men and women around the world for the better part of a century after modern citizenship first emerged. This is not widely known. Histories of citizenship law, for the most part, have been accounts of only half the citizenry. They have been incomplete and inadequate. The fact that there were gendered historical distinctions in the law provides an important key to understanding the evolution of modern thinking about citizenship as a whole. It also offers, as we shall see, a way of rethinking the value of citizenship in the twenty-first century.

Beginnings

Modern citizenship is the creation of the great and irreversible changes that swept through the world between the seventeenth and twentieth centuries, giving rise to what we understand now as the modern nation-state. There can be no single explanation for these phenomena. Historians of state formation have identified innumerable influences, including wars, demographic shifts and economic and industrial developments. States, it is clear, did not emerge on their own; their formation was relational, a process of boundary-drawing, reciprocal recognition and settled coexistence. States emerged as part of an international order, its origins commonly identified as lying in the Westphalian settlement of 1648. The Treaties of Westphalia, which divided up Europe at the end of the Thirty Year War, are regarded as the foundation of modern international relations, governed by the principle of state sovereignty, the foundational principle of modern international law. Under this principle, the borders of states were inviolable, jurisdiction was territorial and states were immune from (legitimate) interference by other states in their governance.

[1] John Torpey, *The Invention of the Passport: Surveillance, Citizenship and the State* (Cambridge University Press, 2000).

The Treaties 'confirmed the supplanting of centralised imperial power by a judicial arrangement of autonomous sovereigns'.[2] Although they applied over only a small part of the world, their influence in the shaping of modern international law is taken to be axiomatic. But Westphalian Europe was a long way from the modern international order in which the citizenship law we recognise today emerged. The sovereignty of Westphalian Europe was that of monarchs and potentates. In such a system, the identification of the population and the attribution of legal status to persons were largely irrelevant. What mattered was the territorial scope of the sovereign's realm. For a modern concept of citizenship to be both possible and necessary, a further step was needed: the displacement of the monarch as sovereign, and the identification of a new sovereign: 'the people'. Only when the idea took hold that the sovereignty of states was (if only rhetorically) based on the consent or authority of their people, did it become important to identify the members of particular states as against each other.

This identification was the product of revolutionary thinking. It is no coincidence that the first countries to recognise citizenship (and naturalisation) in general legislation were those of the great eighteenth century revolutions: the United States and France. The legal status of the members of these new (republican) constitutional communities was 'citizen'. Citizens were, in law, related to each other, not as family members or as members of ethnic or religious communities, nor as fellow 'subjects', but as common bearers of a legal status. They were, in principle, members of a sovereign community, owing their allegiance to that new sovereign, rather than to the monarch (to whom the allegiance of subjects was assumed to be owed). But citizenship law, identifying the legal community to which individuals belonged, was formalised some time later.

Although the idea of citizenship entailed membership of a particular territorial state, its core legal purpose and its core determinants lay in the state's relationship with other states. Modern states were constituted by this relationship, and the identification of citizens was an incremental part of the process. As C. A. Bayly writes, 'A key feature of the nation-state . . . was not its intrinsic nature or its claims and demands on its own population. It was instead the fact that the nation-state operated in a world

[2] Gerry Simpson, 'International Law in Diplomatic History', in James Crawford and Martti Koskenniemi (eds) *The Cambridge Companion to International Law* (Cambridge University Press, 2012) 31.

populated by other, similar nation-states and imperial provinces'.[3] The idea of the citizen as a bearer of rights and obligations, as an individual defined by a national legal regime, with a place governed by a relationship to his or her own state that extended to diplomatic protection by that state through its representatives in other countries, is much more recent. This idea rested on the prior foundation of a complex juridico-political regime of national and international recognition.

In the early evolution of the modern state, 'the individual had no place, no rights in the international legal order'; diplomatic protection emerged as an element of international relations only after the legal classification of the relationship of individuals to states and of states to each other became 'clearly defined in modern public law'.[4] Citizenship law, in other words, was a product of, and a latecomer to, the development of international relations. This (seemingly paradoxical) process, it will become apparent, is central to an understanding of both the policy of conditional marital nationality and its timing.

The idea of the people as the new sovereign generated a demand for the democratic organisation of state power. Jürgen Habermas, writing of the post-revolutionary emergence of citizenship, has observed that '[w]ith the French Revolution . . . the meaning of "nation" was transformed from a prepolitical quantity into a constitutive feature of the political identity of the citizens of a democratic state'.[5] The idea was also critical to the claims of the American Revolution. The American revolutionaries asserted their sovereign right to break the bonds with the British sovereign; their enemy was external, a distant, oppressive executive (styled as the King). The Declaration of Independence claimed a right of rupture, and at the same time identified a new sovereign – the 'people' – who would be named as the sovereign community in the opening lines of the United States Constitution ('We the people of the United States'), at the moment of its transformation into a constitutional community.

And yet, the American Constitution itself said nothing about how citizenship was acquired or transmitted; it mentioned citizens in several sections (regarding eligibility to serve as President or in Congress or the Senate) and it referred to the 'privileges and immunities' of citizens, but

3 C. A. Bayly, *The Birth of the Modern World: 1780–1914* (Blackwell, 2004) 234.

4 Edwin Borchard, *The Diplomatic Protection of Citizens Abroad*, 1913 (PhD dissertation, Columbia University; Nabu Public Domain Reprints) 497.

5 Jürgen Habermas, 'Citizenship and National Identity' (1990), Appendix II, *Between Facts and Norms* (Polity Press, 1997) 494.

it was not until 1868, with the ratification of the Fourteenth Amendment, that American citizenship by birth was given constitutional recognition. (Earlier American naturalisation laws, as we see in the following chapter, set out citizenship eligibility criteria, but only for foreign-born persons.)

A decade after the American Revolution, the Constitutions that followed the French Revolution of 1789 spoke of citizenship more explicitly. The 1791 Constitution described the means of acquisition via multiple paternal pathways. It distinguished between *citoyens français* and *citoyens actifs*: 'The former were nationals or citizens in the modern sense, including all members of the nation-state; the latter comprised the sub-class of persons with political rights'.[6] Citizenship was attached to political participation, and Frenchwomen were initially incorporated in this conceptualisation, but only briefly. Women's identification as 'active' citizens was wound back in 1792, when the right to vote was extended only to all adult males. The rationale was that men who were liable for military service should have the (sole) right to choose their representatives.[7] Still, importantly, women retained their status as members of the constitutional community, as legal citizens. The *acquisition* of citizenship, as a status (independently of the rights and entitlements that might follow) was neutral with regard to gender.

At this stage in the evolution of modern citizenship, no distinction was made between men and women in the laws governing birthright citizenship in either the United States or France. It was the Napoleonic Code of 1804 (as we saw in the Introduction) that introduced the idea that a woman's citizenship was to be dependent on the citizenship of her husband. By the mid-nineteenth century the idea had spread[8]: the citizenship of married women was widely treated as conditional, as transferrable from one state to another in the event of foreign marriage, regardless of the legal or practical consequences for the individual woman.

As modern international relations evolved, persons were progressively allocated under law to a particular state. The state needed to identify its members: it needed to do this in order to draw the line of authority and sovereignty between itself and other states. Citizenship law was the product of this line-drawing, or 'triage': the allocation of individuals to

[6] Brubaker, *Citizenship and Nationhood*, 87.

[7] Charles Tilly, 'The Emergence of Citizenship in France and Elsewhere' (1995) 40 *International Review of Social History* 223.

[8] Robert S. Miller, 'Recent Developments in the Law Controlling Nationality of Married Women' (1932–3) 1 *George Washington Law Review* 330.

one sovereign or another. This process allowed states to identify their own members against those of others, to know which sovereign was to take responsibility for which individuals. Popular sovereignty as the basis of the state demanded this, as did the drawing of modern territorial borders. The laws that instituted women's conditional marital nationality were, to put it simply, the by-product of arrangements for states' reciprocal recognition of each other's citizens.[9]

If the Treaties of Westphalia laid the territorial foundations of international law, the Congress of Vienna in 1815, which redrew Europe's borders after the defeat of Napoleon Bonaparte, laid the foundation for modern international negotiations and for the recognition of constitutional government. While the Congress 'restored the traditional authority of crown and altar',[10] at the same time it resisted claims for territorial divisions based on nationalism and ethnicity. By the 1840s and 1850s, 'attempts to hold together a streamlined version of the old order of states had evidently failed',[11] and the revolutionary movements of those decades gave rise to a Europe divided along both nationalist and constitutionalist lines. The new order of international relations set down in 1815 endured, however, and the modern approach to the legal status of persons began to emerge. Many of the general rules for acquiring citizenship that were found in the Napoleonic Code in 1804 were gradually adopted around the world. Laws that governed women's loss of citizenship through marriage were followed in Europe, and, as we have seen, from the mid-century became almost universal. These laws were progressively adopted regardless of whether the state in question was formed on nationalist or constitutional lines. The internal character of the nation-state, in other words, did not

[9] Karen Knop and Christine Chinkin, exceptionally, recognise the historical international dimension of the rule of common family nationality as an underlying premise of conditional marital nationality. The premise, they argue, 'was deeply bound up with a vision of the international order as a power struggle between states'. If husband and wife had different nationalities, 'the rivalries, tensions, and hostilities that existed between states would be projected onto the marriage'. Knop and Chinkin, 'Remembering Chrystal Macmillan', 523, 558. My account privileges cooperation rather than struggle between states in explaining conditional marital nationality, and reverses the equation: nationality rivalries in a marriage would be projected onto the (respective) states. But cooperation and power struggles are two sides of the same coin; the first is the means of avoiding the second. I find conditional marital nationality, however, to be a secondary effect, a 'by-product' of the cooperative arrangements for the recognition of (masculine) citizenship.

[10] Peter Flora (ed) *State Formation, Nation Building, and Mass Politics in Europe: The Theory of Stein Rokkan* (Oxford University Press, 1999) 162.

[11] Bayly, *The Birth of the Modern World*, 127.

determine whether or not a policy of conditional marital nationality was applied.

Debates abound over the relationship between nationalism and the emergence of the modern state: for some historians, long-standing nationalist identification of 'peoples' or 'nations' provided the foundation for the state, fuelling demands for nationhood and its recognition in the boundaries and institutions of statehood. For others, nation-states were 'constructed' in the process of modernisation; the claims of nationalism, some scholars have argued, followed the establishment of the state. States in the nineteenth century, Bayly notes in his summary of the modernisation view,

> promoted popular education, defined citizenship and its duties, counted and imprisoned people . . . [G]overnments began to institute regular censuses and to control immigration and emigration . . . All this was consciously or unconsciously directed to strengthening the sentiment of nationalism and making people on the margins choose one or another nation-state.[12]

One need not take a position on whether national communities are real or 'imagined'[13] to make several observations: the laws that defined citizenship in the nineteenth century were 'ethnically' open, at least in most countries. Even where the *jus sanguinis* rule applied (basing citizenship upon descent or 'blood', as opposed to citizenship by birth in the territory, or *jus soli*), naturalisation permitted members of other states' or nations' 'peoples' to be assimilated into the citizenry. In some countries, naturalisation of certain classes of aliens was prohibited on racial grounds (the United States and the British Dominions, for example, prohibited Chinese and Japanese naturalisation in the late nineteenth and early decades of the twentieth century) but such lines of exclusion were not drawn around nationalities, in the sense of self-identifying ethno-cultural communities of 'peoples'. The members of the citizenry were always more heterogeneous than the latter, and the qualifications for citizenship were relatively neutral and capacious. But, the denaturalisation of women who married foreign men proceeded, regardless of the degree of nationalism in the relevant jurisdiction. Women who were members of nationalistic communities were stripped of their citizenship on the same footing as women who were members of nationalistically weak states.

[12] Bayly, *The Birth of the Modern World*, 203.

[13] Benedict Anderson, *Imagined Communities: Reflections on the Origin and Spread of Nationalism* (Verso, 1983).

Conditional marital nationality was also applied regardless of a country's rule for the acquisition of citizenship. Under British common law, for example, the status of British subject was acquired by *jus soli* – the simple fact of birth within British territory, regardless of ethnicity or parentage. Exceptions to this rule – the children of ambassadors, and children fathered by members of occupying armies during war – were extremely limited, and served to confirm the rule that nationality was based on a principle of allegiance to the state. This common law rule was followed around the British Empire, and was adopted in the American colonies and subsequently the United States. In contrast, for example, Prussian law conferred nationality upon the basis of paternal descent, *jus sanguinis*, and this rule was followed after German unification in 1871. By the second half of the nineteenth century, however, notwithstanding the German attachment to the principle of citizenship defined by 'blood', German women who married foreigners found their nationality no more secure than that of women who acquired their nationality by birth in Britain or America.[14] Conditional marital nationality for women was also adopted in other countries that followed the *jus sanguinis* rule (Japan, for example), as it was in countries that practised both citizenship by birth and descent, and as it did in countries such as France, which changed its approach over time.[15]

Regardless of the form of constitutional or administrative authority, or whether the 'people' of the state were identified ethnically or constitutionally, women were denaturalised by foreign marriage. Denaturalisation under national laws also occurred in countries where the rights of political participation ('political citizenship') were determined at the local level (the Cantonal level in Switzerland, for example, or the State level in the United States); that is, notwithstanding local eligibility rules for public participation, a national approach to the citizenship of married women prevailed. The law of citizenship was under-determined by the cultural and legislative choices of individual countries or their own particular pathway to statehood.

As in histories of citizenship (noted in the Introduction), in histories of the modern state and its conceptualisation of membership, scholarly neglect of women's legal status is striking. A major work, exploring

[14] Prussian 'Law on the Acquisition and Loss of Confederative and State Citizenship' of June 1870 (section 13); adopted as Reich law, April 1871.

[15] 'Since the Revolution, France has changed its [nationality] laws more often and more significantly than any other democratic nation has'. Weil, *How to Be French*, 3.

the growth of the national state, globalisation and transformations of concepts of citizenship since medieval times includes a discussion of multiple grounds of denaturalisation ('denationalisation') across the historical landscape, but does not factor marriage into the account.[16] A recent global history of the nineteenth century discusses the quest on the part of nation states and empires to establish norms for the 'model citizen'. The author observes that '[m]usings about national identity or "civilized behavior" . . . were a feature of public life in many countries'; nevertheless, he adds, 'the uniform simplicity of nations and "national organisms" remained an illusion. Empires could not conjure away their multinational character and none took the radical step of introducing a single, "color-blind" citizenship'.[17] In fact, Britain did not differentiate in legal entitlement to *birthright* citizenship on the basis of colour and nor did the United States after 1868, but this aside, the analysis overlooks that almost every country in the nineteenth century did take 'the radical step' of introducing a single, *gender-based* citizenship, with women's legal entitlement and imputed identity based on the single variable of marriage.

Allegiance and protection

In feudal England and Europe, an individual's primary status was determined by birth into one of the feudal orders. The place of birth was important too, although less so. The legal significance of birthplace was relatively slight. Common law rules governed entitlements to property ownership, the payment of tithes and taxes, and the performance of certain local duties. The relationship of individual to sovereign was that of subject; the subject was born within the 'ligeance' of the king. The obligation on the part of vassal to the lord on whose lands the vassal was tenant was one of 'fidelitas or fealty' given by oath. Fidelity to the king was expressed as an oath of 'allegiance'.[18]

But, in addition to express declarations, Blackstone notes, there was an 'implied, original, and virtual allegiance, owing from every subject to his sovereign'.[19] Natural allegiance was perpetual and inalienable; it was 'due from all men born within the king's dominions immediately

[16] Saskia Sassen, *Territory, Authority, Rights: From Medieval to Global Assemblages* (Princeton University Press, 2006).

[17] Jürgen Osterhammel, *The Transformation of the World: A Global History of the Nineteenth Century* (Princeton University Press, 2014) 632–3.

[18] Blackstone, *Commentaries on the Laws of England*, 430, 355.

[19] Blackstone, ibid, 356–7.

upon their birth'.[20] A change of residence (or 'local allegiance'), even to another country, could not alter or diminish allegiance to the sovereign.[21] The sovereign, in return, owed a perpetual duty of protection (although temporary protection was offered to resident aliens, this was only during their residency). Women, in this system, enjoyed protection from loss of their subject status, regardless of the status of their husbands, and, like other subjects, they enjoyed security of abode. As subjects they were not susceptible to expulsion from their territory of residence.

In all other legal respects, however, women were the equivalent of aliens. They were subjects with highly circumscribed rights. To be a subject (or citizen) without rights might appear derisory. But the enjoyment of the status was itself significant. In the nineteenth and twentieth centuries, women who campaigned for citizenship equality emphasised the fact that, under the common law, women had enjoyed citizenship in their own right, and that it was only in modern times that legislation had made women's citizenship conditional and its retention or loss dependent on the citizenship of their husbands. Most strikingly, in surveying the shifts in laws governing citizenship from the pre- to the post-revolutionary era, we see a paradoxical *décalage*: in the feudal system, women's citizenship status was independent and secure, while their rights were minimal; in the modern constitutional state, women's citizenship status was contingent and weak, while their enjoyment of legal and political rights was expanding.

Citizenship, as it emerged in the modern constitutional state was built around two enduring pre-modern paradigms: allegiance and protection. The first has attracted disproportionate attention and been prioritised by law. The second has been sidelined, or treated as secondary and contingent. A 1963 publication of the United Nations Commission on the Status of Women opens with the statement: 'Nationality affects allegiance

[20] Blackstone, ibid, 357.

[21] Loss of subject status did occur under British and other law in certain exceptional historical instances, notwithstanding this principle. Territorial relinquishment provided one early and enduring example; in a case concerning Britain's recognition by Treaty of the independence of the United States, the King's Bench held that 'a declaration that a State shall be free, sovereign and independent is a declaration that the people composing that State shall no longer be considered as subjects of the Sovereign by whom such declaration is made'. (*Doe on the Demise of J. Thomas* v. *Acklam*, King's Bench, 1824). (The Court also considered the possibility that dual nationality might otherwise arise.) Certain Acts providing for deprivation of nationality for conduct amounting to treason can also be found. These do not upset the principle that a subject under the common law could not voluntarily 'expatriate'.

and the concomitant right of the individual to protection by the State'.[22] This statement implies that protection is offered as a return or reward for allegiance. Histories of citizenship and case law concerning the legal status of individuals have similarly prioritised allegiance. Their focus, to put it simply at this point, has been on the obligations – putative or actual – owed by the individual to the state. The citizen is said to be 'under allegiance', and consequently to be required to perform certain duties to the sovereign.

Historically, the legal obligations of allegiance were few. Allegiance was owed to the king both in his 'political capacity' and his natural person.[23] The associated duties were primarily those of defence (military and personal), paying taxes, performing military service where necessary, and defending the king's person and honour. The taking of oaths of fidelity expressed the subject's willingness to perform these duties. These duties attached to men and were not available to women. They were masculine duties, masculine tests of 'belonging' or identification. Women did not perform military service, and nor in many countries did they swear oaths of allegiance. More importantly, the duties were conceptually male: the duties of persons with a public identity, duties that overrode family obligations or loyalties. Nevertheless, women born within the ligeance were legally defined as subjects; that is to say, their incapacity to perform duties of allegiance did not disqualify them from 'citizenship'. The sovereign's protection, such as it was, was not withheld from women for non-performance of duty. Allegiance was assumed as a quality of the subject, not as a test of activity or character.

At the same time, the subject's allegiance to the sovereign was not elective or optional, not a matter of choice or volition. It was indelible, perpetual and inalienable. Subjects could not divest themselves of their allegiance any more than they could 'divorce' their family. A sovereign, in some cases, had the power to banish a subject from the realm, but still could not strip that person of subject status. By the mid-nineteenth century, in a radical rethinking of the relationship of individual to sovereign, states had begun to recognise citizenship as alienable, indeed, to recognise voluntary 'expatriation' as an individual freedom.

This mutability (as we see in the following chapter) was essential to the international relations of modern states. In practice, however, this

[22] United Nations, Commission on the Status of Women, 'Nationality of Married Women' (Report submitted by the Secretary-General, New York, 1963) 5.

[23] Blackstone, *Commentaries on the Laws of England*, 359.

new freedom was for men alone. Previously protected by the principle of inalienability and perpetual allegiance, women's citizenship became conditional and precarious. The laws of modern states that first acknowledged voluntary 'expatriation' on the part of individual citizens both indirectly and directly consolidated the emerging vulnerability of women's citizenship. Once allegiance/'citizenship' was no longer perpetual, it became conceivable not only that an individual might change allegiance, but also that the sovereign might strip away an individual's citizenship. This shift in thinking permitted the policy of conditional marital nationality not only to be effected, but (as we shall see) to be treated as necessary and inevitable in cases of a woman's foreign marriage.

To summarise, in the pre-modern legal order, women held inalienable 'citizenship' (or subject status) in their own right, and were offered protection, regardless of their non-performance of specific duties of allegiance. Allegiance was assumed as an attribute or quality attached to being a subject, and inherent to the status, as such. The specific duties of the subject, where relevant, were masculine, but the masculine character of allegiance was not exclusive. As modern citizenship law developed, however, allegiance became conceptualised in performative terms. It ceased to be indelible; a person's choice to transfer allegiance and thus citizenship began to be recognised, even conceptualised as a right. This choice, however, was not available to married women.

As we have noted, in the United Nations statement, nationality (or citizenship) involves allegiance and protection, but allegiance is privileged. Reversing, or at least equalising, these concepts has radical implications. To recognise protection as lying at the core of citizenship shifts the perspective from what is owed by the individual to the state, to what is owed by the state to the individual. Historically, these obligations were reciprocal: allegiance to the sovereign brought protection on the part of the sovereign. The modern conception of sovereignty (constitutional rather than personal) retained this relationship, although in an attenuated form. The state was, in principle, obliged to protect its citizens, but the legal expression of this obligation was, and remains, imprecise, more a matter of 'soft' law than enforceable law.[24] Nevertheless, its expressions – the state's inability to expel its own citizens, and the expectation that diplomatic representation and assistance will be available to its citizens in foreign countries – are important parts of the story of modern citizenship.

[24] Alfred M. Boll, *Multiple Nationality and International Law* (Martinus Nijhoff, 2007).

Seen in this light, the state has a protective, even 'familial' relationship with the citizen.

In the nineteenth century, increasingly, the protection offered by the sovereign or the state to women was delegated to men. Men became, indeed, the family sovereign; they became the (presumptive) object of women's allegiance. This will seem obvious to those familiar with the literature on 'coverture', the transfer of a woman's legal rights upon marriage to her husband, in which (as noted in the Introduction) 'the very being or legal existence of the woman [was] suspended during the marriage, or at least is incorporated and consolidated into that of the husband'. But, paradoxically – or so it may seem – this delegation of the duty of protection, along with the newly found alienability of citizenship, occurred just as women were beginning to enjoy the legal autonomy we associate with citizenship today.

Why marital denaturalisation?

Patrick Weil explains that '[i]n order to exist, every nation-state needs a population and a territory. Since individual human beings have a limited lifespan, states – to ensure their own continuity over time – have had to find legal tools that not only attribute nationality but also transmit it from generation to generation'.[25] This observation is profound, but it invites questions: why were states willing to let go of their women who married foreign men (even if the married couple continued to reside in the woman's country)? Why, indeed, did they choose positively to exclude such women from their population? Had the survival and continuity of the state been the major driver of modern citizenship law, the imperative should have been the retention of as many of the women citizens as possible. The numbers of women who lost their citizenship through marriage were far from small. Marital denaturalisation also meant that their children, and future generations, were in many cases lost permanently to the woman's state.

The primary explanation, I have suggested, was external to the state's legal regime for governing its population. The conferral of citizenship by law was a consequence, rather than a means. It followed, as suggested, from the need to 'sort' the populations of modern states as against each other, from the international triage of populations that was required in

[25] Weil, *How to be French*, 2. Weil references Jean-Paul Niboyet, *Traité de droit international privé français* (1938).

the emergence and evolution of international relations.[26] States needed to identify those of their residents for whom they were responsible in and against other countries, from whom among their non-residents they could demand service as against those who 'belonged' to another state, and whom, outside their borders, they were obliged to protect. Diplomacy, good international relations and international comity were facilitated and embedded in the conferral of legal citizenship upon a defined population.

The story of women's conditional citizenship is not the only avenue for recognising this motor of modern constitutional citizenship, but it is a major part of the story, and the story is largely opaque without it. Married women, in short, were a 'triage problem'. If the right to hold citizenship is viewed primarily as a matter of allegiance, their allegiance appeared compromised by their marriage. A married woman's allegiance, it was assumed, would flow to her husband and through him, to her husband's country. Women 'belonged' to their husbands, rather than primarily to their original state. Just as the international community resisted dual nationality on the grounds that a person could not owe allegiance to more than one sovereign and that, at a practical level, diplomatic relations would be hindered if dual nationality were permitted, women, it was believed, could not owe allegiance to more than one sovereign.

Rather than diminishing as women gained legal and political rights, this conceptualisation of citizenship increased as the twentieth century approached. The fact that marital denaturalisation laws were adopted when women generally, and married women in particular, were incrementally acquiring independent legal rights in other spheres underlines this relationship. The contingent character of women's citizenship was solidified as modern international relations took shape; women's citizenship became more precarious as the modern constitutional state emerged. As the nineteenth century progressed, and the modern rules of international relations evolved, the rules governing citizenship changed. Women now held their citizenship contingently.

The French example is revealing. It is one of striking reversal. Under the revolutionary constitutional law of 1790 that granted citizenship upon residence, automatic naturalisation would follow from five-years, residence in France for those with certain property or business or other association of affiliation. Foreign men, living in France, who married French women

[26] Macklin refers to 'the global filing system that assigns every human being to at least one state'. Audrey Macklin, 'Who is the Citizen's Other? Considering the Heft of Citizenship' (2007) 8 *Theoretical Inquiries in Law* 333, 340.

were automatically considered French, even without their consent (but French men who married foreign women were not denaturalised).[27] The practice of automatic naturalisation for residents was short-lived, however, and was brought to an end under the Constitution of 1795. Marital naturalisation of foreign men endured until 1799, when the Constitution of that year made residency alone the pathway to French nationality.[28] By 1804, the Napoleonic Code, displacing those constitutional provisions, detached civil rights from citizenship, substituted *jus sanguinis* for both *jus soli* and residence, promoted patrilineal transmission of citizenship to children, and stripped citizenship from French women who married foreign men. The break with *jus soli*, writes Weil, 'inaugurated the era of modern nationality law in France and throughout Europe'.[29] Weil notes that the pre-Code model in which citizenship rested upon residence 'had been a sign of allegiance to the sovereign under the Old Regime, and later a sign of support for the Revolution';[30] the new model, based on (paternal) 'blood' denoted allegiance to the French nation-state.

Still, this does not explain why *jus soli* was retained in other modern states that at the same time copied the Napoleonic Code when it came to married women. The identification of the nation 'as the political extension of the family',[31] does not exclude the rule of *jus soli*. Britain and the member states of the British Empire retained this rule until decades after the Second World War. The United States embedded it in the Fourteenth Amendment and continues to apply it. Yet these states developed modern citizenship laws in the nineteenth century, and also followed the Code's novel practice both of naturalising foreign women who married their citizens and denaturalising citizen women who married foreign men. Allegiance, according to the European model, was determined by 'blood'. According to the British model, it was determined by 'soil'. But, common to both models was the idea that allegiance was determined by sex.

By the mid-nineteenth century, the principle that nationality was no longer indelible and perpetual and that a person had a right to change nationality was becoming accepted, although more unevenly. To give a few examples, marital naturalisation and denaturalisation, as we have seen, were adopted in France in 1804, but perpetual allegiance (for men) persisted, signified by the rule that voluntary naturalisation for Frenchmen in another nationality was not permitted without prior approval, which applied until 1889. Marital naturalisation was adopted in Britain in 1844,

[27] Weil, *How to be French*, 17. [28] Weil, ibid, 19. [29] Weil, ibid, 29.
[30] Weil, ibid, 30. [31] Weil, ibid, 29.

and voluntary expatriation was not permitted until 1870 (the same year that marital denaturalisation was adopted); the dates for the United States are, respectively, 1855 and 1868 (and for marital denaturalisation, 1907).

Conclusion

With some few exceptions, pre-modern citizenship was perpetual and indelible. It was a status into which a person was born, a type of non-elective membership or belonging, like the membership of a family. It was existential, but not subjective. Only late in the eighteenth century was it generally accepted that a foreigner might change his allegiance by naturalisation, and with that his citizenship status. However, the principle that a person might cease to be a citizen of his (or her) own state by naturalisation in a foreign state was not generally accepted until the second half of the nineteenth century. With this step, the idea emerged that a state could strip native citizens of their citizenship for other reasons.

The introduction of conditional marital nationality was part of this shift. It also reflected a shift in thinking about the nature of marriage. By the end of the eighteenth century, the practice of arranged marriages had largely ended in Europe and around the common law world. The idea of marriage as a personal agreement between two parties, prior to a legal contract, came to dominate. The (gradual) recognition of divorce (at least in some parts of the world) also expressed this idea.

The associated view that marriage was a matter of choice, entered into not only freely, but in full awareness of the consequences, was repeatedly expressed in discussions of marital denaturalisation. Women who married foreign men, it was said, did so on the understanding that they would lose their pre-marital nationality; it was part of the choice they made. The assumption was that women, weighing up the consequences, were free to choose or decline a particular marriage. The decision to go ahead with a foreign marriage was treated as analogous to other voluntary forms of conduct by which citizenship could be lost (such as naturalisation in a foreign country). Marriage was a voluntary union, willingly embracing what followed, so it was thought, including for the woman's citizenship status: 'if marriage to an alien man is worthwhile, it is worth some sacrifices'.[32]

In 1943, on the eve of reform in Britain's conditional marital nationality laws, one UK Member of Parliament, would sum up the view that had

[32] Lucas Crane, 'The Nationality of Married Women' (1925) 7 *Journal of Comparative Legislation and International Law* 53, 59.

dominated for decades. Marriage, he said, was one of 'the most perilous adventures' of human life, which was not made less perilous 'by making it easier to enter upon it'. Relations with foreigners, he added

> are also extremely perilous adventures. When you do the two things simultaneously, you get a sort of geometrical progression of peril ... [T]here is less risk of human unhappiness ... [if] the woman has to face the fact and say, 'I want this man and I am prepared to face the perils, inconveniences and disadvantages of losing my British nationality'.[33]

It is clear from the records from and about women who experienced marital denaturalisation that not only was this particular consequence in fact little known or, at least, not fully understood, but also that much more than a dispassionate calculation of the advantages and disadvantages was involved in the decision to marry. The question of whether it was reasonable to ask a woman, in love with a prospective husband, to choose between him and her native citizenship was frequently raised in debate over marital denaturalisation laws. The 'choice' offered was, effectively, between the citizenship of the woman's country on the one hand, and family life, companionship, security, respectability, and social approval on the other. This amounted, in the eyes of those who campaigned against marital denaturalisation, to the equivalent of acting under duress. Women who married foreign men were required to make a choice that was neither free nor voluntary nor, in many, perhaps most, cases, informed. Similarly, automatic naturalisation by their husband's country often occurred, again regardless of their consent. Maritally naturalised wives found themselves inserted into a new jurisdiction, one in which the legal status of women may have been importantly different from that of their pre-marital citizenship.

The policy of marital denaturalisation was embedded in deep-seated assumptions about women's relationship to men, including, essentially, the idea that a woman's allegiance to a state was determined by her allegiance to her husband. However, the policy was not primarily driven by principles of women's subordination or legal incapacity, since it emerged and expanded at a time when women were acquiring at least a relatively enhanced capacity to enjoy independent legal rights. It was, rather, a response to two, associated global and transnational developments: the realignment of sovereignty in the modern constitutional state and the growth of modern international relations.

33 United Kingdom, House of Commons, *Debates*, 24 March 1943, 1715.

Early legislative steps in state responses to the latter concerned, not women's citizenship, but naturalisation. New laws of naturalisation laid the seedbed, or perhaps provided the starter motor, for marital denaturalisation. It may seem paradoxical that naturalisation should have offered the first avenue for the emergence of modern citizenship law. Birthright citizenship would appear to be the core – conceptually and legally – and naturalisation (which is not a right) a subsequent or peripheral form of citizenship. Indeed, this is the nature of the two forms today. Yet legislative regimes governing naturalisation emerged, with few exceptions, prior to those governing birthright citizenship. The historical centrality of naturalisation arises, indeed, from the core imperatives of modern state formation and the consequential need for states to recognise each other's sovereignty. Understanding this is a key step in conceptualising what was at stake in the formation of modern citizenship, and the first step to recognising the gendered character of the latter. We turn next to the history of naturalisation.

2

Naturalisation

> Naturalization is not a matter to be taken lightly. To seek and to obtain it is not something that happens frequently in the life of a human being. It involves his breaking of a bond of allegiance and his establishment of a new bond of allegiance. It may have far-reaching consequences and involve profound changes in the destiny of the individual who obtains it.

So stated the International Court of Justice in 1955, in the iconic Nottebohm Case,[1] in which a naturalised citizen of Liechtenstein was held not to be a genuine citizen of that country.[2] The reasoning was controversial,[3] but the Court was nothing but clear-sighted in its characterisation of the impact of a change of nationality. The acquisition of a new nationality and the loss of a former are profound experiences, as citizenship itself is a profoundly important possession. For the women who experienced either marital denaturalisation or naturalisation (or both), 'far-reaching consequences' were often the outcome. Bonds were broken; new bonds had to be forged. One way or another, the destinies of women who married foreign men were changed.

By the time of the Nottebohm decision, the world had begun to see non-consensual citizenship stripping and enforced naturalisation as a breach of human rights. But it had taken a century to apply this conclusion to the

[1] *Liechtenstein* v. *Guatemala* 1955 I.C.J. 4, 23.

[2] Such that Liechtenstein would have had a 'sufficient title to exercise protection in respect of Nottebohm' for the purpose of bringing a claim on his behalf in the International Court of Justice (ICJ).

[3] There are also persuasive doubts that the 'genuine link' test for nationality was actually the judgement's finding: Robert D Sloane, 'Breaking the Genuine Link: The Contemporary International Legal Regulation of Nationality' (2009) 50 *Harvard International Law Review* 1. Sloane argues that the Court cannot have intended its judgement to produce the obviously 'absurd consequences' of concluding that nationality only held where a person had a 'close link' such as spending most of one's life in the citizenship-conferring country. Sloane argues that the ICJ's decision was based on a broader principle: that it is an abuse of rights to exercise a right in order to evade international obligations, which, Sloane points out, is what Friedrich Nottebohm attempted to do.

citizenship of married women. Citizenship itself (regardless of gender) became recognised as a human right only as the consequences of its loss became severe, but the general assumption that the legal status of women was secondary (both in itself and to that of their husbands) meant that women's citizenship subordination attracted little attention, even long after the human rights dimension of citizenship became understood.

An understanding of the effect of marital denaturalisation must be contextualised. The consequences were not consistent throughout history. However, the claim that maritally denaturalised women suffered an existential injury (in addition often to practical disadvantage) is not retrospective or tendentious. It does not assume an equivalence between what follows from citizenship today (or what we believe should follow), and what followed in the past. It is built on the appeals made by citizenship equality campaigners and the women they represented, as well as the words of maritally denaturalised women themselves, as they attempted to explain to governments what they experienced and what they felt.

These appeals began to multiply from the first decade of the twentieth century. The effects of denaturalisation were most evident in the era spanning the start of the First World War and the close of the Second World War. The irony – in contextualising our understanding of the impact of marital denaturalisation – was that (with some individual country exceptions) the laws of marital denaturalisation were at their peak around the world, and governments defended the practice most assertively, at a time when the practical consequences of holding citizenship were multiplying and citizenship was acquiring the characteristics we attach to it today: the right to political participation, to a passport, and to diplomatic protection overseas, among others. In many cases, women, whether single or married, were acquiring these rights. But women who married foreign men were risking them. Most strikingly, they were experiencing the reversal of the particular right that women had historically held, sometimes as their sole equality right under law: citizenship in their own name.

The nineteenth century was the hinge between a world where citizenship meant relatively little and a world in which it was profoundly important to the fate of individuals. Before the revolutions of the late eighteenth century, membership of a polity or juridico-political community had modest weight and few consequences. Status identity and accompanying rights were largely determined by family, religion, class, and the locality into which one was born and lived. Travel to, or service in, other parts of the world were relatively rare. When it occurred, a person's 'nationality' had some importance; nationality was carried with that person and, regardless of presence or residence in another country, could not be alienated. It was, as we have seen, inalienable and permanent. The idea that a subject might change allegiance and thus become the subject of another sovereign was inconceivable, as was the idea that a person could lose nationality or citizenship, either by choice or force. A subject might be banished (and banishment was an especially severe punishment, practised in Britain from at least the twelfth century, then superseded by transportation, beginning in the seventeenth century), but that person did not cease to be a subject.

The idea that a foreign-born person might become a subject by being 'naturalised' was not entirely outside common law thinking, however, and its evolution would prove central to the emergence of modern citizenship law and the legal place of women as citizens. Naturalisation itself was a dramatic idea. It grew slowly and incrementally. Some legal provisions for specific forms of naturalisation can be found in pre-modern instruments, but these were very limited, and they did not involve a transfer of allegiance. Early English laws dealt principally with the 'naturalisation' of children of male subjects born outside the territory or the 'ligeance' (since the *jus soli* rule otherwise conferred subject status only by birth in the territory).[4] Children born of aliens within the ligeance, regardless of the sex or the nationality of either parent, did not need to be naturalised; they enjoyed the status of natural-born subjects.[5] Conferral by royal prerogative of 'denizen' status on aliens (including women) was also possible under English law. This was not the equivalent of full naturalisation, however, but stood somewhere between the status of alien and that of natural-born subject; the primary advantage was the right to hold property, unavailable to an alien until the mid-nineteenth century (and in other countries, much later). No political rights followed.

Naturalisation of aliens was available in Britain, albeit only by individual acts of parliament; the naturalised subject, having taken the oath of allegiance, then enjoyed all the rights of the natural-born subject (except the elite right to sit on the Privy Council or in parliament). Residence

[4] The Statute 7 Ann. c. 5, permitted general naturalisation for foreign Protestants, but was repealed after 3 years and replaced with the statute confining general naturalisation to the foreign-born children of subjects. Blackstone, Commentaries on the Laws of England, 363. The Act of Geo II c. 21, provided for the naturalisation of children of English parentage born outside the King's dominions.

[5] The children of the King's ambassadors were always held to be natural born, since the ambassadors did not shift their local allegiance, despite living in a foreign country. This exception for acquiring citizenship in countries, like the United States, with a *jus soli* rule, still applies.

and service in war also provided limited avenues for acquiring subject status outside birth. Blackstone notes that foreign seamen who served two years on an English ship in time of war were automatically naturalised, and foreign-born Protestants and Jews who lived for seven years in the American colonies were eligible to naturalise.[6] These rules, and the conceptualisation of 'citizenship' they captured, meant that, in the acquisition of nationality by birth, men and women were equally situated, and marriage did not alter women's status (indeed, it could not, since subject status was inalienable). Women were eligible to naturalise, and many foreign wives took the oath of allegiance.[7] (Married women's naturalisation by Act of Parliament ceased to apply in 1844, when automatic marital naturalisation of foreign wives of British subjects was adopted.)

Despite the unavailability of general naturalisation in Britain, and the 'intermittent resistance from the imperial authorities',[8] naturalisation laws emerged early and independently in the American colonies. By the eighteenth century, naturalisation of foreigners (by taking an oath before a State court or a Justice of the Peace[9]) had become regularised. Unlike in Britain, it was, indeed, encouraged. The desire to attract immigrants to the colonies was signified in the minimal restrictions on naturalisation and the rejection of a culture of nativism which would have excluded non-'natives' from the idea of the citizen.[10] The impact was more than technical, however; 'systematic deviations from English patterns . . . carried significant theoretical implications'.[11] The more generous approach to naturalisation in America and a simplified legal distinction between alien and citizen generated a re-conceptualisation of citizenship as a contractual relationship between citizen and political community.[12]

Ultimately, American laws (and judicial decisions) would treat citizenship as a matter of individual 'ownership', involving a type of contractual commitment with the state and with consequences for breach, but with the

6 Blackstone, *Commentaries on the Laws of England.*

7 Todd, 'Written in Her Heart', 168.

8 James H. Kettner, *The Development of American Citizenship, 1608–1870* (University of North Carolina Press, 1978) 106.

9 Weil, *The Sovereign Citizen*, 18. Weil states: 'This first federal law was just the continuation of state laws by which naturalization was effected "by taking an oath of allegiance before a State court of a justice of the peace"', 207–208.

10 Alexander M. Bickel, 'Citizenship in the American Constitution' (1973) 15 *Arizona Law Review* 369.

11 Kettner, *The Development of American Citizenship*, 106.

12 Kettner, ibid, 106–107.

individual's consent essential for the deprivation or forfeiture of citizenship. The contractual concept became more widely accepted after the mid-nineteenth century and was broadly entrenched as the general paradigm of citizenship. It would have profound consequences for women. It would find itself at odds with policies of (non-consensual) marital denaturalisation, and would ultimately serve the campaign to repeal these policies (in this respect, it is significant that this campaign was successful much earlier in the United States than in Britain).

A contractual conceptualisation of citizenship involves a voluntary relationship between person and state, an ability to negotiate its terms and to withdraw on mutual agreement. The relationship cannot be severed by unilateral action on either side. This conceptualisation emerged with the idea of (voluntary) naturalisation: the willing, but conditional agreement between a person and a state that the former could change allegiance and the latter would accept that new allegiance.

A relationship of reciprocal allegiance and protection between citizen and sovereign was carried over from the feudal conception of subjecthood, but as the American Revolution replaced the British sovereign with the American people, a new object of allegiance was created. (This idea of popular sovereignty would, little by little, spread around the constitutional world.) The 1776 Declaration of Independence listed grievances against King George III, amounting to a claim that the King had withdrawn his protection from the American people, and that, accordingly, the people 'declared themselves absolved of their former allegiances as British subjects'.[13] In their place, the United States Constitution became the new object of allegiance, expressing the identity of the American people, the new sovereign. With this break came a 'broad welcome to the foreign-born',[14] extending the more generous approach to naturalisation already adopted in the American colonies. Constitutional allegiance no longer depended on the fact of birth alone; it could be tested, by character and residence, and *declared* by the individual. It became a matter of will, an expression of the heart.

Americans of former British subject status who had sided with the revolutionary cause were assumed to have demonstrated their capacity for citizenship. Non-British foreign-born persons were to be assessed individually. Individual States applied naturalisation tests (race, character, residence, and in some cases, property or religion), but an emerging post-revolutionary sense of citizenship as a national matter, and the 'desirability

[13] Kettner, ibid, 213. [14] Kettner, ibid.

of ending the confusion inherent in a multiplicity of naturalization laws and procedures'[15] led to the inclusion in the United States Constitution, in 1787, of a congressional power over naturalisation. This power, asserted as a sovereign right, was an element in revolutionary thinking about the constitutional state. The Constitution conferred the power on Congress to 'establish an uniform rule of naturalization',[16] but until 1868, it was silent on the means by which birthright citizenship might be acquired, or the qualifications or qualities of the natural-born citizen. The common law provided the rules for the former. Legislation framed acquisition by naturalisation.

The first US Naturalization Act, passed in 1790, provided for naturalisation of 'free white person[s]' of good character, to be conferred by any common law court of record; it set the period of residence as two years. Applicants were required to take an oath to 'support the Constitution of the United States'.[17] The second Naturalization Act, 1795, also provided for naturalisation of 'free white' persons, but required an applicant first to make a declaration by oath or affirmation before a State or federal court, of the applicant's intention to become a citizen and 'to renounce forever all allegiance and fidelity to any foreign prince, potentate, state or sovereignty whatever'. No less than three years later, the applicant (after having resided in the United States for at least five years[18]) was then to make a further oath or affirmation 'that he will support the constitution of the United States; and that he doth absolutely and entirely renounce and abjure all [other] allegiance and fidelity'.

The court was also required to satisfy itself that the applicant had 'behaved as a man of good moral character, attached to the principles of the Constitution of the United States, and well disposed to the good order and happiness of the same'. Any hereditary title or order of nobility had to be expressly renounced in front of the same court. The Act further provided that the minor children of naturalised persons 'dwelling within the United States' would be considered citizens, as would the children

15 Kettner, ibid, 224.

16 Although this was a concurrent power, the Constitution's 'supremacy clause' meant that Congressional laws 'pre-empted' States laws, and the effect of the early federal Naturalization Acts was to make these laws national. The administration of naturalisation remained a State matter until 1906, when an Act established a federal supervisory agency in the Bureau of Immigration and Naturalization. Hattie Plum Williams, 'The Road to Citizenship' (1912) 27 *Political Science Quarterly* 399.

17 Weil, *The Sovereign Citizen*, 18.

18 The Naturalization Act of 1798 extended the qualifying period of residence to 14 years.

born outside the United States of citizen fathers. Persons proscribed by any State or persons convicted of having joined the British army during the revolutionary war were inadmissible for naturalisation (other than with the consent of the legislature of the State). We note here that the 1855 Act that adopted marital naturalisation of foreign wives of American citizens (see below) did not apply any of these tests (other than racial) to such women. That a woman's allegiance was transferred via her marriage to a citizen was taken for granted; so much so that the increasingly complicated steps for ordinary naturalisation were bypassed.

Women were not disqualified from naturalisation under these pre-1855 Acts. In principle, at least, women were free to apply for naturalisation in their own right (although few did) and married women were permitted to be naturalised on their own petition, regardless of the husband's citizenship status or intentions.[19] Many years later, John Cable (the sponsor of the congressional Act that, in 1922, repealed conditional marital nationality for most classes of married women in the United States) wrote that the early rule permitting married women's naturalisation should not be treated as a recognition of women's independence or equality but was 'a rule of convenience only' to be replaced in due course by a further 'utilitarian' rule,[20] prohibiting naturalisation of married women in their own right.

This may be so, at least as far as the intentions of the legislators who later abrogated the rule were concerned, but in the light of subsequent history, it remains a token of citizenship independence, distinguished from the effect of automatic marital naturalisation by its essential voluntariness. Although citizenship by naturalisation (as well as the grounds for losing citizenship) was primarily attached to tests of allegiance that privileged masculine duties such as military service, access by women to independent naturalisation offered an important exception.

Automatic marital naturalisation altered this landscape. It proceeded in two stages in the United States. The wife and children of a man who was naturalised under American law were included in his naturalisation. As early as 1804, the issue of a woman's naturalisation first came to the attention of Congress: the widow and children of an alien who had begun

[19] *Priest* v. *Cummings*, 1837, 16 Wend. (N.Y.), 617, cited in John L. Cable, *American Citizenship Rights of Women* (United States Congress, Hearing Before a Sub-Committee of the Committee on Immigration, 2 March 1933) 12.

[20] Cable, ibid, 13.

naturalisation proceedings but died before their completion were treated as naturalised.[21] The Act of February 10, 1855 extended this principle of single family nationality, providing for automatic marital naturalisation of foreign women who married American citizens. In doing so, it paid no attention to the woman's status or actual allegiance. It stated simply that 'Any woman who is now or may hereafter be married to a citizen of the United States, and who might herself be lawfully naturalized, shall be deemed a citizen'.

The marriage of an American woman to an alien did not, of itself, entail her denaturalisation prior to the 1907 Expatriation Act. The law was not consistent on this matter, but the general conclusion was that only a combination of alien marriage, residence abroad and transfer of allegiance by naturalisation in the husband's country, or active 'adherence' to a foreign sovereign, amounted to expatriation.[22] This early conceptualisation of a married woman's citizenship appeared to give some degree of attention to the woman's particular circumstances; it suggested some element of 'test' of the individual woman's relationship with a sovereign. It mirrored the test applying to persons seeking naturalisation. It included at least an imputation of voluntariness, and it echoed the dominant American principle that citizenship and residence were closely connected. This principle, under the 1907 Act, would be abandoned for married women, and displaced by a simple assumption of transferral of allegiance in a foreign marriage, without regard to either residence or foreign 'adherence'.

The British, less eager to encourage naturalisation, passed their first general Act governing naturalisation (An Act to Amend the Laws Relating to Aliens) in 1844. It empowered the Home Secretary to grant certificates of naturalisation to individuals. Importantly (albeit unnoticed by most historians of citizenship), the Act not only regularised the status and certain property rights of naturalised subjects, but also provided for the automatic naturalisation of foreign women who married British men. Section 16 of the Act stated: 'any woman married to or who shall be married to a natural-born subject or person naturalised shall be deemed and taken to be herself naturalised and have all the rights and privileges of a natural-born subject'.

[21] Report on the Subject of Citizenship, Expatriation, and Protection Abroad, to House Committee on Foreign Affairs (Washington, Government Printer, 1906).

[22] Ernest Hover, 'Citizenship of Women in the United States' (1932) 26 *American Journal of International Law* 700.

Alienability

Such laws made provision for *foreigners* to become citizens or subjects; they did not yet recognise the right of natural-born persons to cast off their own citizenship for any purpose. At this stage, loss of citizenship was only for citizens or subjects of other states. In the United States, prior to 1868, constitutional amendment and legislation providing for deprivation of birthright citizenship in consequence of certain acts (accepting a foreign title, foreign naturalisation, service to or permanent residence in a foreign state, among others) had been proposed, but not adopted. Nevertheless, the laws (and such proposals) recorded a shift in the old view that allegiance was permanent and inalienable.

For naturalisation to be possible, the naturalising country had to accept that, at least for other country's citizens, citizenship was alienable and allegiance transferrable. Until the mid-nineteenth century this idea was anathema for a country's own citizens. Naturalisation, thus, was initially a one-way process: reception by and inclusion in the state into which the alien was naturalised, but without reciprocal acceptance by the alien's former state of the change of status. One state received, but the other did not relinquish. This created practical difficulties in individual cases (particularly if the naturalised citizen returned to his former country). Importantly, it breached a general rule that was conceptually entangled with the rule of non-alienability: the rule against dual nationality.

A state may have accepted that an alien could be transformed into a citizen under its own law, but the idea that a naturalised citizen might continue to be allegiant to his former state – that is to say, might be simultaneously a citizen of both – was unacceptable. Transfer of allegiance might have been accepted for other states' citizens, but divisibility of allegiance was not tolerated. Indeed, the international community would not recognise dual (or multiple) citizenship under well after the Second World War, and even then, reluctantly.

The rule against dual nationality was of particular significance to married women. If, as was generally assumed by the mid-nineteenth century, a woman took the nationality of her husband, the proposition that she might simultaneously retain her own citizenship was unacceptable, since it would inevitably produce dual nationality. The growing idea of alienability of allegiance, albeit only initially recognised for foreign citizens, went hand in hand with the growing prospect of, and consensus against, dual nationality. Both would contribute, in particular ways, to a new view of women's citizenship: acquired under the same rules as for men, but held conditionally, transferrable without consent, exclusive, and therefore susceptible to alienation.

The foot was in the door. That states were willing to accept the principle of alienability for the citizenship of others, but not their own, created conceptual incoherence, and diplomatic nuisance. Indeed, it contributed to hostilities. The idea that a change of allegiance might also be available to a state's own citizens was unavoidable. Eventually, legal agreements between states recognised the inevitable: that, as the receiving state confers citizenship upon an alien, the original state must accept that one of its own has acquired a new nationality and a new allegiance. Relinquishment by the new citizen's former state was conceded. For naturalisation to be fully effective in a practical sense (that is to say, allowing the naturalised person to live and own property in the new country on the same footing as birthright citizens, and freeing him from pre-existing duties of military service) the former state must not challenge the status of the naturalised person. It must accept that citizenship is alienable not only for those citizens of other states, but, ultimately, for its own.

A state's naturalisation laws could not, of course, govern the acquisition of a foreign nationality. A person's eligibility to naturalise was subject to the laws of the state in which naturalisation was sought. But what a state could do with regard to foreign naturalisation of its own citizens was significant and often decisive. It could rule on whether they were permitted to divest themselves of their nationality, including in order to acquire another. Since, as noted, most states did not permit dual nationality, the view of allegiance as inalienable and the corresponding inability to abandon primary citizenship presented, in most cases, an absolute obstacle to a change in citizenship by naturalisation. The recognition that a state's own citizens might voluntarily expatriate or 'denaturalise' themselves that was captured in laws adopted in the middle decades of the nineteenth century, represented a profound conceptual shift (far more difficult than the acceptance that foreigners might choose to become subjects or citizens). This shift in thinking had equally profound significance for the citizenship status of women.

In 1868, the United States Congress passed the first Expatriation Act (Act of July 27, 1868). Enacted in the same year as the ratification of the Constitution's Fourteenth Amendment (which defined the acquisition of American birthright citizenship for the first time) the Act declared that 'the right of expatriation is a natural and inherent right of all people, indispensable to the enjoyment of the rights of life, liberty and the pursuit of happiness'. The following year, a British Royal Commission came to a similar conclusion: the doctrine of indelible allegiance was 'neither reasonable nor convenient. It . . . conflicts with that freedom of action which is now recognised as most conducive to the general good as well as to individual happiness and prosperity'.[23]

The Commission's Report also acknowledged the imperatives of international relations and the inconveniences created by foreign naturalisation of British subjects, and it included a wide survey of naturalisation and nationality transmission laws in foreign countries. It was conscious, too, of the loss of rights that would be suffered by British subjects who, by foreign naturalisation, became aliens in Britain, and it reflected on whether special provisions should be made for them or whether there should be a general change in the law regarding alien rights; it recommended the latter. British law did not at that time permit the holding of real property by aliens (except, with particular conditions and time limits, specifically for those who resided in Britain). This rule, the Commission recommended, should be revisited. Many European countries, it noted, permitted alien property ownership, as did a number of British colonies.

The British Naturalization Act of 1870 followed (and in the meantime, a naturalisation treaty was concluded with the United States). The Act permitted naturalisation of aliens who had lived or been in the service of the United Kingdom for not less than five years and who intended to remain there or to serve under the Crown, on condition that they ceased to be a subject or citizen of their former state, 'in pursuance of the laws thereof, or in pursuance of a treaty to that effect'. Four character references were required, attesting to the applicant's loyalty. The Home Secretary retained discretion to refuse naturalisation (the subsequent British Nationality and Status of Aliens Act, 1914, would provide for the cancellation of a certificate of naturalisation, something unavailable under the 1870 Act). Again, none of these complicated tests was required of foreign wives who were automatically naturalised under the Act of 1844.

The 1870 Act deemed any British subject naturalised in a foreign state to have become an alien. This principle was not found in common law, and was new to British law.[24] The Act, as we have seen, also provided

[23] *Report of the Royal Commissioners for Inquiring into the Laws of Naturalization and Allegiance* (HM Stationary Office, London, 1869) v.

[24] G. Addison Smith, 'British Nationality and Naturalization' (1906–07) 18 *The Juridical Review* 273, 278. The Act did not, in its wording, extend to the self-governing colonies of the British Empire; they remained free to adopt their own naturalisation laws, but until 1914 these laws had effect only within the legislating colony. A naturalised person ceased to be a British subject outside the colony in which naturalisation had been conferred.

(albeit circuitously) for the automatic denaturalisation of British women who married foreign men, by 'deeming' a woman to be 'the subject of the state of which her husband is for the time being a subject'. It permitted a person with dual nationality to make a declaration of alienage, ceasing to be a British subject, but persons 'under disability' were ineligible. 'Disability' was defined in the Act as 'the status of being an infant, lunatic, idiot, or married woman'. Married women were, thus, able to lose their British nationality, without their consent, but were unable voluntarily to renounce it. The effect of the provision was to prohibit married women's voluntarily naturalisation in their own right.

Significantly, the law governing women's citizenship status was merged with laws concerning the naturalisation of foreigners. The Commissioners' Report had not specifically recommended this; it had simply recommended that any British subject who resided in and was naturalised in a foreign country should cease to be a British subject, and that the same 'rule should be applied to a woman who, being a British subject shall become by marriage with an alien the subject or citizen of a Foreign State'.[25] It had also recommended that British-born subjects who had lost their British nationality should be permitted to resume it within two years of their foreign naturalisation, or at any later time, subject to the discretion of the Secretary of State, and that '[t]he same rule as to readmission should apply to women of British birth whose British nationality had been lost by marriage with an alien, on their becoming widows'.[26] The Act adopted the recommendation for a widow's readmission to British nationality, but it made no acknowledgement that the principle in the 'rule' identified by the Commission – that foreign naturalisation should lead to loss of British subject status – appeared to invite at least an inquiry into whether a married woman had or had not been maritally naturalised. It simply asserted the assumption behind naturalisation – that it entailed a transfer of allegiance – and extended this to British women.

In the House of Lords, at the Bill's second reading, the Lord Chancellor explained the rationale for allowing British subjects to be naturalised in a foreign country; it was entirely in terms of international reciprocity.

There was, in other words, no 'imperial naturalisation' at that time. Many variations across the Empire could be found in the extent to which the 1870 Act was followed in colonial legislation, and much confusion surrounded the status of married women under colonial legislation until 1914, or in some cases later.

25 *Report of the Royal Commissioners for Inquiring into the Laws of Naturalization and Allegiance*, v.

26 *Report of the Royal Commissioners*, ibid, x.

He then asked, 'What is to be done with the wife or child of a person so naturalized?' There are, he stated, 'great inconveniences in the wife being a citizen of one country and the husband of another'. He noted, tellingly, that under law the domicile of the wife was that of the husband, 'but with nationality it is different'. The Lord Chancellor interpreted the Commission's recommendations to extend to the principle that the wife should acquire the nationality of the husband.[27]

The question 'what is to be done with the wife?' was revealing. Women with foreign husbands were a conundrum. To whom did they belong? The legislative steps that recognised the alienability of allegiance of a state's own citizens as both possible and reasonable signified an emerging view of citizenship as consensual, but it was a view that applied to men alone. Women still acquired citizenship by birth, but theirs was now a citizenship that was contingent, conditional, and subject to mandatory alienation. Men, whether married or single, could retain their citizenship, or, if eligible, they could alienate it, and acquire that of another state. Married women could do neither. If her husband was foreign, a woman could not retain her own citizenship. If his country automatically naturalised his wife, she could not refuse to be naturalised. She could neither seek naturalisation in her own right, nor retain her primary citizenship if her husband naturalised in a foreign citizenship. The principle that expatriation was 'a natural and inherent right of all people', a source of liberty, happiness and prosperity, was simply and unambiguously, a masculine principle.

Reciprocal recognition

What was occurring, however, was much more than just the 'personalisation' or conditioning of citizenship. Recognition of other countries' naturalisation laws was central to the growth of international law and diplomacy, and this recognition ultimately drove states' laws for recognising their own citizens. In 1812, Britain and the United States had gone to war with each other, and among the many reasons for this conflict was

[27] United Kingdom, House of Lords, *Debates*, 25 February 1870, 1118. In the House of Commons Committee debate, one member (Sir Roundell Palmer) stated that it was 'quite settled as a matter of International Law generally that the status of the wife and that of minor children followed from the status of the husband and father'. United Kingdom, House of Commons, *Debates*, 25 April 1870, 1741.

Britain's refusal to recognise American naturalisation of British subjects.[28] Under American law they were considered former Britons, but in Britain, under the rule of indelible allegiance, they were regarded as permanent subjects, still 'belonging' to the British. Naturalised American seamen, captured by the British, were impressed into the British navy, treated as subjects and forced to serve. This, to the Americans, was a fundamental breach of their sovereignty.

In the United States, the 1868 Expatriation Act carried the memory of this dispute over naturalisation recognition. After declaring the principle of expatriation to be natural and inherent, it continued:

> [W]hereas in the recognition of this principle this government has freely received emigrants from all nations, and invested them with the rights of citizenship; and whereas it is claimed that such American citizens, with their descendants, are subjects of foreign states, owing allegiance to the governments therefor; and whereas it is necessary to the maintenance of public peace that this claim of foreign allegiance should be promptly and finally disavowed...

To the British in 1812, the American naturalisation law had been similarly offensive. Furthermore, the British believed, it had offered incentives to British seamen to make fraudulent claims about their citizenship status and shirk their duty to the sovereign, which was a fundamental breach of the law of citizenship. In the words of one Member of the House of Commons, in 1813,

[28] In the second reading speech on the 1870 UK Naturalization Bill, the Lord Chancellor described the difficulties created by the British rule of perpetual allegiance as 'well exemplified by the events that led to the War of 1812, when the difficulty reached a fearful height'. Terrible threats of retaliation and barbarous reprisals were made, he said, as the opposing countries seized other's nationals. It was 'only by the exercise of great forbearance and temper' on both the British and American sides 'that the most disastrous results were averted'. United Kingdom, House of Lords, *Debates*, 25 February 1870, 1123. In addition to the War, the United States Report on the Subject of Citizenship, Expatriation, and Protection Abroad, to House Committee on Foreign Affairs, 1906, notes conflicts arising from the refusal of recognition of naturalisation between America and Germany, over the arrest of naturalised (former German) Americans for non-performance of German military service, and with Britain over 'numerous arrests' of naturalised (former) Irish nationals charged with political crimes. The conclusions of the 1869 UK Royal Commission that British allegiance was no longer inalienable settled the conflict with America regarding recognition of naturalised British-born United States citizens, but the fact that the 1870 Naturalization Act went beyond a treaty of mutual recognition and extended to other states suggests the wider evolution of the principle of alienability at that time.

> if America conceived that she had the power of absolving men from the allegiance due to their lawful sovereign, and of making British subjects American citizens, she ought to be told that such a principle was unreasonable and unjustifiable, degrading to England, subversive of her interests, and therefore one which she would never cease to oppose.[29]

The Member was mistaken. Fifty-seven years later, as we have seen, Britain ceased to oppose the principle. Still, if we substitute the word 'people' for 'men' (to read: 'the power of absolving people from the allegiance due to their lawful sovereign'), the change of heart was registered earlier and (it was clear) was considered less dramatic. After 1855, American law naturalised foreign wives of citizens, but there is no record (of which I am aware) of opposition on Britain's behalf to the American naturalisation of British women with American husbands. Uncontroversially, too, Britain's own Act of 1844 did the same thing to foreign women who married British men. America's power of 'making British subjects American citizens' in such cases was not regarded as unreasonable, unjustifiable, degrading or subversive.

The point here is not that Britain's conceptualisation of what was at stake in the foreign naturalisation of its subjects should have been different. It is, rather, that the conceptualisation of women's citizenship as derivative and conditional was moving in parallel, but different directions from that governing men's citizenship and that both shifts were, significantly, shaped by the imperatives, at that time, of evolving international relations.

These principles were increasingly affirmed under law and in the courts. In the same year as American law first recognised the 'right' of a citizen to expatriate himself, the United States Supreme Court considered the application of the 1855 Act with respect to a woman's status. The question in *Kelly* v. *Owen* (which concerned a disputed property inheritance) was whether citizenship was conferred upon the foreign wife only at the time of her marriage or at any time during the marriage (in cases where, subsequent to the marriage, the husband became naturalised as an American citizen). The Court held that a man's citizenship 'whenever it exists, confers, under the act, citizenship upon' his wife. To conclude otherwise, it stated, would be to restrict the Act's object which was 'to allow [the woman's] citizenship to follow that of her husband without the necessity of any application for naturalisation on her part'.[30] The Court pointed

[29] United Kingdom, House of Commons, *Debates*, 18 February 1813, 616 (Mr Ponsonby).

[30] *Kelly* v. *Owen*, 74 U.S. 496 (1868) 74 (Justice Field for the Court).

out, however, that the Act restricted marital naturalisation to those eligible for naturalisation: that is, 'free white person[s]' and persons who were not alien enemies.

As Candice Bredbenner notes, this conclusion generated disagreement between the judicial and the administrative authorities. The 1907 Act (discussed below) sought to clarify the law in this respect.[31] What is significant here is the acknowledgement that, at the same time as Congress (as in other countries) was recognising the right of voluntary expatriation – the right of the individual, effectively, to choose the sovereign to whom he owed allegiance – married women were increasingly denied this choice. As noted, the Expatriation Act of 1868, which declared expatriation to be the 'natural and inherent right of all people' did not apply to married women. Eligible women whose husbands were American citizens either at the time of the marriage or who became citizens at any time during the marriage were not free to opt in or out of citizenship. Ineligible women were not free to naturalise either on their own motion, or via their husband's citizenship. Married women, in short, could neither expatriate themselves voluntarily nor acquire an alternative citizenship by naturalisation in their own right.

It was not entirely one-sided: a naturalised citizen was assumed to have relinquished his American citizenship by prolonged foreign residence. International treaties concluded around this time (discussed below) provided for loss of naturalised citizenship on this ground, among others. Territoriality and residence remained an important element in determining a person's citizenship. Still the principle, in practice, was not ungendered; a core (albeit untested) assumption in the policy of marital denaturalisation was that a woman would live in her husband's country.

Similar processes governing naturalisation law, albeit differently staged, were occurring in Europe. The immediate post-Revolutionary years in France saw multiple changes in citizenship law, but by the early nineteenth century, the French had embraced the British view of alienability. French naturalisation of foreigners had been allowed under the 1790 Constitution. The practice was subsequently to permit a foreign man, ten years after he had registered his 'declaration of intent', to assume French nationality. This automatic access to French nationality ceased in 1809; complex procedures and proofs were now required for approval, albeit with a provision that made exceptional naturalisation, without a residency time limit, available to foreigners who had 'rendered important

[31] Bredbenner, *A Nationality of Her Own*.

services to the Republic' or would bring useful talents or benefits.[32] The Civil Code had initially permitted a Frenchman to change his nationality by naturalisation in another country, but the 1809 Code reversed this and mandated perpetual allegiance. Foreign naturalisation of a Frenchman without authorisation from the French government was not permitted until 1889. The point of these increasingly restrictive laws was, among others, to prevent a Frenchman from evading military service or to control his service abroad, and to prevent foreign 'undesirables' from automatically acquiring French nationality.

Naturalisation of foreign women in their own right was no longer available after 1804, other than exceptionally. Applications were rarely approved. Weil describes the case of the wealthy widow of an Irish national who had spent part of her fortune acquiring real property and undertaking a major land restoration project in France. Her application for naturalisation was refused on the ground of her incapacity, as a woman, to exercise political rights. She was granted, instead, the right to residency, appropriate to her entitlement only to civil rights.[33]

The most dramatic and influential step in the French story of women's citizenship was found in the Napoleonic Code of 1804. The Code represented the first systematic classification of persons according to nationality. As we have seen, it included a provision governing the nationality of married women specifically, declaring that a foreign woman who married a Frenchman would 'follow' his citizenship, and that a Frenchwoman who married a foreigner would do likewise. The policy of conditional marital nationality had found its first legislative expression.

This policy would spread throughout Europe and into Britain and the rest of the world in subsequent decades, as the demands of international relations created pressure for mutual recognition by states of each other's naturalised citizens. Treaties were a key part of this process. Around the middle decades of the nineteenth century, bilateral treaties governing the nationality of children born in foreign territories, and treaties on naturalisation began to multiply. The American 'Bancroft Treaties' (first negotiated by United States diplomat, George Bancroft) were a series of agreements between the United States and other countries; they recognised the right of each party's citizens to become naturalised as citizens of the other, and they defined circumstances in which naturalised persons

[32] Weil, *How to be French*, 31. [33] Weil, ibid, 33.

were entitled to renounce their naturalised citizenship or were presumed to have abandoned it and resumed their former citizenship.

Some specified the terms for the recognition of the naturalisation of their citizens by the other party (typically five years uninterrupted residence in the foreign country); some provided for the prosecution of naturalised former citizens upon their return to their former country for crimes committed in that country before their naturalisation. A presumption was included of abandonment of the citizenship acquired by naturalisation if the individual returned to his country of origin and resided there continuously for two years (the principal purpose was to prevent individuals from seeking foreign naturalisation in order to avoid military service in their original country).[34] Numerous bilateral naturalisation treaties – between the United States and European, Scandinavian, South American, British and other countries, as well as Treaties, Protocols and 'Exchanges of Notes' between countries of Europe, South America, Scandinavia, Japan and others – had been concluded by the second part of the nineteenth century.[35]

These treaties were advantageous to the individual state parties. They were also of central importance in progressing international relations in that period. We note, again, that, at the time the reciprocal harmonisation of the principles of acquired citizenship was being negotiated, and with this the recognition of voluntary shifts in allegiance, the status of married women was moving in opposite directions. Married women, as such, were not excluded from being naturalised – they were, indeed, automatically naturalised in many countries either by their husband's existing citizenship or as a consequence of his naturalisation – but they were deprived of the choice or agency that is otherwise conceptually and legally associated with the application to be naturalised. Indeed, marital naturalisation did not require any qualification other than marriage; no oath of allegiance was taken.

In assembling this picture, we need to recognise that Britain and the United States protected the citizenship of their own women over a period when marital denaturalisation was the norm elsewhere. A report by the Lord Chief Justice of England, Sir Alexander Cockburn, claimed in 1869 that 'in every country, except where the English law prevails, the

[34] Charles Gordon, 'The Citizen and the State: Power of Congress to Expatriate American Citizens' (1964–5) 53 *Georgetown Law Journal* 315, 322.

[35] See Flournoy and Hudson, *A Collection of Nationality Laws.*

nationality of a woman on marriage merges with that of the husband: she loses her own nationality, and acquires his'. English law, he pointed out, naturalised an alien woman who married a British subject, but 'an English woman marrying an alien still remains a British subject'. The American law was the same. Cockburn also recognised that Continental law enabled a woman whose nationality had been changed to her husband's to resume her original nationality upon widowhood, upon the condition of residing in or returning to her country of origin (which required, 'in some instances, the authority of the State').[36]

Cockburn's confident comparison was out of date almost as soon as his publication appeared (and the 'anomaly' of dual nationality for certain British women was corrected). In 1870, one year later, as noted, Britain's Naturalization Act was passed. It recognised for the first time the general right of British subjects to change allegiance by foreign naturalisation; it permitted aliens to hold real property, and included the provision that was to be notorious for citizenship equality campaigners, deeming married women to be the 'subjects' of their husbands' state. The provision's purpose, as debate on the Bill made clear, was to follow international trends, and to avoid the international 'inconveniences' caused by the wife's holding of a different nationality from that of her husband. Responding to objections that its effect would be 'oppressive' to British women whose husband acquired a foreign nationality, one MP stated that 'the object of the Bill was to amend our naturalisation law, so as to make it conform more nearly to International Law; and therefore it was necessary to adopt the general rule that the wife should follow the nationality of her husband'.[37]

In America, the Acts of 1855 and 1868 allowed American women who married aliens to retain their citizenship, but they created a 'changed attitude on the part of the courts'; the rule of perpetual allegiance had been abrogated 'and thereafter the courts searched for evidence of an American woman's election to expatriate herself after marriage to an alien'.[38] Neither Act was passed in isolation. Both followed trends around the world and represented changes in thinking internationally. The concept of citizenship itself had changed. Principles of individual autonomy and freedom to expatriate now went hand in hand with increasingly strict

[36] The Right Hon. Sir Alexander Cockburn, *Nationality: or the Law Relating to Subjects and Aliens, Considered with a View to Future Legislation* (William Ridgway, London 1869) 5.

[37] United Kingdom, House of Commons, *Debates*, 25 April 1870, 1742 (Mr Jessel). The speaker added that the objection was merely 'theoretical'; 'except, sentimentally, the legal status of the wife would not be altered by the act of her husband'.

[38] Cable, *American Citizenship Rights of Women*, 17.

laws that identified the sovereign to which the individual owed allegiance. Citizenship was becoming more specifically masculine.

Things were different for women. The woman's allegiance to the sovereign was no longer perpetual, either, but far from being enhanced, her freedom was attenuated, and, in many cases, her 'happiness and prosperity' would be ill-served by the new approach. A married woman's allegiance and, with that, her citizenship, were now outside her control. All she could do – in the event that she knew the law and its consequences – was decline to marry. She would pay a high price for the retention of her citizenship. If, however, she married, as most people did, her allegiance was automatically assumed to shift: to her husband, and through him, to his state.

By the end of the nineteenth century, as we have seen, most countries had adopted marital denaturalisation laws. In 1880, the International Institute of Law, in Oxford, would declare, without qualification, that 'a woman acquires by marriage the nationality of her husband'.[39] The United States had been conferring automatic naturalisation upon foreign wives (subject to a race test) for twenty–five years, but at the time had not yet taken the step of legislating to strip citizenship from American women who married 'out'. In 1907, Congress passed the Act of 2 March, 1907 (the 'Expatriation Act') section 3 of which declared that a woman who married a foreign man took her husband's nationality.

How much the citizenship of married American women had, in practice, been previously protected remains open to question. A report on Citizenship, Expatriation and Protection Abroad, for the Congressional House Committee on Foreign Affairs, in 1906, found significant inconsistencies in judicial conclusions on this matter.[40] In the 1830 case of *Shanks* v. *Dupont* (concerning the estate of an American woman married to a British officer) the Supreme Court had held that marriage did not 'dissolve' a woman's allegiance, even under 'coverture'. In the words of Justice Story:

> The incapacities of *femes covert* (sic) provided by the common law apply to their civil rights and are for their protection and interest. But they do not reach their political rights nor prevent their acquiring or losing a national character.[41]

39 Lutz, 'Nationality of Married Women in the American Republics'.

40 Report on the Subject of Citizenship, Expatriation, and Protection Abroad, to House Committee on Foreign Affairs, 1906.

41 *Shanks* v. *Dupont* 28 U.S. 242 (1830).

Other cases, however, reached different conclusions,[42] and 'much doubt' surrounded the status of American women married to foreign men.[43] Residence in the United States notwithstanding an alien marriage was, in certain cases, treated as significant. Still, before 1907, '[i]t became the accepted rule that if the matrimonial domicile continued in the United States after marriage to an alien, the wife's native citizenship remained unchanged'.[44]

The 1906 Report's purpose was to make recommendations 'to settle some of the embarrassing questions that arise in reference to citizenship, expatriation, and the protection of American citizens abroad'. Arising from this, its first recommendation was that

> in order to render more effective the national policy of regarding voluntary expatriation from one country to another as a right, and to secure the equal protection of American native and naturalized citizens abroad, negotiations should be undertaken to extend and perfect the treaty relations of the United States with foreign countries.[45]

It further recommended that there should be legislation, including a provision

> That an American woman who marries a foreigner shall take, during coverture, the nationality of her husband, but upon termination of the marital relation by death or absolute divorce, she may revert to her American citizenship by registering within one year as an American citizen at the most convenient American consulate, or by returning to reside in the United States, if she is abroad; if she is in the United States, by continuing to reside therein.[46]

42 The Report on the Subject of Citizenship, Expatriation, and Protection Abroad 1906, identified cases that followed the conclusion in *Shanks*, and noted that in the most recent relevant case, *Ruckgaber* v. *Moore* 104 F. 947 (1900), the court held that a woman marrying an alien became a foreign citizen, provided there be 'withdrawal from her native country, or equivalent act, expressive of her election to renounce her former citizenship as a consequence of her marriage'.

43 J. P. Chamberlain, 'Married Women's Naturalization Act' (1923) 9 *American Bar Association Journal* 57, 58.

44 Hover, 'Citizenship of Women in the United States', 704.

45 Report on the Subject of Citizenship, Expatriation, and Protection Abroad, to House Committee on Foreign Affairs, 1906, 7.

46 Report on the Subject of Citizenship, Expatriation, and Protection Abroad, ibid. The other recommended grounds for denaturalisation were: the acquisition of a foreign citizenship by naturalisation, service to a foreign state of the kind that entailed the taking of an oath of allegiance to that state, and domicile in a foreign state for five years without intent to return. Voluntary expatriation was only to be permitted in time of peace.

These recommendations reflected the composite paradigm of modern citizenship: the Committee's inquiry and its recommendations were shaped by international imperatives, by concern for international recognition, and by interest in bringing American law into harmony with the law prevailing in other parts of the world. Its discussion of citizenship loss was conceptualised in terms of foreign state-oriented conduct: expressions of allegiance to another state, rather than conduct in, or relations with, the citizen's own state.

Here, despite the apparent protection of the Fourteenth Amendment, the United States followed world practice. A woman citizen's foreign marriage was to be treated as abandonment of her country, the equivalent of naturalisation or foreign service and consequential transfer of allegiance to another country. The marriage oath was, effectively, the equivalent of the oath of allegiance, an expression of putative disallegiance to the citizen's country. (The irony was that married women, under American law and that of many countries at that time, were not free to take the oath of naturalisation.) The assumption of disallegiance was made, not merely regardless of any test of actual withdrawal of allegiance, but also regardless of the woman's actual circumstances or intention with regard to residence. As with the citizens of other countries, American-born women were rendered aliens in their own country.

The Act and its assumption did not go without challenge. In 1915, in *Mackenzie* v. *Hare*, the American-born Ethel Mackenzie, who lived with her Scottish husband in California, unsuccessfully challenged the constitutional power of Congress to strip citizenship from an American citizen without consent. The United States Supreme Court held that a woman's foreign marriage was 'tantamount to voluntary expatriation' (We consider this case further in Chapter 3.) Fifty years later, one writer would describe the case's holding as capturing a 'new concept': that citizenship 'could be lost without regard to . . . desires'.[47] In fact, the case represented the culmination of thinking, both in the United States and internationally, about the character of citizenship and its mutability. Citizenship law, built around the imperatives of international relations and diplomacy, rested on the principle that citizenship was 'owned' by the state, regardless of individual 'desires'.

At the same time, the seeds of a later view – that citizenship was in principle 'owned' by the individual – were being sown in the concession, from the mid-nineteenth century onward, that individual transfer of

[47] Gordon, 'The Citizen and the State', 325.

allegiance was possible (subject to eligibility rules) upon individual initiative. (The 'state-ownership' view was strenuously challenged by citizenship equality campaigners, and was loosened significantly in the post-Second World War era. Indeed, United States Supreme Court judgements after the 1950s represented the triumph of the idea of citizenship as personal and existential. This is discussed in Chapter 7.)

What significance did the inclusion have in the Act's marital denaturalisation provision of the conditional right of a woman to resume her American citizenship upon termination of her marriage (mirroring the British Act of 1870, but expanding the termination categories from widowhood alone to divorce)? Many years later, in a case challenging the power of Congress to legislate for involuntary denaturalisation (of a man), Chief Justice Warren (in dissent) treated this provision effectively as a statement that a married woman's citizenship was only 'suspended'.[48] This may have been technically so (and, as we shall subsequently see, the provision was broadly interpreted as such) but the assumption that no injury was involved in the citizenship's loss since it might be restored following the husband's loss captured cold logic.

In 1922, the United States Congress passed the 'Cable Act', repealing both marital denaturalisation and marital naturalisation. The Act also abolished the rule that a married woman could not be naturalised while her husband remained a citizen of a foreign state, and provided that 'the right of any woman to become a naturalized citizen of the United States shall not be denied or abridged because of her sex or because she is a married woman'. Foreign wives of American citizens could now be naturalised with a reduced residency requirement (one year, rather than five), and without the requirement of prior registration of intention. American women who had earlier lost their citizenship by marriage could avail themselves of the Act's provision, and apply for re-naturalisation. However, like other alien women, they were subject to eligibility criteria, including race, age, education, and moral character. The husband, too, had to be eligible to naturalise for the wife to be eligible; a former American citizen married to a Chinese husband, for example, or an alien woman of Chinese origin, married to an American husband would not be permitted to naturalise. Residency requirements for naturalised citizens also applied to the woman's restored citizenship: five years continuous residence outside the United States (without registration) or, in the woman's case, continuous residence for two years in the country of

[48] *Perez* v. *Brownell* 356 U.S. 44 (1958).

which her husband was a citizen, were presumed to signal abandonment of citizenship by naturalisation. John Cable later wrote that the provision in the 1922 permitting the restoration and retention of citizenship to American women with foreign husbands, but only in cases where the husband was eligible for naturalisation, was inserted to ensure the passage of the Bill.[49] It was repealed in 1931. (We consider these developments further in following chapters.)

These conditions were not unique to the United States. What we see, again, is the close historical relationship between citizenship laws and laws of naturalisation. The latter, providing the framework for receiving other states' citizens, became in this context a means of transforming birthright citizens – women whose citizenship had been conditioned upon their marital state – into naturalised citizens, whose naturalisation, in turn, was conditioned upon eligibility and residence. It signalled that women's citizenship remained secondary and precarious. It revealed the extent to which the 'triage' rationale still applied in the identification of a country's own citizenry.

Conclusion

The answer – at this point in the history – to the question of why the practice of conditional marital nationality had been adopted almost universally by the end of the nineteenth and the early years of the twentieth century, lies in the problem created by the nationality of married women for the global rule that the allegiance of individuals was owed to a single state. At a time when alienability of citizenship had begun to be conceded, when naturalisation was correspondingly regulated by inter-state agreements, and when dual nationality was accordingly rejected, it was regarded as axiomatic that a married woman could not keep her own citizenship. This conclusion rested on the unquestioned conviction that a woman's allegiance was owed to her husband and, through him, to her husband's country. The independent citizenship of married women, that is, was sacrificed in the triage of persons that followed from the evolution of international relations among sovereign states.

The assumption of derivative allegiance, transferred from the legal doctrine of 'coverture' and other sources of women's legal incapacity, was so embedded in the equation that little explanation or justification was given for the introduction of conditional marital nationality laws. By the

49 Cable, *American Citizenship Rights of Women*, 29.

twentieth century, however, with the erosion of coverture and progress towards equal political rights, this assumption could no longer be taken for granted. Governments were increasingly called upon to justify their continuing commitment to policies of conditional marital nationality. The reasoning became more complex, more explicit, and increasingly defensive, as the impact of marital denaturalisation, in particular, became more severe.

This account provides only the 'objective' perspective on the history of citizenship law and gender. The other side of the story is that of the women who lost their citizenship by (one might say) following their hearts. If the objective history of modern citizenship focuses on allegiance, the existential history of modern citizenship prioritises protection. In the next three chapters, we consider the stories of maritally denaturalised women, as a lens on this existential history, before turning again to the international response, this time, post-First World War, in which protection begins to play a greater part in the characterisation of citizenship, and in the ultimate (if partial and fragile) shift in perspective that allowed primary or 'birthright' citizenship to be thought of as 'belonging' less to the state and more closely to the person.

3

The impact of marital denaturalisation

I say that my nationality is as much a part of me as any of the other rights that I have in law.[1]

By the mid-nineteenth century, the long-standing rules of perpetual allegiance and inalienability of nationality had been largely abandoned. The policy of stripping citizenship from women who married foreign men was part of this trend. The policy was expressed in national legislation, but, as we have seen, was activated and shaped by international interests: the acceptance of the need for reciprocity in naturalisation and the mutual recognition of countries' naturalisation laws, accompanied by the associated rule of single allegiance. These developments took place against deep-seated background assumptions about married women's status that were transformed into assumptions about women's allegiance in an era when the legal status of citizenship was becoming consequentially important. It was at this time that the principle of marital denaturalisation became widespread.

To recap: as the modern system of international relations developed, shaped by the growth of constitutional states, it became imperative to define the members of those states as against those of others; membership rested on a principle of allegiance; multiple allegiances were considered impossible; married women were assumed to be allegiant to their husbands (notwithstanding the growing recognition of women's independent legal capacity in domestic national laws); women who married foreign men were, therefore, a dilemma for the international order of reciprocal citizenship recognition. They were a 'triage problem'; marital denaturalisation (and at least an assumption of reciprocal naturalisation) was, effectively, the solution. A man owed allegiance to, and therefore belonged to his own country; a woman owed allegiance to her husband,

[1] United Kingdom, House of Commons, *Debates*, 28 November 1930, second reading on Nationality of Women Bill (Ellen Wilkinson).

and therefore belonged to her husband's country. A woman lost her citizenship upon foreign marriage, and (in principle at least) gained her husband's citizenship.

The United States introduced marital naturalisation in 1855, but, as we have seen, was a latecomer to legislated marital denaturalisation (although at times during the second half of the century its courts had proceeded as if such legislation were already in place; the case law was inconsistent). In 1907, Congress passed what became known as the Expatriation Act; it included the martial denaturalisation provision. The Act was a response by the United States to the pressures of international relations, including the widespread practice of marital denaturalisation in other countries. A report in 1906 prepared for the Congressional Committee on Foreign Affairs had recommended legislation 'to settle some of the embarrassing questions that arise in reference to citizenship, expatriation, and the protection of American citizens abroad'.[2] According to one international lawyer, the 1907 Act to which it gave rise finally brought the United States law into line 'with the laws passed on the subject by practically all other civilized states of the world'.[3] By this stage, in the early twentieth century, however, certain countries had already begun to make amendments to the laws governing this practice, to address, on an ad hoc basis, the administrative problems they had long been known to generate, and that were increasingly drawn to the attention of governments by the women affected and by those who campaigned for the laws' repeal. The Expatriation Act, itself, included certain 'remedial' provisions (discussed below). Indeed, at the same time as it confirmed the policy of marital denaturalisation for American women, it indirectly, but effectively recognised at least certain of the inequities this produced.

Despite this relative sophistication, the 1907 Act (like the French Civil Code of 1804, the British Naturalization Act of 1870[4] and others),

[2] Report on the Subject of Citizenship, Expatriation, and Protection Abroad, to House Committee on Foreign Affairs, 1906, 1.

[3] J.S. Reeves, 'Nationality of Married Women' (1923) 17 *American Journal of International Law* 97, 98.

[4] Ann Dummett and Andrew Nicol also recognise this 'example of the poor drafting for which the 1870 Act became notorious'. They note the opinion of the jurist, Sir Francis Piggott, in 1907, that the Act was 'the worst drafted piece of legislation that ever found its way on to the Statute Book', and the suggestion that 'the haste with which the Bancroft Convention had to be drafted' as being responsible. Dummett and Nicol, *Subjects, Citizens, Aliens and Others: Nationality and Immigration Law*, 88 and 286 (fn 29). This, however, is not convincing, at least with respect to the marital denaturalisation provision, since it does not account for the similarity in wording and the repeat of the error of law in the other

incorporated an extraordinary, if revealing, error of law. Its declaration that 'any American woman who marries a foreigner shall take the nationality of her husband' was legally incoherent. The 1907 Act (like the others) appeared to legislate for foreign law, but no country could declare or deem what could only be determined under the law of another country. (This is discussed further in the context of international law in Chapter 6.) In denaturalising its own women citizens, a state simply handed them over to a foreign state, guessing, but without inquiring into its actual effect. In most cases, for a time at least, the guess that a woman would automatically acquire her foreign husband's citizenship was correct, although this was beginning to change in the early years of the twentieth century. What was revealing in this strange and erroneous statement of the law was the extent to which women's citizenship was treated as a matter to be determined by other countries' laws.

Seven years after the United States Act, and on the eve of the First World War, the British passed the Nationality and Status of Aliens Act (BNSA Act) of 1914. It reaffirmed Britain's commitment to both marital denaturalisation and naturalisation. This time, it did so in legally sound terms: 'The wife of a British subject shall be deemed to be a British subject, and the wife of an alien shall be deemed to be an alien'. Where the 1870 Act had dealt with naturalisation of foreigners (and denaturalisation of British women married to foreigners) the BNSA Act set out, for the first time, a full, statutory basis for the acquisition of British nationality (and for 'imperial naturalisation': a scheme for a uniform, reciprocally recognised system of British and Dominion naturalisation laws). It included, among other things, provisions for the renunciation of birthright nationality (which had been possible in the past only in very limited circumstances). It made few formal changes to the status of British nationals or the means of acquiring nationality, but it represented a major shift in thinking, one that was characteristic of modern countries generally around that time.

countries' instruments. Catheryn Seckler-Hudson also notes the error of law: *Statelessness: With Special Reference to the United States* (Digest Press, 1934). Revealingly, the legislators were not unaware of the problem. In his second reading speech on the Naturalization Bill, the Lord Chancellor explained why a 'clear definition' of nationality could not be included in the legislation as a means to overcome the inconveniences that arose from the many inconsistencies in the nationality laws of European nations. He explained that such a definition was impossible, 'for we should be legislating in a manner which affects to bind those who are resident in another country, and subject to a totally different jurisdiction, over which we have no control'. Any definition, he added, must arise by 'international accord and treaty'. United Kingdom, House of Lords, *Debates*, 25 February 1870, 1122.

British nationality itself was now a matter of legislation; it was no longer an inherent *common law* right. Legislation meant that nationality was contingent; the rules that governed its acquisition and loss were now subject to the shifting will of elected legislatures. This fact, however, had long applied to married women's citizenship.

The 1914 BNSA Act retained the principle of *jus soli* – the acquisition of nationality by birth in the territory. Allegiance to the sovereign remained the central indicium of citizenship and the central test for a British subject, but the sovereign had decisively changed. The sovereign to whom a British subject owed allegiance was still, in theory (and statutory language), the King or Queen, but the sovereign parliament now determined what that allegiance meant in practice. The Act recorded this change. It also confirmed a previous statutory rule – a type of conceptual companion – that was already a departure from the common law. The Naturalization Act 1870 had already reversed the common law principle that a British national could not lose or change nationality by any voluntary action, and had applied legislation to British nationality. The act of marriage, while voluntary, was deemed also to include the voluntary transfer of allegiance (even if the latter was, in reality, a legal fiction).

The 1870 Act's marital denaturalisation provision (as was subsequently noted by citizenship equality campaigners) had been inserted with little regard for its likely impact – practical or psychological – upon women. It was treated by its framers as a relatively minor measure, a simple gesture of comity with other nations whose laws already incorporated the principle of conditional marital nationality. Nevertheless, despite the apparently casual adoption of the provision, its arrival had already been signalled in the earlier Act of 1844, which had provided, among other things, that an alien woman, upon marriage to a British subject, would become a British subject. Again, the provision applied, regardless of the personal impact on the women in question or whether or not they had consented.

That the BNSA Act of 1914 Act reaffirmed marital denaturalisation was particularly offensive to the women who had been campaigning to amend the 1870 Act since the early part of the twentieth century.[5] However, like the United States Act of 1907, the BNSA Act also included some 'remedial'

[5] Reform of conditional marital nationality laws had been on the agenda of the International Council of Women since 1905. It had been on that of the Women's International League for Peace and Freedom since the war. Mrs Oglivie Gordon's statement: Report, Home Office, September 1918, 'Deputation from Women's Societies to the Secretary of State for the Home Department on the subject of The Nationality of Married Women'. CO 323/778: Special Conference on Nationality and Naturalization.

measures to pre-empt the inequities produced by marital denaturalisation in certain circumstances (discussed below). Both countries, in other words, affirmed the policy of martial denaturalisation and at the same time recognised certain problematic effects.[6] Their recommitment to the policy at this time signalled something larger: as we have observed, married women's nationality was determined by considerations beyond the national level. It was (or so governments thought) locked into place by an international understanding that allegiance, and therefore nationality, must be exclusive, and by international agreement to recognise both the unique citizenship of other countries and their laws governing its conversion by naturalisation. If women with foreign husbands had been allowed to retain their own citizenship the rule of unique allegiance would be broken and, so it was believed, intractable problems in international relations generally, and diplomatic relations specifically, would follow.

In return, many consequences and problems, both for the women affected by the law and for the relations between the relevant countries followed the 'deeming' of a married woman's citizenship to be that of her husband. These arose both from the legal reversal from citizen to alien (and vice-versa) in the countries involved, and from the particular impact of the general classification of married women on those who were maritally denaturalised. Legally, married women were classified as being 'under disability' (as the BNSA Act explained in its definitions, borrowed from the 1870 Act, this meant 'the status of being a married woman, or a minor, lunatic or idiot'). Persons 'under disability' were denied specific legal entitlements (conferred in other relevant Acts). Commonly, the eligibility to apply for naturalisation was one of these. Married women, as we saw, were therefore, in many countries, ineligible to naturalise on their own account. Women with foreign husbands who had lost their native citizenship were incapable of regaining their former citizenship through their own naturalisation.

Marital denaturalisation and its consequences

The instances of grievance and the cases of disadvantage (at least as recorded in official records) were relatively few in the early decades of

6 Indeed, one finds a type of remedial provision already in the Napoleonic Code. A denaturalised Frenchwoman, '[i]f she become a widow... shall recover the quality of Frenchwoman, provided she already reside in France, or that she return thither under the sanction of government, and declare at the same time her intention to fix there'.

marital denaturalisation laws. The great majority of women whose nationality was altered by marriage, we can assume, either enjoyed or suffered their new condition without public comment. Like most persons in history, they lived quietly, their circumstances unchronicled.

Still, those affected were not altogether silent, even at this early stage. Hardships and anomalies created by these laws were brought to the attention of officials right from the beginning. As we have seen, the British Act of 1870, which tucked its marital denaturalisation provision into a general scheme for both foreign naturalisation and the extension of alien property rights, was passed, ironically (so it appears now to present history) in the same year as the first British Married Women's Property Act. The latter Act permitted married women to hold property (derived from their own sources) in their own right. It did not directly engage with the property rights that were provided for in the other Act, but had an unintended effect upon married women's new status as property owners. The effect, as it turned out, was relatively easily corrected, but it illustrated, if nothing else, that the course of applying marital denaturalisation law would not be smooth.[7]

The new statutory right of aliens to hold property in Britain was expressed in the Act so as not to 'affect any estate or interest in property . . . made before the passing of the Act'. In other words, the new property rights of aliens were not retrospective. By that same Act, British women married to foreigners were transformed into aliens. This transformation was undated; such women who had married before 1870 were to be treated ('deemed') as having acquired their husbands' nationality, and thereby having lost their British nationality on the same footing as women who married after the passage of the Act. In the transformation, the existing property rights they had previously enjoyed as British subjects appeared to have been extinguished. In April 1871, the Home Secretary received a communication from the lawyer of a British woman who, on behalf of her sister who was married to a foreigner and living abroad, had written to him 'in great alarm' at what she referred to as 'this new Act of Confiscation'.[8] The sisters, she had explained, were jointly entitled to the ownership of an estate in England, but the married sister, stripped of

[7] Many conundrums surrounding the status of women married to foreign men before the Act's passage but subsequently widowed were also raised with government officials. Dorothy Page, 'A Married Woman, or a Minor, Lunatic, or Idiot'.

[8] UK National Archives, File HO 45/9282/1749E, James Haig to Home Secretary, 20 April 1871.

her British nationality by the 1870 Act, now appeared disentitled to her share of the property. The lawyer was advised by the Home Secretary's office to inform his client that her sister was now an alien and incapable of holding land in England. But (in an internal memo) the Home Secretary was immediately informed that this effect was a 'real blot in the [Naturalization] Act', and a 'blunder' in the drafting.[9]

An amending Bill was quickly drawn up, but in the event was not activated; opinion was given that the word 'affect' would be interpreted to mean 'injuriously affect',[10] presumably saving the sister's share of her estate. Still, under another provision of the Act, the new property rights of aliens had been expressed so as not to extend to property 'situate outside the United Kingdom', which included Britain's colonies. British women married to foreign men and holding property in the colonies would, as aliens, gain no protection from the new law. With regard to this particular effect, the British government realised that there was nothing it could do, other than advise colonial authorities of the need to amend their own laws.

This vignette, albeit with probably few counterparts, illustrates not merely that applying the policy of marital denaturalisation was complex from the start, but that little thought had been given to the effect on the women involved. Looking back, it also reveals the striking lag between laws that were beginning progressively to confer legal personhood on married women generally and laws that, at the same time, conferred derivative citizenship upon a class of the same women. This appears as a paradox, or perhaps, a failure of policy coordination, but (to restate the central argument) it can be understood better as arising from the imperatives of international relations and the willingness of governments to allow their women citizens to be reclassified: a response to the 'triage' problem created by the event of foreign marriage. Cases of hardship experienced by individual women as a result grew over the years and multiplied dramatically as the twentieth century unfolded.

These cases reveal what is difficult to appreciate by treating citizenship law in the abstract. They illustrate the effect on real persons, on human lives. The cases, as recorded in government archives, mainly illustrate the practical side of the story, since, in most instances, entreaties to

[9] UK National Archives, File HO 45/9282/1749E, James Haig to Home Secretary, 7 May 1871.

[10] UK National Archives, File HO 45/9282/1749E, Memo, Office of the Parliamentary Counsel, 12 July 1871.

governments took the form of appeals for practical assistance or intervention. But the existential dimension was also revealed, both in the appeals and in the claims of the citizenship equality campaigners who tirelessly wrote treatises and letters, sent delegations to meet with government officers and ministers of state, and publicised the general effects of marital denaturalisation. Often these were illustrated with reference to practical hardships in individual cases, but they also directly identified and deplored what was both generalised and intangible: marital denaturalisation was an injury in itself. This complaint, indeed, grew louder as remedial amendments were made to the law. Alleviating practical problems, one by one, assisted in certain classes of case, but it confirmed that the legal identity of married women remained subordinate and conditional, and at the same time, it demonstrated official intransigence on this view.

The loss of citizenship upon marriage was difficult to conceptualise as an injury in itself, in particular because, as we have noted, at least until the inter-war period in most countries, foreign women who married citizens 'enjoyed' automatic naturalisation in their husband's country. They appeared immediately to have regained the thing they had lost. In many cases, in a functional sense, this was correct, and undoubtedly in many cases, too, the transfer of citizenship was appreciated by the women in question. An existential or personal satisfaction or sense of belonging may also have been experienced by many women who, on marriage, took not only their husband's name, but also embraced life in his country, and acquired a new sense of home.

This is strikingly illustrated in the case of the Canadian 'war brides' (non-Canadian women who had married Canadian soldiers on service abroad during the war) who, between 1940 and 1947, were officially welcomed as new 'citizens' on their arrival in Canada, and who believed themselves to have automatically acquired citizenship under Canada's law. Although a good number had returned to their former country (the divorce rate of war brides was relatively high) many had become socially and culturally integrated and had come to identify with and love their new country. They would discover many decades later (in many cases only after 2001 when Canadians became required to carry passports for travel to the United States) that, having failed to apply for a certificate of citizenship, they were not (yet) recognised as citizens.[11] The revelation that Canada

[11] Matrix, 'Mediated Citizenship', 68. Matrix reports that it proved difficult in many cases, after such a length of time, to amass the relevant birth and marriage certificates required for proof of status.

was not, in fact, 'their' country, shocked and dismayed many.[12] In 1988, as Sidney Eve Matrix notes, a seventy-five-year-old widow of a Canadian serviceman, having just learned of her alien status, wrote to *The Toronto Star*, inquiring about how to locate her husband's birth certificate. She wanted to apply for the Canadian citizenship that, for forty years, she had believed herself to have held: 'I now want to die with proof of my right to call Canada "my country"'.[13]

The ideal of neutral reciprocity between countries' conditional marital nationality laws had worked, and probably well, in such circumstances, where the woman lived in her husband's country and the relevant country conferred advantages on citizen women that were equivalent or superior to those conferred by her native country. Between 1902 and 1920, for example, an American-born wife of an Australian man, living in Australia, would have enjoyed the right to vote in national elections, a right that would have been denied to her had she stayed in America either as a single woman or married to a fellow American; a Frenchwoman, married to a New Zealander any time after 1893, and living in her husband's country would, similarly, have enjoyed an enlarged political citizenship ahead of female citizens of France until 1944. On the other hand, reversing the nationality of the respective wife and husband, gives a picture of loss of 'citizenship' rights. It was the lottery of love that determined whether the transfer of citizenship brought loss or gain.

Opportunism and marital citizenship

While it is unlikely that many foreign marriages were entered into order to attract political rights, there were many recorded cases of

[12] Under the Canadian Citizenship Act 1946, they had, in fact, automatically become citizens if they had been admitted to Canada for permanent residence before 1 January 1947, and if their husbands were Canadian citizens or had been born in a Commonwealth country and had lived in Canada for at least five years immediately prior to the marriage. George T. Tamaki, 'The Canadian Citizenship Act, 1946' (1947) 7 *The University of Toronto Law Journal* 68. What was required was (merely) to obtain a certificate of Canadian citizenship to prove that they had acquired citizenship, in order to receive the entitlements of citizens. The confusion between legal citizenship status and its recognition in eligibility for the entitlements attached to citizenship is revealing. The war brides described by Matrix experienced the requirement to 'prove' their citizenship as a denial of something inherent to their person. The difficulty in obtaining the requisite documents was, it seems, experienced less as an inconvenience than as an element of this denial. (After the Act came into force in 1947, alien wives of Canadian citizens no longer automatically acquired Canadian citizenship.)

[13] Matrix, 'Mediated Citizenship'.

opportunistic foreign marriages, the primary goal of which was to gain citizenship, and with this the right of residence and protection from deportation. Opportunistic marriages, governments knew, were the risk created by the practice of marital naturalisation. Laws were amended accordingly, or new laws passed, in the attempt to control this effect. An American law passed in 1875 prohibiting the importation of women or girls for the purpose of prostitution, was expanded in 1910, to make it a felony to import into the United States 'any alien woman or girl for the purpose of prostitution, or for any other immoral purpose'.[14] The 'Dillingham Commission'[15] also investigated immigrant women's marriages to American citizens entered into as a means of evading deportation.[16] The United States Act of February 5, 1917 excluded women of 'sexually immoral classes' from marital naturalisation in cases where the marriage occurred after a woman's arrest 'or after the commission of acts which make her liable to deportation' from the United States.[17]

Governments also made efforts to track down and take action against sham marriages, in particular those entered into to give foreign-born prostitutes the opportunity to work without doubts about residency entitlements (or, to allow their pimps to be free of such concerns). In the interwar period, the British authorities warned imperial governments about the practice of men being paid to marry foreign prostitutes. A 'strictly confidential' memo for the General Register Office in London asked Superintendent Registrars and passport authorities to 'exercise particular care' in obtaining valid identities from foreign women engaging in British marriages: 'in most cases the male party is either a criminal or a wastrel who for a consideration [of money] is prepared to enter into matrimony with a woman whom he does not know and will probably never see again'.[18]

[14] Act of June 25, 1910 ('Mann Act').

[15] A Congressional committee formed in 1907 to investigate the distribution and effects of recent immigration to America, the recommendations of which led to sweeping immigration restrictions.

[16] Bredbenner, *A Nationality of Her Own*, 31.

[17] Bredbenner, ibid 123, describes one 'controversial case involving the exclusion of a citizen's wife' on such grounds; the husband lobbied, advertised, and conducted legal proceedings, ultimately successfully, to secure an amendment to the United States Immigration Act in 1930, excluding the law's application to women who were minors at the time of their offence, and had received only a short sentence no more than five years before the amendment's passage. The amendment corresponded to his (former German) wife's circumstances and allowed her to be admitted to the United States.

[18] Library and Archives Canada, RG25 Issue of passports to Married Women Regulations 1934–1936, Vol 1679 (Superintendent Registrar, November 1931).

A British Foreign Office circular for 'His Majesty's Consular and Passport Officers' included a list of around fifty names and details of 'undesirable' women married to British men: including Marie Laurence Cecile McG, née L, who married a British subject '[w]hilst on remand on a charge of being an unregistered alien'; Suzanne Germaine S, married under the name of D, falsely using the identity of a 'respectable dressmaker resident in Paris'; and Anna Maria Louisa G, convicted of soliciting, and subject to a Deportation Order.[19] In Canada in the 1930s, a ring of prostitutes of French origin was identified, working through a branch in Montreal, several having undergone false marriages with Canadian citizens. A memo from the Metropolitan police listed cases of such marriages, including that of a French woman who had obtained a British passport by marriage to a Canadian, and who then travelled to London to work as a prostitute.[20]

Even 'nuisances' who could claim British citizenship by marriage were under suspicion. One Foreign Office circular, dated 17 November 1927,[21] was devoted entirely to the case of Mrs Amy (or Aimee) L, 'an undesirable character, who was recently expelled from Russia, and has since been a source of annoyance to His Majesty's Consul and the British community at Riga'. Amy L, we learn, was 'believed to have married originally a Russian, Count K, who was either killed during the war or is at present a refugee in Paris, and subsequently a Russian named V, from whom she is stated to have been divorced'. She then married a British subject, 'a master mariner, named L, now deceased, and was granted a passport' at Leningrad in April 1925. Mrs L's passport, officers were advised, should be impounded until she produced documentary evidence that both her former husbands were either dead or that she had been legally divorced in both cases, prior to her British marriage, in addition to evidence that her husband was a British subject at the time of their marriage. What Mrs L's colourful case revealed was, in fact, the intractability of marital naturalisation laws applied to genuine marriages. The British were searching for evidence that her claim to be lawfully married to a British subject was not genuine; in the absence of illegal activity or misrepresentation on her part, her undesirable 'character' was not a disqualification.

There was another dimension to the opportunistic side of conditional marital nationality. Certain women, maybe many, were rescued by

[19] National Archives of Australia, Series A1, 1932/3357, 'List of undesirable alien women acquiring British nationality through marriage – Passports "L"'.

[20] Library and Archives Canada, RG25 Issue of passports to Married Women Regulations 1934–1936, Vol 1679.

[21] National Archives of Australia, Series A1, 1932/3357, 'List of undesirable alien women acquiring British nationality through marriage – Passports "L"'.

marriage to a foreigner whose country offered refuge from persecution in their own, and for whom the husband's citizenship sheltered them from deportation. There were celebrated examples. In 1935, Erika Mann, the German-born cabaret artist (and daughter of Thomas Mann) whose anti-Nazi satire had brought her under political suspicion, entered into an 'arranged' marriage with the homosexual British poet, W. H. Auden. The same year, the German-born, part Jewish novelist, Sybille Bedford, also a critic of Nazi policies, made a similar marriage with a British homosexual. The marriages transformed both women into British subjects and denaturalised them as Germans, thus allowing them to travel with British passports and to live outside the reach of German authorities. The Russian-born anarchist, Emma Goldman, married a British anarchist in 1925 also for reasons of self-protection. Having been deported in 1919 from the United States (where she had lived since 1885) to the Soviet Union under the US Alien Act of 1918, and having subsequently lived insecurely in several other countries, she was now, as a British subject, shielded from further deportation, including from Canada, where she ended her years. There were, no doubt, other marriages arranged for such purposes.

Such happy endings, however, were not an advertisement for conditional marital nationality laws. The reality was that opportunistic marriages were invalid under law. The security they appeared to offer was fragile. Archives record prosecutions of individuals participating in false marriages in order to secure passports for Jewish refugees.[22] The cases of such marriages, however, illustrate what is conceptually true about citizenship. It offers protection, in the sense of a place in the world from which a citizen cannot (legitimately) be expelled. That is not to say that, in each case, the individual citizen is protected from harm in his or her country. Indeed, Mann and Bedford were escaping from the harm that was threatened under their native citizenship. But none of these effects required or depended on the simultaneous denaturalisation of married women. What followed from the automatic conferral of citizenship upon marriage was not in itself incompatible with the retention of the woman's own native citizenship.

Problems relating to conflicts of law also arose from conditional marital nationality, and attempts to resolve these also extended to marriages entered into in purely to facilitate naturalisation. The validity of a marriage

22 Library and Archives Canada, RG25 Issue of passports to Married Women Regulations 1934–1936, Vol 1679.

was determined by the law of the country in which it took place (and principles of international comity required the inter-state recognition, at least in most cases, of foreign marriages); where a marriage between a foreign women and a citizen had been performed in another country in order to evade the immigration laws of the husband's country (including laws banning foreign prostitutes) the naturalised wife's deportation was permitted.[23]

Conflicts of law

The international consensus against dual nationality was at the heart of these conflicts, and (as we have observed) it contributed, in some cases, to statelessness. There were many alternative scenarios, less drastic, but nevertheless consequentially severe: cases where the husband's country restricted women's rights generally or married women's rights specifically; cases where the husband was himself an alien of the country in which the couple lived; cases where the woman had been deserted by her husband or had otherwise lost his support or protection; cases where the marriage (which gave rise to the woman's loss of native citizenship) was not recognised as valid under the law of the husband's country; cases where the couple were divorced, but either the divorce was not treated as a ground for the restoration of the woman's native citizenship, or the country in which the couple lived did not recognise divorce generally or did not recognise the divorce laws of the particular country in which the divorce had been granted. Furthermore, the ideal only applied if, in fact, a denaturalised woman acquired her husband's citizenship. For a time at least, the latter was a reasonable assumption, but it was not incontrovertible. While almost all countries denaturalised their women who married 'out', some did not automatically do the reverse, and, as the twentieth century progressed, this asymmetry increased in laws around the world.

The ideal of neutral symmetry in countries' conditional marital nationality laws also depended upon countries' recognition of each other's marriage and divorce laws; there were multiple differences in rules governing, among others, marriageable age, definitions of relationships or degrees of consanguinity governing the prohibition on intra-family marriage,

[23] In the United States, regarding a particular 1910 case, an Attorney-General's opinion held that the alien wife of an American citizen must be admitted regardless. Catheryn Seckler-Hudson, *Statelessness: With Special Reference to the United States*, 48.

requirements of civil or religious ceremonies, what counted as consent on the part of the parties to a marriage, recognition or non-recognition of divorce,[24] whether marriages by proxy or polygamous marriages were accepted, and many more.[25] The common law rule that a married woman's domicile was that of her husband, with jurisdiction concerning divorce, testamentary capacity and related matters based on domicile, further complicated the determination of a woman's marital status. Additional questions also arose concerning the recognition of nationality status, going to the heart of recognition of the state itself.[26] Determinations on these issues had vital, life-changing consequences. The non-recognition by one country of another country's marriage laws, in cases where the first country denaturalised its women upon foreign marriage, produced statelessness. This effect was the most severe of all.

Even if none of these misfortunes was experienced, the ideal of neutral reciprocity only applied if the woman was happy for her citizenship to be altered without any active acquiescence on her part. Most significantly, the ideal did not function well – indeed, it lost its character of reciprocity – where the woman continued to live in her country of origin, and now found herself transformed into an alien. In this transformation, she lost not only the citizenship entitlements she may have formerly held, but also found herself subject to the disentitlements that applied specifically to aliens. For many women, stripped of the citizenship they cherished, the existential injury was as severe as any material or practical hardship.

[24] Including conflicts between different religious laws and state laws in the same jurisdiction. The myriad complexities were noted, for example, in marriages between English women and Indian men which, by the early years of the twentieth century were 'by no means infrequent'. E.J. Trevelyan, 'Marriages between English Women and Natives of British India' (1917) 17 *Journal of the Society of Comparative Legislation* 223.

[25] Lennart Palsson, *Marriage in Comparative Conflict of Laws: Substantive Conditions* (Springer, 1981).

[26] Unless the first country had adopted the rule (stated in the Hague Nationality Convention of 1930) that marital denaturalisation would only apply when the foreign-marrying woman acquired the nationality of her husband's country. In such a case, the non-recognition of marriage by the first country also involved the question of whether that country would recognise, not merely the marriage, but also the nationality conferred upon the woman by her husband's country. For example, in the interwar period (after the Hague Convention rule was adopted in Britain, in 1933), a British executive decision was taken that 'a woman British subject who acquires Palestinian citizenship through marriage with a Palestinian citizen is not deemed to lose her British nationality by reason of her marriage, as Palestinian citizenship is not regarded as nationality within the meaning of... the British Nationality and Status of Aliens Act'. National Archives of Australia, Series: BP234/1 Control symbol: SB1937/3236.

The status of an alien

The hardships of marital denaturalisation were felt most commonly in this transformation of women into aliens in their own country. Women, married to foreign men, but living in their native country, came under Aliens Acts (and their legislative counterparts), as well as numerous provisions applying specifically to aliens in the various laws of every country. The consequences of alienage varied, but were typically substantial. (In wartime, the classification as an enemy alien brought dramatically heightened consequences. We consider such cases, as they applied to denaturalised women, in Chapter 4.)

In assessing the impact of denaturalisation, we cannot treat the historical context as identical to our own. Just as the effects of holding citizenship were different in the nineteenth century and early twentieth centuries, the effects of denaturalisation and alienage changed over time. In most cases, they became more complex or harsher. Passports or transit visas were not generally required for travel until the First World War, and they were internationally standardised only after the war, following the League of Nations 'Passport Conferences' in 1920 and 1926. Most people travelled less than today in any case. Relatively few countries had public pension schemes where an eligibility distinction between citizen and alien might have been drawn, and the idea that social welfare was a matter for government only began to emerge in the second half of the nineteenth century (having been previously understood primarily as the responsibility of families, churches and charitable organisations, much of this borne by women, but where citizenship status was unlikely to be relevant). By such measures the distinction between citizen and alien was relatively weak.

In some countries, however, the difference between being a citizen and being an alien had a chronologically early impact on ordinary life. In nineteenth century France, for example, citizenship was a qualification for registering a patent or for practising certain occupations. In some regions, it was attached to local or communal rights, such as the use of common lands or forests. Jennifer Ngaire Heuer has chronicled the moving claims made by foreign men who lived in rural regions and were married to native-born French women, for the right to collect firewood or graze animals on the commons. Not only were they reminded that they were disentitled as aliens, but they were also informed that their marriages had rendered their wives foreign too.[27] Many exclusions could

[27] Heuer, *The Family and the Nation*, 175.

be found in other countries in the early part of the nineteenth century. A wide-ranging survey of alien 'disabilities', included as an Appendix to the British Report of the Royal Commission inquiring into naturalisation in 1869, revealed numerous cases where citizenship was required for certain professions, occupations or positions, along with multiple specific exclusions, most commonly governing employment or engagement in civil service and membership of political organisations, as well as a good number of restrictions on property ownership and inheritance.[28]

There were advantages, on occasion, in the status of alien. In post-revolutionary France, for example, Frenchmen and women who had left France to live in another country during the Revolution were, as émigrés or émigrées, subject to severe penalties (also applying to their families). But native-born French women who had lost their citizenship by marriage to a foreign man and who had left France with their husbands were treated leniently, since, as (marital) foreigners, they had no patriotic obligation to remain in their (former) country. They had not, in effect, emigrated. In 1812, the Minister for Justice 'wrote to administrators throughout the empire telling them to remove names of women from the lists of subjects who were to be penalized for having left France without permission'.[29] The particular test of allegiance applied specifically to citizens.[30]

Regardless of any advantages, aliens were typically the object of many more exclusions from entitlements or rights. In many countries, aliens were ineligible for employment in the public service or as teachers, or in occupations requiring official licences. In many countries, aliens were also barred from holding or inheriting property, and in some from the use of public lands.[31] In the history of the United States, as Alexander Bickel observed, 'as one or another wave of xenophobia or unemployment

[28] *Report of the Royal Commissioners for Inquiring into the Laws of Naturalization and Allegiance* (HM Stationary Office, London, 1869): Appendix No. II, 'Disabilities of Aliens – Reports from Foreign States'.

[29] Heuer, *The Family and the Nation*, 163.

[30] It is worth noting, however, that, counter-intuitively, the more common test of allegiance historically associated with citizenship, namely, the performance of military service, does not offer an example of the advantages of alienage. Aliens are not necessarily precluded from the obligation to perform military service in the country of their residence (in any case, women, whether citizens or aliens, were not historically subjects of military conscription). This creates a paradox in the conceptualisation of the relationship between citizen and state: the paradigm of allegiance has little positive or behavioural content (disallegiance is another matter). The 'companion' paradigm of protection is positive and concrete.

[31] Waltz, *The Nationality of Married Women*, 94.

swept over the country, state statutes excluded aliens from various callings, employments, and activities'. He listed these:

> optometrist, dentist, doctor, nurse, architect, teacher, lawyer, policeman, engineer, corporate officer, real estate broker, public accountant, mortician, physiotherapist, pharmacist, pedlar, pool or gambling-hall operator, all or some government or public works employment, hunting and receiving public charity, ownership of land.[32]

These laws, in some cases, had been challenged as unconstitutional before the United States Supreme Court, but (with limited exceptions) the challenges were unsuccessful,[33] while other alien exclusion laws had gone unchallenged. Many, we may add to Bickel's observation, applied during the years when marital denaturalisation laws were in operation. While the exclusion of women generally from many of these occupations and married women specifically from others, would have lessened the impact of the loss of citizenship for women, in numerous cases, marital aliens found themselves locked out of occupations they had previously enjoyed or for which they had previously been eligible in their own country.

In the interwar Depression years the specific problems caused by alienage were exacerbated. In 1932, a communication from the Committee of Representatives of Women's International Organisations to the League of Nations explained that women were 'suffering to-day, as never before in recent times, from the disastrous consequences of unequal nationality laws'. Now, 'in time of economic distress', large numbers of married women were 'unable to get employment because [they were] classified as aliens even in the land of their own birth'. Some had had their professional licences taken away; others had encountered new restrictions on trade or occupations, or had lost their pensions, or access to State hospitals: 'the woman who is destitute finds that she has no claim upon her own country for help'.[34]

Melissa Feinberg describes the 'devastating' consequences of alien status for many women who were denaturalised by foreign marriage under

[32] Alexander M. Bickel, 'Citizen or Person? What is Not Granted Cannot be Taken Away', *The Morality of Consent* (Yale University Press, 1975) 46–7.

[33] It had, however, invalidated an Arizona law that imposed a maximum quota on alien employment in private industry. *Traux* v. *Raich*, 239 U.S. 33 (1915). Bickel, 'Citizen or Person?', ibid.

[34] National Archives of Australia, A446 1964/46452 League of Nations, Nationality of Women, 7 September 1932.

the Czechoslovak citizenship law of 1920.[35] As aliens in their former country, they were unable to practise a range of professions or to be employed in the civil service or as teachers, or in the postal service, or the state tobacco factories (in which the majority of employees were women); they and their children were also ineligible for social services, welfare assistance and medical care. Particularly affected were Czech women whose husbands had emigrated to the United States (in anticipation of their families joining them later) and had been naturalised there as Americans. Their naturalisation led to the denaturalisation of their wives under Czech law. These wives were, consequently, unable to obtain Czech passports for travel to America to join their husbands. After marital naturalisation was ended in the United States in 1922, foreign wives were no longer maritally naturalised as American citizens and were therefore ineligible for American passports. They had to wait, as stateless persons, sometimes for years for visas to travel. After the repeal of marital naturalisation in the Soviet Union, Czech women who were married to Russians also became stateless (as did the men who had fled from Russia after 1917 and were, under the Soviet law of 1921, denaturalised); foreign or stateless men seeking naturalisation (which would have had the effect also of (re)naturalising their denaturalised wives), had to reside for ten years in the country to be eligible under Czech naturalisation law. There were, Feinberg observes, many 'harrowing stories' of destitute Czech women and families caught by the combination of these laws.[36]

Such effects did not go unnoticed, including by political representatives. In 1926, the sponsor of an Australian motion favouring the repeal of marital denaturalisation (discussed in Chapter 5), Member of the Australian House of Representatives, John Duncan-Hughes, referred to 'the very great loss which a woman suffers under the present law when she marries an alien'. In the first place, he said, she loses her nationality; secondly, she loses the franchise, and in some circumstances, her property: 'a great many women, both Australian and British, lost their property during the war because of their marriages with aliens'. Women, he declared, 'are not less susceptible to sentiment than men, and to lose nationality is as great a loss to a woman as to a man'.[37]

In 1927, Agnes Macphail, first woman Member of the Canadian House of Commons, observed that there were 'scores of' Canadian women, denaturalised by marriage, but resident in Canada, who were 'unable to

[35] Feinberg, *Elusive Equality*. [36] Feinberg, ibid, 79.

[37] Commonwealth of Australia, House of Representatives, *Debates*, 4 February 1926, 680.

claim the protection of any government, unable to vote, unable to teach or to accept any civil position . . . and, in the event of their husbands' death, unable to participate in the mother's allowance for the benefit of their children'.[38]

In 1932, British Member of Parliament, Victor Cazalet proposed a new law to address such hardships. Introducing his (unsuccessful) Private Member's British-Born Alien Women (Civil Rights) Bill, Cazalet described the situation of many of them as 'piteous, helpless and tragic'. A woman in this position, he said,

> is an alien, she is subject to police supervision, she is forced to register and to inform the police of her movements, she is disqualified for certain benefits under the Insurance Acts, the Old Age Pension Act and the Widow's Pension Act, and although she may pay rates and taxes she has no vote.[39]

He added: 'I know of hundreds of such cases, and I get a letter almost daily explaining the pitiful position of some women in these circumstances'.

In 1920, an (unsuccessful) American proposal to amend the naturalisation law, including to allow maritally denaturalised American women to retain their citizenship so long as they resided in the United States came before Congress. In debate, attention was drawn to the high rate of desertion by alien husbands, leaving the wives ineligible for public assistance, and vulnerable to denial of employment and possible deportation.[40] In an account of the history behind the US Cable Act of 1922, Congressman John Cable, its sponsor, also listed cases of hardship caused by the marital denaturalisation law in the United States. Aliens were disbarred from practising medicine in many States, from teaching in public schools, from taking State or Federal civil service exams or holding government office. In some States, aliens could not practise law. One woman of whom he knew, Cable explained, had become qualified as a lawyer in New York and had built up a successful practice; after she married a Dutch national, she 'lost her law business and the right to practice law in New York'.[41] She also lost her right to an American passport or consular assistance abroad: 'In fact, by exercising a power incidental to its sovereignty the United States could even have expelled her . . . as an alien, although she was native born and her ancestors had been closely connected with the

[38] Dominion of Canada, House of Commons, *Debates*, 6 April 1927, 1983.
[39] United Kingdom, House of Commons, *Debates*, 6 July 1932, 449.
[40] Bredbenner, *A Nationality of Her Own*, 83.
[41] Cable, *American Citizenship Rights of Women*, 26.

early struggles of our great republic'.[42] Bredbenner also notes the case of an American woman, Florence Bain Gual, a former public school teacher, married to a Cuban who had deserted her and their child; Gual reported that, disqualified as an alien from teaching, she had been deprived of her livelihood, 'because of the citizenship of a man'.[43]

Rights of residence were less tightly controlled in the nineteenth and early twentieth century, and the comprehensive system of visas or visit limitations with which we are familiar today had not yet developed. But the right of aliens to remain in a foreign country was increasingly insecure. The British Aliens Act of 1905 targeted both 'undesirable' immigrants and 'undesirable aliens' within the United Kingdom. The first category included those who were unable to establish that they had the means of 'decently supporting' themselves and their dependants (as well as 'lunatics' or 'idiots', and the diseased or infirm, persons who were likely to become a charge upon the public or a detriment to the public; and those sentenced in a foreign country of a crime for which extradition from Britain was available).[44] The Act also made provision for the expulsion of 'undesirable aliens'; those convicted of serious, non-political offences in either the United Kingdom or a foreign country with which there was an extradition treaty; those in receipt of 'any parochial relief as disqualifies a person for the parliamentary franchise', and those 'found wandering without ostensible means of subsistence, or . . . living under insanitary conditions due to overcrowding'.

The UK Aliens Restriction Act of 1919 added further restrictions. In practical terms, its prohibitions on aliens' acting as ships pilots or masters, chief officers, chief engineers on British merchant ships, or skippers or second hands, on British fishing boats (as well as on employment on ships at a lower rate of pay than standard on British ships) were unlikely to have affected women. Also, in contrast to the restrictions on enemy aliens during the war, the 1919 Act exempted women who were at the time of their marriage British subjects, from the special restrictions applying to former enemy aliens (including prohibition, for a three year period, on acquiring property in land or shares or interests in British 'key industries',

[42] Cable, ibid.

[43] Bredbenner, *A Nationality of Her Own*, 83. Quoting letter from Gual to Harriot Stanton Blatch, 5 April 1921.

[44] Exemptions were made for persons seeking to avoid prosecution or punishment on religious or political grounds, or those, having previously resided in the United Kingdom, who had been refused admission in another country from which they had immediately returned to the United Kingdom.

or companies carrying on such industry or owning British-registered ships).[45] More significant, however, was the blunt prohibition in section 6: 'After the passing of this Act no alien shall be appointed to any office or place in the Civil Service of the State'. The former marriage bar on women's employment in the civil service had (at least formally) been lifted with the passage of the 1919 Sex Disqualification (Removal) Act, which provided that 'a person shall not be disqualified by sex or marriage from the exercise of any public function . . . or from entering or assuming or carrying on any civil profession or vocation'. Ironically, this protection of married women's entitlement to work could not assist marital aliens, whose very marriage had disqualified them. Additionally, the School Teachers Superannuation Act of 1910 had provided that 'no superannuation allowance or gratuity shall be payable to any teacher who is not a British subject and no death gratuity shall be payable in respect of any teacher not being a British subject'. British women who worked as teachers before their foreign marriage would, as brides, lose their nationality, probably their job, and any pension entitlements they had accumulated.

As aliens were frequently ineligible for social benefits, these effects were particularly harsh for poor alien women who were also denied employment, and even more so in the case of the husband's desertion. Notwithstanding the recognition of injustice in such cases, the consensus against dual or multiple nationalities within a family repeatedly led to deadlock. So long as the marriage was 'subsisting in law',[46] the citizenship of the woman in question was governed by marital denaturalisation law, and could not be reversed. Despite hardships, even destitution, she could not retain or regain her own nationality.[47]

[45] It also exempted married women from the prohibition on the assumption or use by an alien of any name 'other than that by which he was ordinarily known' on 4 August 1914.

[46] Some countries, at least after the First World War, made provision for the restoration of a woman's pre-marital nationality in cases of 'judicial separation'. Rumanian law of 1924 provided for such cases, as well as for widowhood and divorce, subject to the woman's making a formal declaration of her desire to 'recover' her Rumanian status. Yugoslavian law of 1928 included a similar provision, but 'renewal' was subject to proof of the woman's permanent residence in Yugoslavia. Flournoy and Hudson, *A Collection of Nationality Laws*.

[47] Hardship associated with denaturalisation in cases of separation had been recognised as early as 1870. In debate on the UK Naturalization Act, one member of the House of Commons pointed out that the marital denaturalisation provision 'did not seem to be sufficiently guarded'. A British woman might have been made an alien through her husband's foreign naturalisation, and 'although residing . . . in this country, and judicially separated from her husband, who lived abroad, would be made a foreign subject against her own will . . . [and] would be deprived of all the rights, privileges and protection to which

Women without a country

Being treated as an alien in the country of their pre-marital citizenship was a grievance in itself, but in some cases, maritally denaturalised women were unable to reside in their own (former) country. This occurred where the law of a denaturalised woman's native country excluded aliens of particular nationalities from immigration or from the relevant immigration quota, and the woman had been maritally naturalised in one of the excluded nationalities. It occurred in cases where the woman's particular circumstances (such as suffering from certain contagious illnesses, or 'immorality' of character) excluded her individually from entitlement to a resident's visa. A sense of exile in many cases attached to all such types of exclusion.

The American parable, *The Man Without a Country*, published in 1863, provided a poignant and powerful insight into this experience.[48] The story, by Edward Everett Hale, was of an American man who, having bitterly renounced his citizenship, is condemned to spend the rest of his life on a ship at sea, forbidden to hear any news of his former country. He is well-provisioned and comfortable; he has social company, music, books to read, things to do. But, soon, he experiences his life as unbearable. He is a man 'without a country' not merely because he is stateless, but because he has lost the 'home' that nourished him (and, by implication, his fellow citizens.) The story became widely known, and the parallel with the condition of maritally denaturalised women did not go unnoticed.

Women self-identified as fellow sufferers,[49] assuming the reference would be familiar to their audience. 'Even' a woman does not like to feel herself 'a man without a Country', wrote Marion W F to the Canadian Prime Minister in October 1932. The law under which women lost their nationality, she continued, was 'antiquated' and 'ridiculous'. She had a young Canadian friend – 'all her ancestry are Canadian' – who had married an American and found 'to her surprise' when she came back after a few months that she was no longer a Canadian; nor was she an

a British subject would be entitled'. The Attorney General objected that 'it was almost impossible to provide against every conceivable case of hardship; and [the] question was what rule, on the whole, was most expedient'. United Kingdom, House of Commons, *Debates*, 25 April 1870, 1740.

48 *The Atlantic Monthly*, Vol 12, 1863.

49 Emma Goldman wrote of her experience of deportation from the United States in 1919 under the title 'A Woman Without a Country' (1933): Reproduced in Weil, *The Sovereign Citizen*, Appendix 1, 187.

American (marital naturalisation having been repealed in the United States by then):

> [O]f course, no law could make her in reality anything but a Canadian, or British; to call herself such would be somewhat in the nature of a joke . . . If such a law had in some way implied the losing of citizenship among men I am quite sure it would have been rectified long ago. Women may have been supine under such a law before they received the franchise, but not now. Alas, it is driving a number of Canadians into becoming Americans, who do not really wish to do so. You may be sure that American women would not give their citizenship so readily.[50]

Marion F was correct that American women had challenged the 1907 marital denaturalisation law (and many women had also been vigorously campaigning against counterpart laws in many other countries). In 1915, Ethel Mackenzie, an American-born women, denaturalised by her marriage, had brought a constitutional challenge to the law. Mackenzie, a resident of San Francisco, had married a British subject, also a resident, in 1909. The couple had made their marital home together in San Francisco. Mackenzie had been active in the campaign that had resulted in an amendment to California's constitution, granting the State franchise to the women citizens of California in 1911. In 1913, when she applied to be registered as a voter, she was rejected as a non-citizen. She sought a writ of mandamus against the Board of Election Commissioners in the Supreme Court of California, seeking to compel them to register her. Her initial argument was not against marital denaturalisation as such, but against its application to women, like herself, who, although married to foreign men, lived in the United States.[51] Defeated in California, she challenged the constitutional validity of the Act in the United States Supreme Court. Her claim that the Act had been intended solely to govern the status of citizens living abroad was quickly dismissed. She now argued that American citizenship by birth in the United States was a right that could not be taken away other than as a punishment for a crime or by voluntary expatriation. Congress, in her view, was not constitutionally empowered to 'denationalize a citizen without his (sic) concurrence'. Concurrence,

[50] Library and Archives of Canada. Letter, 4 October 1932. Microfilm: Reel M1110.

[51] 'Rights of Women Married to Aliens', *Ogden Standard* 12 November 1915. Report of Mackenzie's application to the United States Supreme Court: 'In the brief submitted in her behalf, it is said that the decision is of vast importance to American women because of the European War, in particular in traveling on the ocean'.

Mackenzie maintained, could only be 'evidenced by emigration, coupled with other acts indicating an intention to transfer one's allegiance'.[52]

An earlier case, *United States* v. *Wong Kim Ark*, had concluded with the Supreme Court's holding that Congress did not have the power 'to restrict the effect of birth declared by the Constitution to constitute a sufficient and complete right to citizenship'.[53] Mackenzie cited this case in support of the birthright interpretation of the Constitution's Fourteenth Amendment – 'All persons born or naturalized in the United States and subject to the jurisdiction thereof, are citizens of the United States' – overlooking the difference that *Wong Kim Ark* concerned the acquisition of citizenship by birth, not its subsequent loss. The Supreme Court responded:

> The identity of husband and wife is an ancient principle of our jurisprudence. It was neither accidental nor arbitrary, and worked in many instances for her protection. There has been, it is true, much relaxation of it, but in its retention, as in its origin, it is determined by their intimate relation and unity of interests, and this relation and unity may make it of public concern in many instances to merge their identity, and give dominance to the husband. It has purpose if not necessity in purely domestic policy; it has greater purpose, and, it may be, necessity, in international policy.[54]

The condition of marriage, the Court continued, was voluntarily entered into 'with notice of the consequences'. Citizenship, the Court conceded, was 'of tangible worth', and a change of citizenship could not be arbitrarily imposed; that is, 'without the concurrence of the citizen'. While expressing sympathy for Mackenzie's desire to retain her citizenship, the judges nevertheless concluded bluntly:

> The marriage of an American woman with a foreigner . . . is made tantamount to voluntary expatriation. This is no arbitrary exercise of government. It is one which, regarding international aspects, judicial opinion has taken for granted would not only be valid, but demanded.[55]

International 'embarrassments' and 'controversies' might follow, if the law were otherwise.

As it happened, Ethel Mackenzie had acquired British citizenship through her marriage, but the Court made no reference to this fact; nor did it attempt to inquire into whether she had any nationality at all.

52 *Mackenzie* v. *Hare*, 239 U.S. 299 (1915) 310.
53 *United States* v. *Wong Kim Ark*, 169 U.S. (1898) 703.
54 *Mackenzie* v. *Hare*, 239 U.S. 299 (1915) 311.
55 *Mackenzie* v. *Hare*, 239 U.S. 299 (1915) 312.

The Court's statement that conditional marital nationality arose from an 'ancient principle' of American jurisprudence was a mere assertion. It was also inaccurate, if by 'ancient' it intended the common law. Alternatively, if the reference was to the principle of coverture, this too was inaccurate, as coverture did not directly apply to marital nationality. Under the common law, the citizenship of a wife was not tied to that of her husband; her allegiance was not dissolved upon marriage. It was true that the United States legislation of 1855 had had the effect of automatically naturalising foreign women who married American citizens, but this practice (to which the Court made no reference) was scarcely 'ancient', and regarding the issue in Mackenzie's case – marital denaturalisation – American practice prior to the 1907 Expatriation Act had been inconclusive, but had for the most part confirmed married women's independent citizenship.

Over prior decades, different conclusions had been reached concerning the status of American born wives of foreign men. Significantly, in *Shanks* v. *Dupont* – the leading case that preceded both the Fourteenth Amendment and the 1868 Expatriation Act in which the rule of perpetual allegiance was abandoned – the Supreme Court had concluded that 'marriage with an alien, whether friend or enemy, produces no dissolution of the native allegiance of the wife'.[56] There, the Court had tied its conclusion to 'the general doctrine . . . that no person can, by any act of their own, without the consent of the government, put off their allegiance and become aliens'.[57] In a similar case, in 1893, a federal court had asserted that '[a] change of the allegiance due to the United States . . . involves, . . . on the part of the citizen, the manifestation of the purpose to expatriate himself by some unequivocal act, which act must also be recognized by the government to be adequate for that purpose'. It concluded: '[A] woman, a citizen of the United States, does not lose that citizenship by marriage to an alien, at least so long as she continues to reside in the United States'.[58] A range of alternative perspectives was, however, produced in other cases, in lower courts, over the years.

In 1925, without reference to *Mackenzie*, a federal court asserted that 'the decided weight of judicial authority is that a woman did not at common law lose her citizenship here [in the United States] by marrying an alien unless she removed from the country';[59] such women had not lost their American citizenship, so long as they were resident. The case concerned whether Mrs Fitzroy, an American who had married a British

[56] *Shanks* v. *Dupont* 28 U.S. 242 (1830).
[57] *Shanks* v. *Dupont* 28 U.S. 242 (1830) 246.
[58] *Comitis* v. *Parkerson et al*, 56 F. 556 (1893).
[59] *In re Fitzroy*, 4 F. 2d 541 (1925).

subject in Boston in 1905 and resided in the United States, was an alien. But the Court's comment that 'there is no evidence that Mrs Fitzroy ever expected or intended to lose her citizenship in the United States' was revealing. She had married before the Act of 1907, but what women in her position 'expected' had been altered by the Act, or at least was taken to be altered, as the reasoning in Mackenzie's case suggested. Although the judge in the Fitzroy case commented that '[i]t is pretty artificial to say . . . in the absence of any controlling statute, that the marriage expatriated her and imposed upon her the duty of allegiance to the British sovereign' given her continuing domicile in the United States, this, at least under British law, was the effect.

Summing up the case law in 1932, an American naturalisation expert concluded that marital denaturalisation had only been effected in the United States prior to 1907 in cases where the wife of a foreign man both acquired his citizenship by marriage and permanently lived abroad.[60] Nevertheless, as Bredbenner explains, the State Department 'began to treat women married before 1907 as aliens and reject their requests for passports'.[61] The 1907 Act did not state whether or not marital denaturalisation applied retrospectively to women whose marriages to aliens took place before its passage. The Mackenzies were married in 1909. What was certain about Ethel Mackenzie's status was that she had been, since her marriage, an alien in her own country. Within a year of the judgement, it was reported that Peter Gordon Mackenzie had applied for naturalisation as an American citizen.[62] His naturalisation would automatically (re-)naturalise his wife. Ethel Mackenzie, born an American citizen and denaturalised under American law, would now become an American again. Her difficulty, as it turned out, was resolved by an act relating not to America's own citizens, but to foreigners. Since Britain permitted its nationals to naturalise, Mr Mackenzie would now be the party to change citizenship. Unlike his wife, however, his transfer of allegiance could only occur as a consequence of both his action and consent.

It was a practical solution that did not, of course, resolve the underlying grievance: women's citizenship remained a shadow of their husband's, vulnerable to his choices and essentially precarious. Although the Court asserted that the 'consequences' of marriage were on notice, it is striking that an educated, politically active woman such as Ethel Mackenzie,

[60] Hover, 'Citizenship of Women in the United States', 705.

[61] Bredbenner, *A Nationality of Her Own*, 66, fn 52.

[62] 'To be Citizen to Aid Wife', *New York Times*, 9 March 1916.

had been unaware of the law by which she lost her citizenship until she attempted to register for the vote for which she had campaigned. But, even had she been aware, the choice – between citizenship and marriage to the person of one's choice – scarcely rendered the outcome consensual.

The stronger argument revealed in the case, that which the Court referred to as the Act's 'greater purpose' and, perhaps, 'necessity', concerned its 'international aspects'. The 1907 Act, as we have seen, was a specific response to imperatives of international relations, primarily intended as an adjustment to international trends and to the need to bring the United States in line with world practice. A matter exclusively within the jurisdiction of the nation-state and a core incident of state sovereignty – nationality law – was shaped, if not determined, by international considerations, even where these worked against the asserted interests of the state's own citizens.

Personal accounts

The response recorded by Marion F to marital denaturalisation (astonishment, dismay, outrage) was a common experience of women who found their national status changed without their prior knowledge. It was, in a functional sense, the result of the weak notification of the law, with the accompanying legal presumption that women knew the consequences. But it was most revealing of the fact that marriage, a deeply personal matter, is much more than a legal undertaking. In most cases, at least at the start, any conflict between love of an 'intended' and love of country is unlikely to have occurred to most women. Even if it had, the putative choice was scarcely a genuine choice, and a man, it was assumed, could love both country and wife without sacrificing either.

Government records are rich in letters written by or on behalf of individual women, accounts of cases that created special administrative problems, requests for information from consular or other officials on the part of women who had sought advice about their status, and many other inquiries or entreaties. Many cases were also recorded in the speeches and writings of political reformers, in legislative debates, and occasionally in the newspapers. Although some of the records concern 'ordinary', even poorly educated women (the larger number of maritally denaturalised women were found among the poorer sectors of society, in communities dominated by immigrants) many belonged to the articulate and educated classes. Some featured women who could claim the attention of political champions or could activate elite connections, or whose circumstances might even have threatened political embarrassment. But neither marital denaturalisation nor marital naturalisation could be waived for individuals or reversed by the exercise of discretion.[63] Although, special arrangements (such as issuing identity papers for travel or exceptional passports[64]) were sometimes made, alleviating the impact for some individuals, the law itself applied equally, regardless of 'class'.

Individual members of government or of legislatures were frequently sympathetic and responsive to accounts of hardship (as we see in Chapter 5, there were many examples of interventions, including Private Members Bills, seeking to amend the law).[65] The press, too, increasingly noticed the effects of marital denaturalisation. The appreciation of what was at stake in tying a woman's citizenship to her husband's depended significantly on stories of personal adversity and of family and domestic privations, and sympathy could most easily be aroused by tales of undeserving individual women whose birthright citizenship had been taken from them merely for following their hearts. In contrast, there was relatively little outrage to be generated in the recognition that a class of women, upon marriage, had lost the right to vote that they had previously held as citizens in their own country, and even less in the abstract proposition that women were entitled to their own citizenship, on the same footing as a man (although this argument would gain in force over the interwar years). Citizenship equality campaigners therefore frequently proceeded by anecdote. In doing so, they conveyed, indirectly, that citizenship is an experience in itself, that it shapes and profoundly affects all life histories, and that it does so in a way that is unique among legal or administrative classifications.

That conditional marital nationality was both global and 'democratic', applying equally to rich and poor, was an advantage for campaigners. Attempts on the part of the well-connected to 'pull strings' also brought the problems created by martial denaturalisation to the personal attention

[63] The old system of naturalisation by individual Act of Parliament was still available in the United Kingdom and occasionally applied, but married women were not eligible to apply for naturalisation in their own right, even if this route had been considered applicable to their individual circumstances.

[64] In Argentina maritally denaturalised Argentinian women who resided in their country, were entitled to a passport, and to receive 'succour and aid from the Representatives of the Republic'; although the passport would record that they were not Argentine citizens. Chrystal Macmillan, 'Nationality of Married Women: Present Tendencies' (1925) *Journal of Comparative Legislation and International Law* 142, 152.

[65] As M. Page Baldwin has shown, in Britain at least, obstacles to amendment were more frequently asserted or erected by senior civil servants. Baldwin, 'Subject to Empire', 522.

of members of government. In 1932, Mary W E, from Ontario, wrote to the Canadian Prime Minister, Richard Bennett, reminding him that they had met in Paris several years earlier. Her grandfather and father, she recounted, had been active Conservatives in Canada; her father was friend of the legendary former Prime Minister, Sir John A McDonald (who had visited her family 'frequently'); her brother was the first Speaker in the Legislative Assembly of Saskatchewan and had held a seat in the Alberta Legislature. She had just learned, she wrote, that her marriage to an American many years earlier had led to her denaturalisation, a double denaturalisation, as it turned out (although, in this case, with a happy ending). Her husband had died, and 'I took my two daughters to Paris in 1912, and have lived there ever since'. She had done war work in Paris, had received the Mons Medal from the British government, and medals from France and from the Red Cross. 'During all these years I held an American pass port (sic). Last year when I asked for a renewal of it, in order to go to England... [i]t was refused by the American Consul in Paris. He said in order to keep it I should go to the United States every two years, and it was five years since I had been there'. She was advised that in order to get British nationality, she would need to spend six months in the United Kingdom or a colony, and to reacquire her Canadian nationality, she would need to reside in Canada for a minimum of five years. She did not want to leave Paris, where her daughters, now adults, lived.

Prime Minister Bennett replied personally, advising her that he was 'having enquiries made with regard to the situation'. Advice from the Under Secretary of State to Bennett pointed out that hers was 'a very simple case'. Mary E was a Canadian born women who had married an alien, and after the death of her husband had returned to Canada. The Canadian Naturalization Act of 1914 provided that a woman who was a British subject prior to her marriage to an alien and whose husband had died or whose marriage had been dissolved, could reacquire her nationality, without the usual residence requirements applying. A note of 16 December 1932, attached to her letter, recorded that a Certificate of Naturalization had been issued to her. Mary E was saved from statelessness by the law's amendment in 1914, recognising that the husband's death severed the bond of allegiance to his country, but her story remains one of vulnerability, an account of the vicissitudes in women's lives as wives (and mothers) that, while personal and affective, shaped their public, legal status.

In 1935, Dorothy W also wrote to Prime Minister Bennett, in an even more intimate tone:

> Are you in the mood to play knight-errant to a distressed lady? In other words, are you disposed to exercise your great power to get me out of an absurd position in regard to my nationality? You are the only man who can do it. I am, as you know, Canadian born (my father was the late Sir Edmund W) but by my first marriage I lost my nationality, and for some years had none at all.[66]

She set out her circumstances in an account that reads like a potted history of marital denaturalisation:

> In 1931 when I was in Canada I applied for re-nationalization (sic) and was given a certificate and a passport, but I was disgusted to see a note on the latter saying that I was only a naturalized British subject. (The French are kind enough, in such cases to use the words 'by re-integration'.) Being however in reality Canadian born it never occurred to me that I had to do anything to keep my nationality and no one warned me that I was in danger of losing it again. In November last I married again, an American, and as I want to go away for winter sports I went to the Legation yesterday to have my passport re-issued in my new name . . . They tell me that I have lost my citizenship again, that I should have returned to Canada each year or filled out some papers, and that they cannot issue a passport for me without special instructions from you. As I want to keep my Canadian citizenship and as I expect to remain in Europe, and as I am really Canadian born, I wonder if you could not give instructions to the Legation here to issue me a passport without the clause about naturalization. Could not you do it for me? I simply hate being treated like an alien and being told that I cannot enter my own country . . .

In New Zealand in 1934, Prime Minister, George Forbes, received a letter from the New Zealand High Commissioner in London, Sir James Parr, urging the government to proceed with a proposed amendment of the country's marital denaturalisation law,[67] and illustrating its urgency with the story of his daughter's predicament. The proposal, he wrote,

> should . . . be passed speedily, to remedy the anomalous and unfortunate position under which many New Zealanders labour . . . [A] New Zealand woman marrying an American loses her own nationality and, because of the American laws, does not gain any other nationality. With the result that she is entirely without any nationality status. My own daughter, Betty,

[66] Library and Archives of Canada. Letter, 6 February 1935. Microfilm: Reel M1110.

[67] The proposal was for amendment to permit maritally denaturalised New Zealand women, resident in New Zealand, to reacquire their political and other legal rights as if they were British subjects. It was not for their restoration of citizenship, although many people misunderstood it as the latter. As a resident of Australia, Betty S would not have benefited from the NZ law. (This law is discussed in Chapter 5.)

> recently married a citizen of the USA, and is therefore in this unfortunate position.[68]

Parr also wrote, in confidence, to Alexander Young, Minister of Internal Affairs, about the proposed amendment:

> I am personally very keenly interested. My daughter, Betty, a year ago married a very nice American man with a large business in Melbourne (where they at present live), and she is, of course, very upset over the fact that she now has no national status... [A]ll that I... ask [is] that you will, as an old friend and former colleague, see that your Bill goes through the upper House next sitting[69]

Betty S herself also wrote to the Private Secretary in the New Zealand Postmaster-General's Office, asking for a copy of the Bill and signing off poignantly: 'Hoping to hear something satisfactory from you. I should like a nationality'.[70]

Such attempts at string-pulling served the purpose of alerting governments to problems caused by marital denaturalisation, but whether public sympathy would have been attracted, had they become known, depended upon the relevant country's culture. As Bredbenner notes of the United States, newspapers paid attention to 'socially prominent' marital 'expatriates'. There were three prominent cases in California, for example, and 'Californians who read the society pages... may have sympathized with the baronesses and duchesses of American birth who lost their citizenship, but elsewhere such stories risked arousing contempt rather than pity'.[71]

Elsewhere, stories of innocent 'celebrities' made good copy. Under the revealing heading, 'That Nationality Again!', a news report told of 'Mrs Jascha Spivakovsky, an Adelaide girl, who met her famous [Russian-born] husband in Berlin in 1926'. Leonore Spivakovsky, the report went on,

68 Archives New Zealand, R19964 605, Ref no. IA1 2824, Record no 116/6. 22 November 1934.

69 Archives New Zealand, R19964 605, Ref no. IA1 2824, Record no 116/6. 27 November 1934.

70 Archives New Zealand, R19964 605, Ref no. IA1 2824, Record no 116/6. 19 November 1934. Betty S's statelessness arose from the combined effect of the New Zealand marital denaturalisation law (which mirrored the British Act) and the United States Cable Act of 1922 that, we have seen, ended marital naturalisation (and partially repealed marital denaturalisation) in that country. She had lost her New Zealand nationality, without gaining her husband's citizenship, but was not eligible to be naturalised in the United States, as she was not a resident.

71 Bredbenner, *A Nationality of Her Own*, 68–9.

> is delighted that work at the Melbourne University Conservatorium will keep him in Australia for the greater part of the year... [She] is waiting for the English law to let Englishwomen married to foreigners retain their own nationality, for, as the Russian law does not deprive a wife of her nationality, and under Australian law she assumes that of her husband, she says that at present she has lawfully no nationality at all.[72]

Stateless women, in such a position, would soon be rescued. In the 1930s, Australia and many other countries, adopted amendments to their laws to give effect to the principles of the 1930 Hague Convention on Nationality (discussed in Chapter 6), which confined denaturalisation to cases where the woman acquired her husband's citizenship. Spivakovsky's Australian citizenship would be restored under these principles, as the Soviet Union did not confer citizenship upon foreign wives. However, notwithstanding her understanding of the proposed 'English law', marital denaturalisation would continue to apply under Australian law in cases where a woman gained the foreign nationality of her husband.

As late as 1949 (when the relevant law had already been repealed in Britain and the Dominions), the effects were still being felt and personal pedigrees asserted. Mrs Hazel C M, from Oakville, Ontario, wrote to the Passport Division in the Canadian Department of External Affairs. She had married an American in 1918, and only now, wishing to travel and having applied for a passport, she had 'made some disturbing discoveries concerning my citizenship'.[73] When, believing herself to be an American citizen (by marital naturalisation) she applied for a US passport, she discovered that long-term residence outside the United States was a ground for loss of citizenship by naturalisation, and that her residence in Canada had meant that she was no longer an American citizen. The Canadian authorities then informed her that she was an alien under Canadian law and would have to apply for naturalisation. The process, she learned, would take one and a half years. Although the practical impact (it can be assumed) was primarily inconvenience, Hazel M expressed her grievance in terms of identity and belonging:

> This [conclusion] is difficult for me to believe as I am directly descended from two Loyalist families who settled in Upper Canada in 1791. My

[72] Archives New Zealand, R19964 605, Ref no. IA1 2824, Record no 116/6. Press clipping [July 1934].

[73] Library and Archives of Canada. File RG26-A-1-a, Volume 82 File Part 1, File no. 1–24–29. Department of Citizenship & Immigration. Deputy Minister's Office. 'Convention on Nationality of Married Persons'. 16 March 1949.

> great-grandfather, William C was founder of the town of Oakville in 1827 and Member of Parliament for many years. With one exception my immediate family and children are Canadian citizens . . . Therefore, I cannot believe that I must be treated in the same manner as foreigners entering Canada for the first time.

Such well-placed women may have been advantaged in their personal connections and confidence, but the position of poor women was not entirely overlooked. In Britain, as in other countries, social welfare benefits were an issue. The problem created by the exemption of aliens from the old age pension, for example, was recognised soon after the passage of the UK Pensions Act in 1908. The Act was amended in 1911 to extend the pension to denaturalised widows and divorcees of foreign men who, as aliens, were previously ineligible (in common with persons in receipt of poor relief, or those who were work-shy, or who had been convicted of drunkenness or imprisoned within the previous ten years for a serious crime). In 1913, the National Insurance Act of 1911 was similarly amended. Under the BNSA Act of 1914, widows and divorcees of foreign men became eligible to apply for the resumption of their British nationality, but denaturalised wives whose foreign husbands were alive remained ineligible for social benefits, and other benefits were insecure.

In debate on the 1914 BNSA Bill in the House of Commons, representatives of poor constituencies drew attention to these effects. Willoughby Dickinson, Liberal Member for St Pancras North, pointed out the 'serious matters' that had arisen before the Pensions Act was amended, and forecast further 'disastrous' effects of maintaining the policy of marital denaturalisation.[74] William Glyn-Jones, Liberal Member for Stepney, commented that problems arising from the policy were often associated with the holding of property abroad, but, he said, 'my concern is for the very many poor women in Stepney who are not affected by property abroad, but are much more affected by the [National] Insurance act'.[75] He was joined by Thomas Harvey, Liberal Member of Leeds West: 'I think those who know the conditions of East London – and I think the same applies to some extent in seaport towns – know that women often marry aliens without being aware that they are aliens at all'. Women should be permitted to exercise 'some option' on marrying, he said, 'so that they shall not be treated as though they were semi-servile beings passing into

[74] United Kingdom, House of Commons, *Debates*, 13 May 1914, 1208.
[75] United Kingdom, House of Commons, *Debates*, 13 May 1914, 1206.

the power of their husbands'.[76] Frederick Booth, Member for Pontefract, added:

> [A] British woman who marries an alien . . . is treated as of no account whatever, and immediately she becomes an alien . . . Those who can conceive and defend an idea of that kind are hopelessly behind the times, and they are voicing the conditions of an Eastern harem. I am amazed that anyone should have the cool audacity to put such Clauses in the Bill. It is perpetuating the idea that woman is the slave and the chattel of a man as soon as she is married to him.[77]

Reassurances were received from Lewis Harcourt, Secretary of State for the Colonies, that the issues raised would be considered during the Committee stage, 'with a view, if possible, of meeting the objections'. However, his cautionary additional note that '[w]e must not interfere with the existing legislation of the Dominions' was revealing. The commitment to a 'common code' of British nationality law across the Empire (as we see in Chapter 5) was to make the amendment of marital denaturalisation laws especially difficult in its member countries. Britain and the Dominions, despite the outrage of representatives like Booth, would cling to marital denaturalisation until after the Second World War.

This particular British difficulty was, however, indicative of the general status of married women's nationality. As we have seen, citizenship laws were shaped by considerations of international relations. Any change in the laws of one country would unsettle the associated laws of other countries. At a minimum, the repeal of one country's marital denaturalisation law would allow that country's women to retain their citizenship regardless of foreign marriage, while at the same time, in many cases, acquiring the citizenship of the husband under the laws of his country. In such a case, a woman would have dual nationality, something that was regarded as intolerable. Alternatively, in the event that her husband's country did not naturalise foreign women who married its citizens, the couple would hold different nationalities, something that was also regarded as unacceptable. In cases where a country repealed its marital naturalisation law, women who married a citizen of that country but whose own country still practised marital denaturalisation would find themselves stateless.

In the British Empire, additionally, the proposition that the status and therefore the rights of British subjects would vary from country to country was considered offensive to the idea of common membership

[76] United Kingdom, House of Commons, *Debates*, 13 May 1914, 1209–10.

[77] United Kingdom, House of Commons, *Debates*, 13 May 1914, 1211.

and imperial 'family' unity. Despite Mr Harcourt's undertaking and Mr Booth's subsequent complaint that there had been no proper consideration in Committee, the unamended Bill became the Act (the 1914 BNSA Act) that maintained the marital denaturalisation policy that was first set down in 1870.

Remedial measures

Alien status is, of course, relative to the jurisdiction in which a person finds him or herself. All persons become aliens as soon as they move outside the country in which they are citizens. Had women who lived in their foreign husbands' country retained their native citizenship, assuming that that country (in common with most of the world) did not permit dual nationality, such women would have been aliens in their new home. Similar hardships to those of the maritally denaturalised woman who lived in her own native country would have followed.

This fact was stressed by those who defended the policy of conditional marital nationality. Their response to opponents was to point out, among other things, that repeal would result in the alien status of countless women who lived in their husband's country. In turn, this problem was not overlooked by opponents. Among the many alternatives proposed was to allow the wife to retain her native citizenship, while allowing her to apply, if she chose, to be naturalised in her country of residence, including on facilitated or expedited terms (this was the model adopted in the United States after 1922 and eventually in other parts of the world, and anticipated in the 1957 Convention on the Nationality of Married Women). The law might also be reformed, it was suggested, so that dual nationality was tolerated, allowing a woman who was automatically naturalised in her husband's citizenship to retain her pre-marital nationality, or, alternatively, allowing a woman the choice of nationality upon foreign marriage (presumably to be based on to the country of conjugal domicile). Another alternative – that adopted by the League of Nations in the Hague Convention of 1930 – was for married women to lose their pre-marital citizenship only in cases where they simultaneously acquired the citizenship of their husband's country.

For many citizenship equality campaigners, however, alternatives that did not offer women full independence to retain their own citizenship were unacceptable, standing as remnants of the former merging of a wife's whole legal identity with that of her husband. For such campaigners, the principle that there should be 'no distinction based on sex in law and practice relating to nationality' (expressed in the Montevideo Convention of 1933 and in the 1935 Irish Citizenship Act, which, as we see in Chapter 5, allowed the husband and wife, in certain circumstances to choose a common citizenship on equal terms) was non-negotiable. Some, however, were concerned that even this principle would not adequately protect women: that 'it would give rise to laws that required either the husband or wife to change their nationality; [and that] tradition . . . would dictate that the woman would lose her nationality'.[78]

The division between those who accepted pragmatic, incremental reforms and those who were intransigent with regard to principle unsettled the unity in the citizenship equality campaign. But the alternatives further illustrated the complexity of the policy's impact, and divisions over their desirability did not destroy the essential focus of the campaign. Common to all alternatives was the conviction that non-consensual loss of citizenship was an injury in itself, even where adjustments could be made to avoid practical hardship. As the 1930s progressed, the impact of martial denaturalisation became increasingly severe. As international conflicts of law multiplied, the campaign became more urgent. (We consider this period further in Chapter 5.)

Governments remained convinced that citizenship equality between married couples would lead to diplomatic conflict, deadlocks of interest, and the erosion of family unity, and maintained that, unless all the countries of the world simultaneously adopted identical laws governing the citizenship of married women, intractable conflicts of law would arise. However, under the impact of the equality campaign and a growing awareness of problems created by conditional marital nationality, some governments adopted remedial measures. The remedies varied, and their variety revealed both the extent of the problems and official intransigence on the policy itself. The most extreme problem, as noted, was statelessness resulting from cases where the wife was denaturalised under her country's law, but not naturalised under her husband's.

By the time of the 1930 Hague Convention's commitment to the reduction of maritally induced statelessness, a handful of countries had already amended their laws to pre-empt marital statelessness for their own citizens. The first to legislate for conditional marital nationality, France was one of the first countries to mitigate this effect. Article 19 of the Civil Code of 1889 provided that a French woman did not lose her citizenship through marriage unless she automatically gained that of her husband.

[78] Miller, 'Geneva – the Key to Equality', 229.

The Japanese Law of 1899 offered similar protection, inverting the relationship between loss and gain: 'A Japanese who, on becoming the wife of an alien, has acquired her husband's nationality, loses Japanese nationality'. By 1924, comparable provisions precluding statelessness could be found in the laws of Belgium, China, Italy, Netherlands, Norway, Persia, Portugal, Russia, Salvador, Siam and Venezuela (Guatemala and Honduras denaturalised women who married foreign men only if they became domiciled abroad).[79]

In some cases, limited administrative remedies applied. Passports could be issued, in certain circumstances, to allow non-citizens or stateless persons to travel, without attribution of the nationality of the issuing country. 'Deeming' instructions could be issued, for example, regarding changes in nationality laws by the Soviet Union that led to concerns about the status of British-born wives. The case of Mrs Jessie S, and another (unnamed) woman, was brought to the attention of the British Home Office and led to the decision that

> for administrative purposes . . . British-born wives of former Russian subjects who were married after the 7th November 1917 shall be deemed prima facie not to have ceased to be British subjects in virtue of [the BNSA Act] . . . Similarly, a British woman whose husband became naturalised in the Soviet Republic at any time after the 7th November 1917 should be regarded as having retained British nationality.[80]

The BNSA Act of 1914, as we have seen, had reaffirmed the conditional marital nationality policy of the earlier British Acts, but allowed a British woman the choice to take or decline her husband's (new) nationality in the event that he was naturalised in a foreign country; this new provision stated that the woman remained British unless she made a 'declaration of alienage'[81] or unless the Secretary of State 'directed otherwise'. It did not provide fully for her choice of nationality, leaving open the exercise of executive discretion to 'alienate' her. The 1914 Act also allowed for maritally denaturalised British-born women whose marriage had been terminated by death or divorce to apply to be 're-naturalised' (the 1870

79 Richard W. Flournoy, 'The New Married Women's Citizenship Law' (1924) 33 *Yale Law Journal* 159, 164.

80 UK National Archives, File FO 612/238. 'Women of British Nationality married to aliens who have not acquired husband's nationality'. Foreign Office, to Godfrey Haggard, HM Consulate General, Paris (no date).

81 The provision was amended in the UK Nationality Act in 1933, requiring the declaration of alienage to be made within twelve months of her husband's foreign naturalisation.

Naturalization Act had already allowed denaturalised widows to obtain a certificate of 're-admission to British nationality'), without having to fulfil the normal residency requirements for naturalisation, albeit at the discretion of the Secretary of State.

In 1918, four years later, the Act was amended, giving further recognition to the problems produced by martial denaturalisation: it now permitted British-born women, married to foreign men who were 'the subject of a state at war with His Majesty' (that is, men whose nationality classified them, during wartime, as 'enemy aliens') to apply to the Secretary of State for the resumption of their British nationality through the grant of a certificate of naturalisation. (We consider the operation of this provision in Chapter 4). The assumption in such cases, and in the event of divorce or widowhood, provided for in the 1914 Act, was that the woman in question no longer embraced her husband's allegiance, that she was, as in her pre-marital state, free again from the pull or taint of foreign allegiance. Re-naturalisation was not, however, automatic, and nor did it occur simply at the request – or declaration of 'desire' – of the woman concerned. Eligibility criteria for naturalisation applied. 'Undesirable' former British women were not eligible to return to the community of British subjects. However, the strategy of sifting out undeserving women, by applying criteria of suitability for membership as if they had never been members, was incomplete with respect to the foreign-born woman who had been naturalised by marriage to a British national. Such a woman, who found herself divorced or widowed, the Act stated, 'shall not by reason only of the death of her husband, or the dissolution of her marriage, cease to be a British subject'. She retained her British nationality, in other words, on the assumption that her post-marital allegiance endured. Even 'undesirable' foreign women were protected from loss of citizenship acquired by marriage, following its termination.

Assumptions about allegiance must explain this paradox; the policy of conditional marital nationality, we have emphasised, assumed an automatic transfer of allegiance from the woman to her husband, and thus to his country, in the case of a (genuine) marriage. 'In-marrying' women were assumed to retain that allegiance even after the marriage had terminated, as were those who had married 'out'; for the latter, this assumption was rebuttable, subject to the tests of allegiance that applied in ordinary naturalisation.

The United States Expatriation Act of 1907 included a similar provision, but its test for the restoration of citizenship after the termination of a marriage was simpler. The 'sifting' between desirable and undesirable women occurred more evidently at the point of acquisition of American citizenship by foreign wives who, unlike in Britain, were always subject to racial and character disqualifications. To the statement in section 3 of the 1907 Act – 'That any American woman who marries a foreigner shall take the nationality of her husband' – was added:

> At the termination of the marital relation she may assume her American citizenship, if abroad, by registering as an American citizen within one year with a consul of the United States, or by returning to reside in the United States, or, if residing in the United States at the termination of the marital relation, by continuing to reside therein.[82]

Similar provisions could be found in, among others, the laws of Japan, France (subject to residence) and Switzerland (subject to Federal Council approval); in Canada; in Italy (following widowhood); and in Hungary (following divorce).[83] But, in none of these countries did women who were deserted by their foreign husband qualify for restoration of their citizenship and thus relief from the deprivations that were, in many cases, multiplied by the loss of their husbands' support. The insistence that conditional marital nationality applied to any marriage that was 'subsisting in law' was revealing of how rigidly the attribution of allegiance underpinned the policy. Women, regardless of their degree of real attachment to their husband, were assumed, by the simple fact of marriage, to 'belong' to his country. Women who had been ill-treated or deserted by their husband but had no way of regaining their former citizenship were a frequent object of equality campaigners' concerns.

Chrystal Macmillan related the story of Mrs B who in 1917 had married an American who had subsequently deserted her. In 1928, Mrs B applied to the Home Office to restore her British nationality, but was told that she could not do so until she had divorced, which she was unable to do in either the United States or England. It was hard to be regarded as an alien, Mrs B wrote to Macmillan, being British-born, as both her parents were, and holding British property: 'I have given up all hope of being anything but an "alien" and a "woman living apart from her husband"'.[84]

[82] The Act, however, allowed women who had been naturalised as American citizens by marriage to retain their citizenship after the termination of the marriage if they continued to live in the United States or, if they lived abroad, by registering before a Consul within one year of the termination of the marriage. Such women also had the option of making a formal renunciation of their American citizenship.

[83] Phillimore, 'Nationality of Married Women', 165.

[84] UK National Archive. File HO 45/15147: 'Nationality of Married Women'. 'Deputation from the Women's Organisations received by Secretary of State on 29 January 1932'. Macmillan, 'The Nationality of Married Women', January 1931.

In a proposal to amend the Australian Nationality Act of 1920, which (following the BNSA Act of 1914) denied naturalisation to persons 'under disability', the Australian government pointed out in a submission to an Imperial Conference, that the provision had 'resulted in the infliction of considerable hardship upon certain women of British birth who have married aliens and have been deserted by them, but who are nevertheless not eligible to reacquire their former British nationality'. The submission offered, as an illustration, the case of an English-born woman who had emigrated to South Australia where, in 1885, she had married a German national. In 1912 her husband had deserted her and returned to Germany:

> Since his departure he has not written to her, [nor] sent her money, and she has had to earn a living as best she could. She was the mother of ten children. The eldest son served in the Light Horse in the late war and returned to Australia a cripple. In 1920 the woman had a paralytic stroke and was ill for a considerable time, and partially lost her memory. Fourteen of her male relations, including sons, grandsons, and nephews, served in the late war, and three of them were killed, yet this woman is not entitled to the privileges of a British subject.[85]

Women who deserted their husbands suffered further disadvantages, compounded by the general rule against naturalisation of 'immoral' women. In an example also related by Macmillan, we find multiple dimensions in the experience of marital denaturalisation and the assumption that a marriage, short of divorce or the death of a spouse, was 'subsisting under law'. The story reads like a piece of bad fiction, peppered with theatrical stereotypes. It is all the more revealing, as Macmillan intended, as an account of a real human experience:

> Mrs C. a young and very pretty woman, was seduced in her teens by an elderly Spaniard, a paying guest in her father's house. Her parents insisted on marriage and, after the birth of the child, the man returned to Spain, taking his wife with him. She there discovered that her husband was concerned in very questionable traffic and was determined to add to his income the immoral earnings of his pretty wife. Though penniless and ignorant of the language, she saved herself by flight, and, aided by a British official, reached the French coast. Had she not lost her British nationality she would have had no difficulty in crossing the Channel, but her husband having, in revenge, falsely declared that she had left him in order to lead

[85] Irish National Archives, Roinn An Úachtaráin [Dept of the President] File no. s 3439. 'Imperial and Imperial Economic Conferences 1923'. Cabinet File. Appendices to the Summary of Proceedings', Imperial Conference 1923. Appendix VI, 'Papers regarding Nationality Question', Memorandum from the Australian Government.

> an immoral life, she was for a long period regarded as an undesirable alien and not allowed to return to her parents' home in England. Finally, after much wire pulling, she was allowed to land, but she cannot regain her nationality and owing to her husband's false representations, is liable at any moment to deportation as 'undesirable'.[86]

The 1923 British Imperial Conference recommended that there should be a power 'to readmit a woman to British nationality in cases where the marriage state, though subsisting in law, has for all practical purposes come to an end'. Despite the moving messages conveyed in these stories, the recommendation was never adopted by any of the Commonwealth countries represented.

Less dramatic, but similarly hortatory anecdotes were frequently recounted, including by elected representatives who supported the repeal of marital denaturalisation laws. British Member of the House of Commons, Dr Ethel Bentham, illustrated the importance of the private member's Nationality of Women Bill (submitted to the House of Commons seven times in the interwar years: discussed in Chapter 5), with several examples of hardship, including that of a woman who was

> so determined to retain the protection of her country's laws and her own nationality that she and the man she was proposing to marry deliberately determined to live together without marriage in order that she might retain her nationality. A woman should not have to choose between her nationality and the legitimacy of her children.[87]

In contrast, the United States campaign succeeded relatively quickly. America, as we have seen, repealed its policy of conditional marital nationality in 1922. This would set off a cascade of further difficulties in other countries, generating the need for further amendments. By the 1930s, the original purpose for which marital denaturalisation was designed – to facilitate the classification of individuals as members of one particular state as against others according to attribution of single allegiance, and with this to smooth the wheels of international relations – was no longer being served. Macmillan wrote in 1925 that '[t]en years ago the most common objection to change was that it would upset the legal symmetry which by that time had been almost universally established in Europe'; but since the United States and the USSR and, 'to a limited extent, Belgium,

[86] Macmillan, 'The Nationality of Married Women' (pamphlet) January 1931.

[87] United Kingdom, House of Commons, *Debates*, 28 November 1930.

Norway, Denmark and Sweden' had given married women an independent nationality, '[t]his objection is of less force today'.[88]

An already complicated landscape of conflicting laws and ad hoc responses would become even more complicated. The experience of one war, and the approach of another, would offer particularly dramatic examples of these effects. We consider conditional marital nationality and war in the following chapter.

[88] Macmillan, 'The Nationality of Married Women', 145.

4

Marital citizenship and war

War and citizenship are historical companions. The idea of citizenship – what it is to be a citizen, and the duties that attach – has been profoundly shaped by the contemplation of war. The privileging of military duty as an attribute of ancient citizenship (exemplified in the Greek conferral of citizenship on men who had completed military training) has been well documented.[1] The association between citizenship and military service was not exclusive in the classical model, but it was embedded in the ideal of the citizen (as an attribute of men of suitable age and physical capacity). An evolving conceptualisation of citizenship as a relationship of political allegiance between the individual and the state animated the modern constitutional order, but, over the course of history, despite the fundamental differences between classical and modern citizenship, the association between allegiance and military defence endured. The term 'citizen' was employed to designate members of a republic; although, in monarchies, the term was 'subject', the logic in this respect was similar and the difference irrelevant. Subjecthood and citizenship alike were associated with service and duty to defend the sovereign.

Laws governing modern citizenship emerged from a context in which war, or the threat of war, was a key background factor. War captured the clash of sovereigns and heightened the battles over whom, among the population, the sovereign was entitled to claim, to press into service, to hold as prisoners of war, or to punish for insubordination or desertion. Citizenship law provided a modern framework for settling these claims. The international consensus against dual nationality captured, among other things, a recoil against the prospect of treason being committed by

[1] See Rubio Marin, 'The Achievement of Female Suffrage in Europe', 4. For a counter-perspective on the citizenship roles played by women, see Cynthia Patterson, 'Citizenship and Gender in the Ancient World: The Experience of Athens and Rome' in Seyla Benhabib and Judith Resnik (eds) *Migrations and Mobilities: Citizenship, Borders, and Gender* (New York University Press, 2009).

a national of one country against another country of which that person was also a national. Among the many objections to the idea of married women's independent nationality was that '[w]here a wife retains her . . . nationality but also acquires that of her husband, she might find it impossible to avoid in time of war committing high treason against one or other of her two allegiances'.[2] The Napoleonic Code, the first legal instrument in which the principle of conditional marital citizenship and the practice of marital denaturalisation were expressed, was adopted by France during the ratification of peace treaties with England and European powers.[3] Among its grounds for loss of French citizenship, in addition to a woman's foreign marriage, was engagement in military service with a foreign power or enrolment in any foreign military association. In this same era, as noted in Chapter 2, England's refusal to acknowledge the foreign naturalisation of British subjects (and its consequential attempts to impress naturalised American sailors into the British navy), stands as one of the uncontested explanations for the 1812 war between Britain and America.[4] Such events demonstrated the high stakes attached to competing sovereign claims over persons, and the imperative of regularising the system of citizenship 'triage', so that duties could be claimed by a state against particular citizens without the risk of (legitimate) counter-claims by other states. They illustrate, graphically, that the citizenship status of individuals can be a flashpoint, leading to conflict in international relations, and that the regularisation of the recognition of citizenship claims, as between states, was an important element in forestalling conflict.

With the adoption and formalisation of naturalisation laws in the nineteenth century, came the composition of modern oaths of allegiance. The connection between citizenship and defence of the sovereign was captured in such oaths. Among the common grounds for loss of native and naturalised citizenship alike was taking an oath of allegiance to a foreign country and service in the armed forces of a foreign power; and

[2] UK National Archives. File HO 45/15147 Title: 'Nationality of Married Women', 'Report of conclusions of Inter-Departmental Meeting of D.O., F.O. and H.O. on the question of nationality of married women'. February 1932. Memorandum, Foreign Office, 29 January 1932.

[3] Weil, *How to Be French*.

[4] Warren H. Goodman, 'The Origins of the War of 1812: A Survey of Changing Interpretations' (1941) 28 *The Mississippi Valley Historical Record* 171. The British were unequivocal about this as a cause of the War, as the Lord Chancellor described it during the second reading speech on the UK Naturalization Bill in 1870. United Kingdom, House of Lords, *Debates*, 25 February 1870, 1123. See Chapter 2, n 28.

among the common assumptions governing naturalisation was that the new citizen would be released from duties of military service in his former country. With this, came the correlate that naturalisation could not serve as an excuse for evading military service in a man's former country.[5] Again, citizenship laws and naturalisation treaties between states were intended to pre-empt conflicts that would otherwise arise.

Reciprocal recognition of citizenship was, indeed, seen by some as offering the basis for a type of peace treaty or treaty of friendship. Writing in 1897, the leading English jurist, A. V. Dicey, proposed a common citizenship between England and the United States. Among his identification of points of commonality favouring the scheme, he observed that both England and the United States 'stand apart from that admiration for military power which prevails throughout Continental Europe'.[6] Neither country, he noted, imposed conscription and, although there was 'something fine, and even noble, in the idea that every man should, for a portion of his life, take a personal share in the defence of the State', the absence of conscription 'removes the sources of disagreement which always abound whenever the citizens of the one country flee from it to another in order that they may escape the burden of military service'.[7]

Dicey's account of the pacific concept of citizenship in both countries still measured citizenship in military terms, depicting shared citizenship as an alternative to conflict. It would soon be overtaken by events. Military associations with citizenship, never far from the surface, were strengthening at that time. In the United States, under the law of 1796, the naturalising citizen had been required to swear that 'he will support the Constitution of the United States, and that he absolutely and entirely renounces and abjures all allegiance and fidelity to every foreign prince, potentate, state, or sovereignty'. In 1906, following a report on citizenship and naturalisation commissioned by the House of Representatives Committee on Foreign Affairs[8] (which led to the adoption of the 1907 Expatriation Act) the US oath became strikingly more defensive, requiring an additional promise to 'support and defend the Constitution and laws of the United States of America against all enemies, foreign and domestic';

[5] For example, *The Bancroft Naturalization Treaties with the German States; The United States Constitution and the Rights and Privileges of Citizens of Foreign Birth* (Wurzburg 1868) 39.

[6] A. V. Dicey, 'A Common Citizenship for the English Race' (1897) 71 *Contemporary Review* 457, 468.

[7] Dicey, ibid, 469.

[8] Report on the Subject of Citizenship, Expatriation, and Protection Abroad, to House Committee on Foreign Affairs, 1906.

during the war, it became routine to ask applicants, specifically, if they were willing to 'take up arms' in defence of the United States.[9]

The oath became indirectly, albeit tellingly, relevant to the repeal of America's conditional marital nationality policy in 1922. American-born women, previously denaturalised by foreign marriage, were now entitled to apply for the resumption of American citizenship. Their application, however, was subject to the eligibility criteria (except the general residency requirements) in the Naturalization Act, and included an assessment of their suitability to take the oath of allegiance. On the naturalisation application form at that time, applicants were asked whether they were willing 'to take up arms in defence of this country'. What, specifically did this mean for women? As Bredbenner points out, the question was not routinely asked of female applicants by naturalisation judges,[10] but it could be. When it was, the fact that women were not admitted into the armed forces of the United States (as in other countries) made the commitment a curious one, requiring, one might have thought, particular attention to the alternative ways in which 'defence' might have been demonstrated.

In 1929, the United States Supreme Court touched upon the issue in a case concerning the naturalisation application of an (unmarried) Hungarian woman, Rosika Schwimmer.[11] Schwimmer, a pacifist who believed in 'the human family' (as opposed to the 'national family'), stated her preparedness to take the oath, since she considered herself duty-bound to defend America, not militarily, but against ideological or philosophical attacks on its democratic values and governance. The Court rejected her claim for pacific defence, and insisted that the oath required both specific nationalistic allegiance, and a willingness to fight in a military sense: 'the duty of citizens by force of arms to defend our government against all enemies whenever necessity arises is a fundamental principle of the Constitution'.[12] On women's disqualification from military

[9] In *Girouard* v. *United States* 328 U.S. 61 (1946), the United States Supreme Court held that '[t]he oath required of aliens does not in terms require that they promise to bear arms'. It added: 'The bearing of arms, important as it is, is not the only way in which our institutions may be supported and defended, even in times of great peril'. The Court concluded that *Schwimmer* and similar others, had been wrongly decided. Under the Naturalization Act of 1952, conscientious and religious pacifists were exempted from pledging to bear arms.

[10] Bredbenner, *A Nationality of Her Own*, 184.

[11] *United States* v. *Schwimmer* 279 U.S. 644 (1929).

[12] *United States* v. *Schwimmer* 279 U.S. 650 (1929).

service, it observed that persons who were 'by reason of sex, age or other cause . . . unfit to serve' were nevertheless capable of influencing others against the use of military force, and that Schwimmer's objection to military service 'rest[ed] on reasons other than mere inability because of her sex and age personally to bear arms'. In a dissenting opinion, Justice Oliver Wendell Holmes made the obvious point that, as 'a woman over fifty years of age . . . [she] would not be allowed to bear arms if she wanted to',[13] but the issue was not pursued.

It became more directly relevant to the circumstances of a maritally denaturalised woman, only two years later. Rebecca Shelley, an American-born religious pacifist had married a German national in 1922, just one month before the passage of the Cable Act. Her application for re-naturalisation was, like Schwimmer's, rejected. As Bredbenner points out, the naturalisation judge initially 'concluded that since women were not required to serve in the military, he could administer the oath of allegiance to a female pacifist without violating her principles or the government's requirements for naturalisation'.[14] His subsequent change of mind and denial of naturalisation set in train a process of appeals that would last for more than a decade. Shelley, whose principal argument rested on her claim that American-born women were now full citizens (following the ratification of the Nineteenth Amendment and the passage of the Cable Act) and thus protected from denaturalisation, did not press the point about women's exclusion from taking up arms or the associated inconsistency in the requirement to promise that they would. The Federal Court decided her case perfunctorily as a matter of statutory interpretation: the Act, unambiguously, required the taking of the oath, and this meant that a person unwilling or unable to take it could not be naturalised.[15]

The issue found no resolution: citizenship was based on a test of allegiance (or a presumption of allegiance) imbued with duties that women citizens could not perform. The fact made no difference to birthright citizenship, but the precariousness of the latter for women and its conditioning on their marriage highlighted the masculine character of allegiance, along with the embedded assumption that women's citizenship

[13] *United States* v. *Schwimmer* 279 U.S. 653 (1929).

[14] Bredbenner, *A Nationality of Her Own*, 185.

[15] *Shelley* v. *United States* 120 F. 2d 734 (1941). The United States Supreme Court denied her application for further appeal. Shelley was ultimately permitted to take the naturalisation oath in 1944.

was not true citizenship. It was an assumption that transferred readily into the idea that women with foreign husbands, whether they knew or consented, had shifted their allegiance, derivatively (albeit with no public duties attached) and therefore belonged to a different sovereign.

While the British naturalisation oath was relatively simple and open-ended as to the content of allegiance (focusing on defence of the Queen),[16] in 1908, Britain's distinguished legal historian, F. W. Maitland, would explain British nationality thus:

> The Englishman, the Scot, the Irishman, the Canadian, the Australian – all of these have a nationality in common; if there be war between the United Kingdom and a foreign power, say France, all of them are enemies of the French, any of them who side with the French are traitors.[17]

It was not far from the 'admiration of military power' as a defining character of citizenship that Dicey had attributed to other countries.

To 'serve one's country' remains universal shorthand for military service, regarded as the exemplary token of citizenship. Paradoxically, however, military duty has not been exclusive to legal citizens (resident aliens have frequently been entitled and, at relevant times, obliged to join the armed forces of their country of residence). Nor has it been the sole measure of normative citizenship. But the association is powerful, and attached to it is the idea of recognition and 'reward' from the sovereign. In many countries, a record of military service has expedited or facilitated naturalisation, and in most, it has brought special post-service entitlements or benefits. If benefits were offered to aliens and citizens alike for military service, what, then, was the reward specifically for the citizen's allegiance? What did the citizen get in return?

Protection is the reciprocal face of allegiance, and protection has a particular meaning in this context. The benefits offered in return for an alien's military service were limited; they did not extend to the sovereign's protection against expulsion from or denial of entry into the territory of the state. As long as a person remained a non-citizen, there was no

[16] The naturalising subject swore: 'I do sincerely promise and swear that I will be faithful and bear true Allegiance to Her Majesty Queen Victoria, and will defend Her to the utmost of my Power against all Conspiracies and Attempts whatsoever, which may be made against Her Person, Crown, or Dignity . . . ' The oath was simplified in 1868, requiring the person to swear to 'be faithful and bear true Allegiance to Her Majesty Queen Victoria, Her Heirs and Successors according to Law . . . '

[17] F. W. Maitland, *The Constitutional History of England* [1908] (Cambridge University Press, 1963) 341.

guarantee of remaining in, or returning to, any country other than that of his or her own citizenship. Without citizenship, there could be no certainty of reception or harbour, even in the country in which a person otherwise lawfully resided. Nor was there certainty of protection in a third country. Lawful residence counted for something (consular assistance could, and can, extend to the permanent residents of the relevant country) but it guaranteed nothing.

This was the essential loss that followed from marital denaturalisation. The transformation of citizen women into aliens as a consequence of their foreign marriage did not, in most cases, immediately limit their residency rights or make them liable to deportation from their pre-marital home. Many continued to live, as aliens, in 'their own' country. If the husband was deported, or if he belonged to a class of person liable to exclusion or expulsion (for racial or political reasons, for example), maritally denaturalised wives also became liable. Otherwise, in an era when the right of residence for non-citizens was, in most countries, more generous and less restricted than now, their domicile was reasonably secure. But vulnerability still attached to alienage.

The withdrawal of the former sovereign's protection, even without threats to residency rights, manifested itself concretely in multiple other ways. As we have seen, it lay in restrictions applying generally to aliens regarding employment, eligibility for public office and social benefits and, in some countries, extending to limitations or prohibitions on property ownership, among other legal disabilities. But, at its core, it manifested itself existentially in the vulnerability to expulsion (whether or not this occurred), and the sense of defencelessness or exposure that attaches to alien status. Citizenship equality campaigners stressed this experience. They described marital alienage as akin to infantalisation, as a loss of personhood, a unique form of vulnerability. Married women were legally 'under disability', and that disability had a peculiar, existential character when alienage came with it.

Ideals of citizenship associated with military service routinely disregarded the fact that women were historically excluded from such service (note Dicey's statement about the nature of conduct that was 'fine' and 'even noble'). This association became heightened as the nineteenth century turned into the twentieth and the international strains leading to world war began to be felt. The shaping of modern citizenship that began with the formalisation of naturalisation law in the later years of the eighteenth century and first half of the nineteenth century reached its peak in the lead-up to the First World War (as we have seen, Britain's first nationality legislation was adopted in 1914, displacing the common law that had hitherto generally governed British subjects). Marital denaturalisation laws also reached their peak at that time.

The association of citizenship with military service played a part in the idea that an individual's allegiance must be exclusive (albeit, from the mid-nineteenth century onward, alienable, at least in peacetime).[18] Exclusivity of allegiance, however, applied differently to men and women. Married women were not stripped of citizenship because they had failed to perform military service (after all, single women who did not perform military service held and retained citizenship, as did women married to fellow citizens). Loss of citizenship was gendered, not merely in the sense that marital denaturalisation applied only to women. Service to a foreign country was the primary, common ground of denaturalisation specifically for men; marriage was the primary ground of denaturalisation specifically for women. Foreign marriage was treated, effectively, as an act of disloyalty, as representing the withdrawal of the woman's allegiance to her country, akin to service to a foreign sovereign.

These were, of course, not the only grounds for loss of citizenship. Indeed, an individual's naturalisation in a foreign country almost always resulted in loss of the individual's native citizenship. This ground was general and superficially gender-neutral (at least in the abstract, since in many countries married women could not be naturalised on their own account). However, as we have noted, at least until the 1930s (when many countries amended their relevant laws) women who married foreign men suffered denaturalisation even in cases where they did not acquire their husbands' citizenship. The naturalisation analogy was false or, at the least, weak. Acquisition of citizenship by regular naturalisation was, for adults, a choice, a voluntary transfer of allegiance with the certainty of having a legal citizenship status at the completion of the process. In contrast, although foreign marriage was often spoken of as the equivalent of foreign naturalisation, it was critically different in effect. Married women had no choice. They were 'deemed' or assumed to acquire their

[18] Declarations of alienage – renouncing one's citizenship – had become available in many countries from the mid-nineteenth century. However, at least under British law, during wartime, 'the power to make a declaration of alienage could not be exercised by a person who possesses an enemy nationality in addition to his British nationality, upon the ground that to do so would in effect be an act of treason'. UK National Archives, File HO 45/11902 Title: 'Nationality of Married Women': Nationality and Naturalization: Special Conference. Memorandum prepared in the Home Office on the subject of Dual Nationality for consideration by members of the Conference. October 1918.

husbands' nationality, whether they did or not. Foreign marriage was not the equivalent of foreign naturalisation.

Loss of citizenship for reasons other than marriage was a punishment for disallegiance. Years after the repeal of most marital denaturalisation laws, in a case concerning the stripping of citizenship from a man who had left America to avoid military service, Justice Brennan of the United States Supreme Court described citizenship deprivation as a 'drastic, ... truly terrifying remedy'.[19] In this case, as in others, it went unnoticed that the numbers of individuals denaturalised on grounds such as avoidance of military service was infinitely smaller than the numbers denaturalised as a consequence of marriage. It was assumed both that maritally denaturalised women had simultaneously gained another citizenship (and that the substitution of a foreign for a native citizenship entailed no loss) and also that citizenship was, in essence, a masculine status. It was assumed that women's marital denaturalisation was not 'truly terrifying'.

Nevertheless, the recognition of the severity of the loss was an important step for a retrospective understanding of what was existentially at stake for married women. Citizenship equality campaigners had stressed this severity for decades. At no time was this more powerfully illustrated than during war.

Citizenship, loyalty and war

The injury of losing citizenship was compounded by the conditions of war. Individuals holding citizenship of a country at war with the country in which they found themselves were classified as enemy aliens. In addition to the conditions applying generally to aliens, additional, specific restrictions applied to enemy aliens, typically, with respect to their occupation, residence, travel, and right to hold or access property. During the World Wars, enemy aliens were interned in many countries. They were physically separated from the general population, regardless of how long they had previously lived in the relevant country and, in some cases at least, regardless of how well integrated they were. Internment also extended, in some countries, to persons of enemy nationality origin, notwithstanding their citizenship of the interning country. Australia, for example (with a population of less than five million in 1915) interned close to 7,000 people during the First World War, extending internment to residents who were British subjects of German ancestry, as well as aliens of enemy

[19] *Kennedy* v. *Mendoza-Martinez* 372 U.S. 144 (1963) 187.

nationality. Nationality or ancestry were regarded as inherently dangerous, as potential reasons for, or sources of, treason.[20]

As we have seen, a woman was assumed to acquire her husband's citizenship, regardless of her country of origin. In their own (now-former) country, the wives of enemy aliens, who, by marriage, were already 'statutory' aliens, were transformed further into enemy aliens. On the assumption that women's allegiance was subjective and derivative, a woman was assumed also to share her husband's predisposition to disloyalty. She thus attracted the restrictions and deprivations that applied to him.

Generally, however, women's disloyalty was considered less likely to be concretely manifested and consequently less dangerous. The majority of interned persons were therefore men. The Australian government's (Second World) War Book included the 'general rule' that women, regardless of nationality would not be interned, although '[w]hen the interests of public safety so demand, they will be kept in custody'. It was not anticipated that large numbers would be affected, 'as women are not generally so involved in organising activities inimical to the Empire as men of enemy nationality'.[21] In those cases where individual women were detained, concerns were raised that the conditions were harsher than those applying to men.[22]

Native-born women who had become enemy aliens simply through marriage were unlikely to have been among those detained, although there is evidence from news reports and government records that individual women with enemy alien husbands were treated with suspicion. To the dismay of citizenship equality campaigners (a complaint re-voiced in the Second World War, and made in many countries regarding conditional

[20] The law of treason did not distinguish between citizens and aliens as traitors, since resident aliens owed 'temporary allegiance' to the sovereign.

[21] National Archives of Australia, A816 (A816/1) 54/301/3. Memo, 'Enemy Women', from Secretary of Department of Defence Co-ordination, 8 August 1940. The Commonwealth War Book Part 1, Chapter VII, 'Internment of Aliens'.

[22] There was some concern about keeping women in custody – that is, in prison, rather than in internment camps. National Archives of Australia, A816 (A816/1) 54/301/3. Correspondence Note 'Internment of Aliens': from Secretary to the Military Board, 15/9/1939: 'I am commanded by the Military Board to invite attention to the provision of Cable Circular A. 4 from the Secretary of State, London, dealing with aliens. . . . The provision of Commonwealth War Book, Chapter XII, Part 1, Paragraph 3, that women will not be interned but kept in custody is at variance with British practice. Custody must mean detention in a jail, which is much more rigorous than internment, and there is no apparent reason why women should be treated more harshly than men. It is submitted that the relevant portion of the War Book should be amended. The policy of restricting internment to the absolute minimum will, of course, continue'.

marital nationality), foreign women naturalised by marriage to citizens were exempt from the restrictions applying to maritally denaturalised wives of aliens. There were, however, exceptional cases of women, naturalised by marriage, whose former nationality and conduct (or associated suspicions) attracted the penalties that applied to enemy aliens. In one notorious First World War case, Hildegarde Burnyeat, German-born wife of a former English Member of Parliament (and, therefore, by her marriage, a British subject), was interned at England's Aylesbury Prison under the Defence of the Realm Act. She was believed to have harboured pro-German sympathies; 'her house in Whitehaven is supposed to have been spared by a German submarine' during a bombardment, and 'peculiar lights are supposed to have been observed near the house' at the time. Her parents in Germany were much concerned about her fate, and made urgent inquiries about her welfare.[23]

Still, enemy status was not attributed to native-born women without equivocation. Governments began to recognise that stripping citizenship from one of their 'own' and treating her as an enemy at a time when loyalty had heightened content with harsh consequences for breach, was, at least, culturally uncomfortable. Late in the First World War, this discomfort was addressed and given partial legal relief.

Wartime re-naturalisation of marital enemy aliens

In 1918 (as we noted in Chapter 3), the British Nationality and Status of Aliens Act was amended, allowing women who had lost their British nationality through marriage to an enemy alien to apply for re-naturalisation (the amendment was also adopted in Dominion nationality laws). House of Commons debate over this amendment began with the issue of reviewing the naturalisation status of those whose previous citizenship would have qualified them as enemy aliens. The initial proposal was for the denaturalisation (at the discretion of the Home Secretary) of British women in cases where their foreign born husband, naturalised as a British subject, had had his certificate of naturalisation revoked for disloyalty or absence from Britain. In the course of debate the hardship of citizenship stripping was rehearsed. The consequences and

[23] UK National Archives. File FO 388/80 Title: 'Prisoners. German Files. 1915'. Correspondence about case of Mrs Burnyeat, who has been interned, under Defence of the Realm Regulation 14 B. Memorandum, Berlin, 26 November 1915. (One year later, she was released from the prison on health grounds.)

disabilities for loyal British-born women married to Germans were severe, the Conservative MP, John Butcher, observed; these included 'the extremely serious comments that are made on persons of German nationality'.[24] Still, doubts about the allegiance of wives of enemy aliens remained close to the surface.

Denaturalisation, Herbert Samuel (Liberal MP, former Home Secretary) conceded, generally 'create[d] grave injustice in many cases'; the 'process of denationalisation', he added (in words ironically reminiscent of the marriage service), 'is not one to be lightly undertaken'.[25] But the matter was complex, he said, and to be judged by 'circumstances'. English women who lost their nationality through marriage to Germans who subsequently failed to be naturalised in Britain suffered, but at the same time, the wife, in most cases, was 'greatly under the influence of her husband', especially in business matters. If, 'for good reason', he was denaturalised, and she was permitted to retain her British nationality, he might transfer his business arrangements into her name. 'She will still act under his direction and influence, and you will find that the provisions of the law . . . are defeated'. Additionally, when an enemy alien was required to leave a prohibited area, in the ordinary course, his wife (and children) would go with him, but if she retained her British nationality, she might remain in the prohibited area and 'probably be in constant communication' with her husband; the reasons for removing him from area would be defeated.[26]

Nevertheless, Samuel and other speakers recognised that there was injustice in denaturalising British-born women whose loyalty was not in doubt, at the same time as the law continued to provide for the unqualified marital naturalisation of German women who married British men. Butcher (who would later introduce a private member's Bill into the House of Commons, seeking the repeal of marital denaturalisation law[27]) commented that the current provision whereby a British born woman, denaturalised by marriage, could regain her British nationality upon

[24] United Kingdom, House of Commons, *Debates*, 12 July 1918, 642.

[25] United Kingdom, House of Commons, *Debates*, 12 July 1918, 628.

[26] United Kingdom, House of Commons, *Debates*, 12 July 1918, 629.

[27] First introduced in 1922 as 'The Nationality of (Married Women) Bill'. Its proposed provisions included the repeal of marital denaturalisation and the restoration to British women of the nationality they had lost through alien marriage (with the option to make a declaration of alienage); the repeal (prospective) of marital naturalisation; and foreign wives' naturalisation to be subject to the same conditions as were required of alien men applying for naturalisation.

widowhood should be extended. There was, Butcher said, 'no difference in substance' between death and divorce. 'Either the hand of God or the hand of man has got rid of her husband'.[28] He illustrated the point:

> A British woman married a German some time ago, before she perhaps knew very much about that particular German or Germans in general. She has separated... and never intends to return to him and desires to purge herself of all German connection and association for the rest of her life.

Liberal MP, Willoughby Dickinson (a dedicated supporter of women's suffrage), read out a letter from a denaturalised British born woman:

> I have been separated from my husband, a German, who was interned nearly four years ago. He has got nearly all my money in Germany and is trying to starve me into submitting to do what he wishes me, namely, to go to Germany, a thing I will never do. As the law stands, I can neither divorce my husband nor yet appeal to my own country for protection, or for my money. Equally I cannot apply to Germany... I cannot even find suitable work to do, though well qualified in one or two lines, as the question of nationality stands like a spectre at every turn, beating me back into helplessness.[29]

Several speakers recognised the strength of feeling among women as well as in the public against both marital denaturalisation and the assumption that the wife's nationality was determined by her husband's. The spectre of unimpeachable British women being treated as disloyal simply because they were married to German men prompted this recognition, and the war offered an abundance of anecdotes that demonstrated the injustice. What is significant in these stories is not just their poignancy (which they certainly capture) but also the heightened conjunction of the principles of allegiance and protection in conceptualising citizenship. At a time when allegiance was powerfully and directly relevant, the protection offered to (a class of) those who demonstrated their actual allegiance was, inconsistently, withheld. The war also created a heightened opportunity to recognise this inconsistency; it polarised responses to the policy of conditional marital nationality. Revealingly, the decision to marry a foreign man was treated by many in the course of debate (including many in the public) less as an act of disloyalty, than as an accident, for which the

[28] United Kingdom, House of Commons, *Debates*, 12 July 1918, 643.
[29] United Kingdom, House of Commons, *Debates*, 12 July 1918, 1171.

woman paid an unjust price. Liberal MP, Arthur Sherwell, pointed out that legislation was

> introduced in response to what is understood to be the feeling of the country, [and] there cannot be any dispute that at the present time there is an overwhelming number of our citizens – practically the whole body of organised and even unorganised women's opinion in the country – in favour of seizing this opportunity to redress . . . a very grave injustice.[30]

Liberal MP, Charles Roberts, noted that there were, at that time, 3,000 women, originally British subjects, who were married to Germans:

> Many of them, I suppose, did not in the least know that they were losing their British citizenship, for these matters to the lay mind are wrapped in very great obscurity . . . You will only get into difficulty by the application of a general principle, and you will never get out of the difficulty unless you say that the wife must be treated independently on her own merits, irrespective of this ancient legal fiction.[31]

Concerns about espionage, he added, were misplaced, given the continuing policy of naturalising foreign wives of British men: 'Much the safest position for the female spy of German birth is to get married to a British subject . . . I should have thought that position was one that would appeal to any clever spy who was prepared, in the interests of her profession, to take any kind of step'.[32]

Sympathy for denaturalised British women was strong, but not uniform. Liberal MP, Richard Holt, challenged the view that it was unfortunate for a British woman to have married a foreigner:

> It appears to me to be fundamentally ignorant of what are the real objects of marriage . . . I suppose when [a woman marries a foreigner] that the matter is one of mutual satisfaction! . . . I should imagine that an English woman who married a German would naturally identify herself with things German. Otherwise, I do not understand why she married at all . . . [W]hen an Englishman marries a foreign wife he certainly expects her to identify herself with his interests . . . If you are going to intern the husband and declare the wife to be of a different nationality, then you ought to divorce the two, and terminate the marriage altogether . . . The woman must follow the nationality of her husband, and so must the children. They must stand

30 United Kingdom, House of Commons, *Debates*, 12 July 1918, 651.
31 United Kingdom, House of Commons, *Debates*, 12 July 1918, 661.
32 United Kingdom, House of Commons, *Debates*, 12 July 1918, 662.

> or fall together . . . If the husband has behaved so badly that he ought to be turned out of the country, then the wife ought to have a divorce.[33]

Many objections were voiced to Holt's declaration (Mr Wilson: 'A woman marries a man not because he is German or Austrian, but because he is a man'[34]; Mr Newman: 'There is hardly a member [in the House] who would not feel that to be turned from an English subject into a German subject would be little short of the death penalty itself'[35]). Alternative suggestions that married women should have full autonomy in citizenship were not supported, however, but sympathy for women married to enemy aliens won the day.

The Act was amended. The new provision gave a degree of agency to the British-born wife, unlike the original proposal. In place of the previously unbending rule that a woman's citizenship followed her husband's (at least while he was alive), it offered the alternative. Section 10 (6) of the BNSA Act, as amended, read:

> Where an alien is a subject of a state at war with His Majesty, it shall be lawful for his wife, if she was at birth a British subject, to make a declaration that she desires to resume British nationality, and thereupon the Secretary of State, if he is satisfied that it is desirable that she be permitted to do so, may grant her a certificate of naturalization.

But, despite the high level of sympathy in the House, and the many moving stories and expressions of public outrage against the conferral of enemy alien status on British-born women, the provision was applied narrowly at this time. Only twenty-eight naturalisation certificates were recorded as granted between the Act's amendment and the official termination of the war, and only in cases where the woman in question had been separated for a long time from her husband and the separation was judged likely to be permanent.[36] The general efficacy of this new policy was questioned. In debate in the Australian parliament on an unsuccessful motion to repeal marital denaturalisation (and allow women instead to make a declaration of alienage, if they chose), the motion's mover, John Duncan-Hughes, described the provision as 'more a pious aspiration than one which is likely to be freely utilized. In any case a woman who is allowed to resume her original nationality in these circumstances is obviously in

[33] United Kingdom, House of Commons, *Debates*, 12 July 1918, 1175–6.

[34] United Kingdom, House of Commons, *Debates*, 12 July 1918, 1178.

[35] United Kingdom, House of Commons, *Debates*, 12 July 1918, 1177.

[36] UK National Archives, File HO 213/1675, 'Married Women: Naturalization under Section 10 (6)'.

an inferior position to one who has never been deprived of it'.[37] Still, the fear remained among legislators that, in an existing marriage, the wife's allegiance to her former country would be compromised by her emotional allegiance to her husband, and the provision was not taken further.

The provision was reactivated in the Second World War. In 1939 instructions governing the application of British-born women of enemy alien husbands for naturalisation suggested that the limited approach to the provision's application should be repeated:

> If the applicant is living with her husband, her application cannot be considered until her husband's position has been reviewed by one of the Tribunals appointed by the Secretary of State to examine cases of Germans and Austrians and unless her husband has been exempted from the restrictions applicable to enemy aliens . . . An application from an applicant who is not resident in the United Kingdom will only be considered in an exceptional case.[38]

It the event, however, it was applied more generously. An official memo regarding its reintroduction noted that its application during the First Word War had been very limited, applying in practice only in cases of likely permanent separation from the enemy alien husband, and 'If the matter were to be treated as one of logical theory, it would no doubt be right to follow the same procedure during the present war. Our nationality laws are based on the principle that married couples should be treated as a unit for nationality purposes, but breaches have been made in this principle by the Act of 1933' (which allowed British women to retain their nationality in cases where they did not acquire their husband's foreign nationality through marriage). There were also 'notable' cases of prominent British women who were likely to be affected:

> Lady Elizabeth P, the second daughter of the Marquis of Anglesey, married in June 1939 an Austrian who appears to have severed his connection with Austria, but has not had continuous residence in Great Britain so as to qualify him for British nationality. The daughter of Sir Findlater S married

[37] Commonwealth of Australia, House of Representatives, *Debates*, 4 February 1926, 678.

[38] UK National Archives, File HO 213/1675, 'Married Women: Naturalization under Section 10 (6)'. 'Instructions as to an application for a certificate of naturalization'. Additionally, '[w]here the applicant is separated from her husband and has the custody of any child of the marriage, who is of minor age, it will be open to her to ask that the name of such child (or children) be included in the certificate of naturalization'.

in December 1938, a German refugee. The daughter of Sir Henry P C married in November 1936, a German refugee.[39]

The memo concluded that '[o]n the whole...where a British born woman is married to a German or Austrian and the husband is classified as a friendly or neutral alien and exempted from the restrictions in [the Aliens Order], the Home Office should be prepared to consider an application for naturalisation from the woman'. If this policy was adopted, it continued, applications might be received from between 1,000 and 1,500 women.[40] In the first two years of the war, numerous applications for re-naturalisation under the Act were indeed received by the Home Office (up to 80 per month, with long backlogs in assessing them).[41] In 1943, in debate in the House of Commons on the proposed repeal of conditional marital nationality it was noted that some 2,000 certificates of naturalisation had been issued to married women since the start of the war.[42]

While the amendment had been adopted in the acknowledgement that women's loyalty did not always follow that of their husband, in some cases, the test of loyalty was especially onerous. A Home Office memo in 1942 concerning applications for section 10 (6) re-naturalisations singled out the wives of Japanese men: 'The wives appear to be decent, genuine British women and speak very well of their husbands. In view, however, of the extreme subtlety of the Japanese race it is very doubtful if the women are actually aware of the real feelings and activities of their husbands'. Naturalisation, none the less, was recommended for most of these applicants, with the exception of Mrs Margaret O, 'where we have definite evidence of the husband's strong anti-British feeling and reason to believe that the wife may also be similarly tainted'. Impressions of the wives' propensities were based on personal interviews and character references (with, in addition, where relevant, reference to the Security Service and to police

39 UK National Archives File HO 213/1675, 'Married Women: Naturalization under Section 10 (6)' 24 October 1939.

40 UK National Archives File HO 213/1675 'Married Women: Naturalization under Section 10 (6)'. (The policy, it was noted, should first be discussed in the Inter-Departmental Committee for the Control of Aliens in Wartime to ascertain the views of MI5, the Foreign Office and Dominions Office).

41 UK National Archives File HO 213/1675 'Married Women: Naturalization under Section 10 (6)', 'Married Women. Section 10 (6) B.N.S.A. Act 1914'. 3 November 1941. The Memo of 24 October 1939 had indeed commented that a more expansive application of the provision would create administrative difficulties, and that extra temporary Home Office staff might be required, with extra resources and time needed for police investigations.

42 United Kingdom, House of Commons, *Debates*, 24 March 1943, 1724.

'remarks'); similar information was also sought about the husband. Mrs O, it was noted, had lived in the United Kingdom for twenty-four years and had a child. She was a '[p]leasant woman but not 100% trust-worthy', although there was nothing specifically against her. Her husband, a former employee of the Japanese Embassy in Britain, had been '[d]escribed by a reliable witness as thoroughly untrustworthy and anti-British'. In contrast, other wives of Japanese were found to be genuinely 'British': Florence Y was a 'Good – homely superior type', and Kate Y, a 'Genuine loyal type'.[43]

Applications from denaturalised British wives, married to enemy alien men and living outside Britain, had not been permitted in the First World War, but were now allowed. This generated further policy challenges. In early 1940, the British Home Office recorded inquiries from close to forty such women, and many more were expected once the new policy became known.[44] Uncertainty, in the government's view, was created by the fact that British naturalisation 'was linked with security measures' (and loyalty was determined by the Enemy Aliens Tribunals), but, 'except in France, nothing comparable is available abroad as a guide'. Two applications from (former British) women married to German men, but living in France, had already been received. These were treated sympathetically since, in each case, the woman's health prevented her returning to Britain to make her application. Both also had had periods of recent residence in Britain, 'so that a good deal was known of the applicant and the husbands had been freed from internment'. Although residence in British territory was no longer treated as legally necessary for such a naturalisation application, it was still regarded as 'useful (and an indication of the extent of the British connection)'.

There was another adjustment in the exercise of discretion. Questioned in the House of Commons about the government's policy, the Home Secretary stated that he did not propose to restrict naturalisation to women separated from their husbands, but would limit his discretion only to the extent necessary 'to avoid impairing measures of control which must be

[43] UK National Archives File HO 213/1675 'Married Women: Naturalization under Section 10 (6)'. 'Applications for naturalization under s 10(6): Japanese cases (spouses not separated)'. 29 November 1942.

[44] Between February and the end of June 1942, for example, it was reported that over 100 naturalisation applications were received from wives or widows of subjects of 'the new belligerent States', including Hungary, Rumania, Bulgaria, Finland and Japan. UK National Archives File HO 213/1675 'Married Women: Naturalization under Section 10 (6)', 13 July 1942.

maintained in time of war over persons of enemy nationality'. The test, however, rested with the husband's qualities: if the German or Austrian husband was subject to the special restrictions applicable to enemy aliens, 'it would not as a rule be right to naturalize the [British-born] wife':

> [But] many of the Germans and Austrians now here are in sympathy with this country in the struggle in which we are engaged, and arrangements have been made to exempt such persons from the special restrictions applicable to enemy aliens. In such cases no security measures would be impaired by naturalizing a British-born wife. I have accordingly decided that any such woman may, as soon as her husband has been exempted from the special restrictions, apply for naturalization and that arrangements shall be made to deal with such applications expeditiously.[45]

Nevertheless, the Home Office was later to observe, the cases to be regarded most favourably were still those of the separated wife. Women long-resident abroad were a problematic category, although those 'more closely connected with dominions and colonies' were treated as a distinguishable sub-set. Certain cases contained a myriad of challenges. One applicant, born in the United Kingdom in 1883, had married a German in Copenhagen and had lived abroad for twenty years, latterly in Egypt. She now lived in Athens. Through her brother she applied to be naturalised in Athens, 'as she is afraid of travelling with her German passport. She probably does not want to return'. Another was born in Australia of a Chinese father who had been naturalised in that country. She lived from 1908 to 1931 in Australia, but in 1934 had married a German in Canton.

Applications for such naturalisations required two supportive character references from British-born persons, householders who were 'intimately acquainted' with the applicant. For overseas applicants, much seemed to depend upon reports furnished by the relevant British Consul. The reliability of these reports, the Home Office recognised, depended on the Consul's familiarity with local fellow and former fellow nationals, as well as with the qualities, in individual cases, of foreign husbands. The Home Office had received assessments from Consuls, including several cases 'in which the husband's record is suspicious'. In one, the husband, in Shanghai, was 'thought to have received money to provide the Germans with information'; in another, 'the husband is a Nazi in Madrid, and may be trading with the enemy'; in a third, he was 'an "ardent Nazi" still in

[45] UK National Archives File HO 213/1675 'Married Women: Naturalization under Section 10 (6)': 'Form of Certificate of Naturalization', 5 November 1939.

Germany, but his wife seems to have gone to Switzerland on the outbreak of war'.[46]

A further complicating factor had to be taken into account: an applicant, notwithstanding a long period of residence abroad, may have been relatively recently married. The length of the marriage, however, was not necessarily a useful guide. Sympathetic treatment was recommended where the applicant had recent British associations and her record was known. There was a further critical matter: 'in many cases [the woman's] German passport will be of limited validity or stamped with a "J," and the German Consul will not be helpful to her in the country she goes to'.

Separated wives, including those legally divorced in a country, the divorce laws of which were not recognised under British law (Mexico was given as one example) were to be treated sympathetically, as they had been during the First World War, and the principle now extended to separated wives living abroad, although careful scrutiny, it was suggested, should apply to cases of temporary separation where the husband was in Germany 'and a Nazi'. The file on the cases concluded with the observation that,

> apart from the natural desire of the woman to possess in law the nationality she in fact preserves, the grounds on which the wives of Germans ask for naturalisation are two. The first is that their property in some parts of the Empire is held by the custodian of enemy property . . . The other difficulty is the unpopularity of a German passport, which is greater, of course, in allied countries, and in some neutral countries more than in others.[47]

Still, despite the recognition of these complexities and hardships, marital denaturalisation, as such, was not abandoned in Britain (or in many other countries) until after the Second World War. Marital naturalisation also continued, and this led to the anomalous situation – the source of the additional grievance also expressed by citizenship equality campaigners in the First World War – in which women of enemy alien national origin who were married to citizens were exempt, as citizens themselves, from the restrictions applying to native born women, now classified as enemies. Although increasing sympathy towards the British-born wives of enemy aliens and cultural suspicion of foreign wives of British citizens blurred

[46] UK National Archives, File HO 213/1675, 'Married Women: Naturalization under Section 10 (6)'.

[47] UK National Archives, File HO 213/1675, 'Married Women: Naturalization under Section 10 (6)'.

the distinction, and amendments to the law in principle permitted 'reclassification' (through naturalisation) of previously denaturalised wives of enemy aliens, the distinction, legally and in principle, still rested on the husband's status.

A marital enemy alien wife, whose marriage was intact, would not be regarded as worthy of restoration to her native citizenship if her husband (whose citizenship she had been assumed to acquire) was tainted with disloyalty or disloyal propensities. The loyalty of an enemy-born woman, maritally naturalised, was presumed derivatively to follow the loyalty of her citizen husband. The general conflation of a woman's citizenship with her husband's, not only under law, but as to character, and the core question of character concerning loyalty or allegiance, became clear in discussion of re-naturalisation. In determining applications for British-born women for readmission to British nationality at the end of the war, the Home Office pondered 'How far should we continue to take the husband's history into account?' In assessing such applications, it noted,

> we have always taken the view that it is necessary to be satisfied that not only the wife but the husband are in sympathy with the Allied cause . . . on the ground that where there is any doubt about the husband's loyalty, it is impossible for the Home Office to judge how the wife might behave if there were a conflict between her loyalty to her husband and her loyalty to her country, and that accordingly a woman whose husband's loyalty is doubtful cannot herself be regarded as of unquestionable loyalty.[48]

The policy of approving eligibility if the husband was 'neither detained nor subject to special restrictions under the Aliens Order provided that there was nothing against the wife on personal grounds' had been reconsidered in mid-1944, since a large number of enemy aliens, especially Italians, had been released from both internment and special restrictions, and assigned to public programs of work; therefore, 'it could no longer be assumed that enemy aliens who were not subject to restrictions were necessarily friendly to this country'. Where evidence suggested that the husband could not be regarded as friendly, 'it would be justifiable to refuse to naturalize the wife'.

Even with the war concluded, 'it would not be right to grant a certificate of naturalization to a woman whose sympathies appear to be more with

[48] UK National Archives, File HO 213/1675, 'Married Women: Naturalization under Section 10 (6)'. 'Naturalization of British-Born Women who are Married to Aliens of Enemy Nationality'. Memorandum on Policy, September 1945.

her husband and his country than with her own'. A cautionary note was added regarding the British-born wives of refugees who would be required to return to their country of origin; the fact that they would regard it as their duty to accompany their husbands did not necessarily indicate that their 'affection and sympathy' for Britain did not remain 'alive'. The only clear rule was not to re-naturalise a woman whose husband remained interned or subject to enemy alien restrictions; in such cases, it seemed, 'the husband has never identified himself with this country and is never likely to, and where, so far as we can judge, the wife is as much influenced by her loyalty to her husband as she is by the fact of her British birth'. Among other considerations, it had

> hitherto been the policy to refuse to naturalize women whose husbands are resident abroad. The reason for this is that is has been impossible in such cases to make enquiries about the husband's loyalty... We have made some exceptions in favour of women who have satisfied us that they are finally separated from their husbands... on the grounds that in these cases the husband can be ignored.[49]

Generally, 'in cases where the husband [was] resident in what was enemy territory and where we cannot be sure that the wife will not rejoin him', policy would suggest the refusal of the wife's application. Although the policy could be applied less strictly, where there was 'good evidence that the wife is wholly loyal', the fact that the war had ended, the writer concluded

> does not, to my mind, entail any fundamental change in the principles on which our existing practice is based... So long as it remains the law that a British woman loses her British nationality if, by reason of her marriage to a foreigner, she acquires his nationality, we should hardly be justified in taking advantage of the provisions of section 10 (6), which operates only while a state of war exists, to restore British nationality to women who happen to be eligible... irrespective of the merits of the individual case'.[50]

Beyond the cases surrounding applications for readmission to British nationality by naturalisation, numerous other cases concerning individual women denaturalised by marriage to men, now classified as enemy

49 UK National Archives, File HO 213/1675, 'Married Women: Naturalization under Section 10 (6)'. 'Naturalization of British-Born Women who are Married to Aliens of Enemy Nationality'. Memorandum on Policy, September 1945.

50 UK National Archives, File HO 213/1675, 'Married Women: Naturalization under Section 10 (6)'. 'Naturalization of British-Born Women who are Married to Aliens of Enemy Nationality'. Memorandum on Policy, September 1945.

aliens, were brought to the attention of governments via personal appeals, political speeches, and news reports. The majority concerned hardships suffered by women who experienced both separation from their interned husbands and constraints on daily life, often alone. There were two major classes of maritally denaturalised women to whom official attention was drawn and for whom some sort of legal response was required: first (the majority of cases), native-born women, married to men of enemy alien citizenship, who were living in their country of birth, and secondly, maritally denaturalised women, living in another country, whose circumstances or treatment in that country were harshly affected by the fact of their having been, before their marriage, citizens of a country with which their country of residence was now at war.

Marital enemy aliens: the First World War

Following the passage of the United States Expatriation Act in 1907, the number of women around the world affected by the practice of marital denaturalisation was at its peak during the years of the First World War. In Britain, Chrystal Macmillan's chronicle of the numerous hardships experienced by maritally denaturalised women included the period of the war. Mrs E, for example, was married before the war to a German-born man who had been in England since he was two months old. She had not known that her husband was not British and the question had never arisen until the war broke out and he was interned and his business ruined:

> The wife was compelled to endure all the hardship inflicted on Germans at that time, although she had never been out of the country. After the war the man was taken to a lunatic asylum and the wife has to bring up the children unaided, being heavily handicapped by her alien nationality in obtaining paid work, yet while her husband is alive she is not allowed to regain her British nationality.[51]

British women married to foreign men in seaport regions of England, where the rates of female exogamy were high, provided other moving examples, as Laura Tabili found. Mrs Eleanor Otto, 'a poor woman', British-born, but a German national by marriage, was living in South Shields, which had been designated a 'prohibited area'. Since enemy aliens required a permit each time they travelled more than five miles in a

[51] Macmillan, 'The Nationality of Married Women'.

prohibited area, even to work, Mrs Otto was unable to take a much-needed job as a nurse.[52] In New Zealand, the 'Ladies Page' of a newspaper reported in 1915 on the case of an English woman, the wife of a German national who was prosecuted for going into a prohibited area when she was returning to her parents' home. A magistrate fined her £5 (with the option of prison): 'We have not such magistrates here', the New Zealanders commented, 'but unfortunately, until amended, we have the same laws operative in many ways prejudicial to the NZ wives of aliens'.[53]

In 1923 a UK Parliamentary Committee on the Nationality of Married Women, reported cases of 'British women married to enemy aliens whose property rights and interests had been appropriated under . . . the Treaty of Versailles'. During the war, the Committee heard, such wives, living in Britain, retained their right to property.[54] After the ratification of the Treaty in January 1920, however, they were included in the definition of enemy nationals, and their property rights came under embargo, 'just as entirely and completely as the property rights and interests of a German who had never been here at all', even extending to life interests and property settled on the marriage. Although exceptions were possible, over the previous three years, 2,000 individual cases, revealing unthinkable 'hardship and misery' had come before the Committee.[55]

Even the wives of friendly aliens suffered deprivations during the war. In House of Commons Debate in 1918, Willoughby Dickinson described one case concerning a British woman who had married an Italian subject:

[52] Tabili, 'Outsiders in the Land of Their Birth', 807. Tabili notes that readmission to British nationality for the widows of foreign men was made less expensive during the war, and many petitions were granted; still character testimonials were required to testify to the 'respectability' and 'loyalty' of the applicant.

[53] Archives New Zealand, Ref no. IA1 2824, Record no 116/6, R19964 603, pt 1. Department of Internal Affairs, 'Naturalisation – Nationality of British Women married to Aliens – General file re'. Clipping, 15 September 1915.

[54] In Britain during the war, enemy aliens, although subject to many restrictions, extending to internment, were not deprived of contractual or property rights (as they were in the United States). Under the various UK Trading With the Enemy Acts, businesses in the United Kingdom under the control or for the benefit of enemy subjects could be wound up or impounded. Ernest J. Schuster, 'The Peace Treaty in its Effects on Private Property' (1920–21) *British Year Book of International Law* 167.

[55] Select Committee appointed to join with a Committee of the House of Commons on The Nationality of Married Women, *Report* (His Majesty's Stationery Office, London, 1923) 144. The Report noted that, under the UK Trading with the Enemy Act, 1916, nationality was not relevant (since the Act concerned business with or in enemy countries).

> She separated from him because of his cruelty. He claimed [their] child under the law and she could not take it away. She has been in England all this time, while he has been in Italy. He is a friendly alien, but, because she is married to an Italian subject, she has been subjected to all the hardships of police inspection. Until quite recently, when the Home Office exempted her, she could not travel anywhere without a permit, and she could not change her address. She was treated exactly as an alien because she was an alien, although she had married a friendly alien and had been separated from him for several years. That is only one instance of thousands of cases.[56]

Such cases were not confined to Britain. Congressional debates on the Cable Act of 1922 in the United States included stories of the disadvantage suffered during the war by American-born women married to German men. Proclamations ordering the Germans out of the District of Colombia, resulting in the separation of some married couples, had caused distress. During the war, it was said, some American women who were married to German men had 'expatriated themselves', embracing their husbands' enemy allegiance, but, 'to the everlasting credit of American womanhood... cases of the woman's transfer of her moral allegiance... were not very numerous'. Thousands of women with German husbands, 'never lost one particle of [their] own loyalty to our flag and our country... Yet their property was sequestered and they were subject to the legal duress and restrictions and the social suspicion and ostracism which attached to the status of alien enemies'.[57] The claim was illustrated by an anecdote:

> A girl who went to school with me [the Congressman] at home and whose noble old father had lost an arm in the Civil War married while she was studying music in German a young German officer. The marriage was not a happy one, and she returned after a very few years to the United States and lived with her parents.... [B]ut being of a religious faith which frowns upon divorce she never obtained a legal separation. This splendid young woman took an active part in Red Cross and other military relief work, and was broken-hearted when she was required to stop on the ground that she was an 'alien enemy'.[58]

Congressman Cable, later explaining the need for repeal of the law, also cited cases of hardship during the war. The Austrian husband of a

56 United Kingdom, House of Commons, *Debates*, 19 July 1918, 1347–8.

57 United States, House of Representatives, *Congressional Record*, 20 June 1922, 9040.

58 United States, House of Representatives, *Congressional Record*, 20 June 1922, 9040 (Mr Vaile).

denaturalised American-born woman, resident in the United States, was killed in a mine accident in the State of Washington and, as an alien enemy had his workmen's compensation payment seized during the war by the Alien Property Custodian.[59] An American-born woman, married in 1886 to a German man had inherited a fortune, both in an estate and in a trust. Her husband was entitled to her estate under German law; he took possession of it and dissipated it, but without access to the trust. However, during the war, she was declared an enemy alien and her income from the trust fund was seized by the Alien Property Custodian under the provisions of the Trading with the Enemy Act of October 6, 1917. Separated from her husband, the woman, Cable reported, was destitute when she returned to America in 1919, unable to get a divorce for at least six months, and unable to acquire an American passport.[60] The Senate Committee on Immigration, which had the power to recommend special Acts for exceptional naturalisation cases granted her application: 'Mrs de Haven-Alten thereupon immediately regained her American citizenship and recovered her property from the Alien Property Custodian'.[61]

This happy ending masks the reality that her petition to Congress was her only recourse. It was a private act 'for the benefit of one particular person', and, in Cable's opinion, it may have exceeded Congress's constitutional power 'to establish an uniform rule of naturalization'.[62] The need for exceptional powers, and the fact that many other such cases came before the committee, demonstrated, in Cable's words, 'the inadequacy and unfairness of the laws then governing the citizenship of married women'.[63]

Even relatively minor discrimination was experienced as a grievance. In 1915, the New Zealand Canterbury Women's Institution commissioned a report on women's nationality during the war. They petitioned the government, asking that women married to enemy subjects be readmitted to British nationality,[64] so that 'in this way they would not be deprived of the right to participate in patriotic funds raised for the benefit of women and children on whom the War had imposed financial hardship'.[65]

[59] Cable, *American Citizenship Rights of Women.* [60] Cable, ibid, 23.

[61] Cable, ibid, 24. [62] Cable, ibid. [63] Cable, ibid, 25.

[64] Ironically, it was not realised that these women remained British subjects in New Zealand. (See Chapter 3.)

[65] Archives New Zealand, Ref no. IA1 2824, Record no 116/6, R19964 603, pt 1. The Canterbury Women's Institute to Minister for Internal Affairs, re Enemy Subjects Commission, 25 June 1915. The Institute employed Miss Rout, a professional reporter, to write a newspaper article in reference to nationality from a woman's point of view. Published in the *Lyttelton Times*, and elsewhere, 5 June 1915.

The 1930s: approach of war

The ratification of the Hague Nationality Convention and its incorporation into the legislation of at least some of its signatory states saw the reduction of maritally induced statelessness (as we see in Chapter 6). The post-Hague era was anything but settled, however. Women who were naturalised by marriage under the law of their husbands' country continued to be denaturalised in their own country, and the hardships multiplied in the inter-war years, in particular with the growing preoccupation of Nazi Germany and fascist Italy with the 'purity' of their national citizenship.

Until the outbreak of war, non-Jewish alien-born women married to German men, and living in Germany, could be assumed to have benefitted, at least practically, from the law that transformed them into German citizens, including in acquiring the benefits enjoyed by native-born women generally. Such maritally naturalised wives were, most significantly, free from fear of deportation or expulsion from their country of residence, and free to remain with their German husbands. After the declaration of war, however, women whose country of origin was that of an enemy of Germany suffered hostility (as happened in reverse in their former countries). The converse of the protection they enjoyed from deportation was the restriction or denial of the opportunity to return to their country of origin, including to seek shelter with members of their original family.

These experiences were common in a war context. What was different in the 1930s, and endured to the end of the war, were the racial citizenship laws that had the effect of doubly denaturalising certain alien wives of German and Italian nationals. Under the German law of 14 July 1933 naturalisations granted between November 1918 and January 1933 were revoked; the object of the law was the denaturalisation of 'undesirable' naturalised Germans, primarily Jews. The Nuremburg Citizenship Law of 15 September 1935 divided Germans into citizens and subjects: all Jews were classified as subjects and accordingly deprived of rights attached to citizen status. In 1941, the law was extended, and all German Jews residing abroad were denaturalised, with confiscation of their German property.

The 1941 law had a particular effect on foreign Jewish women married to Germans (and thereby maritally naturalised as German) whose country of origin still practised marital denaturalisation. Foreign Jewish wives of Germans were rendered stateless if they lived outside Germany.

Under the laws of countries that had incorporated the Hague Convention relating to married women's nationality, such women were, in principle, protected from loss of their native citizenship. To apply this rule to the circumstances of foreign women married to German men meant, however, the recognition in the woman's original country of the Nazi law that stripped citizenship from Jews. This created policy dilemmas for opponent governments.

Eda F, the British-born wife of an Austrian refugee, living in England, refused, like her husband, to identify as German and sought to regain her British nationality as a stateless wife. After much head-scratching, the Home Office advised: '[W]e are telling the police to cancel her registration under the Aliens Order and to hand her back her British passport'. It added: 'The issue to the wife of a British passport in such a case as this causes some embarrassment here in so far as it almost amounts to an admission that the husband is stateless'.[66]

The automatic attribution of German citizenship to wives of Germans (and their consequent loss of their pre-marital nationality) had tragic consequences for some. Margrith Bigler-Eggenberger identifies the marital denaturalisation as amounting, 'in the context of Swiss women married to [German] Jews . . . to abandoning them to the German National Socialist concentration camps':

> Had the wives of German, French, Hungarian, Austrian and Polish Jews who were dragged away to concentration camps been able to keep their Swiss citizenship, Switzerland, via its diplomatic posts, would have been able to save lives from certain and gruesome extermination. [It] would at least not have been allowed, or able, to close its borders to former Swiss female citizens with their families who wished to return, or who were forced to flee, between the years of 1938–39 and 1945.[67]

In Italy, a decree of 17 December 1938, as in Germany, cancelled all naturalisation certificates issued to Jews after 1 January 1919. Similar laws

[66] UK National Archives, FO 612/238 'Women of British Nationality married to aliens who have not acquired husband's nationality'. Home Office (Aliens Department), 29 June 1943.

[67] Margrith Bigler-Eggenberger, 'Bürgerrechtsverlust durch Heirat: Ein dunkler Fleck in der jüngeren Schweizer Rechtsgeschichte' (1999), extract translated in Boll, *Multiple Nationality and International Law*, 245–6. Brigitte Studer's research on marital denaturalisation in Switzerland illustrates individual cases of such a fate for Jewish women who had lost their Swiss nationality through foreign marriage. After December 1942, however, such women were able to acquire refugee status. Studer, 'Citizenship as Contingent National Belonging'.

were passed in other Axis countries.[68] Marriages between non-Jewish Italians and Jews (whether foreign or Italian) were no longer recognised as valid. The Italian non-recognition of divorce was also a complicating factor. A British-born woman married to an Italian citizen in Libya under Italian law, Karin T, was saved from loss of her British nationality only because she had been previously married and divorced. As her Italian marriage was not considered valid in Italy, she came under the British amendment in 1933 to the BNSA Act that limited marital denaturalisation to cases where the wife acquired the husband's nationality. She was granted a British passport that was marked: 'British subject by birth, the wife of an Italian subject'.[69]

In Spain, the law regarding citizenship had remained uncertain during the years of the Civil War. The 1931 Constitution of the Spanish Republic included a provision offering alien women who married Spanish men the choice of retaining their native citizenship or acquiring their husband's Spanish citizenship. British authorities, at least, were unclear as to whether this applied in law: 'it has been the practice to regard the position of a [British] woman who is married to a Spaniard as extremely doubtful'. Passports issued to any such woman who had not prima facie opted for Spanish nationality were restricted to a maximum period of twelve months 'and the grantee [was] warned that the question of her national status is in doubt'.[70] In one particular case, Mrs C, having produced a certificate from the Spanish Consul in Liverpool certifying that she had not applied for a Spanish passport and nor had her marriage been registered at the British Consulate, was given the benefit of the doubt and granted the British passport for which she had applied. Mrs C would have enjoyed her renewed British nationality only briefly. In November 1939, a decree promulgated by General Franco provided that all foreign women married to Spaniards, whatever the date of the marriage, were deemed to have Spanish nationality. British officers were advised that passports issued to British-born wives of Spanish men between 1931 and 1938 should be impounded and the holders informed that they had acquired Spanish nationality by marriage and had lost their British nationality under the BNSA Act: 'They are therefore no longer

[68] United Nations, *A Study of Statelessness*, New York, August 1949.

[69] UK National Archives, FO 612/238, 'Women of British Nationality married to aliens who have not acquired husband's nationality' (no date).

[70] UK National Archives, FO 612/238, 'Women of British Nationality married to aliens who have not acquired husband's nationality'. Home Office, 25 August 1939.

eligible to hold British passports and cannot be afforded British diplomatic protection'.[71]

Marital enemy aliens: the Second World War

By the mid-1930s, the United States had fully repealed its conditional marital citizenship laws, and several other countries had followed. The majority, however, had only amended their laws to reflect the commitment of the 1930 Hague Nationality Convention which, as we have noted, was designed to pre-empt maritally induced statelessness in cases where the wife did not automatically acquire her husband's nationality. Britain, the Dominions, and many European countries still retained the general rule of conditional marital nationality.

As in the First World War, this rule caused many hardships and grievances for denaturalised women living in their native country. In 1940, British Member of Parliament, Irene Ward, inquired about the policy regarding British-born wives of Italians. 'As I understand the situation', she wrote, 'we were given an assurance that women British born would receive back their British nationality if married to enemy aliens'.[72] She enclosed a letter from Mrs Alice L, the wife of a well-connected Italian national, a prominent banker who had spent much time in Britain, and had been awarded an Order of the British Empire during the First World War for services to the Ministry of Munitions. Mr L had left Italy in 1938 'owing to the Fascist Anti-Jewish laws', and notwithstanding his distinguished status was now interned in England as an enemy alien. Mrs L's letter set out her current circumstances:

> My children, one of whom is British born, are at school in a protected area, and I am completely cut off from them. In accordance with instructions, I reported to the local police to have the particulars of my aliens registration book endorsed on my National Identity card. The officer merely endorsed the number, saying he was forbidden to add 'British born'. Therefor[e] at any time I may be called on to produce my identity card, this leaves me in exactly the same position as any foreign born alien who may have come to this country immediately before the war. A disgraceful situation.[73]

[71] Ibid, 9 January 1940. 'Examiners Please Note': 'British Women Marrying Spaniards'.

[72] UK National Archives, HO 213/1675: 'Married Women: Naturalization under Section 10 (6)', 27 July 1940.

[73] UK National Archives, HO 213/1675: 'Married Women: Naturalization under Section 10 (6)'. Minutes. 'Noted' 13 November 1940.

'I suggest that in cases of this kind', wrote Ward, 'it is perfectly reasonable to grant certificates to the wives'. In reply, Ward was told that no assurance had been given that British-born women married to enemy aliens would have their British nationality restored, and was reminded that section 10 (6) of the Act conferred no right to recover British nationality, but only the right to apply to the Home Secretary for permission to do so. The special Aliens Tribunals, she was informed, operated under a scheme of assessments placing Germans and Austrians, resident in Britain, in different categories according to individual security risk assessment (and thus liability to internment). The Home Secretary was prepared favourably to consider applications from British-born women married to Germans and Austrians whose assessment was favourable, but had indicated that 'it would not normally be possible to grant applications in other cases'. Nor would it be possible to modify those general rules: 'It would not be right to permit a British-born woman to recover her British nationality if there were any doubts about her husband's friendliness towards this country, unless she could show that she was genuinely separated from him'.[74]

All Italians whose names appeared upon the Security List, and all Italian men between the ages of 16 and 70 with less than twenty years continuous residence in Britain had been interned at this stage[75]: 'Consequently no more can be said about British-born women married to Italians than that if the Home Secretary is satisfied on such information as is available at the Home Office that the husband is well disposed to this country, he will be prepared to consider naturalising the British-born wife'. There was enough information about Mr L to enable the Home Office to consider an

74 UK National Archives, HO 213/1675: 'Married Women: Naturalization under Section 10 (6)'. Osbert Peake (Parliamentary Under-Secretary of State for the Home Department) to Irene Ward, 19 August 1940.

75 Similar hardships arose from the removal of enemy aliens from prohibited areas (including farms) in the United States, extending to the American born wives of Italian citizens, notwithstanding the repeal of conditional marital nationality laws in 1922 and 1931. As Lawrence Distasi explains, in some cases American women who had married foreign men before 1922 and had thereby lost their citizenship did not know of, or had not availed themselves of, the re-naturalisation procedure available after that date. In early 1942, an official from the Immigration and Naturalization Service, attempting to clear up the confusion, recognised that many women had unnecessarily registered under the various alien and enemy registration orders. The official's explanation of the applicable law, while helpful, still left much uncertainty. Additionally, many '[w]omen who had lost their citizenship by marriage were simply allowed, and in some cases, compelled by zealous officials to follow a mistaken interpretation of the law'. Lawrence Distasi, 'Derived Aliens: Derivative Citizenship and Italian-American Women During World War II' (2011) 9 *Italian Americana* 23, 30.

application from his wife for naturalisation. But nothing in her husband's case, it was reported, indicated grounds to differentiate his from any others with respect to release from internment.

In assessing the extent that restrictions should apply to British-born wives of non-interned enemy aliens, the Aliens Tribunals were advised that, regarding travel and the possession of motorcars, cameras, and other restricted items,

> husbands and wives, who are living together, should stand on the same footing. They should either both be exempted from these restrictions or both be subjected to them. The ground for this recommendation is that if it is necessary for security purposes to restrict the husband's power of moving about the country, the wife ought not to be placed in a position in which she could move about the country freely as her husband's agent. Where, however, the tribunals are satisfied that both husband and wife, though German in nationality, are friendly to this country and unlikely to do anything to assist the enemy, they are empowered to exempt the alien from these restrictions, and such exemptions have been granted in a very large number of cases. If, therefore, a British born woman is married to a German who is classified by the Tribunal as friendly, she is not in practice subject to any of the special restrictions applicable to enemy aliens.[76]

The memo summarising these instructions concluded revealingly. Notwithstanding the exemptions granted to 'a very large number of cases' of husband and wife of enemy alien status, the British-born wife was still required to register with the police as a German, 'and it is this German label that constitutes her real grievance'. It may be said, the memo continued, that 'if the woman is subjected to no practical inconvenience by being labelled a German, there is the less reason for giving her British nationality, but such an argument ignores the very real sentimental grievance'.[77]

The end of the war brought further grievances. Where enemy aliens who had been interned were deported, the wives, including those of former native nationality, were deported with their husbands. In occupied countries, maritally denaturalised foreign-born wives created humanitarian dilemmas for their country of origin. British-born wives in Germany, it was decided, could apply for Red Cross food parcels as if they were still British subjects. Widows were offered repatriation to Britain, 'as it was

[76] UK National Archives, HO 213/1675: 'Married Women: Naturalization under Section 10 (6)'. Communication to Peake and Secretary of State, 24 October 1939.

[77] UK National Archives, HO 213/1675: 'Married Women: Naturalization under Section 10 (6)'. Communication to Peake and Secretary of State, 24 October 1939.

felt that these women, who are only technically German, had probably suffered considerably during the war because of their British origin'.[78]

This recognition that the German nationality of such women was 'technical' was a small, but significant token of the changing attitude at this time regarding the nature of foreign marriage. Although in 1947 the official instruction was 'to revert to the normal practice' and treat the women as German nationals,[79] in less than two years, British law would be conclusively altered, bringing conditional marital nationality to an end. Maritally denaturalised women would automatically reacquire their British citizenship, without the requirement of undergoing (re)naturalisation.[80] Women would no longer face the penalty of loss of citizenship for performing that most commonplace, indeed routine, human act of marriage.

Although this study has not considered the transmission of citizenship from parents to children, one further rule is relevant to an understanding of the gendered impact of war on women's citizenship. Among the general exceptions to the rule of *jus soli*, practised in, among others, the United States, Britain and the Dominions, was the rule that a child whose father was an enemy alien and who was born within territory that at the time of the person's birth was in hostile occupation could not acquire nationality. The injustice of this rule was recognised in a 1946 report of an Australian Parliamentary Committee, appointed 'to consider the Practical and Legal Difficulties involved in the Possession, by Husband and Wife, of Different Nationalities' (it was chaired by Dorothy Tangney, the first woman elected to the Australian Senate). In addition to recommendation that British women should not lose their nationality on marriage to a foreigner, and nor should a foreign woman automatically acquire her British husband's nationality, the Report recommended that this particular *jus soli* exception should be repealed. The rule, the Committee stated, 'placed an undeserved

[78] UK National Archives, FO 940/12: 'Marriage of British Women with German Nationals – General Information'. Circular issued by British Consulate-General, March 1948: 'Guidance on Treatment of non-Official British Subjects in the British Zone of Germany'.

[79] UK National Archives, FO 940/12: 'Marriage of British Women with German Nationals – General Information'.

[80] British Nationality Act 1948 (which came into effect on 1 January, 1949) (section 14). Such women, having regained their British nationality, became entitled (section 19) to make a declaration of renunciation of their British citizenship (sic) (subject to exceptions during time of war). Section 19 also included the statement that, for the purposes of the right of renunciation, 'any woman who has been married shall be deemed to be of full age'. The irony is evident. Having previously treated married women as the equivalent of minors for the purposes of nationality law, the law now deemed actual minors to be competent adults, by virtue of their married status, for the purposes of nationality law.

stigma on the child and caused it and the mother unmerited hardship'.[81] The rule, it may be added, presumed a type of complicity on the part of the mother, as if her bearing of a child were an act of disloyalty, and it took no account of the practice of rape by invading soldiers. It was, perhaps, the starkest illustration of the conflation of the sexual 'union' between a woman and a foreign man with the assumption of disallegiance underlying the loss of citizenship.

Conclusion

The 'sentimental grievance' identified in the memo to the British Secretary of State on enemy alien assessment was at the heart of marital citizenship deprivation, and the circumstances of war brought this, literally, home. The imputation of disallegiance, always present in the denaturalisation of a married woman, was foregrounded, and both the sense and the reality of insecurity and vulnerability were heightened. The historical association between citizenship and defence of the sovereign re-emerged powerfully. The experience of existential injury in citizenship loss found its full expression. The reciprocal recognition between states of each other's citizens that had, in its evolution, nourished modern international relations and avoided conflict, was tragically strained. The laws of conditional marital nationality that had been the product of this arrangement had begun to lose their rationale. The automatic attribution of a married woman's allegiance to her husband's country now produced deep ambivalence in the governments that maintained it.

Following the Second World War, with the abandonment of marital denaturalisation in Britain, a newspaper comment summed up the injuries that the practice had inflicted. British-born women with alien enemy husbands had been

> literally disowned by their own people, with almost punitive thoroughness. A British woman marrying an alien husband was regarded as an alien, refused a British passport, and denied the protection of the British Government abroad. Even if she did not leave her own land and could speak no word of her husband's language, the British wife was treated in the same way.[82]

[81] National Archives of Australia. Record series: A446/182 Control symbol: 1960/67025. Department of Immigration: 'Nationality of Married Women'. The Committee noted that Norway was intending to repeal this rule. It recommended, however, retaining the rule that the citizenship of the father in a marriage should determine the citizenship of children.

[82] *Evening Post*, 'A Right Restored to British Wives', 25 February 1948.

The situation of such women, the report concluded, was 'fantastically cruel and unjust'.

This assessment cannot be treated as an exaggeration. The wartime cases (of which the above are just a small sample) reveal what is essential to understanding citizenship generally: it attaches to human lives and shapes their circumstances in ways that are profoundly existential, and that go well beyond the functional entitlements or political rights often associated with citizenship. The wartime situation of marital enemy aliens starkly illustrates how vulnerable citizens are to changes in international relations and the international climate, and just how dramatic the withdrawal of the state's protection can be.

5

Marital denaturalisation begins to unravel

> You have to consider . . . whether the wife is a kind of handbag which the man carries about with him to and from a foreign country . . . a mere chattel and appendage with no will of her own. That, I confess, does not correspond to the new facts of the time.[1]

By the 1920s, the effects of marital denaturalisation on women's lives were well-recognised. The International Council of Women (with branches in more than twenty countries) had been advocating reform of the law since 1905, and other national and international women's organisations had followed suit in the years immediately after the war.[2] The campaign for citizenship equality had begun to have an impact. While most countries still clung to the policy of conditional marital nationality, many had made amendments to their laws in the attempt to mitigate some of the problems to which these gave rise. A few now permitted a choice of nationality on the part of the out-marrying woman: the Belgian law of 1922, for example, provided for denaturalisation where a woman automatically acquired her husband's nationality, but permitted her to a make declaration within six months of her marriage of her desire to retain her Belgian nationality. The Rumanian law of 1924 was similar, other than in requiring the declaration to be made before or on the occasion of the marriage. The French law of 1927 offered the converse, permitting a woman married to a foreign man to remain French unless she made a declaration that she desired to take her husband's nationality.[3] Some countries had repealed marital

[1] United Kingdom, House of Commons, *Debates*, 19 July 1918, 1351 (Mr Roberts).

[2] Macmillan, 'Nationality of Married Women', 142.

[3] If, however, her first matrimonial domicile was outside France and she had automatically acquired her husband's nationality, she ceased to be French. The Belgian law of 1909 and the French law of 1889 already provided that a citizen woman was denaturalised only in cases where she acquired the nationality of her husband. At the time, this would have been the majority of cases. The nationality laws were not otherwise gender egalitarian. The 1922 Belgian law still maintained marital denaturalisation of foreign wives. The French law of 1927 allowed for marital naturalisation of foreign wives (with certain provisos concerning

denaturalisation, while retaining other incidents of the policy (including marital naturalisation, and loss of a wife's citizenship in the event of her husband's foreign naturalisation[4]). Few, however, had gone as far as to repeal all conditional marital nationality laws.[5]

Russia had ended the practice after the 1917 Revolution. A Decree in 1918 made it permissible for a married women to become naturalised in her own right. A 1921 law made loss of citizenship conditional only upon overseas residence or counter-revolutionary activities. Mass denaturalisations of expatriates followed, but foreign marriage did not count as disallegiance. A Soviet Decree in 1924 stated specifically: 'When a marriage is concluded between a person who is of [Soviet] Union citizenship and a person who is of foreign citizenship, each retains his or her own citizenship'. Foreign governments (and the League of Nations) took notice of these laws, but in terms of impact specifically on women's status, both numerical and substantive, the United States Cable Act of 1922, was the most significant and the single greatest catalyst for further change.

The Cable Act

As we have seen, the Cable Act repealed both the marital naturalisation section of the United States Act of 1855,[6] and the marital denaturalisation

their native country's law) subject to their making a declaration of intention before the marriage ceremony. Flournoy and Hudson, *A Collection of Nationality Laws.* See also Beroë Bicknell, 'The Nationality of Married Women' (1934) 20 *Transactions of the Grotius Society* (British Institute of International and Comparative Law) 106. (Bicknell identifies Belgium as the first European State to offer the option of choosing between her own or her husband's nationality.)

4 Swedish law of 1924, for example, provided that marriage to a foreign man did not of itself result in loss of Swedish nationality, but the general rule that Swedish citizens who naturalised in a foreign country and established domicile outside Sweden, applied to women who acquired their foreign husband's nationality upon marriage. Marital naturalisation of alien women who married Swedes continued, and was not conditioned upon domicile.

5 Feinberg reports that by 1926 only six countries allowed complete gender equality in citizenship laws: the United States, USSR, Argentina, Cuba, Paraguay, Uruguay. Feinberg, *Elusive Equality*. This list must be qualified: the United States law at that time did not permit the restoration of citizenship lost by marriage in cases of women ineligible to naturalise, or whose husband was ineligible.

6 Specifically, section 1994 of the Revised Statutes (August 9, 1888), taken from the Act of Congress of February 10, 1855: 'Any woman who is now or may hereafter be married to a citizen of the United States, and who may herself be lawfully naturalized, shall be deemed a citizen'.

section of the Expatriation Act of 1907.[7] It began with a statement regarding naturalisation: 'That the right of any woman to become a naturalised citizen of the United States shall not be denied or abridged because of her sex'. Elaboration followed: a foreign woman who married a United States citizen, or the wife of a man who became naturalised as a United States citizen would no longer 'by reason of such marriage or naturalisation' become a citizen herself. She would, however, be entitled to apply to be naturalised in her own right, in an expedited and simpler process than that which was required for ordinary naturalisation.[8]

The repeal of the 1907 law did not by itself restore citizenship to maritally denaturalised American-born women. Such women were required to undergo naturalisation, as provided for under the 1906 Naturalization Act.[9] This requirement, indirectly, offered a significant disqualification from the restoration of an American woman's citizenship lost under the 1907 Act, and also for the acquisition of American citizenship by a foreign wife. The woman in question needed to be 'eligible to citizenship'.[10] The main ground of ineligibility was racial; only 'white' or African American persons could qualify for naturalisation. Persons of Asian ethnicity were ineligible. Under the Cable Act, the race criterion also applied to the woman's husband (notwithstanding that her re-naturalisation would have had no impact upon his citizenship status). Section 3 of the Cable Act read: '[A]ny woman citizen who marries an alien ineligible to citizenship shall cease to be a citizen of the United States'. Other qualifications applied, albeit less numerically significant. The applicant for naturalisation had to be of 'good moral character'; he or she could not be a 'disbeliever' (an atheist), or opposed to organised government; or a polygamist or a believer in the practice of polygamy. The applicant also

7 Section 4 of the 1907 Act: '[A]ny American woman who marries a foreigner shall take the nationality of her husband'.

8 No declaration of intention was required, and in lieu of the regular requirement of at least 5 years' continuous residence in the United States, she had only to reside continuously for at least one year. However, she had to be eligible for naturalisation: Cable Act, section 2: 'if eligible to citizenship, she may be naturalized upon full and complete compliance with all [other] requirements of the naturalization laws'.

9 Law of June 29, 1906 (with amendments, 1918 and 1926, having no direct relevance to the citizenship of married women).

10 Cable Act, Section 4. 'That a woman who, before the passage of this Act, has lost her United States citizenship by reason of her marriage to an alien eligible for citizenship, may be naturalized' under the (simplified) naturalisation procedure, with eligibility restrictions applying.

had to be willing to swear the oath of allegiance, and commit herself to defending the United States.[11]

Tying the restoration of birthright citizenship to the procedure (and concept) of naturalisation meant that women's marital citizenship remained conditional. Notwithstanding the words of the Fourteenth Amendment, all persons born in the United States were not, in fact, birthright citizens. They could begin as such, but might be transformed into naturalised citizens, via their loss of citizenship upon marriage and their subsequent resumption of citizenship by naturalisation.[12] Although, after 1922, no American-born woman who married an eligible alien man would be denaturalised through marriage, those who had previously lost their citizenship might not get it back, either on their own account or because of the status of their husband.

A maritally denaturalised woman might meet the eligibility criteria and become, once again, an American citizen, but even in such circumstances her birthright citizenship was not actually restored and nor was it secure. If the (re-naturalised) woman resided continuously for two years in her husband's country of citizenship or for five years elsewhere outside the United States, she was subject to the presumption of loss of citizenship that applied to ordinary naturalised citizens. This condition, indeed, represented a reversal of one of the provisions of the 1907 Act that had allowed for the restoration of citizenship in the event of the termination of a woman's foreign marriage, if (among other things) she registered as a citizen at a United States consulate, even while living outside the United States.[13]

[11] English language competency was also required, as was the renunciation of any hereditary title or order of nobility.

[12] The US Nationality Act of 1940 allowed maritally denaturalised American women to recover 'the same citizenship status as that which existed immediately prior to its loss'; in other words, to treat them as birthright citizens. However, such women were still subject to processes applying to naturalisation, and were not exempt from the requirement to take the oath. As Candice Bredbenner points out, in light of the guarantee captured in the Act, this requirement was 'even more illogical . . . than it had been'. Bredbenner, *A Nationality of Her Own*, 192.

[13] Section 4 of the 1907 Act provided 'That any foreign woman who acquires American citizenship by marriage to an American shall be assumed to retain the same after the termination of the marital relation if she continue to reside in the United States, unless she makes formal renunciation thereof before a court having jurisdiction to naturalize aliens, or if she resides abroad she may retain her citizenship by registering as such before a United States consul within one year after the termination of such marital relation'. The reversal arose because, in repealing the 1907 Act, the legislators had failed to notice that no

The residency anomaly was corrected with the Cable Act's amendment in 1930, and the racial disqualification for restoration of pre-marital citizenship was removed in 1931. In 1934, a new Act permitted the transmission of American citizenship to children by either parent in a marriage. By 1940, United States citizenship law made no distinction between men and women, or between married and single women, or regarding the citizenship status of the husbands of married women. But the incremental steps between the in-principle commitment to the reversal of the policy in 1922 and the actual achievement of full citizenship equality were indicative of the difficulty legislators had in treating women as independent citizens.

By the time of the Cable Act's introduction into Congress, the subject of conditional marital nationality had been on the agenda of the House of Representatives Committee on Immigration and Naturalization for several years; its proposed repeal had been endorsed in the 1920 platforms of both the Republican and the Democratic Parties.[14] Debate over the proposal revealed a long-standing concern about the injustices and disadvantages caused by marital naturalisation, mixed with objections to the practice of automatic naturalisation of alien wives of citizens. The view expressed were not, however, uniformly favourable. They also revealed ambivalence over the entitlement of American women to hold citizenship in their own right and scepticism about women's motivation in marrying foreign men.

Debating the Cable Bill in Congress, speakers recognised that serious complications (in particular regarding property rights) were created by marital denaturalisation. As in other countries, anecdotes about women affected by the law featured prominently. Again, as elsewhere, the position of socially prominent women was raised, offering, in this context, an opportunity to caricature the personal circumstances of individuals. Such cases also provided an avenue for amplifying the claim that foreign marriage was, for a woman, an act of disallegiance. American heiresses with impoverished, but titled foreign husbands were a particular target for opponents of reform.[15]

companion provision had been inserted in the Cable Act. Hover, 'Citizenship of Women in the United States', 700.

14 Reeves, 'Nationality of Married Women', 99.

15 They were not an imaginary class. According to one source, as at 1914, there were 60 British peers and 40 younger sons of peers married to wealthy American women. Kathleen Burke, *Old World, New World: Great Britain and America from the Beginning* (Atlantic Monthly Press, 2008).

The proposition that such women suffered an injustice in their loss of citizenship was dismissed. Oklahoma Congressman, Manuel Herrick, claimed that it was 'a well-known fact that no American farmer's daughter, no American labourer's daughter, no small business man's daughter marries a foreigner'. Only the wealthy did, he said, only the members of the 'profiteer class' who little value their American heritage. They 'coin American citizenship into gold, which they may use to purchase some Count No Account, some degenerate from over the seas'.[16] There was laughter from the House.

Other Congressmen, less comically, emphasised the unity of the family, and the desirability of retaining the law that allowed alien wives to naturalise. New York Congressman, Meyer London (suggesting a compromise amendment that would provide that an alien woman who married an American citizen should still become a citizen, unless she renounced her American citizenship within ninety days) described the proposed legislation as 'a piece of political candy that is being given to the women' who were campaigning for citizenship equality.[17] His objection, he said, was to the withdrawal of automatic marital naturalisation; that was the 'poisoned candy' that would be handed out to 'millions of poor devils who are taking care of their children and of their husbands, and who make happy homes'.[18]

Defending his Bill, Congressman Cable agreed that 'the rich American woman who marries a title and lives abroad should cease to have the privileges and benefits of an American citizen', but, he said, there were many American 'girls' married to foreigners who continued to live in America. 'Their loyalty and fidelity' remained with America: 'An American citizen who marries an alien girl still retains his citizenship; so also should the American girl who marries the alien man. We should not withdraw our country's protection from these natural-born American women'.[19] Examples were given of individual women, from honourable, patriotic families, and with impeccable personal qualities, who had suffered for the mere fact of marriage. As we saw in Chapter 4, Augusta De Haven-Alten, an American-born daughter of a United States Naval Captain (as the press reported) had married a German in 1886, and had lost her citizenship twenty-one years later following the passage of the Expatriation

[16] United States, House of Representatives, *Congressional Record*, 20 June 1922, 9053.
[17] United States, House of Representatives, *Congressional Record*, 20 June 1922, 9060.
[18] United States, House of Representatives, *Congressional Record*, 20 June 1922, 9060.
[19] United States, House of Representatives, *Congressional Record*, 20 June 1922, 9046.

Act.[20] In the war, her American property had been seized by the Alien Custodian: 'Reduced from wealth and luxury to absolute poverty, this woman, who had never ceased to be an American at heart, came here to appeal to the chivalry of the American Congress to restore her citizenship'.[21] Individual 'corrections' through Acts of Congress, such as that of April 1920 by which her citizenship was restored, would no longer be needed, so Congress was told, if the new Bill were passed.

These anecdotes gave human colour to the argument over policy. But, importantly, as in 1907, the debate also rested on claims (albeit not necessarily well-informed) about international trends. Support or opposition was repeatedly justified in such terms. Responding to opponents in the House, Cable emphasised the international context, observing, among other things, that a Private Member's Bill proposing to repeal marital denaturalisation (the unsuccessful Nationality of Married Women Bill) had been introduced into the British House of Commons, and that the International Council of Women, meeting in 1920 in Copenhagen, had passed a resolution supporting women's independent citizenship. The French Senate, he added, had recently introduced a Bill providing that French women who married aliens retained their French citizenship unless they made a formal declaration that they preferred to take the nationality of their husband.[22]

The international context was also represented as grounds for opposing Cable's Bill. New York Congressman, Ogden Mills, asserted that marital denaturalisation was still practised in most countries, and that it was the 'universal practice' that a woman's home was her husband's home (American men who married foreign women, he said, 'stay at home'). The proposition that women who married foreign men could keep their native citizenship violated 'all existing legal notions, and . . . the essential principle of family unity'.[23]

The international perspective was reaffirmed in 1934, with the passage of the 'Equalization' Act[24] which gave American women the same right as

[20] Or had been assumed to have lost it, by virtue of marital naturalisation and residence in another country. Hover, 'Citizenship of Women in the United States', 700.

[21] United States, House of Representatives, *Congressional Record*, 20 June 1922, 9041.

[22] United States, House of Representatives, *Congressional Record*, 20 June 1922, 9046.

[23] United States, House of Representatives, *Congressional Record*, 20 June 1922, 9061.

[24] Act of May 24, 1934. The Act also gave equal rights to women and men with foreign spouses to make a declaration of renunciation of citizenship, and equal conditions for spouses governing naturalisation eligibility, including the same residency requirement of three years (formerly, after 1922, one year for foreign wives). The effect of the equal

men to transmit citizenship to their children, and allowed husbands and wives both to renounce their citizenship and to become naturalised on the same terms (with the same residency test). A Memorandum setting out the proposed changes and their reasons focused less on principles of equality and American values than on international comparisons: lists were offered of countries that had 'radically' amended their laws to give women equality in citizenship with men,[25] as well as relatively few (so it was claimed, albeit not entirely accurately) that still compelled their women citizens to assume their husbands' nationality. 'The constant trend of world legislation on nationality is toward the full recognition of the right of equality in nationality for both men and women', said one Congressman.[26] It was further noted that an Equal Nationality Treaty, signed by the twenty-one nations of the Pan American Union in Montevideo (discussed in Chapter 6), had committed its members to equality for women in all matters to do with nationality, citizenship and naturalisation. In addition, at least thirteen countries, it was said, already gave mothers the same right as fathers to transmit citizenship to their children.

As in 1922, critics also sought to situate the proposed measures in the international context: '[D]oes it not run counter to the laws of all the

residency rule, one contemporary observed, would in fact be unequally 'harsh' for women, since many countries still applied marital denaturalisation to their out-marrying women citizens. As the United States had not adopted the Hague Convention statelessness pre-emption provisions, the law would render such women stateless for at least a three year period. Lester B. Orfield, 'The Citizenship Act of 1934' (1934–5) 99 *Chicago Law Review* 111.

25 The Memorandum listed: Great Britain, Canada, France, Spain, Norway, Sweden, Denmark, Finland, Iceland, Belgium, Estonia, Rumania, Jugoslavia (sic), Turkey, China, Persia and Albania. It also listed thirteen countries that allowed mothers to transmit citizenship on all equal basis. 'Only' twenty-two countries of 'the 77 principal countries of the world', it noted, compelled their women citizens to assume the nationality of the alien husband. These were: Afghanistan, Bolivia, Czech, Germany, Australia, British India, Irish Free State, Newfoundland, New Zealand, South Africa, Haiti, Hedjaz (sic), Honduras, Hungary, Iraq, Liechtenstein, Luxembourg, Netherlands, Palestine, San Marino, Transjordania, Vatican City – 'but in several of these countries laws giving men and women equal nationality rights are now being drafted'. Of the remaining fifty-five countries 'of the civilized world', fourteen gave their women citizens 'the absolute right to retain their nationality under all circumstances on marriage to an alien'. Six more – Albania, Belgium, Estonia, Guatemala, Rumania and Jugoslavia – gave a woman citizen the right to retain her nationality upon alien marriage if she took legal action to preserve it. Of the remaining thirty-five countries, women citizens lost their nationality on marriage only under certain circumstances.

26 United States, House of Representatives, *Congressional Record*, 25 April 1934, 7332 (Mr Dickstein).

great powers of the world affecting nationality', one Congressman asked; 'Is it not the law in all of the first-class powers that the father transmits his nationality to the child?'[27] Would not the Bill create problems of dual nationality? The first objection was met with lists of countries that practised citizenship equality, and the second by the observation that the problem could be 'settled only by treaty action between nations'; however, it was added, 'the fact that this complication exists – for men as well as women – is no reason for any country, under its own laws, to deny justice and equality to women'.[28] Against this sweeping international landscape, individual women's circumstances and choices were once more depicted. Again, as in 1922, the image of wealth marrying title was raised, and the sneer repeated: 'many of these women who marry foreigners deserve no sympathy when they find that they have bargained for a count and get a no account'. But the tone was less vehement. 'Still', said Congressman Jenkins, 'there are, no doubt, some deserving cases. I am sure that some of the women . . . will be American citizens of the best kind'.[29] By 1934, there were women in Congress. Congresswoman Edith Rogers of Massachusetts (who reminded them that her late husband had introduced the Cable Bill in 1922) declared that 'the men of the United States are fairer and kinder to the women of their country than are the men of any other nation'. Any Member of the House, she said, who had a daughter married to a foreigner ('of course he would prefer to have her marry a citizen of the United States') 'would want his grandchild to become an American citizen'.[30]

The change of heart which began with the 1922 Act was not driven purely by sympathy for American-born women who found themselves stripped of their citizenship. As with many citizenship equality campaigners, Cable had also deprecated the automatic conferral of citizenship upon alien women who married American citizens. Such women, he pointed out, were not required to speak English or to know American customs or law. They did not 'even have to renounce allegiance to [their] foreign ruler and take the oath of allegiance to Uncle Sam'. Conversely (since married women were still ineligible to naturalise in their own right), a married foreign woman who had lived in America for many years and had become loyal could not become an American citizen unless her husband

[27] United States, House of Representatives, *Congressional Record*, 1934, 7330–1 (Mr Cox).
[28] United States, House of Representatives, *Congressional Record*, 1934, 7332 (Mr Dickstein).
[29] United States, House of Representatives, *Congressional Record*, 1934, 7339 (Mr Jenkins).
[30] United States, House of Representatives, *Congressional Record*, 1934, 7344.

was naturalised. Such cases, Cable said, also meant that the 'mother's influence and guidance [are] lost to the family without the education that naturalization proceedings provide and require'.[31]

Ending marital naturalisation, it appears, was an equally strong incentive for repeal of conditional marital citizenship, and a more consistent theme among American citizenship equality campaigns than in Britain and at least some of its Dominions. In Canada, however, opposition to the marital naturalisation of immigrant wives was also strongly focused on their acquisition of British nationality (under the Canadian law of 1881 that followed the British Act of 1870). But Canada, locked into a 'common code' of nationality law with the rest of the British Commonwealth (as we see below) could not simply repeal such laws as the Americans had done. Instead, after 1918 (when Canadian women were federally enfranchised) the legislative 'solution' was to place restrictions on the franchise, in order to qualify the access of uneducated women to the vote.[32]

As Bredbenner has demonstrated, Americans (and Canadians) were increasingly anxious about undesirable immigration in the early decades of the twentieth century, and laws imposing restrictions on immigration from Asian countries and on the naturalisation of Asian immigrants were adopted. But this trend was not new. America's marital naturalisation law of 1855 had already provided for automatic naturalisation of alien wives only in cases where the woman was eligible for naturalisation, and the 1907 Expatriation Act had not altered this condition. The Cable Act had ensured that Asian wives of American citizens and American-born wives of Asian men were not eligible to take advantage of the new law, but the racial disqualification, as noted, was repealed in 1931. The principal concern in Congressional debates in 1922 appears to have been less about the race of wives gaining citizenship, than about the in-marrying woman's qualifications for American patriotism. Certainly, members of 'undesirable' races were regarded as unsuited to patriotism, but repeatedly, the likely lack of allegiance of foreign women in general was stressed. Asian women were not singled out for presumed disallegiance. Indeed, the nationality most frequently cited with suspicion and as underserving of American citizenship was German.

Notwithstanding these concerns, at least until 1922, the law made no distinction between American-born women of any race, or between those who resided in the United States and those who lived in foreign

[31] United States, House of Representatives, *Congressional Record*, 20 June 1922, 9045.

[32] Girard, "If two ride a horse", 28.

countries, with respect to loss of citizenship upon marriage to a foreign man. But, as the British Nationality and Status of Aliens Act had done in 1914, regarding the resumption of British nationality by widows and divorcees of foreign men, the re-naturalisation requirement in the 1922 Act provided a 'filter', sifting out the women, originally American citizens under the Fourteenth Amendment, who were considered undesirable for reasons additional to having married a foreign man. It was an opportunistic means of achieving what the original denaturalisation law had missed. It also allowed for a woman's commitment to her re-acquired American citizenship to be demonstrated by her residence in her country. The problem that the Cable Act appeared designed primarily to correct was the loss of citizenship to the (presumptively) allegiant American woman.

The residency test for the restoration of American citizenship by married women created lingering dilemmas. Nationality 'gives a warrant to the government of one country to protect the person and property of its nationals in another country',[33] wrote one international lawyer in 1930, and, under principles of diplomatic protection, a state may claim redress for an injury caused by another state to one of its nationals. The 'rule of continuous nationality', however, required the claimant state 'to prove that the injured national remained its national after the injury itself and up to the date of the presentation of the claim'.[34] Laws that made nationality contingent on residence were implicated in this rule. An individual whose citizenship was presumed to have ceased (even if it was merely suspended) became disentitled to the treaty rights that otherwise extended to nationals. The jurisdiction of international claims commissions and arbitral tribunals governing disputes between the United States and other countries, for example, did not extend to Americans whose citizenship was presumed to have ceased during overseas residence.

Addressing this issue, Margaret Lambie asked: 'Are native [born] Americans ever liable to a presumption of cessation of citizenship' under these laws?[35] Any American born woman, married to a non-citizen, she noted, 'might find herself barred from having her claim presented, even though she had taken no steps to divest herself of her American citizenship, and had not been divested of it under the laws of the United States'. Although

[33] Margaret Lambie, 'Presumption of Cessation of Citizenship: Its Effect on International Claims' (1930) 24 *American Journal of International Law* 264, 271.

[34] United Nations, Draft Articles on Diplomatic Protection. *Yearbook of the International Law Commission*, 2006, Vol II, Part Two.

[35] Lambie, 'Presumption of Cessation of Citizenship', 277.

such a woman was entitled to regain her citizenship if she returned for permanent residence in the United States, 'apparently no claim of hers having arisen when a presumption under that Act was against her may ever be presented to an international claims tribunal'. Given that, in the words of a Commissioner of the General Claims Commission, 'the status of a great number of parents and children, as well as property rights... must have been affected... over a long person of time', there were particular ramifications for married women.[36]

In short, for a time at least, the Cable Act (and its successors) left American women vulnerable to legal complications and potential disadvantage arising from their altered citizenship status. But the principal impact was felt by women in and from other countries. The Act created a cascade of problems. The fact that the United States no longer naturalised 'in-marrying' foreign women meant that women who married American men, but whose country still denaturalised its 'out-marrying' women, became stateless. Statelessness was already recognised as an outcome of asymmetrical conditional marital nationality laws, but the dramatic increase in numbers of cases following the Act's passage prompted the international community to recognise married women's nationality as an international issue. The issue had long attracted international or transnational attention, but in 1920s it generated an unprecedented level of interest and debate. Multiple initiatives were undertaken, and numerous proposals circulated, culminating in the provisions governing married women's nationality that were inserted in the League of Nations Nationality Convention, adopted in The Hague in 1930. (We will see this in Chapter 6.)

Britain and the Dominions

Unlike many other countries, Britain and its Dominions retained their conditional marital nationality laws until after the Second World War. This did not, however, signal lack of sympathy for the principle of citizenship equality or inattention to the legal framework for achieving it. The topic of married women's nationality appeared on the agenda of almost all Imperial Conferences[37] after the First World War: in 1917 (the Imperial War Conference), 1918, 1921, 1923, 1926 (with a sub-committee

[36] Lambie, ibid, 277.

[37] The Imperial Conferences were meetings of government representatives of Britain and the Dominions, regularised in 1907 for the purpose of discussing questions of common

dedicated to the subject), 1930 and 1937. It was the first item at a Special Conference on Nationality and Naturalization in 1918, and a major item at a second Special Conference on Nationality in 1921. It was the subject of a parliamentary committee in 1923 and of a committee at the Conference of Commonwealth Prime Ministers in 1935. It was discussed at the 1929 Expert Conference on the Operation of Dominion Legislation, at the 1932 Imperial Economic Conference (held in Ottawa) and by the 1947 Commonwealth Expert Committee on Nationality.

These gatherings included official representatives – variously, Prime Ministers, Ministers of State, politicians, and senior administrators – from around the self-governing states of the Empire (and on occasion, from certain colonies). Support was repeatedly expressed for the principle of citizenship equality, and many representatives favoured reform of the law governing married women's nationality. But just as repeatedly, there were objections, and even when something resembling consensus on a principle was reached, stalemate resulted from the attempt to secure agreement on how reform of the law might be achieved. Unanimity was repeatedly elusive.

At the 1918 Special Conference on Nationality and Naturalization, delegates, still very uncertain of the scope of the issue or the facts of the relevant laws, identified the key matters concerning married women's nationality that would dog governments and lead to frustration and stalemate over the next three decades. A Home Office memorandum submitted to the Conference suggested that

> a reasonable course to take, without too many practical difficulties would be to allow women on marriage to make [a] declaration within one month either before or after date of marriage that they desire to retain their nationality of origin, to be registered with [the Home Office]. Also, that British woman who retains her nationality after marriage to [an] alien will not be entitled to diplomatic protection outside [the] Empire; and alien born woman who retains her nationality after marriage to [a] British man will not be entitled to be regarded by British Authorities anywhere as British. Women already married and resident in the Empire should have [a] period of, say, 6 months, after end of war to make similar declaration.[38]

interest among the self-governing parts of the Empire. From 1921, the Conference also became the forum for discussing imperial foreign policy.

[38] UK National Archives, CO 323/778: 'Nationality and Naturalization': Special Conference. 'Memorandum prepared in the Home Office on the subject of the Nationality of Married Women for consideration by members of the Conference', 1918.

The Conference, however, reached no agreement on these proposals. Canadian representative, High Commissioner to the United Kingdom, Sir George Perley, spoke of Canada's particular interest in the subject of married women's nationality, now heightened by the acquisition by Canadian women of the right to vote. He expressed the distinctive Canadian concern: that foreign women acquired British subject status by marital naturalisation. Such women now enjoyed a right that Canadian women with foreign husbands did not: 'I do not know how you managed in Australia', he commented, 'where the women have had votes for a good deal longer'.[39] The New Zealand representative, Sir Joseph Ward, replied that his country had had universal suffrage for '22 years or more' (it was actually twenty-five years) and 'all the women vote'. But, responding to a further question, Ward revealed the general confusion about the status of New Zealand nationality law: 'In practice we do not follow what is the Law here at present, that if a man marries a foreigner she becomes the subject of the same country as her husband – not in the matter of voting'. Quizzed further, he claimed never to have heard the issue of a married woman's denaturalisation raised in regard to voting. British representative from the Home Office, Sir John Pedder, pointed out that, under the 1914 law, a British woman whose husband was naturalised in foreign nationality now had the right to retain her British nationality. 'That is quite new in English Law, is it not?' asked the Australian representative, Solicitor-General, Robert Garran. There was a good deal to be said for citizenship equality claim, Garran added, but it was a difficult question, involving, among other things, the issue of dual nationality in the one household.

Dual nationality, threats to family unity, the tension between nationality and political rights, and the strain placed on the policy of conditional marital nationality by incremental concessions in favour of women's independent citizenship, were hurdles to surmount, but again and again, their resolution appeared to raise further obstacles. In an atmosphere of general uncertainty about the current law regarding women's citizenship, the Conference took a decision that would be repeated up to the end of the Second World War: to gather more evidence, write a memo, consult among the Dominions, and plan a further meeting. Perhaps they might reconvene in a fortnight, the Home Office representative suggested;

[39] UK National Archives, HO 45/11902: 'Nationality of Married Women'. Minutes of Proceedings at a Special Conference' [on] Nationality and Naturalization. Held at Home Office, 31 July 1918.

perhaps they might also meet with a deputation of women, 'and then we shall be carrying out our promise to them'. Against one member's suggestion that the meeting could be 'done vicariously', the Home Secretary objected: 'I expect the women would like to exercise their persuasive powers on you as well as on me'. 'Then, if possible', he concluded, without identifying any date, 'we will meet again'.

In a memo on the nationality of married women prepared by the Home Office for the 1929 Conference on the Operation of Dominion Legislation, sympathy for the goal of citizenship equality was expressed, but again the problems to which it would be expected to give rise were stressed: dual nationality, conflicts of law, diplomatic clashes, 'international friction', risks to the unity of family life. And, it was added, in cases of dual nationality, in the event of war, a woman 'would almost inevitably find herself in the unfortunate position of having to commit acts which would legally amount to high treason to one or other of the two countries of which she was a national'.[40]

The conferences and meetings were inevitable targets for the campaign for citizenship equality, and numerous representations from citizenship equality advocates were made in the lead-up to and during their deliberations. At the Imperial Conference of 1926, the Report of Nationality Committee commented that '[v]ery serious pressure [was being] brought to bear in this country and, no doubt, in other parts of the Empire from Women's Societies urging that women of British nationality by birth should not lose that nationality on marriage'. It noted, however, that the demand gave rise to serious practical difficulties:

> The ideal would be that every person should have one, and no person should have more than one, nationality; whereas, in view of the present state of nationality law of most countries, the permission to married women to retain their original nationality would give rise to a large number of persons having two nationalities.[41]

It too recommended that the question should be postponed pending further discussion at a planned future conference on Dominion legislation.

Domestic initiatives were equally inconclusive. In 1923, one year after the passage of the Cable Act in the United States, the British Parliament appointed a joint select committee to examine British law regarding the

[40] UK National Archives, HO 45/20163, 'Conference on the Operation of Dominion Legislation'.

[41] UK National Archives, HO 45/20163, 'Conference on the Operation of Dominion Legislation', Minutes, 17 October 1929.

nationality of married women, the legal and practical issues involved in the possession by a husband and wife of the same or of different nationalities, and the operation of the laws of foreign countries. It was asked to report on 'what, if any, alteration of the British Law is desirable'.[42] The Committee (five members each of the House of Commons and the House of Lords) gathered copious evidence and considered many proposals to amend the current law. It acknowledged the 'inconveniences' created by the Cable Act, which 'though only dating from September 1922', had 'by creating international divergence in the subject of nationality already caused serious embarrassment' to Britain 'in the matter of passport facilities'.[43] But this Committee, too, could not reach a consensus, and made no recommendations. A Chairman's Report (expressing the view of the Lords) found unconvincing the argument that the world trend was towards change, and expressed the opinion 'that it will be time enough to consider a change in British law . . . when the majority of the more important States have signified their readiness to adopt the principle of a woman's nationality being unaffected by her marriage'. Despite the growing demands of women's equality campaigners, the Lords concluded that they could not

> overlook the fact that by marriage a woman is merged in the unit of the family, and that within the family it is at present the husband who is head, who bears its legal responsibilities . . . and whose occupation in most cases is the decisive factor as to where that home is to be established, and who among other things gives his nationality to the children. It is their opinion therefore that in this important sphere of family life the nationality of the husband should be the governing factor and determine the nationality of the wife.[44]

Britain's 'unique position' in having British communities in various non-Empire countries that wished to maintain their British identity was also emphasised. If the proposed amendment to the law governing a woman's marital citizenship were adopted, the Report stated, the alien wife of a British subject living abroad would not acquire British nationality and would be ineligible for naturalisation. The family's British identity would soon be lost. It concluded: 'If two ride a horse one must ride in front'.[45] Notwithstanding this restatement of the law as if it were the reason for

[42] *Report by the Select Committee appointed to join with a Committee of the House of Commons on The Nationality of Married Women*, His Majesty's Stationery Office, London, 1923 (ii).

[43] *Report by the Select Committee*, ibid, xvi.

[44] *Report by the Select Committee*, ibid.

[45] *Report by the Select Committee*, ibid.

the law (and the inapposite metaphor), the Committee did recognise one 'special case' where amendment was needed: where the law gave rise to statelessness, for example, where a British woman married an American citizen.[46]

The Report did not settle the matter. The Committee was split, and a minority report (authored by Sir John Butcher) was submitted, recommending that both marital naturalisation and marital denaturalisation should be repealed, and that married women should be allowed a choice of nationality, either, in the case of the British wife of an alien, by making a declaration of alienage, or in the case the foreign wife of a British subject, by applying for expedited naturalisation: 'We are unable to accept the main argument – that change would impair family and matrimonial harmony'. The Report conceded that inconveniences might arise in the home in cases where a couple held different nationalities, but differences of religion or political opinion might also lead to disturbances:

> No one proposes compulsorily to impose on a married woman the religion of her husband . . . But you can no more compel a woman on her marriage to surrender her national sentiment than you can compel her to surrender her religion.

Butcher's Report pointed out that there was 'nothing to show that matrimonial harmony was disturbed prior to 1870', that there were no references to the unity of family in the 1869 Royal Commission report which had led to the inclusion of marital denaturalisation in the Naturalization Act of 1870, and that jurists were divided on the general principle governing married women's nationality. There was, he wrote, also no evidence of the inconveniences or complications with foreign states that other members of the Committee claimed to arise in the absence of single family nationality. The idea that Britain should wait until there was general agreement among nations on change was 'entirely contrary to the principle on which this country has proceeded in adapting our naturalisation laws to altered circumstances'.[47]

Individual members of Parliament, including Butcher, had already begun a campaign to amend the law, and from 1922 for the next eleven years, the Private Member's Nationality of Married Women Bill (drafted by the National Council of Women[48]) would be presented to the House of

[46] This was conceded at other meetings. UK National Archives, HO 45/20163, 'Conference on the Operation of Dominion Legislation'.

[47] *Report by the Select Committee*, xxi.

[48] Baldwin, 'Subject to Empire', 522.

Commons by Conservative and Labour Members alike: Sir John Butcher 1922; Ellen Wilkinson 1928; Captain Victor Cazalet 1930; Dr Ethel Bentham 1931; Sir John Sandeman Allen 1933. The Bill, prepared in essentially the same form on each occasion, proposed that a British woman should not lose her British nationality by marriage with an alien; that a British woman who had already lost her British nationality by marriage with an alien should be deemed to be a British subject unless she made a declaration of alienage within a certain period; that an alien woman should not become a British subject by marriage with a British subject; that a woman who was already a British subject by marriage should continue to be a British subject unless she made a declaration of alienage; and, that a woman, notwithstanding her marriage, should be competent to apply to receive a certificate of naturalisation in her own right.

Although the Bill was repeatedly defeated, it received strong, sometimes passionate support from individual members of parliament. The existential, and not merely the practical impact of denaturalisation, was well understood. Ethel Bentham, for example, evoked the 'endless personal hardships and injustices' to which the law gave rise: 'it very often increases and endangers the domestic relations and happiness of families', she said, 'and it definitely imposes upon women a condition of inferiority as citizens which they resent more emphatically with every month that passes'.[49]

There were further expressions of official support for the principle of citizenship equality. In February 1925, the House of Commons resolved: 'That, in the opinion of this House, a British woman should not lose or be deemed to lose her nationality by the mere act of marriage with an alien, but it should be open to her to make a declaration of alienage'. In 1931, at the League of Nations Assembly, the British government delegate, Dame Edith Lyttelton, read a declaration:

> The British Government considers that it is right that all disabilities of married women in matters of nationality should be removed, and that so far as nationality is concerned, a married woman should be in the same position as a man, married or unmarried, or any single woman.

Similar developments were taking place in the Dominions. In 1926, the Australian House of Representatives passed an identical resolution to that of the House of Commons. Its mover, John Duncan-Hughes, spoke at length about the changes that were occurring in marital nationality laws

[49] United Kingdom, House of Commons, *Debates*, 28 November 1930, 1675.

in other countries, the decline of the rule of inalienability of allegiance, the advance of women's political and legal rights, the 'tremendous service' rendered by women during the war, and the claims of 'ordinary justice':

> [I]t is a terrible situation in which to put a woman who desires to marry a man who was not born under the English flag, to say to her that she must forfeit her nationality in order to do so, that she must forfeit all her civic rights, and possibly her right to property. I go a step further. I do not think it is desirable . . . that we should force our women against their will out of our community or nation . . . The people of a country who have loyal and cordial feelings towards it should be regarded as a national asset.[50]

The resolution's seconder, Edward Mann, dismissed objections that problems would arise in international relations if women were given a choice regarding their post-marital nationality (the British, he said, must have considered this before they passed their own resolution) or in family relations (women, he said, were as capable as men of determining this). He acknowledged the weight of opinion behind the motion, the numerous national and international women's organisations that supported it and the democratic right of women to have their demands heard. As evidence for the advancement of women's legal equality, he made reference to the British Sex Disqualification (Removal) Act of 1919, which protected women against disqualification 'by sex or marriage' from exercising public functions or working in civil professions. One Member's cry, that '[i]f British women married men of their own race there would be no trouble', found no echo, but hints in several other Members' responses, noting the imperative of imperial uniformity in nationality laws, would prove more telling. This imperative, as noted, would be the decisive stumbling block for reform over the next twenty years.

None of the problems identified in any of the British discussions or reports was unique to Britain. Other countries, faced with similar obstacles, managed to undertake at least some degree of reform in their marital nationality laws. The special obstacle facing the British was the imperial idea that there should be a single, reciprocally recognised status of British subject: a 'common code' of nationality law. Notwithstanding the multiple expressions of sympathy for the principle of citizenship equality,[51]

[50] Commonwealth of Australia, House of Representatives, *Debates*, 4 February 1926, 682.

[51] It was the government and members of parliament who were most sympathetic. Senior civil servants were much less so; indeed, they frequently raised objections or identified obstacles to proposed alterations to the policy. M. Page Baldwin has also noted this: Baldwin, 'Subject to Empire'. Prior to the Imperial Conference of 1921, for example,

Britain and its Dominions remained deadlocked. Although nationality law was a matter for individual Dominion parliaments, commitment to the common code meant (so it was understood) that any changes to any member country's laws could only occur if the others unanimously agreed to amend their laws accordingly. (Although technically this was not the case in the international scene, the imperial stalemate represented in miniature the international landscape in this period.)

Even before the passage of the BNSA Act in 1914, the Dominions had followed British policy regarding women's nationality in laws governing local naturalisation, and in assumptions in their common law. The BNSA Act specifically stated that its naturalisation provisions only applied if Dominion legislation adopted them.[52] However, in providing for a scheme of 'imperial naturalisation' (so that naturalisation in any part of the Empire would be recognised across the whole Empire) the law created increased pressure for conformity in nationality laws, and this extended to policy governing the nationality of married women. By the end of the 1920s, with the exception of the Irish Free State, the Dominions had, one by one, adopted or copied those relevant parts of the BNSA Act in their own legislation.[53] The British government, with the agreement of the Dominions (placed on record at the Imperial Conference, in 1930) maintained that:

> It is of the greatest importance that no member of the [British] Commonwealth should introduce legislation on the subject of the 'common status' without previous consultation and agreement with the other members... and if the Parliament at Westminster were to legislate on this

internal Home Office and Colonial Office memos noted that nationality questions (second generation citizenship, dual nationality and the nationality of married women) had been held over from the 1918 Imperial War Conference, but expressed the hope that these could be given low priority, or left off the agenda at the 1921 conference: 'There is no great urgency about the questions but a certain amount of pressure is brought from time to time in Parliament and elsewhere by persons who think (loosely and without knowledge) that there are all sorts of points in which the British Nationality law requires drastic revision... ' (J.P [Sir John Pedder] 12/2/21). UK National Archives, HO 45/11902 'Nationality of Married Women'.

52 This provision did not appear in Part III governing the nationality of married women, thus creating some confusion over whether Part III was intended to apply around the Empire without the necessity of local adoption. The consensus emerged, however, that it did not apply of its own force.

53 Canada's Naturalization Act of 1914; Newfoundland's Consolidated Statutes of 1916; Australia's Nationality Act of 1920; New Zealand's British Nationality and Status of Aliens (in New Zealand) Act of 1923; South Africa's British Nationality in the Union and Naturalization and Status of Aliens Act, 1926.

> subject independently and with the knowledge that the other members of the Commonwealth would not legislate similarly, this would be not only a breach of the agreement reached at the Imperial Conference but also a precedent for independent legislation by any Dominion which might involve a still more serious breach of the principle of uniformity.[54]

With this commitment in the background, and despite the record of constant stalemate, proposals for women's equal citizenship were repeatedly circulated in the hope that these might prove agreeable to all.

The Commonwealth post-Hague

The Imperial Conference of 1930, like its predecessors, failed to reach agreement on reform of marital nationality law, but that year marked a major change in the international perspective. The Hague Convention on Nationality had been adopted, including Articles designed to pre-empt statelessness among women who were married to alien men, at the same time as preserving the policy of conditional marital nationality. (These are discussed further in Chapter 6.) The Imperial Conference concluded that it could not make 'any recommendation for the substantive amendment of the law' other than to adopt the Articles of the Convention. Adoption by one or more members of British Commonwealth of further measures would be a 'breach of the principle of unanimity to which His Majesty's Government . . . attach the highest importance':

> Divergencies (sic) of law in different parts of the Commonwealth on the subject of the nationality of married women could not be regarded as minor provisions designed to meet particular local conditions. The very fact that the question has aroused so much controversy and given rise to differences of opinion which it has not been possible, in spite of prolonged efforts, to reconcile, shows that this matter cannot be regarded as a minor issue, but must be treated as a matter of principle.[55]

The Hague Nationality Convention, however, gave the imperial representatives a baseline for consensus, and Canada quickly acted on it, adopting the statelessness pre-emption provisions, in anticipation that the rest of the Dominions would follow suit. In addition, the Imperial Conference introduced a new point of permissible differentiation in policy. While it

[54] UK National Archives, HO 45/15147: 'Nationality of Married Women'.

[55] National Archives of Australia, Series A435, 1948/4/102, 'Imperial Conference 1937' (extract of record of the Imperial Conference 1930).

had agreed not to take any action affecting the common nationality code, its Report emphasised that the agreement

> clearly does not debar any member of the Commonwealth [of nations], who desires to do so, from conferring local rights within its territory on British-born women who have ceased to be British subjects by marriage with an alien. The question of the law relating to the status of British subject is quite distinct from that of the law relating to the enjoyment of local rights, and a law conferring local rights on women who do not possess the status of British subject is not a matter for consultation between members of the Commonwealth.[56]

Still, proposals for further reform circulated. A British government memorandum on the Nationality of Married Women circulated to the Dominions in July 1931, set out further alternatives for their consideration: that British women should not to lose their nationality by marriage whether or not they acquired their husband's nationality; that alien women should not automatically acquire British nationality by marriage to a British subject; that '(as the law already in substance provides)' the wife of a British subject should not automatically cease to be a British subject if her husband acquired a foreign nationality; that when an alien was naturalised as a British subject, his wife should not automatically become a British subject; that a foreign wife should be eligible to apply for naturalisation under the ordinary statutory conditions; that 'where a woman who remains British notwithstanding her marriage with an alien acquires foreign nationality by a voluntary and formal act of her own she shall thereupon cease to be a British subject'; that a woman who had lost British nationality by marriage should be eligible to make a declaration within limited time that she wished to resume her British nationality.[57]

Once again, these proposals, revealing the labyrinthine complexity of conditional marital nationality, were to prove incapable of attracting

[56] National Archives of Australia, Series A435, 1948/4/102: 'Imperial Conference 1937' (extract of record of the Imperial Conference 1930). Emphasis (underlining) in the original.

[57] UK National Archives, HO 45/15147: 'Nationality of Married Women'. The memorandum stated that the government was not prepared to accept a proposal from women's organisations that the nationality of children should be derived from a parent without giving preference to one parent over another, 'the consequences of which may not have been fully realised by its authors. Not only would the child of a mixed marriage in every case possess two nationalities under the *jus sanguinis* (sic), but there will be not a few cases where the child would possess three nationalities, e.g. if it were born in a country where the jus soli applies, of parents of different nationalities, neither being the nationality of the country where the child is born'.

unanimous support. A deputation of citizenship equality campaigners in 1932 was informed by the Home Secretary that there was 'at present no prospect of [the Dominions] being persuaded to change their opinions' and that it was not possible for Britain to pass legislation limited to Britain since Cabinet was in favour of uniform national law throughout the Commonwealth. There were four possible courses, they were told: (1) Indefinite postponement of the question; (2) Postponement, to give women's organisations the opportunity to 'carry out propaganda' in the Dominions in the attempt to persuade them to change their minds; (3) Legislation to provide that British-born women in the United Kingdom would not be treated as aliens for the right to vote or stand for Parliament (the Home Secretary observed that he 'could not promise approval' on this[58]); and finally (4) legislation giving effect to the Hague Convention (that is, repealing marital denaturalisation only in cases where a woman did not automatically acquire the nationality of her husband), perhaps combined with (3).[59]

One member of the deputation, Maria Oglivie Gordon (from the National Union of Women Workers) assured the Home Secretary that they appreciated the inter-Imperial difficulty, but insisted that a long postponement was undesirable, in light of the fact that so many British women were suffering hardships. Chrystal Macmillan pointed out that the existing law already recognised special cases (for example, the retention of British nationality by a wife if her husband became naturalised abroad), and she noted that Canada had legislated to give effect to the Hague Convention and, in doing so, 'had already created an exception from the principle of uniformity throughout the Commonwealth'.[60] The proposal to restore political rights to denaturalised British-born wives, Oglivie

[58] At the UK Conference on the Operation of Dominion Legislation in 1929 a proposal was noted for 'a provision under which the general law relating the British nationality should remain unaltered, but that each part of the Empire should be at liberty to provide, if it wishes, that a woman of British nationality by origin, notwithstanding her marriage to an alien . . . retain in such part such civil and political rights as she would otherwise have possessed'. In 1918, the Canadian House of Commons had discussed a similar proposal, without resolution. UK National Archives, HO 45/20163: 'Conference on the Operation of Dominion Legislation'. Memorandum on Nationality of Married Women. The suggestion, as we shall see, would attract the interest of at least some of the Dominions.

[59] UK National Archives, HO 45/15147: 'Nationality of Married Women' 'Note of Deputation received 14 March 1932'.

[60] Canada, responded the Home Secretary, was relying on the United Kingdom and other Dominions to pass similar legislation.

Gordon said, 'would be quite inadequate'. As for the Hague Convention option, she commented, they were not in a position to say whether the women's organisations would accept it, but they might make enquiries. But the Convention, Macmillan added, 'was entirely irrelevant to their demands as it did not touch the question of principle'.[61]

The women already knew that the majority of women's organisation did not support the limited option of giving effect to the Hague Convention, and Macmillan's analysis was representative of their reasons. The principle was citizenship equality. The Convention's solution to statelessness still retained the idea that married women's nationality was conditional and therefore, so the campaigners understood, inferior. In return, the Home Secretary already knew that nothing more would be conceded. One month before the meeting with the deputation, an Inter-Departmental meeting of the British Dominion Office, Foreign Office and Home Office on the nationality of married women, had reached the conclusion that, from an administrative point of view, to legislate as Canada had done in 1931 'is the course least open to objection'. It recognised that increasing administrative inconvenience and practical difficulties would arise, but concluded that this could not be 'regarded as a decisive argument against the law'. To the meeting's minutes, a handwritten note was added:

> If the whole world had maintained the principle that husband and wife had one nationality, the difficulties in practice . . . would either not have arisen or have been of less importance. [The] U.K. has hitherto done her best to maintain the principle, and her law still provides that a woman loses her British nationality on marrying a foreigner (and vice versa). But that point has now been given up – almost inevitably.[62]

What had been given up was not the policy as such (although it certainly generated increasingly mixed and unsettled responses), but the attempt to maintain an unqualified legal regime of conditional marital nationality. Repeated local amendments, ad hoc and makeshift administrative arrangements, the pressure of changes in other countries' nationality laws and thus in international arrangements, had by the 1930s, seen the policy's core eroded. While some countries – in particular certain countries with

[61] UK National Archives, HO 45/15147: 'Nationality of Married Women', 'Note of Deputation received 14 March 1932'.

[62] UK National Archives, HO 45/15147: 'Nationality of Married Women', 'Note of Deputation received 14 March 1932'.

strong religious views – still held fast to the idea that family unity compelled a wife to take her husband's nationality, this had long ceased, both in reality and in principle, to be the primary reason for the policy. Inconveniences in international relations and diplomatic embarrassments were increasingly cited, but these were now mostly focused on the issue of dual nationality. Once countries allowed that domino to fall, the rest would go with it. But, contrary to the British perspective in 1931, the law of conditional marital nationality had many years left to run. In the British Commonwealth, with multiple, far-flung legislatures involved, the law appeared impossibly tangled, and a minority of members simply blocked any attempt to find a way through it.

The United Kingdom amended the BNSA Act in 1933, to give effect to the Articles of the Hague Convention that pre-empted women's statelessness arising from marriage. The principle of conditional marital nationality was, however, retained ('the wife of a married British subject shall be deemed to be a British subject, and the wife of an alien shall be deemed to be an alien') but the Act now stated:

> Where a woman has (whether before or after the commencement of this Act) married an alien, and was at the time of her marriage a British subject, she shall not, by reason only of her marriage, be deemed to have ceased to be a British subject unless, by reason of her marriage, she acquired the nationality of her husband.

And

> Where a man has, during the continuance of his marriage, ceased (whether before or after the commencement of this Act) to be a British subject, his wife shall not, by reason only of that fact, be deemed to have ceased to be a British subject unless, by reason of the acquisition by her husband of a new nationality, she also acquired that nationality.[63]

[63] The Act also maintained the provision from the 1914 Act that allowed a maritally denaturalised British-born woman whose marriage had terminated by the death of her husband or divorce to apply for re-naturalisation as a British subject, without needing to satisfy the regular residence criteria for naturalisation; as well as the provision that a husband's naturalisation did not automatically result in his wife's naturalisation, but required her consent; and from the 1918 amendment allowing for a British-born woman, whose husband was a subject of a state at war with Britain, to make a declaration that she desired to resume her British nationality, which might be granted subject to the discretion of the Secretary of State. The 1933 Act added a provision permitting a British-born woman whose husband naturalised in a foreign country the law of which automatically naturalised wives, to make a declaration within twelve months from the date of his naturalisation that she desired to retain British nationality (and the converse applied for foreign women whose husbands were naturalised as British subjects).

The Dominions' response

It was expected that the British Dominions would do likewise, but the British government had doubts about the likely harmony of their responses to any further proposals for amendment. A 'secret' Cabinet memo in 1932 summarised the positions in the Dominions at that time. Canada's problem was 'acute', because of the high rate of marriages between Canadians and Americans (giving rise to statelessness among the Canadian-born wives);[64] the Canadian parliament had already amended its law to give effect to the Hague Convention, but delaying the operation of this legislation, at the request of the British government. Canada had its own additional, internal reasons for this limited response. The Canadian representative (at the League of Nations Assembly), it was recorded, had

> intimated in private conversation that, while the Canadian Government regarded this legislation as urgently necessary to meet the practical difficulty... they were not, so far as he knew, likely to wish to go further at present on the grounds that there was no general demand for further changes in the direction of theoretical equality, while any such changes would probably be strongly resisted by the large Catholic population in Quebec and elsewhere.[65]

Australia, the memo continued, was in favour of the principle of citizenship equality, so long as it was endorsed by other governments, especially the United Kingdom. New Zealand, in the past, the memo noted, had held a similar view to Australia's, but its representative at the League Assembly had indicated that the New Zealand government would probably not wish to go further than the statelessness provisions in the Hague Convention. South Africa was not prepared to go further, either, and 'although the [South African] Union Government did not refer to the point, it is probable that their position is largely based on religious considerations, namely the attitude of the Dutch Calvinist Church'. The Irish Free State government 'have consistently made it clear that they are not prepared to

[64] At the 1926 Imperial Conference, the Canadian representative had raised the matter: 'there was a constant interchange of population between Canada and the United States [and] they had several cases in which Canadian women who married American citizens wished very strongly to retain their British nationality'. Irish National Archives, Department of External Affairs, File no. DFA2/1/20. 'Nationality of Married Women'.

[65] UK National Archives: HO 45/15147: 'Nationality of Married Women', 'Secret' Memo for Cabinet from Home Secretary, 25 January 1932.

go beyond [the Hague Convention]. This attitude is undoubtedly based upon that of the Roman Catholic Church'.[66]

This summary, however, indicated only the Dominions' attitude at a moment in time, and with particular governments in power. The Commonwealth was not only heterogeneous across its various countries, there were also variations in the countries' policies over the years as governments came and went, multiplying the difficulties in achieving the uniformity and the stability required for a uniform policy to find expression in complementary pieces of individual Dominion legislation. As elsewhere in the world, British nationality laws applying to married women had grown increasingly complex, with the number of exceptions from the basic principle of conditional marital nationality multiplying. As each country amended and adjusted its marital nationality laws (and its associated naturalisation laws), the international asymmetries multiplied.

In the event, Canada, having debated, but failed to proceed with, a proposal in 1918 that would have deemed Canadian-born women with foreign husbands to be British subjects for the purpose of the right to vote, went no further than the Hague position in the 1930s, but, by the 1940s, it was leading the Commonwealth towards independent nationality laws, including in the repeal of marital denaturalisation. South Africa's concern with gender equality in citizenship remained secondary, and it never even went as far as to adopt the Hague provisions. The Irish Free State took the most idiosyncratic path. It did not adopt the provisions of the Hague Convention, but rather, framed a new Nationality and Citizenship Act in 1935, complete with a unique solution to the dilemmas surrounding the issue of citizenship equality. This (as we see below) would, at least on its face, meet the religious interest in family nationality, the principle of gender equality, and the opposition to dual nationality. It would also provide a tool in Ireland's long-standing campaign for independence from Britain.

New Zealand and Australia both adopted the Hague provisions. As the first among the world's pioneers in granting women the (parliamentary) vote (1893 and 1894, respectively), they were acutely conscious of the paradox of stripping citizenship from their women merely for marrying a foreign man. Their laws would also incorporate a suggestion made as early as 1918 and repeated in Imperial Conferences: maritally denaturalised women could reclaim, if they wished, the political rights that they had lost in becoming marital aliens.

[66] UK National Archives: HO 45/15147: 'Nationality of Married Women', 'Secret' Memo.

Political rights without citizenship

New Zealand had been relatively slow to include marital denaturalisation in its legislation; its British Nationality and Status of Aliens (in New Zealand) Act of 1923 had incorporated the relevant marital denaturalisation provisions of the 1914 BNSA Act, but the delay, ironically, appears to have arisen from a New Zealand assumption that the British Act operated directly across the Commonwealth without need for separate legislation.[67] Only eleven years later, it was the first to adopt a scheme for the restoration of rights to maritally denaturalised women. The relevant provision of its Act as amended in 1934 stated that

> every woman who, at the time of her marriage to an alien . . . was a British subject and, who, by reason of her marriage, has acquired the nationality of her husband . . . (whether her marriage is still continuing or not) may, at any time within twelve months after the passing of this Act (in the case of a woman married to an alien before the passing of this Act), or within twelve months after the date of her marriage (in the case of a woman married to an alien after the passing of this Act), or in either case at such later time as the Minister of Internal Affairs may in special circumstances allow, make a declaration in the prescribed form and manner that she desires to retain while in New Zealand the rights of a British subject, and thereupon she shall, within New Zealand, be entitled to all political

[67] The British government had become uncomfortably aware of this aspect of New Zealand's law in 1923, as indicated in a 'private' letter and note to MP, Sir John Butcher. In the parliamentary Joint Committee on the Nationality of Married Women, Butcher had asked a 'rather awkward' question, to which no answer could immediately be given, about whether the conditional marital nationality provisions of the British BNSA Act applied in New Zealand. It turned out, from inquiries, that although the New Zealand Aliens Act of 1908 provided for the marital naturalisation of alien women who married British subjects in New Zealand, no marital denaturalisation provisions had subsequently been adopted: '[I]t would appear that the status in New Zealand of a British born woman married to an alien man, not being governed by any statute either Imperial or local, must be determined by the common-law as existing before the English Act of 1844 was passed'. This meant that New Zealand women did not lose their nationality through alien marriage. The British government felt that 'controversy' would be stirred by making this known. Sir J. S. Risley, of the Colonial Office, recorded that he had written the private letter to Butcher, 'in amplification of the Note – which I hope will have the effect of preventing his pursuing further the question whether sec 10 of the Act of 1914 applies to persons in New Zealand'. UK National Archives: CO 323/915: 'Nationality of Married Women – opinion of Colonial Office Legal Assistant'. This fact was subsequently noted, without secrecy, in the *Report of the Select Committee on The Nationality of Married Women*, United Kingdom, House of Commons, July 1923, xii. The matter was soon settled with the adoption of the British Nationality and Status of Aliens (in New Zealand) Act 1923 which included an express marital denaturalisation provision. The legal treatment of New Zealand women with foreign husbands prior to this enactment remains troubling.

> and other rights, powers, and privileges, and be subject to all obligations, duties, and liabilities, to which a natural-born British subject is entitled or subject.[68]

The provision, leaving marital denaturalisation intact, had no prospect of satisfying the demands of citizenship equality campaigners, but many denaturalised women, including some who had married many years earlier, took advantage of it.

On 17 May 1935, Mrs Ellen Z, of Auckland, wife of Hermann Z, 'native of Germany', came before a Stipendiary Magistrate to sign a declaration that, having acquired her husband's nationality by reason of her marriage in Auckland on 3 October 1898, she now wished to retain the rights she would have exercised as a British subject.[69] She was probably the first to do so. That same month, two other wives of Germans, and the wives of French, Italian, American and Danish men, stepped up to make the same declaration. Over the following years, many more women would do the same thing, including, in 1939 in particular, a significant number with German husbands.[70]

The motivation of such women can be readily imagined. Some, in all likelihood, shared a widespread confusion over the effect of the law, believing that it re-conferred British nationality on maritally denaturalised wives. Others, better-informed, no doubt wanted to identify again as full, participatory members of the national community, or at least to go as far in this direction as was offered. Either way, it is moving to see that even illiterate women were similarly motivated. On 22 February 1936, Mary H S, married to a 'Chinaman' in 1895, signed her name with a cross. Forty years after her marriage, forty-three years after New Zealand women gained the right to vote, and an indeterminate number of years after her country's law stripped her of her British nationality, her former status was still prized by her.

[68] Section 3 (1) and (2) of the British Nationality and Status of Aliens (in New Zealand) Act of 1934 (which amended its 1928 Act).

[69] Archives New Zealand: Item ID R17549 067; Ref no. 1A53 81/84, 'Letters of Naturalization . . . [and] Declarations under British Nationality and Status of Aliens (in New Zealand) Amendment Act 1934–35'. The Act came into operation on 26 March 1935.

[70] The irony was that, notwithstanding their reacquired rights and duties, the wives of Germans (and its allies) would soon be classified as enemy aliens, along with their husbands, and their rights and duties would accordingly be suspended again, unless they were able to avail themselves of the provision of the New Zealand Act that, following the BNSA Act (as amended in 1918), permitted applications, subject to ministerial discretion, for re-naturalisation of former British women who were married to a subject or citizen of a state at war with Britain.

Confusions about the effect of the law abounded. This was unsurprising. New Zealand effectively trialled the legal and administrative obstacles. The initial proposal, indeed, had been to permit a maritally denaturalised British-born woman, not only to make a declaration that she desired to regain the rights of a British subject, but also, for the purposes of New Zealand law, for her 'to be deemed never to have acquired the nationality of her husband but to be, and at all times since her marriage to have been, a British subject'.[71] The proposal stirred alarm in Britain. There were fears that the New Zealand law would 'impair' the uniformity of national law throughout the British Commonwealth, as well as fears that New Zealand women would be entitled to assert the rights of British subjects in other parts of the Commonwealth. A telegram from the British Secretary of State for Dominion Affairs began by assuring the New Zealand Governor-General that the decision to proceed was 'entirely for the consideration of His Majesty's Government in New Zealand', and then expressed hope that New Zealand would omit the 'deeming' provision.[72]

The retrospective operation of the provision was also of concern. The New Zealand Under-Secretary for Internal Affairs raised the possibility that retrospective claims for old age or widows' pensions or family allowances, unavailable to alien women (including 'statutory aliens'), were likely to be made by women who were 'deemed' never to have lost their British subject status upon marriage. Advice from the Commissioner of Pensions reassured the Minister that such claims were unlikely.[73] Still, the deeming words were removed before the amendment was passed by the Parliament.

Australia followed New Zealand's lead. Section 18A of the 1920 Nationality Act, as amended in 1936, was expressed in almost identical words to the New Zealand provision. Procedurally, the Australian Act allowed for a declaration to be made before a Justice of the Peace on a form that provided details of the applicant woman's marriage to a foreign man, stating her desire to exercise, within Australia (or its Territories), 'all political

[71] Archives New Zealand, Ref no. IA1 2824, Record no 116/6, Item ID R19964 604. Department of Internal Affairs, Under-Secretary, Wellington. 'Naturalisation – Nationality of British Women married to Aliens – General file re'. 'Supplementary Order Paper', House of Representatives, 16 August 1934.

[72] Archives New Zealand, Ref no. IA1 2824, Record no 116/6, Item ID R19964 605. Copy of telegram, 8 November 1934, Secretary of State for Dominion Affairs, UK to Governor-General of New Zealand.

[73] Archives New Zealand, Ref no. IA1 2824, Record no 116/6, Item ID R19964 604. Memos for Minister of Internal Affairs from Under-Secretary, 13 August and 15 August 1934.

and other rights, powers and privileges, and be subject to all obligations, duties and liabilities, to which a natural-born British subject is entitled or subject'. (The Australian authorities, for uncertain reasons, required a fee of ten shillings; the New Zealand, a fee of five shillings.) As with the New Zealand Act, it permitted a discretionary extension of the deadline requirement.

In February 1939, Mrs Vera I, married five years earlier, wrote to the Australian Secretary of the Department of the Interior with a request for copies of the declaration form. She was informed that she should have made her declaration within twelve months after the passage of the Act, but was also asked for information about why she had failed to comply. She replied quickly, explaining that she was married at 'only 17½ years of age'. She added: 'My husband told me that he would make himself a Naturalized Subject, but has not done so, and I being so young did not trouble, not knowing that I would lose my rights. Last year when I went to enrol myself [to vote], they refused . . . as I had lost my rights through marriage'. Official approval was given; her declaration was made, endorsed, and returned to her, with the advice that it was 'to be retained by you as evidence of the acquisition by you of British nationality'.[74]

Even here, the advice was inaccurate. The confusion over the effect of the law that occurred in New Zealand was repeated in Australia. No doubt Vera I was pleased that her delayed application had succeeded, but, contrary to what was stated in the letter she received, she had not acquired or even reacquired British nationality. Not only were the maritally denaturalised women still no longer British subjects, they remained citizens of their husband's country, and thus (whether they knew it or not) under a foreign allegiance.[75] The principle that citizenship and allegiance to a particular sovereign were co-dependent was simply stretched or relaxed here to rectify an inequity that the law itself had created.

Communications from women's groups in New Zealand and Australia, and newspaper reports to the effect that British citizenship had been restored to denaturalised women, repeatedly frustrated administrators and required correction, and even the administrators, as in Vera I's case,

[74] National Archives of Australia, A659/1 1939/1/8440. Department of Interior File.

[75] The decision to make political rights available to denaturalised women in Australia also reflected a degree of inattention to constitutional obstacles: Australia's amendment to the Nationality Act was probably unconstitutional, at least with respect to the right to stand for parliament, since to be a member of Australia's parliament, a person must be a 'subject of the Queen' (that is, a British subject), and to have no other citizenship or allegiance. Commonwealth of Australia Constitution Act, sections 34 (ii) and 44 (i).

got it wrong. Three years after the passage of the Australian amendment, officials were still clearing up misunderstandings. A letter from Miss M V B in 1939 informed the Australian Department of the Interior: 'I am about to marry a Hungarian Joseph N... and would like to apply for permanent British Nationality, could you arrange it for me before March 20th?' The law, the reply advised her, only allowed for its retention in cases where the woman did not acquire her husband's nationality under the laws of his country, and Hungary was not such a country:

> It is not competent for you to take any steps to retain your British nationality, but provision has been made in the Commonwealth Nationality Act whereby a woman, so situated, may make a declaration that she desires to retain, while in Australia, the rights of a British subject. If you wish to make this declaration you should, after you become married, complete the attached forms in the presence of a Justice of the Peace and return them direct to the Department, accompanied by the sum of 10/- for registration of the declaration and copies of your Birth and Marriage Certificates... The matter will then receive prompt attention.[76]

The New Zealand and Australian initiatives were not intended to disturb the nationality 'common code', but they set off ripples in its increasingly troubled consistency. In the British House of Commons, the Prime Minister Ramsay MacDonald was questioned over Britain's failure to reform the laws governing married women's nationality in light of New Zealand's progress. Conservative MP, Nancy Astor (American-born, but married to a British subject) challenged him to consider the disparity between the 'hundreds of thousands' of alien wives who acquired citizenship by British marriage, and the Englishwomen married to foreigners who 'get no rights at all'. MacDonald responded that the New Zealand legislation was simply about making a declaration of rights, and was not in conflict with imperial uniformity. There was no useful purpose, he said, in once again raising the matter of amending the common code. The retention of political rights was 'one thing in New Zealand and another here'.[77]

The Imperial Conference of 1937, however, revealed Australian and New Zealand efforts to make the matter relevant to the common code, and to use it as a lever for further change. Australia, having outlined the action it had taken, asked if Britain would give 'local' rights in the United Kingdom to women marrying aliens who held these rights in Australia

76 National Archives of Australia, A659 (A659/1) 1939/1/8273: 'Inquiry re retention of British Nationality'.

77 *Evening Post*, Wellington, 14 June 1935.

and in New Zealand. The British Secretary of State for Dominion Affairs replied that to do so would involve an 'invidious discrimination' against British women belonging to the United Kingdom who married aliens. The Canadian representatives then indicated that Canada might be prepared to give any British woman marrying an alien 'the opportunity of making a declaration so as to preserve her status as a British subject'. South Africa deflected the debate (a special committee, its representative noted, would shortly examine 'the whole question of the application of the equality principle'), but its representative's personal view was that South Africa 'should recognize as a possessor of the common status any woman who under the law of any Dominion was a [British] Subject, notwithstanding her marriage to an alien'. The British Attorney General responded, in turn, that he 'could not see how the common status could in such circumstances be maintained'.[78]

Debate arose over the wording in the draft Conference Report. The Australian delegation, supported by New Zealand, it was reported, had 'initiated a discussion on the subject of the enactment of legislation to provide that the nationality of married women should not necessarily be dependent upon that of their husbands'. Notwithstanding that this violated the established practice of not attributing particular views to particular Dominions in Imperial Conference reports, they wanted their contribution to be minuted.[79] It was a sensitive matter, and indicative of the growing fragmentation of views on the subject. The British responded that the proposed minuting 'tended to suggest that the particular Delegation had pushed the question of legislating in the direction desired by the Women's Organisations, thus implying that other Delegations (including the United Kingdom) had not done so at the Conference'.[80] Alone at the Conference, the Australians persisted. They submitted a new draft paragraph for the Report, recognising the discussion of reciprocal arrangements 'on [the] basis of legislation "recently passed" by Australia and New Zealand' that enabled women to make a declaration of their desire to retain political rights. Further debate ensued, and the wording

[78] UK National Archives, HO 213/388: 'Married Women'. Inter-Imperial/Aliens Department – Home Office: Imperial Conference 1937. Minutes of Discussion by Constitutional Committee on 8.6.37.

[79] UK National Archives, HO 213/388: 'Married Women. Inter-Imperial'/Aliens Department – Home Office, Minutes Folder. 'Imperial Conference 1937, [To] Secretary of State: Imperial Conference, 1937, Nationality of Married Women.

[80] UK National Archives, HO 213/388: 'Married Women'. Inter-Imperial/Aliens Department – Home Office: Imperial Conference 1937.

was finally settled: 'The Australian and New Zealand delegations opened the discussion by calling attention to the further legislation'.[81] Once again, however, no uniformity in favour of any change in the existing law could be achieved, and the Conference concluded without recommendations. Again, it was merely accepted that further consideration and consultation between the respective governments should follow.

The Irish response

In the meantime, Ireland had gone further than any of the others. Indeed, Irish representatives at Imperial Conferences during the years (1922–37) when the Irish Free State held Dominion status, were, it is clear, incrementally treating the nationality law question as a means of advancing Irish nationalism. The issue of married women's nationality had arisen early in the life of the 1922 Constitution,[82] with the Irish conclusion that the BNSA Act did not apply in Ireland. The 'case for adopting' the BNSA Act in order to secure uniformity in British subject status was 'overwhelmingly' opposed. Irish legislation governing citizenship was the alternative. A government memo in 1924, pointed out that the Constitution had left open the acquisition of citizenship for those born after its operation, and was neutral on whether the transmission of citizenship to children was to be through the father or mother: a decision on the principle of

81 UK National Archives, HO 213/388: 'Married Women'. Inter-Imperial/Aliens Department – Home Office: Imperial Conference 1937, Memo, Secretary of State. It was recorded that Mr Lyons wanted it to be made clear that he had acquiesced 'with the sole object of reaching unanimity and in order to avoid embarrassing the U.K. Govt.... Mr Lyons felt that it would be essential for him to explain on his return to Australia what had happened, – i.e. that the Commonwealth [of Australia] delegation had pressed for improvement in the position of married women in various directions but had been unable to achieve their objective.... Mr Lyons would be careful not to indicate from what quarter opposition had arisen but observed that if explanations... were given by the Commonwealth and New Zealand Prime Ministers, it would become fairly obvious where the difficulties arose!'

82 Article 3 of the 1922 Irish Constitution read: 'Every person, without distinction of sex, domiciled in the area of the jurisdiction of the Irish Free State (Saorstát Eireann) at the time of the coming into operation of this Constitution, who was born in Ireland or either of whose parents was born in Ireland or who has been ordinarily resident in the area of the jurisdiction of the Irish Free State (Saorstát Eireann) for not less than seven years, is a citizen of the Irish Free State (Saorstát Eireann) and shall within the limits of the jurisdiction of the Irish Free State (Saorstát Eireann) enjoy the privileges and be subject to the obligations of such citizenship: Provided that any such person being a citizen of another State may elect not to accept the citizenship hereby conferred; and the conditions governing the future acquisition and termination of citizenship in the Irish Free State (Saorstát Eireann) shall be determined by law'.

transmission through the male line was needed, as was further discussion as to whether a female Irish citizen would lose her citizenship upon marriage to an alien. The memo noted that a 'special difficulty' had arisen from the operation of US Cable Act, which, in many cases, rendered the alien wives of Americans stateless. It commented that the British government had found it necessary to make special arrangements for such cases, and was currently considering a Bill to provide that a woman would not lose her nationality unless she acquired her husband's: 'A similar provision might perhaps be inserted into the proposed [Irish] Bill'.[83]

The idea of a common British nationality code increasingly troubled the Irish delegates (in particular because it denoted shared allegiance to a common sovereign, a proposition entirely rejected by the Irish Free State), and the nationality of married women became a sub-theme in the emerging commitment to independence outside the imperial context. The British recognised this. As a Dominion, the Irish Free State had signed the Hague Convention in 1930, and was expected to introduce legislation to give effect to its provisions. As early as 1931 (two years before passing their own amending legislation) the British were contemplating the likelihood of Ireland's failure to do so. There was 'danger', it was suggested, that Ireland would fail to make provisions for the common status of British subjects. These fears were well-founded. No references to British subjects could be found in legislation of the Irish Free State, and the Irish Nationality and Citizenship Act of 1935 would declare that the British common law of nationality and the BNSA Acts of 1914 and 1918, 'if and so far as they respectively are or ever were in force' in Ireland were 'hereby repealed'. On the eve of the conference of nationality experts, in 1947, the Irish government noted that Britain had always regarded persons born in Ireland as British subjects, but '[w]e have always protested against this claim and have insisted that Irish citizens were never British subjects'.[84]

The issue of married women's nationality offered an avenue for attracting support for this perspective. This irritated the British government. In the words of Oscar Dowson, Legal Adviser to the Home Office:

[83] Irish National Archives: Roinn An Úachtraráin [Department of the President] File no. S 6501: 'Irish Nationality and Citizenship Act 1935': Memo, 13 October 1924, to 'Each Member of the Executive Council', from the Minister of Justice.

[84] Irish National Archives: Roinn An Taoishigh [Prime Minister's Department] File no. S 14002A (3/471/6 (1065)) Department of External Affairs, Memo for Government, 16 January 1947.

> The Irish Free State are quite impossible; they want to have the best of both worlds. [John] Hearne [Legal Adviser to the Irish Department of External Affairs] made a speech the other day to the League of Nations Union... in which he talked about Irish nationality... and he said in effect that they had nothing to do with British nationality. At the same time he indicated considerable sympathy with the women's point of view in claiming a position of equality with men in regard to nationality, and indicated vaguely that the Irish Free State might give effect to this principle in their legislation about Irish nationality. It is obvious to me that in future the Empire or Commonwealth for purposes of nationality will consist of the UK and the Dominions other than the Irish Free State. If we try to reconcile the position of the Irish Free State with that of the rest of the Commonwealth... we shall get into trouble. We can only hold South Africa to the British Nationality Act by ignoring the I.F.S. claims.[85]

A further source of irritation was the British perception that the Irish had changed their minds on the question of married women's nationality. This was partly true, although there were continuities. At the imperial conferences of the 1920s Irish representatives opposed citizenship equality for women on family unity grounds. The Irish representative at the 1926 Conference, Minister for Justice, Kevin O'Higgins, expressed his government's view '[a]s regards the proposal... to give women who are British subjects a legal right to declare their nationality upon their marriage with aliens':

> I wish to say that we are against that proposal. There is not in the Irish Free State the same pressure from Feminist movements which... exist[s] in Great Britain... There is no doubt that the War gave rise to problems of nationality which created great hardships in individual cases... [But] [w]e should not, I suggest, depart under pressure of War problems from the main principles which have in normal international life governed the law of nationality... [T]he proposal to allow husband and wife to have different nationalities... [would] place husband and wife in the relation of aliens each to the other, possibly alien enemies. I do not think I could hold out any hope that a Bill embodying the proposals contained in the memo would be accepted in the Irish Free State. We are a conservative people despite superficial evidence to the contrary...[86]

85 UK National Archives, HO 45/15147: 'Nationality of Married Women'. 'Correspondence with Mr Dowson at Geneva', 23 September 1931 (Dowson to Sir John Pedder).

86 Irish National Archives, Department of External Affairs. File no. DFA2/1/20: 'Nationality of Married Women'. Copy of Speech of Mr O'Higgins to Imperial Conference 1926, Committee on Nationality.

He was mistaken about the prospects for Irish law. Although the commitment to family nationality endured, the policy of the 1930s offered a reconciliation between family unity and the claim for citizenship equality. Receiving a delegation of citizenship equality campaigners from the Women's International Organisations at the League of Nations meeting in Geneva, in 1931, John Hearne advised them that the Irish government 'had always felt that in principle it was right that the husband and wife . . . of the marriage should have the same nationality and that there should be absolute equality between spouses in this regard'.[87]

The conjunction 'and' was significant. Previously, it had been assumed that family nationality required the subordination of the wife's citizenship, but the Irish were, by this time, devising a scheme that would uncouple the two, and that would, as the British complained, give them the best of both worlds. Against protests that the Hague Nationality Convention, in allowing for a woman's loss of her native citizenship in cases where she automatically acquired the nationality of her husband (albeit expressed conversely), maintained women's citizenship subordination, Hearne assured the deputation that further advances were not ruled out. The Hague Convention was not to be treated as the final code on the nationality of married women, and Ireland was committed to the view that 'international law must advance with the changing needs of international society'.[88] The British had deliberately misrepresented both the Irish position and the importance of the common code, the citizenship equality campaigners were told.

Hearne wrote to the Irish High Commissioner that he had discussed the matter of the nationality of married women many times with the group:

> I have warned them over and over that the Home Office view that 'Imperial Unity' is essential so far as the nationality of married women is concerned is absolute nonsense. There is no reason whatever why the British law relating to the nationality of married women should be the same as ours. British policy has been to inform the . . . feminist organisations that but for South Africa and the Irish Free State Great Britain would be prepared to accept the point of view of those organisations. Nothing could be further from the

[87] Irish National Archives, File no. DFA2/1/20. 'Nationality of Married Women', Copy of paper, 'Issued to Press 24.9.31'.

[88] Irish National Archives, File no. DFA2/1/20. 'Nationality of Married Women'. The Minister was also determined that the report of the meeting should be made available to the press, 'for political reasons connected with his constituency'. Letter to Secretary, Irish Delegation, League of Nation, 24 September 1931.

> truth ... At a Commonwealth meeting held in Geneva during last year's Assembly I requested the British delegation to desist from the practice of informing international feminist organisations or national feminist organisations ... that the British government would be prepared to accept their point of view but for the Irish Free State or any other Member of the Commonwealth. The British government have been wholly reactionary on the subject of the nationality of married women. They wanted if possible to retain the principle of their own statute that the wife of an alien is an alien ... I agree entirely with the South African view ... that in so far as the British Commonwealth is concerned the law relating to the nationality of married women is a purely domestic matter for the government of each Member of the Commonwealth to decide for themselves. The British reply to that would be that there is only one nationality throughout the Commonwealth and that the conditions governing acquisition and loss should be uniform throughout the Commonwealth. That of course is not the case ...[89]

The Irish did not adopt a Citizenship Act until 1935, but (to the frustration of the British) they continued to treat British nationality law as not applying to the Irish Free State. Discussing the nationality of married women at the 1926 Imperial Conference, the Irish Representative (O'Higgins) stated that the BNSA Act of 1914 did not apply to Ireland, that it was an 'imperial statute', one that did not apply unless it was adopted by Irish law, in accordance with Section 3 of the Constitution.[90] The official Irish view was that this meant that the nationality of an Irish woman was protected from the Act's denaturalisation provision.

A communication from the Irish Department of External Affairs in 1927 over passport facilities for Irish women married to Americans captured this view; it pointed out to American passport officers that,

> although [Irish women] through their marriage lose their status of British subject it does not follow that they also lose their Saorstát [Irish Free State] citizenship. At present there is no law determining the circumstances under which a person's Irish Free State citizenship automatically ceases, although in practice a definite overt act such as the voluntary acquisition of another nationality would be regarded as terminating it. In the case of women nationals of An Saorstát who marry American citizens without acquiring the husband's nationality, it is considered that although no longer British

[89] Irish National Archives, Department of External Affairs. File no. DFA2/1/20. 'Nationality of Married Women', copy of paper 'Issued to Press 24.9.31'. Copy of letter, 27 August 1932.

[90] Irish National Archives, Department of External Affairs. File no. DFA2/1/20. 'Nationality of Married Women', Report/Speech of Mr O'Higgins to Imperial Conference 1926, Committee on Nationality.

> subjects, they may still be regarded as Saorstát citizens for the period which under American law must elapse before they can acquire U.S. citizenship.[91]

The Irish Nationality and Citizenship Act of 1935 was an assertion of this view. It gave detailed attention to the question of women's nationality, and it included a provision that offered one solution to the obstacle erected by the imperative of family unity in nationality against the principle of citizenship equality. The Act retained the principle of *jus soli* acquisition of citizenship (and transmission of citizenship by descent from the father alone in most cases[92]). But it did not exclude married women from naturalisation, and it permitted the Minister for Justice to confer naturalisation on a 'spouse' of a person deemed to be a natural-born Irish citizen without requiring fulfilment of the residency criteria.[93] A similar provision applied to maritally denaturalised widows of alien men;[94] and a further provision permitted a maritally denaturalised widow of an alien man, who was a resident and intending to remain a resident of Ireland, to lodge a declaration to that effect; 'such woman shall be deemed to have resumed her [Irish] citizenship'.[95] The revocation of citizenship by naturalisation did not, of itself, affect the citizenship status of a 'wife or husband'. Importantly, the Act stated that marriage to a non-citizen 'shall not of itself operate or be deemed ever to have operated to deprive the party to such marriage' of Irish citizenship or to confer citizenship 'on the party to the said marriage who is not a citizen' of the Irish Free State.

The Act was unusual in effectively restoring citizenship to Irish women who had been denaturalised by marriage without requiring (re-)naturalisation; indeed, deeming them never to have lost their citizenship (as well as repealing marital naturalisation). In a marriage between an Irish citizen and a non-citizen, if the married couple lived permanently outside Ireland, the citizen spouse would be denaturalised, unless (within a prescribed period of time) 'he or she' made a 'declaration of election to retain Saorstát Eireann citizenship as his or her post-nuptial citizenship'.[96]

91 Irish National Archives, Department of External Affairs. File no. DFA2/1/20. 'Nationality of Married Women', Letter to P. Galway Foley, IFS passport control office, New York, 14 November 1927.

92 Section 2 (4) allowed for persons born before 6 December 1922 (the date of the adoption of the first Irish Constitution) to acquire Irish citizenship if, among other criteria, one parent at least was born in Ireland.

93 Irish Nationality and Citizenship Act, 1935, Section 4 (4).

94 Irish Nationality and Citizenship Act, 1935, Section 4 (5).

95 Irish Nationality and Citizenship Act, 1935, Section 14.

96 Irish Nationality and Citizenship Act, 1935, Section 16 (1) and 16 (3).

In the case of marriages between an Irish citizen and a non-citizen, if the couple intended to live permanently in Ireland, the non-citizen spouse could apply for naturalisation in a facilitated procedure (providing he or she ceased to be a citizen of another country); however, if the non-citizen spouse was a man, he was required to have resided in Ireland for two years; if a woman, the residency requirement was dispensed with. Neither the acquisition of another country's citizenship nor the loss of Irish citizenship would of itself affect the citizenship status of a 'wife or husband'.

'The essential thing', wrote Hearne, commenting in 1933 on the policy captured in the then Nationality and Citizenship Bill, 'is that a choice of nationality is given equally to the parties'. The Bill would conform not only to the principles of family unity and citizenship equality, he said, but also to the resolution of the Thirteenth Assembly of the League of Nations in 1932, 'whereby States were requested in drawing up their nationality laws to conform as far as possible to the wishes of the International Organisation of Women'.[97]

These specific equality commitments did not endure. The Citizenship Act of 1956 (which repealed the 1935 Act) conferred citizenship upon any person born in Ireland and on all persons with an Irish mother or father, and it protected any person from loss of Irish citizenship merely by virtue of marriage, or by the spouse's loss of Irish citizenship. But, only narrowly conforming to the commitment of the 1937 Constitution (adopted following a plebiscite of the Irish people) that Irish citizenship should not be denied to any person by reason of sex, the Act permitted only an alien woman married to an Irish birthright citizen to lodge a declaration any time after the marriage 'accepting Irish citizenship as her post-nuptial citizenship'.

Conclusion

Ireland's vigorous constitutional nationalism was not repeated in the other Dominions, although Canada and New Zealand went ahead with new citizenship legislation in 1946, notwithstanding Britain's request to wait for the report of the 1947 committee of nationality experts.[98] An

[97] Irish National Archives, Roinn An Úachtraráin [Department of the President]. File s 6501, 'Irish Nationality and Citizenship Act 1935', Memo, Department of External Affairs, 'Nationality Bill 1933'. The gender discriminatory provisions were amended in 1986.

[98] Baldwin, 'Subject to Empire', 554.

apparently intractable problem created by the desire for autonomy in Dominion nationality within a scheme for imperial uniformity had found a resolution. It was not the first time. The BNSA Act of 1914 had been completed after lengthy inquiries and debates surrounding (among other things) the proposal for a scheme of 'imperial naturalisation'. Previously, the self-governing colonies had been able to legislate for their own local naturalisation, but such naturalisation had purely local effect and was not portable across the Empire. Like the subsequent issue of women's citizenship equality law, any new scheme, and any amendment to British law, required all the Dominions to be consulted and all to approve. But, as Secretary of State for the Colonies, William Harcourt, said in 1914, in discussion on the proposed Act, '[a]ll the problems which seemed so difficult have turned out to be comparatively simple, and under this Bill they are solved'.[99]

Following the deliberations of the 1947 Commonwealth Conference on Nationality and Citizenship (the 'Conference of Experts') another 'comparatively simple' solution was adopted: Britain would pass an Act (a draft was circulated) recognising Commonwealth citizenship; the Dominions' Acts would follow similar lines to those already adopted in Canada in 1946. Laws establishing separate citizenship for each country would be nested in a scheme for shared British subject status. And that was what transpired. The old rule of paternal transmission of citizenship was retained, but none of the new Acts reintroduced the policy of conditional marital nationality.

Notwithstanding the earlier view that administrative complexities, among other things, were so great as to prevent any fundamental reform of the law, governments would devote many years after its repeal to sorting these out (for example, would a woman, originally German, who acquired British nationality by her first marriage to a British subject, then lost it following her divorce, and re-acquired German nationality by subsequent marriage, now be able to re-acquire her British nationality?[100]).

[99] United Kingdom, House of Commons, *Debates*, 13 May 1914, 201

[100] The Consular Department, Foreign Office, London, received an inquiry from the British Consulate-General, Germany, 2 November 1948, on behalf of Mrs Else F: 'She is German born; married British subject, in 1913, in Berlin; lived with her husband in London, 1920 to 1927; then together with their child in Berlin, where husband deserted her in 1927. In 1941, she obtained divorce in Berlin; married German, whom she divorced in 1942. Wants to know if she will regain British nationality'. UK National Archives: FO 372/6493 Title: 'Treaty. 1948. Nationality'. The inquiry adds the observation that there would be 'numbers of these cases, and many persons in similar circumstances'. A further note adds:

Temporary arrangements were also made in anticipation of international impact: a 'Warning slip', for example, was printed, 'to be affixed to passports of British-born women who recover British nationality after having lost it by marriage'. The slip warned that such women might hold dual nationality, but

> [w]hen in the country of their second nationality they are not entitled to the protection of His Majesty's representatives and consular officers and may be claimed as nationals of that country, whether or not they are in possession of British passports, and in such cases their British passports may be liable to confiscation.[101]

In many other countries around the world, similar shifts and similar administrative adjustments were occurring. Within another decade, the international community would signify its realignment in the 1957 Convention on the Nationality of Married Women.

Multiple territorial claims for constitutional sovereignty arose from the war and would mark the decades that followed. However, few, if any, would again involve the denaturalisation of a whole class of otherwise loyal and desirable legal citizens. Having followed each other a century earlier in deeming those of their women who married the citizens of each other's countries to be aliens in their own country, most states resolved to the contrary. The international understanding and the imperatives in the evolution of modern international relations that had compelled the policy of conditional marital nationality were now relatively settled.

Citizenship law would always remain a matter in the borderland between national sovereignty and international concern. In its development, it was treated primarily as a tool of the state's interest in relations with other states. But the shift was now towards conceptualising citizenship as an attribute of persons in their capacity as members of the state. The legal nationalism that had begun to mark at least the rhetoric of the citizenship policies of many countries in the years following the First World War made a striking contrast with the orientation towards international comity of the previous century. Paradoxically, as the international community began to formalise its interest in common nationality policies, the sense of citizenship law as a national matter was strengthening. The

'Section 14 [of the 1948 Act] does have the effect of bestowing British nationality to Mrs F, if in fact she ever lost it' (emphasis in original). But, without further explanation, it cautions, that '[i]t is just possible that an English court might not regard her second marriage as valid'.

101 UK National Archives, FO 372/6493: 'Treaty. 1948. Nationality'.

United States, for example, having accepted in 1907 that its out-marrying women must be denaturalised in order to conform with international practice, was by the 1920s boasting to the world of its citizenship equality laws, and urging other states to follow its example.

We turn now to the international community, and to the intense debate in which it engaged over nationality law in this era, in particular in response to the increasingly fractured topic of the nationality of married women.

6

The international response

In the interwar years, problems arising from the application of conditional marital nationality laws continued to multiply. Inquiries into the subject had been held, sometimes repeatedly, and governments had made incremental and ad hoc adjustments to legislation and administrative practices. Such measures assisted some classes of women, but did not touch the core policy commitment. In any case, national initiatives, applicable only within the territory of the relevant country, were necessarily limited in their scope and effectiveness.

Citizenship laws – albeit an incident of national sovereignty – depend for their effectiveness, indeed their rationale, on their recognition in and by other countries. Even within a state, rights that are available only to citizens engage the distinction between citizens and non-citizens, and in the demarcation exercise, identification of the latter involves other countries' laws. What is essentially national in jurisdictional terms is essentially international in impact and logic, and yet it remains outside the control of international law. This was the paradox that served as both motor and roadblock to change in the policy of conditional marital nationality.

As late as 1947 one international lawyer would describe it as 'tragically true' that '[i]n the present state of international law . . . no uniform agreement on nationality problems can probably be reached'.[1] The statement is both poignant and revealing: it recognises that nationality laws are inextricably bound up with international relations; it acknowledges the existential impact of nationality laws, and it reminds us that, at one time at least, there was a type of 'uniform agreement' on women's nationality, one that itself had tragic dimensions that could only be ultimately mitigated by further international agreement. On the latter, the author was correct for 1947. Another decade would pass before the international community reached agreement on protecting women's nationality.

[1] Tamaki, 'The Canadian Citizenship Act, 1946', 84.

The evolution of modern citizenship law, as we have seen, was shaped by the emerging imperatives of international relations and reciprocities of recognition, exemplified in the treaties on naturalisation that flourished in the mid-nineteenth century. By the 1920s, the desirability of international agreement on nationality laws had 'long occupied the attention of international jurists'.[2] From its beginnings, the Institut de Droit International, founded in 1873, while accepting 'the principle of the liberty of each State in the attribution of nationality', had concerned itself with 'the limits that international law imposed on that liberty'.[3] A report on conflicts of nationality laws was commissioned at its 1891 meeting, and international principles to guide nationality laws were recommended in 1895; these included rules for domestic legislation and diplomatic conventions on the subject of nationality.

Married women's nationality was an early and obvious part of this inquiry. At the Institut's 1904 meeting, the principle that a man's change of nationality by naturalisation should also effect the naturalisation of his wife (and minor children) was accepted, but it was qualified by the recommendation that the wife in such circumstances should have the right to retain her original nationality by making a declaration to that effect.[4] For decades, not even this small concession towards citizenship independence for married women would be accepted by the international community (although some countries individually embraced it), since its adoption would inevitably have given rise to dual nationality in many cases. (The Institut, however, did not 'deal with the situation of double nationality . . . resulting from marriage'.[5])

The identification of international guidelines for national citizenship law revealed deep discrepancies with the policy of conditional marital nationality. Among the Institut's other rules was that no one should lose or be permitted to renounce citizenship without a demonstration of eligibility for acquiring another nationality. Although its application to married women was not addressed, the rule was clearly breached by the policy of marital denaturalisation; denaturalisation took place, in almost all countries (for many years at least), regardless of, and without any inquiry into, a woman's eligibility for acquiring a new nationality.

2 J. W. Garner, 'Editorial Comment, "Uniformity of Law in Respect to Nationality"' (1925) 19 *American Journal of International Law* 530, 552–3.

3 Institut de Droit International, *Livre de Centenaire 1873–1973* (Karger, Basel, 1973) 133.

4 Institut de Droit International (1904) 20 *Annuaire* 291.

5 Garner 'Editorial Comment, "Uniformity of Law in Respect to Nationality"', 550.

Another Institut rule, that denaturalisation 'can never be imposed as punishment',[6] could not apply directly to the policy (marital denaturalisation was never styled as punishment in a legal sense), but it is worth noting for two reasons. One is that maritally denaturalised women, in some cases at least, articulated their loss of pre-marital citizenship in analogous terms, and this experience was associated with the underlying assumption behind the policy that foreign marriage entailed transfer of allegiance and represented a type of disloyalty. The second is that the rule recorded an emerging, albeit faint, shift in thinking about citizenship at that time, an alternative conceptualisation in which the individual, rather than the state, is seen as the 'owner' of his (or, eventually, her) citizenship. It was many years before this shift was more widely embraced, but its incremental spread would, ultimately, assist the campaign for women's citizenship equality, as the existential impact of denaturalisation began to be understood. At the time, however, citizenship was conceptualised as a matter almost entirely for state determination, alienable under circumstances decided purely by the legislating state. It was even more so for married women. The laws governing married women's nationality did not allow even for the small degree of contingent individual influence that persons might exercise over their citizenship status via applications for naturalisation.

National citizenship laws had been framed around the categorical understanding that married women with foreign husbands could not retain their pre-marital citizenship. The system built around it, as we have seen, was always precarious. It could only work, at least as anticipated by legislators, if it was effectively uniform and symmetrical; that is, if all countries stripped citizenship from 'out-marrying' women and all countries, at the same time, conferred citizenship on 'in-marrying' women. There had always been some variation in countries' legal regimes governing women's citizenship, but the equilibrium had more or less held until after the First World War. By the 1920s, however, marital nationality laws were increasingly divergent, and amendments to individual countries' laws had begun to generate unintended consequences, resulting in (among other things) further hardships for many women. In the words of Emma Wold, reporting in 1928 to the United States Congress Committee on Immigration and Naturalization on the 'Effect of Marriage upon Nationality', the principle of male dominance in nationality in marriage 'has tended to create confusion and produce complexities more

[6] Institut de Droit International (1904) 20 *Annuaire*, 291.

perplexing than have the divergent factors of [citizenship acquisition by] jus sanguinis and jus soli'.[7] The whole subject of nationality, a contemporary commented, 'bristle[d] with difficulties' and was rich with potential for conflicts of law; the confusions to which it gave rise were 'so great, so universal, and so embarrassing, not to say exasperating' that it would be recognised as one of the first three subjects to which the world's first conference on the codification of international law was dedicated.[8]

The first multilateral nationality agreement to which this conference gave rise – the 1930 Hague Convention on Certain Questions Relating the Conflict of Nationality Laws (the Hague Nationality Convention) – would, as we have seen, incorporate major provisions on the subject of the nationality of married women in the attempt to address one core aspect of these 'confusions': marital statelessness. It did not, however, settle the matter. In 1937, Waldo Emerson Waltz wrote that 'in the regulation of nationality, and consequently the nationality of married women, the individual state must recognize certain limits on its power, though these limits, existing in the rules of international law, can be only broadly defined'.[9] Contemporaries repeatedly observed that nationality was shaped according to the needs of each state, including 'social, political, military, economic' factors, and was thus a subject over which 'no state is willing to surrender its sovereign prerogative',[10] but, at the same time, was fundamentally influenced by international imperatives.

The multiplicity of citizenship laws in a context of increasing transnational intercourse was the issue: 'If we could suppose that there was but one state in the world' (or even just two states 'provided . . . each lived in solitary isolation'), wrote a leading American international lawyer, it would be a matter of indifference how nationality was determined. But, since citizens of one state visit and settle within the territory of the other, the question of nationality becomes unavoidable. With an increase in the number of states comes 'an increase of the difficulties, until we . . . find ourselves in the uncertainty, confusion and perplexity of the present

7 Quoted in Catheryn Seckler-Hudson, *Statelessness: With Special Reference to the United States*, 25.

8 James Brown Scott, 'Nationality, *Jus Soli* or *Jus Sanguinis*' (1930) 24 *American Journal of International Law* 58.

9 Waldo Emerson Waltz, *The Nationality of Married Women*, 99.

10 Richard W. Flournoy, Jr, 'Nationality Convention, Protocols and Recommendations Adopted by the First Conference on the Codification of International Law' (1930) 24 *American Journal of International Law* 467.

day'.[11] One of the greatest and earliest sources of this perplexity in the post-revolutionary world was that of the woman citizen who married 'out'.

As with all laws governing the acquisition and loss of citizenship, jurisdictionally, the status of women could only be addressed by national legislative action. It was a different matter, however, if statelessness – the condition of having no nationality – was produced by national citizenship laws. Some degree of statelessness had always arisen in marriages involving particular combinations of countries' laws. The most common case, as we have seen, arose where a woman automatically lost her citizenship through foreign marriage but did not or could not acquire that of her husband (for example, marriages between American men and foreign women denaturalised under their own countries' laws but racially ineligible for naturalisation under United States law). There were, however, many other routes to marital statelessness (see below).

State disregard of, or indifference to, the possibility of maritally induced statelessness was recorded in the earliest nationality laws that 'deemed' a woman to take the nationality of her husband. The Napoleonic Code of 1804, the British Naturalization Act of 1870, and the United States Expatriation Act of 1907, among others, all simply asserted – without legal foundation – that a woman married to a foreigner took her husband's nationality. The fundamental error of law went unnoticed, or was disregarded[12]; the Acts merely assumed, and could do no more than assume, the practice of other countries. However, if the husband's country did not extend naturalisation to a foreign wife, her original country had no power to alter this fact. Once a woman ceased to be a citizen under her country's law, that country had no control over her subsequent citizenship status and had no capacity to determine her legal position in any other country. The error and the failure to inquire into whether the assumption of foreign marital naturalisation was correct in individual cases, indicate that, despite some protests to the contrary,[13] women's

[11] Scott, 'Nationality, *Jus Soli* or *Jus Sanguinis*', 59–60. Scott had served on the State Department Commission that made recommendations to Congress, leading to the adoption of the 1907 Expatriation Act.

[12] Note the British Lord Chancellor's words in 1870 on the impossibility of 'legislating in a manner which affects to bind those who are resident in another country, and subject to a totally different jurisdiction, over which we have no control'. See Chapter 3, fn 28.

[13] In debate on the UK Naturalization Bill in 1870, two Members of the House of Commons protested specifically about the provision's application to cases where a British husband

membership of the constitutional community was regarded as both negligible and disposable. It was, effectively, a pawn in the more significant negotiation of international relations, and in the associated demarcation exercise of allocating persons to one particular sovereign state or another.

It still has the power to surprise that such laws were practised, and even introduced in some countries, at a time when women were beginning to gain legal equality and, even further, were acquiring the political rights we understand now as attached to citizenship, and when citizenship was becoming more significant in its general effects. By the twentieth century (and in particular after the First World War) citizenship status was, universally, both a matter of close international interest as between states and also of enormous functional importance in a person's life.

At the same time, in the years following the war, the international harmonisation of law was being increasingly promoted as a critical vehicle for international cooperation, and advanced as a means of avoiding a repeat of the conditions that had led to world conflagration. Among the first substantive tasks of the young League of Nations was the attempt to codify laws (giving rise to the codification conference in 1930, at which the Hague Nationality Convention was adopted). This codification initiative represented an important advance on the view that had prevailed at the League Assembly in 1921, where South African representative, Lord Robert Cecil, had persuasively objected that he 'did not think that a stage had yet been reached in international relations at which it was desirable to attempt the codification of international law'. Indeed, Cecil warned, it would be 'a very dangerous project at this stage in the world's history'.[14]

Over the immediately following years, however, pressure had built to reconsider this conclusion. The American Society of International Law, for example, advanced the view that international agreement on laws

acquired a foreign nationality, thereby automatically effecting his wife's foreign naturalisation, and depriving her of 'all the rights, privileges, and protection to which a British subject would be entitled' (Mr Lawrence) and forcing her 'against her will to become the subject of she knew not what power' (Mr Kinnaird). United Kingdom, House of Commons, *Debates*, 25 April 1870, 1741.

[14] Cecil was speaking to an unsuccessful motion (to the Assembly in Conference, 1921) that:

> The Assembly of the League of Nations invites the Council to address to the most authoritative of the [world's] institutions which are devoted to the study of international law a request to consider what would be the best method of co-operative work to adopt for the more precise definition and more complete co-ordination of the rules of international law which are applied to the relations of states.

was essential to avoid the 'world revert[ing] to chaos and savagery',[15] and it identified nationality laws as a key subject. With such views in the background, notwithstanding Cecil's warning, the harmonisation of laws, including nationality laws, was soon accepted as a priority of the League of Nations.

Towards the Hague Nationality Convention

In 1924, the Council of the League of Nations appointed a Committee of Experts on the Progressive Codification of International Law. The Committee (consisting of representatives of 'the main forms of civilisation and the principal legal systems of the world'[16]) was asked to prepare a provisional list of laws, the international regulation of which seemed both urgently desirable[17] and ready for the first attempt at codification. The Committee consulted authoritative organisations,[18] and sought the opinion of governments around the world on priorities. It then reported to the League's Council with conclusions 'on the questions which are sufficiently ripe and on the procedure for preparing eventually for conferences for their solution'. The issue of nationality laws, as noted, was one of only three that emerged from these deliberations,[19] and in the event, it was the only one to give rise to a substantive agreement among member states at the 1930 Conference.

[15] Editorial Comment, 'The Annual Meeting of the American Society of International Law' (1925) 19 *American Journal of International Law* 530, 539.

[16] Its members consisted of government representatives, jurists and academics from: Upsala, Turin, Oxford, France, Salvador, the Netherlands (the President of Permanent Court of International Justice), Portugal, Czechoslovakia, Poland, Berlin, Buenos Aires, Belgium, and China (Judge of Permanent Court of International Justice); it included also the President of American Law Institute (a former Attorney-General of USA) and 'a legal expert in Moslem law' from Spain.

[17] Nationality, Territorial Waters, Diplomatic Privileges and Immunities, Legal Status of ships owned by the state and used for trade, Extradition and criminal jurisdiction re extraterritorial crimes, State responsibility for damages suffered by states within their territory by foreigners, Procedure of international conferences and conclusion and drafting of treaties, Suppression of Piracy, Limitation (sic), Exploitation of the produce of the sea, List of subjects of private international law.

[18] The Institute of International Law, the American Institute of International Law, the International Law Association, the *Institut ibérique de droit comparé*, the *Union juridique internationale*, the American Society of International Law, the International Maritime Committee, the *Société de legislation comparée*.

[19] League of Nations, Official Journal, February 1925, as referenced in Editorial Comment, 'The Annual Meeting of the American Society of International Law' (1925) 19 *American Journal of International Law* 530, 534.

The changing international landscape in marital nationality laws, in particular following the passage of the United States Cable Act in 1922, was one of the major prompts for this choice of subject as a matter of growing international attention. The International Law Association had adopted a resolution at its 1922 meeting in Buenos Aries, affirming that 'it would be desirable to fix uniformly by treaty the nationality of married women, reserving to a married woman, so far as possible, the right to choose her own nationality'.[20] It discussed the subject again at its Stockholm meeting in 1924. In the same year the United States House of Representatives passed a resolution authorising the President to call a world conference with the aim of concluding a convention on the nationality of married women. While the proposal did not come to fruition, it signalled the nature of the attention now attached to the topic.

Representatives of forty-three nations meeting at a congress of the International Woman Suffrage Alliance, in Rome, in May 1923, adopted a suite of 'rules', resting on the general principle of independent nationality for married women and the principle that a woman's nationality should not be changed without her consent 'except under conditions which would cause a change in the nationality of a man without his consent'. The rules also included that a woman's nationality should not be changed solely because of her marriage or her husband's naturalisation; and a woman's loss of her pre-marital nationality should not occur without her having made a declaration of alienage. Similarly, a woman should not automatically acquire her husband's nationality, although 'special facilities' for naturalisation might be made available, extending also to the husband's acquisition of his wife's nationality. The restoration of nationality lost by marriage should be granted to a woman upon divorce or widowhood, 'should she return to her own country', and nationality lost by marriage or changed by the husband's naturalisation before the passage of amending legislation should be re-acquired 'upon making a declaration to this effect'. Special protection for 'the woman without a country' should be available; if upon marriage a woman lost her own nationality she should be 'entitled to a passport and to protection from the State of which her husband is a national'.[21]

A tug of war between aspirations for full citizenship equality, such as these, and a policy of pragmatic incrementalism, would mark the next

[20] Editorial Comment, 'Uniformity of Law in Respect to Nationality' (1925) 19 *American Journal of International Law* 530, 551.

[21] Macmillan, 'The Nationality of Married Women', 142.

two decades. The League of Nations Committee of Experts considered the Alliance's model and pronounced it 'very desirable' but concluded that it was not a practical or realistic option at present, since it would require too many countries to change their laws.[22] This, again, was the nub of the problem. Policies of conditional marital nationality involved labyrinthine complexities, with multiple national laws, inevitable conflicts of law and international complications, but without sufficient consensus even to establish broad international principles of soft law as guidance for national reform. The deadlock underpinned a status quo that was growing increasingly fragile.

The League's Committee of Experts concentrated on the only nationality subjects with respect to which some degree of international agreement could be discerned, at least as needing attention: multiple nationality and statelessness. Contemporary commentary endorsed this choice. According to the American Journal of International Law, 'it may be doubted whether there is any matter upon which uniformity of legislation and practice among the different states of the world is more needed at the present time'.[23] However, '[t]he acquisition and loss of nationality', the Journal commented, 'are matters which are hardly regulated at all by international law'.[24]

Technically, this was true. But, the coincidence of marital denaturalisation laws in the world, and the endurance of principles of conditional marital nationality over many decades, notwithstanding variations in detail, revealed an international understanding, tantamount to international 'regulation'. It was precisely because of the breakdown of the international consensus, signalled most dramatically in the United States' change of heart in 1922 (and, with lesser impact, that of several other countries), that the by-then fragmented world approach to women's nationality law was revealed. For all this, the policy of conditional marital nationality was still dominant. Alone the rectification of statelessness resulting from marital denaturalisation attracted international resolve at this time.

In anticipation of the League of Nations codification conference, a Research Committee of the Harvard Law School (composed of eminent American international lawyers) prepared a 'Draft Convention on

[22] As Feinberg notes. Feinberg, *Elusive Equality*, 80. What seemed unrealistic at that time would later become possible: this model closely resembles the 1957 Convention on the Nationality of Married Women.

[23] Garner 'Editorial Comment, "Uniformity of Law in Respect to Nationality"', 547.

[24] Garner, ibid.

Nationality'. Its twenty-two Articles included principles of customary international law, as well as several provisions, which, if adopted would have formulated new law.[25] This Draft Convention has been treated as an authoritative statement of international law, both at that time and enduringly.[26] We may note, in this light, that several of the draft Articles, had it not been for specific exceptions carved out for married women, were breached by laws of conditional marital nationality.

The Harvard Committee considered whether naturalisation should be conferred in cases where the naturalised person was not domiciled in the naturalising country. Its Article 14 stated that '[e]xcept as otherwise provided in this convention, a state may not naturalise an alien who has his habitual residence within the territory of another state'. However, the provision, the Draft's comments noted, 'does not prevent a state from conferring its nationality upon a woman through her marriage to one of its nationals' and explained that '[t]he laws of most states conferring their nationality upon alien women through marriage to their nationals make no mention of residence'.[27] In its discussion of the naturalisation of children, however, the Harvard Committee confirmed that there seemed to be 'strong arguments' for retaining the rule against naturalisation through the father until the children acquired residence in the naturalising state. It drew attention to Article 3 of the Resolution of the Institut de Droit International – 'No individual can by naturalisation acquire a foreign nationality so long as he resides in the country whose nationality he possesses' – and section 4 of the 1924 Model Statute of the International Law Association:

> [T]he nationality of a conforming State shall not be acquired otherwise than by naturalization on the application of the person concerned . . . and the conditions imposed on applicants for naturalization shall include a

[25] Francis Déak, 'Research in International Law, Draft Conventions on Nationality, Responsibility of States, Territorial Waters; League of Nations, Conference for the Codification of International Law' (Review) (1930) 30 *Columbia Law Review* 142. The League's Conference Preparatory Committee acknowledged the value of the Harvard Committee's work.

[26] 'A comparison . . . between the Harvard draft on Nationality and the League Bases of Discussion relating to the same subject shows that while the Harvard draft omitted two points which were considered by the League Committee, the League material leaves out of consideration about a dozen questions which were carefully analysed in the comments of the Harvard draft'. Déak, 'Research in International Law', 143.

[27] Harvard Law School, 'Draft Convention on Nationality' (1929) 23 *American Journal of International Law*, Special Supplement, 51. Collective naturalisation following the acquisition of the whole territory of one state by another state (Article 18) was also treated as an exception.

> condition that the applicant must be domiciled within the State of which he or she desires to become a citizen and must have resided within that State or been in the service of that State during a specified period.[28]

The Section added, however, that 'a woman marrying a national of a conforming State shall be dispensed from the said condition as to domicile and residence'. The Harvard Draft additionally addressed the requirement of consent. Its Article 15 stated: 'Except as otherwise provided in this convention, a state may not naturalise a person of full age who is a national of another state without the consent of such person'. The Harvard Committee commented: 'Perhaps the commonest case of naturalisation of an adult without consent, is that of the naturalisation of married women through the naturalisation of their husbands'. It would be in line with 'the modern ideas of the status of married women to require that their consent should be given to their naturalisation when their husbands are naturalized', it stated; its Article had been framed to have that effect.[29]

The Harvard Committee noted several sources for this principle of consent, including the draft report of the League of Nations Committee of Experts, which stated: 'Naturalisation may not be conferred upon a foreigner without his having shown the will to be naturalised or at least without his being allowed to refuse naturalisation'.[30] The Experts' principle, however, was not confined to derivative naturalisation, as the Harvard Committee's was. The latter's insistence on consent only addressed the effect of a husband's naturalisation on his wife's nationality, and did not extend the consent requirement to the naturalisation of women upon marriage. Notwithstanding the identification of 'pre-modern' ideas in the automatic naturalisation of a woman via her husband's naturalisation, the Harvard Draft Convention still accepted the principle of marital naturalisation, albeit requiring at least acquiescence or passive consent, and the application of a residency test. Article 19 stated:

> A woman who marries an alien shall, in the absence of a contrary election on her part, retain the nationality which she possessed before her marriage, unless she becomes a national of the state in which her husband is a national and establishes or maintains a residence of a permanent character in the territory of that state.

[28] Harvard Law School, 'Draft Convention on Nationality', 52.

[29] Harvard Law School, ibid, 55.

[30] League of Nations Document, C. 196, M. 70, 1927 V. The Draft was communicated to governments by the League's Committee of Experts for the Progressive Codification of International Law, with questionnaires, January 1926.

In the event, the Hague Nationality Convention would also retain the principle of conditional marital nationality for women, and affirm the policy of marital denaturalisation, subject only to the qualification that the latter should depend upon the woman's acquisition of her husband's citizenship, as a formula designed only to avoid statelessness as a consequence of marital denaturalisation. Unlike the Harvard Committee, the League did not even support the requirement of no 'contrary election', nor of residence in the husband's state as a requirement for marital naturalisation.

What we see in these statements of principle and the attempted formulation of corresponding rules of international law is a consistent, if indirect, awareness that marital naturalisation and denaturalisation were, in fact, contrary to, or at least in tension with, the broader customary international law of nationality, and that these practices required the carving out of tailored exceptions. We see also, in the Harvard Committee's reservations about the application of conditional marital nationality in certain cases, an emerging ideological objection to the practice of non-consensual naturalisation and denaturalisation. The Harvard Committee noted that,

> [i]n many western countries, modern legislation has tended toward a greater emancipation of married women, and this tendency has not been without some effect on the law governing the nationality of married women. As a consequence of the retention of the older law by many countries and the enactment of new laws by others, the present situation is very confused. Instances are numerous in which some married women have become stateless, and others have acquired dual nationality.[31]

The principles of family unity and of common marital nationality (that of the husband) were having 'the effect of changing the wife's nationality without her consent, and there is a growing disposition to say that it unnecessarily places her in a position of subordination'.[32]

Citizenship equality campaigners were not impressed with the efforts made by these preparatory committees. The Chair of the National Association of Women Lawyers commented in 1930 that '[t]he deep significance of nationality to women was apparently overlooked by' experts on the

[31] Harvard Law School, 'Draft Convention on Nationality', 69. (The list of countries still practising automatic marital denaturalisation and naturalisation, in the Draft Convention's Appendix No. 1, suggests that the distinction between 'western' and other countries with respect to the independence of married women's citizenship was not clear-cut.)

[32] Harvard Law School, 'Draft Convention on Nationality', 69.

League of Nations and Harvard Committees, among others, 'who were engaged in making preparations for the world law':

> Nationality is the relation one bears to one's country. With men nationality is a birthright; it is precious to them. It is the source of their patriotism; and it is the basis on which the state claims their loyalty. Women, on the other hand, have a relation to the state which is indirect. Upon marriage, this relation, which is held so dearly by men, has been severed by the state through no choice and for no fault of the women concerned.[33]

These issues were to generate intense debate and conflict at the Hague Conference in 1930. There the codification of nationality laws, as recommended by the Committee of Experts, was debated at length, and the nationality of married women was a central topic. In the end, however, the most that the international community was willing to concede was a provision for the avoidance of statelessness. We visit that Conference – critical in the history of married women's citizenship – below. First, we turn attention to problem that had begun to trouble the international community: statelessness, especially among married women.

Marital statelessness

Statelessness is a condition of extreme vulnerability, as well as a conundrum for state law. It was increasingly recognised in this era as a particularly 'distressing' condition,

> worse than that of the alien enemy... for the latter might possess rights under treaties between his country and that in which he was domiciled, but the *heimatlos*, being without a country, can have no rights under treaties, because treaties confer rights only upon the nationals of the contracting party.[34]

Occasional cases of statelessness could be tolerated or cured by discretionary executive action, or even simply ignored. But statelessness in large numbers was a new phenomenon. Multiplication of statelessness was identified in the territorial realignments following the First World War and the revocation after 1921 by the Soviet Union of the citizenship of Russian expatriates; it was also witnessed in the dramatic increase

[33] Laura M. Berrien, 'The Campaign of the National Association of Women Lawyers for Equal Nationality Rights' (1930) 18 *Women Lawyers' Journal* 8–9.

[34] Garner, 'Editorial Comment, "Uniformity of Law in Respect to Nationality"', 548.

resulting from conflict of nationality laws, specifically regarding marriage. The change of policy in the United States in 1922 was, as we have seen, the major source of this increase. After that date (the majority of) American women were immune from statelessness arising directly from foreign marriage, but, in providing for their immunity and at the same time discontinuing the practice of naturalising foreign wives, the Cable Act generated countless cases of statelessness for women of other nationalities.

It was not the only source of marital statelessness. Statelessness was, indeed, produced by marriage via multiple routes. Women whose country of origin practised denaturalisation but whose husband's country did not naturalise alien wives became stateless. If the husband of a woman whose country of origin practised martial denaturalisation became stateless as a consequence of his own denaturalisation, his wife typically also became stateless. Women whose maritally acquired citizenship was revoked upon divorce or the death of their husband, without reciprocal restoral of their original citizen under their former country's law, were also rendered stateless. Conflicts of marriage laws could have the same effect. A United Nation's report in 1949 explained the latter:

> [I]f a woman, in virtue of her marriage, assumes the nationality of her husband and loses her nationality of origin, such marriage in order to produce those effects must be a valid marriage . . . If, on the one side, the wife's country regards the marriage as valid and if the wife has lost her first nationality in virtue of the marriage and if, on the other side, the husband's country regards the marriage as invalid or fictitious and refuses to the wife the nationality of the husband, then the wife becomes stateless.[35]

Additionally, in cases where an alien man with an alien wife became a citizen of his country of domicile by naturalisation, the wife's statelessness also followed if that country did not automatically naturalise wives along with their husbands, and, at the same time, her country of citizenship denaturalised her in virtue of her marriage to a man who was (now) a foreigner. Her statelessness could be cured by her own naturalisation, but only if her husband's (new) country permitted married women to naturalise on their own motion, or if her former country permitted re-naturalisation in cases of post-marital statelessness, but then only if the woman was eligible to naturalise (and not excluded for, for example, racial or character reasons). Where eligible, however, a period of stateless was

[35] United Nations, 'A Study of Statelessness' (NY 1949).

typically experienced, while the woman in question fulfilled the residency requirements for naturalisation (even if the length of residency was reduced for alien wives of citizens). A woman who did not live with her husband in his (new) country of citizenship would not qualify for naturalisation in her husband's country and, if maritally denaturalised by her husband's naturalisation, would remain stateless.

Regarding the impact of American law alone upon American-born wives of aliens, Seckler-Hudson identified six ways in which (between 1907 and 1922) a marriage produced statelessness: First, if a woman's husband expatriated himself during wartime, without acquiring another nationality; second, if she married a stateless man; third, if she married an alien whose country did not confer citizenship upon alien wives; fourth, if she married a Greek man other than through a ceremony performed by an orthodox priest and was thereby not recognised as validly married under Greek law; fifth, if widowed and living abroad, she lost her husband's nationality but failed to meet the statutory requirements for resumption of her American citizenship; and finally, if, after the termination of her marriage, having failed to regain her citizenship, she left the United States to reside in a third country.[36] Other combinations of countries' laws generated further examples.

In 1925, the American Journal of International Law, noting several circumstances in which statelessness arose, highlighted the effect of America's repeal of conditional marital nationality. Many consequential hardships, the journal observed, as well as 'confusion and possibly injustice will be inevitable'.[37] Any state, it declared

> which deliberately enacts legislation the effect of which is to denationalize any class of its own or of foreign nationals, except as a punishment for their own misconduct, deprives them of one of the most fundamental rights which belongs to the individual in modern society.[38]

The recognition of citizenship as a fundamental right was increasingly prompted by the contemplation of statelessness, and the effects of statelessness became increasingly harsh as wide-ranging and exclusive legal entitlements were attached to citizenship. The United Nations report noted that statelessness had relatively few consequences prior to the First World War, since residence, employment, and other incidents of

[36] Seckler-Hudson, *Statelessness: With Special Reference to the United States*, 41.
[37] Garner, 'Editorial Comment, "Uniformity of Law in Respect to Nationality"', 550.
[38] Garner, ibid, 552–3.

ordinary life were generally unregulated with regard to nationality. 'Relatively' must be stressed here, however. As we saw in Chapter 3, there were many cases where particular occupations and entitlements were denied to non-citizens long before the war. But as the twentieth century unfolded, citizenship increasingly appeared as a criterion in access to occupations, social benefits, and many other entitlements.

With regard to disentitlements, stateless persons were similarly situated to aliens. But, legally, stateless persons were an anomaly. By the very fact of their statelessness, there could be no applicable state law, no state that was obliged to protect them and little international guidance as to the norms that should govern their treatment. The obligations owed by a state to any stateless persons within its territory were uncertain.[39] What could be demanded of another state, the laws of which had brought about statelessness, was similarly unclear. The United Nation's study explained:

> Administrative authorities which have to deal with stateless persons, having no definite legal status and without protection, encounter very great and often insurmountable difficulties. Officials must possess rare professional and human qualities if they are to deal adequately with these defenceless beings, who have no clearly defined rights and live by virtue of good-will and tolerance.[40]

Statelessness was an extreme condition, qualitatively different from alienage. It was in itself a condition of wretchedness. Since the 'organisation of the entire legal and economic life of the individual residing in a foreign country depends upon [the] possession of a nationality', the fact that the stateless person has no nationality 'places him in an abnormal and inferior position which reduces his social value and destroys his own self-confidence'.[41]

Marital statelessness added a further layer. A stateless wife was dependent on discretionary or extra-legal protection that might be offered by her husband or his country, and in cases where this was denied or was inadequate, or if the husband was absent, she had no alternative source. Furthermore, in countries which constrained the rights of married women generally, the vulnerability was compounded. For example, where the property rights of wives were restricted, '[h]aving become stateless and being resident . . . a woman in this position often finds her

[39] The United Nations 1954 Convention relating to the Status of Stateless Persons, and 1961 Convention on the Reduction of Statelessness have mitigated this uncertainty.

[40] United Nations, 'A Study of Statelessness' (1949). [41] Ibid.

rights actually disputed. She can neither sign a lease, acquire property nor open a bank account. Her economic activity is hampered and her chances of settling down and becoming assimilated are jeopardized'.[42] The Inter-American Commission of Women (established in 1928 by the Pan American Union: see below) 'received more appeals for help because of nationality difficulties than from any other source'.[43]

Marital statelessness was growing. Prior to 1933, when Britain (in conformity with the Hague Nationality Convention) amended its nationality law, numerous British women became stateless. Canada had already amended its nationality law along these lines in 1931. Until the law took effect, Canadian women (who were British subjects) were '[p]erhaps the largest single group of women nationals of any country who have been left stateless as a result of marriage'.[44] The numbers were not small in other countries. In 1922 alone an estimated 1,000 American soldiers married German women, some 200 after the passage of the Cable Act;[45] these wives, denaturalised under German law, were rendered stateless.

In mid-1934, following the amendment of the British law, a newspaper article claimed that the first British passport had just been granted to a British-born woman whose foreign marriage would previously have rendered her stateless:

> An English girl of twenty-one has turned a new page in the story of English women's fight for equal rights with men. For pretty Ina Ginn... has become Mme – or rather Mrs Lucien Albert of Paris – and retained her British nationality. She is the only Englishwoman to have married a Frenchman – or any foreigner – and remained British. Shyly she told me today of how she wrote to the Home Secretary on her engagement explaining her patriotic desire; of the long negotiations with French and British authorities. She came to Paris to be married – on Boxing Day. Since then, presumably, she has had no nationality – until this week. She showed me her new British passport, in her married name, which she has just received.[46]

Britain's Chief Passport Officer was displeased. His office forwarded the newspaper clipping to the British Consul General in Paris, with the comment that it 'contains a number of ridiculous and entirely inaccurate

[42] United Nations, 'A Study of Statelessness' (NY 1949).

[43] Waltz, *The Nationality of Married Women*, 89. [44] Waltz, ibid.

[45] Seckler-Hudson, *Statelessness: With Special Reference to the United States*, 95.

[46] UK National Archives, FO 612/238, 'Women of British Nationality married to aliens who have not acquired husband's nationality'. *Daily Express*, 31 May 1934 (file clipping).

statements'.[47] A following letter observed that '[f]ar from being the first British woman . . . [Mrs Albert] probably comes about two hundred down the list'. The first passports 'of this nature were issued from this Office the day after the Act of 1933 received the Royal Assent and a constant stream of women have been supplied with passports ever since'.[48]

Then non-retrospective application of the Cable Act provided a further path to statelessness. After 1922, American women previously denaturalised through marriage were entitled to regain their citizenship by naturalisation, but this was not automatic. It too applied only where a woman was eligible to naturalise. Eligibility exclusions based on race or 'character', among others, left many former American women denaturalised, and in certain cases stateless. So too did residence requirements. Although permitted in some cases to travel to the United States on special passports, once there, the wives of American citizens (including the wives of servicemen) were required to wait a year before applying for naturalisation.[49] Marriage to a citizen, however, did not always attract a travel permit. Where the immigration quota from the particular country of which the foreign wife was a resident had been filled, the wife would be denied entry to her husband's country, and would thus be unable to begin her eligibility period of residence. This, in the United States, applied in practice even in cases of the denaturalised wives of American diplomatic and consular officials serving abroad, who were ineligible for regular travel documents; special legislation was required to correct this effect.[50]

Exceptional measures governing rights of entry, however, only benefitted women who were eligible for naturalisation in the first place and assisted only those who intended to live in the United States. Mrs A, for example, Chrystal Macmillan wrote, was married to an American businessman living in England. She had lost her British nationality upon marriage, but could not acquire American citizenship without residing for at least twelve months in the United States:

47 UK National Archives, FO 612/238, 'Women of British Nationality married to aliens who have not acquired husband's nationality': Passport Office. To His Majesty's Consul General, Paris, from HGM, Chief Passport Officer, 5 June 1934.

48 UK National Archives, FO 612/238, 'Women of British Nationality married to aliens who have not acquired husband's nationality'. HGM to Haggard, 13 June 1934.

49 Waltz, *The Nationality of Married Women*, 91. (In 1934 the period of residence for the naturalisation of an alien wife was raised from one to three years.)

50 Seckler-Hudson, *Statelessness: With Special Reference to the United States*, 94.

> [S]he is stateless and has no legal status. She pays rates and taxes [in England], but has neither municipal nor Parliamentary vote. Neither the United States nor Britain will provide her with a passport and when she goes abroad she must travel on her husband's as his appendage, or with an 'identification paper' issued by the Home Office on which she is stated to be an American, a statement which the American authorities deny . . . [On re-entering Britain, she] must walk among the aliens. While abroad British Consuls give her no assistance.[51]

Claims of statelessness were sometimes received sceptically, with the intimation that they were a device on the part of women seeking restoration of their citizenship. 'A great number of applications are received from women who claim that their husbands were stateless persons at the date of the marriage and, therefore, they acquired no nationality by their marriage', a 1935 New Zealand government memo explained: 'Strict proof should be required that the husband was in fact stateless . . . and this is sometimes difficult to obtain. The fact that the husband is in possession of a Nansen certificate or a document of identity cannot in every case be regarded as adequate proof'.[52]

Measured against the circumstances of such women, whose very claim to be stateless was treated with suspicion, how much sympathy do women like Mrs A (and Leonore Spivakovsky and Betty S, whom we saw in Chapter 3) deserve? Their cases appear trivial. They, and no doubt many others, were supported by their husbands, treated well and informally assisted in their former countries, mitigating the worst effects of statelessness. Their circumstances were not desperate. They attracted attention, indeed, because they were well connected. But this is too simple. However else one responds, these cases demonstrate something significant, essential to the character of citizenship. Even where little or no material hardship followed, the loss of citizenship was experienced as an injury, and the fact of statelessness as profoundly injurious in itself.

This fact was recognised, if indirectly, in the prioritising of the reduction of statelessness arising from marriage in the League of Nation's attention to nationality law. The 'corrective' adopted at The Hague in 1930 did not measure the degree of material or personal hardship experienced by classes of stateless person, but treated statelessness, in itself, as a harm. This, as we shall see in the following chapter, provides a significant perspective on

51 Macmillan, 'The Nationality of Married Women'.

52 Archives New Zealand, IA1 2824, Record no 116/6, H. G. Mumford to C. B. Burdekin, 4 April 1935. (Nansen certificates were travel documents issued to stateless persons and refugees after 1922 by the League of Nations.)

the value of citizenship, on what it is that is lost when a person ceases to be a citizen and becomes stateless.

Dual nationality

For policies of conditional marital nationality to be abandoned, three principal objections needed to be defeated, or at least weakened: the need for family unity in nationality, the prospect of conflicts arising where a husband and wife held different nationality, and the likelihood that some women would hold dual nationality.

The commitment to family unity as an ideal that included a single, common (masculine) nationality was powerful. O'Higgins, the Irish Minister for Justice, representing his country at the 1926 Imperial Conference, declared that there was 'something in the proposal allow [a] husband and wife to have different nationalities which is not quite in accord with the concept of Christian marriage'.[53] The view was attributed in particular to Catholic countries, but there were important exceptions (in the Latin American countries: see below) and it did not animate the policy in all countries. It was, in practice, always subordinate to objections based on practical and legal considerations. Notwithstanding many heartfelt claims about the value of the family, most countries would ultimately be prepared not only to accept that family members might hold different nationalities, but also to dismiss, in practice, the automatic right of a husband and wife to share a nationality.

The irony was that, as laws governing married women's nationality were amended, patching up inequities on an ad hoc basis, but retaining the policy, the second objection – against separate nationality in marriages – grew. By 1933, Britain's Nationality and Status of Aliens Act included six exceptions to conditional marital nationality, allowing a husband and wife to hold different nationalities in certain circumstances: if the wife did not automatically acquire her husband's nationality through marriage; if the husband was naturalised in a foreign nationality and the wife was not also automatically so naturalised; if the husband was naturalised in a foreign nationality and the wife made a declaration that she desired to retain British nationality; if the husband was naturalised as a British subject and the alien wife did not make a declaration that she desired to acquire British nationality; if the husband was an enemy alien during

[53] Irish National Archives, Department of External Affairs. File no. DFA2/1/20. 'Nationality of Married Women'.

war; if the husband's naturalisation certificate was revoked.[54] The idea that there was something special, and also particularly awkward, about diplomatic dilemmas involving the nationalities of married people, was sometimes raised or intimated, but the general objection against multiple nationality, implying multiple allegiance in the same person, would prove the overriding factor. Once the idea was accepted that a woman was not the same person as her husband for the purposes of citizenship law, the focus could then turn to this last objection.

The international consensus against dual nationality generally was the greatest obstacle to the proposition that a woman's citizenship might be independent of her married status. Several arguments were made against it: patriotic (military service might be demanded of the same person by countries that were hostile to each other); affective (sentiments of allegiance or loyalty could not be divided or shared); legal (conflicts of laws would be generated); and diplomatic (disputes would arise between countries obliged to offer protection to the same person). Repeatedly, and increasingly, resistance to the repeal of marital denaturalisation laws was mounted on the basis that dual nationality would follow.

The fact that dual nationality sometimes arose was recognised in international law, but was seen as a condition to be rectified. The Harvard Committee's Draft Convention on Nationality, for example, included Article 11 which provided that one state of person's nationality could not subject him to military service while he resided habitually in the territory of his other state; Article 12 required a person with more than one nationality to take, at the age of 23 (sic) the nationality of the state in which he had his habitual residence; and Article 13 stated: 'Except as otherwise provided in this convention, a state may naturalise a person who is a national of another state, and such person shall thereupon lose his prior nationality'.

So long as the assumption held that a woman must share the citizenship of her husband, the retention of her original citizenship, would, in principle at least, give rise to dual nationality where her husband's citizenship was different from hers. The compromise offered by the Hague Convention in 1930, allowing women to retain their own citizenship if they did not acquire the citizenship of their husband's country, reflected a similar principle.

Conflicts of laws and tensions in international relations were a constant threat in dual nationality cases. Waltz chronicles several examples arising

[54] Bicknell, 'The Nationality of Married Women', 106.

from mixed nationality marriages in which the nationality of the country against which a widowed woman was entitled to seek compensation for the death of her husband was at stake. One illustrates the complexity: Mary Barchard Williams, American-born, had lost her American citizenship upon marriage in 1909 to a British subject domiciled in the United States. Under British law, she had acquired British nationality. However, upon her husband's death in the Lusitania in 1915, the United States claimed that her American citizenship had been restored, since she was, and had always been, a resident of the United States, and the 1907 Expatriation Act permitted domiciled widows to regain their American citizenship.[55] But, did the provision of the Act require positive action, or 'election' on the woman's part? Was Williams a British or an American citizen? The answer would determine whether a claim against Germany over her husband's death could be heard by the German-American Mixed Claims Commission (established under the Treaty of Berlin in 1922). Germany claimed that Williams was British and was therefore outside the Commission's jurisdiction. The American government claimed that her American citizenship had been restored at the moment she became a widow. It submitted that no deliberate election on the part of the claimant to restore her citizenship was required, and that the fact that the government of the United States presented the claim on her behalf was itself evidence.[56] This conclusion prevailed (and the Commission ordered compensation to be paid to Williams who had, it was reported, become

[55] 'That any American woman who marries a foreigner shall take the nationality of her husband. At the termination of the marital relation she may resume her American citizenship . . . if residing in the United States at the termination of the marital relation, by continuing to reside therein'.

[56] The Commission's Umpire ruled that 'By virtue of this statute and of a similar British statute the claimant by her act in marrying a British subject was *eo instanti* deprived of her American citizenship and coincidentally became a British subject. This statutory rule had its source in the ancient principle of the identity of husband and wife and was designed to prevent domestic as well as international embarrassments and controversies (*Mackenzie* v. *Hare*, 1915, 239 U.S. at pages 311–312). But the statute in effect provided that the operation of the rule should cease upon the termination of the marital relation in which the reason of the rule had its source. Because of her residence and domicile in the United States the claimant owed temporary allegiance to it even while she was a British subject. When the marital relation was severed by her husband's death she continued to reside in the United States and that temporary allegiance became permanent by virtue of the statute above quoted which *ipso facto* clothed her with American citizenship without any further act or volition on her part. She *eo instanti* relinquished her American citizenship when she married a British subject. She *eo instanti* resumed her American citizenship upon the termination of the marital relation by his death' United Nations, *Reports of International Arbitral Awards* (2006), http://legal.un.org/riaa/cases/vol_VII/1-391.pdf.

destitute as a widow), notwithstanding that the American Department of State had previously 'considered that the termination of the marriage did not automatically produce a change of citizenship'.[57] It remains ironical that America, having stripped Williams of citizenship without either her consent or a positive act on her part, now imputed its restoration, also without either.

Had dual nationality been tolerated, the practical problems arising from marital denaturalisation would, in cases such as these, have been relieved. A woman would have retained her native citizenship even while acquiring that of her husband, thus allowing for a common family nationality and for her protection in her country of residence (assuming it to be either her own or her husband's). Dual nationality would not have satisfied the in-principle objection to a woman's legal status being merged with that of her husband, but the existential impact would have been less dramatic. However, not only was dual nationality not conceded (until well after the Second World War), but the possibility that a person might be the legal citizen of more than one country was tellingly 'likened to bigamy',[58] treated as 'a stain on a person's character, an immoral status akin to bigamy'.[59]

There is much irony, too, in the fact that, women whose foreign marriage produced dual nationality, but who did not want both citizenships, could do nothing about it. In 1940, the United States Consul in Melbourne, Australia, sought advice on behalf of an American-born woman, naturalised as a British subject by her marriage to an Australian. She had not lost her American citizenship by her marriage, and 'does not wish . . . to be other than an American citizen'; she had 'handed in her British passport' and wanted to register herself as an American, and therefore alien, in Australia. 'Can a person in such circumstances take any action to divest herself of British nationality conferred on her by marriage?', the Consul asked. The advice was uncompromising. There was no provision in

[57] E. M. Borchard, 'Opinions of the Mixed Claims Commission, United States and Germany' (1926) 20 *American Journal of International Law* 69, 73.

[58] David A. Martin and T. Alexander Aleinikoff, 'Double Ties' *Foreign Policy* No. 133 (November–December 2002) 80.

[59] Peter J. Spiro, *Beyond Citizenship: American Identity After Globalization* (Oxford University Press, 2008) 59. The marriage analogy was deeply flawed. Had the analogy been consistent, conditional marital nationality laws would have been, at the very least, questionable. A woman would not have acquired her husband's nationality, as happened, without regard to her pre-existing citizenship/marital status. Citizenship would not have been lost, without consent, in order to force a new, monogamous 'marriage' on a woman.

the Australian Act allowing a woman naturalised by marriage to make a declaration of alienage. Such a woman possessed dual nationality, regardless of her desires. Furthermore, the international practice regarding dual nationals was to treat the nationality of the country in which the person resided as the 'dominant' one with respect to protection abroad.[60] This woman was – and so it must have seemed to her – doubly trapped in her marital nationality.

Dual nationality is still not tolerated in many countries for their own citizens, but, Alfred Boll writes, after a long resistance on the part of the international community, '[a]rguments favouring the avoidance of multiple nationality appear to have given way in many countries to the equality and choice of individuals . . . [and] there is no doubt that equal treatment of women has led to a greater number of multiple nationals'.[61] Boll notes, however, that the 'contention that states have always been opposed' to multiple nationality or that it has 'invariably been seen as undesirable, is belied by historical evidence'.[62] There were, indeed, many instances in the past, including as a result of foreign marriage, where multiple nationality occurred and was recognised.[63] Women's citizenship equality campaigners commonly made the same point in responding to the claim that repeal of conditional marital nationality was impossible, because of its likely contribution to dual nationality. However, notwithstanding this historical reality, the contention that states were (virtually) uniformly opposed to dual nationality arising from a woman's foreign marriage is correct. Whether in disregard of the reality or for hortatory purpose, states consistently objected that married women's independent citizenship could not be permitted for this reason.

[60] National Archives of Australia, Record series A659, Control symbol: 1940/1/1902, 'British subjects with dual nationality – Question of making decision of alienage in time of war'. Department of the Interior, Memo to Director, Commonwealth Investigation Branch, 24 April 1940.

[61] Boll, *Multiple Nationality and International Law*, 247.

[62] Boll, ibid, 2.

[63] The Explanatory Report to the 1997 European Convention on Nationality notes the growing number of problems concerning nationality since the adoption in 1963 of the Council of Europe's Convention on the Reduction of Cases of Multiple Nationality (which did not, itself, exclude multiple nationality arising from marriage). Among the relevant developments are 'the growing number of marriages between spouses of different nationalities' and the acceptance of 'the principle of equality between the sexes' in acquisition and transmission of nationality to children. Multiple nationality, thus, is permitted (Article 14) in the case of spouses of mixed marriages and their children (as well as several other categories). Council of Europe, *Explanatory Report to the European Convention on Nationality* (ETS No. 166) para 8.

That allegiance could not be divided was a powerful principle, and women's foreign marriages added a further dimension to it. Such marriages involved not only two pre-marital nationalities, and therefore two allegiances, but also the particular subjective allegiance assumed to be owed by a woman to her husband, as, effectively, the state in miniature. The woman's allegiance to her country was assumed to be slight or negligible; her allegiance to her husband was assumed to be powerful. She could not retain her own citizenship because her heart now belonged to her post-marital sovereign.

The Hague Nationality Convention

The League of Nation Conference for the Codification of International Law met at The Hague from 13 March to 12 April 1930, with representatives of forty-eight governments, including the non-member United States. Its primary outcome – indeed, its only convention-based outcome from among the topics singled out for possible codification – was the Convention on Nationality.[64]

The Conference began with the appointment of three subject committees (Greek delegate, former diplomat and former Minister of State, Nikolaos Politis, chaired the Committee on Nationality). Whether to make the Committees' discussion open to the public was left to each Committee, but in the event (to the dismay of women's citizenship equality campaigners) no public meetings were held. On the evening of 1 April, however, the Committee on Nationality 'invited certain ladies to speak; but in form, at least, that meeting was not public'.[65] The women had already been told by the Chair of the Committee, so one reported, that 'nothing we might say would influence a solitary vote in the committee'.[66]

From the start, the Committee confronted problems of great difficulty. Among others, '[t]he question of the nationality of married women involve[d] ... deep-seated differences of a fundamental nature, resting upon sentiments regarding the national life, the family and the

[64] Three Protocols were also adopted: The Special Protocol on Statelessness; Protocol Relating to a Certain Case of Statelessness; and the Protocol Relating to Military Obligations in Certain Cases of Dual Nationality.

[65] David Hunter Miller, 'The Hague Codification Conference' (1930) 24 *American Journal of International Law* 674, 677.

[66] Doris Stevens (Chair, Inter American Commission of Women), 'America Takes Her Stand Among Nations for Equality' *The Congressional Digest*, November 1930, 280.

individual, which are inherently irreconcilable'.[67] Still, the Conference reached a conclusion on this question. It was to be the only conclusion to which general agreement among the delegations could be secured; indeed, it was the most that many could be brought to concede. Paradoxically, as was noted in a report on the Conference, 'the subject that had least to do with international law... was the one on which most agreement was reached'.[68]

The Nationality Convention began with general principles about reciprocal recognition of nationality, and covered the rights to diplomatic protection of dual nationals, expatriation, and the nationality of children. Article I stated the categorical principle: 'It is for each state to determine under law who are its nationals'. An immediate qualification, however, followed: 'This law shall be recognized by other states in so far as it is consistent with international conventions, international custom, and the principles of law generally recognized with regard to nationality'. Lack of international consistency was precisely what had brought the Conference together. The problem for married women was that 'international custom' regarding their citizenship status and accompanying state laws were inconsistent with other principles of international law. The long-established consensus among states still favoured conditional marital nationality, and, as we have seen, this consensus was justified both in local terms (maintaining family unity) and international terms (avoiding diplomatic inconvenience and conflicts). At the same time, an emerging international perspective promoted the view that married women's nationality should be protected on the same terms as nationality generally, arising both from the principle of the right to legal equality and as a means of avoiding the terrible alternative to dual nationality, statelessness.

When it came to the nationality of married women, upon what consistent principles would the world agree? The delegation from Chile had proposed a commitment to complete equality of sex in matters of nationality. Such a proposal had no chance of adoption and was not pressed to a vote: 'Probably ninety per cent of the Delegations at The Hague would have voted against it'.[69] The Conference did, however, adopt a

67 Hunter Miller, 'The Hague Codification Conference', 678.

68 Edwin Borchard (response to report by Hunter Miller, Chair, American delegation), 'The First Conference for the Codification of International Law', (1930) 24 *Proceedings of the American Society of International Law at its Annual Meeting* 213, 221.

69 Hunter Miller, 'The Hague Codification Conference', 681.

recommendation that captured something of the sentiment of citizenship equality. A resolution was presented by United States delegate, Ruth Shipley (Head of the Passport Division of the State Department), which embraced the idea in the Chilean proposal but offered a compromise. The Conference should recommend to the member states the study of whether 'it would not be possible to introduce into their law the principle that in their law and practice relating to nationality there shall be no distinction based on sex'.[70]

Shipley's recommendation included an additional matter 'of importance': the study of the principle of citizenship equality should be conducted 'with particular consideration of the interests of children involved'. The United States, she declared, had 'gone very far in its legislation toward the removal of discrimination based on sex, in matters of nationality'. Everyone 'who has made any study of questions of nationality knows very well the complexity of the whole subject'. Any change that related to the status of married women also involved complex question concerning the nationality of children and children's interests: 'The two problems, one the problem of the nationality of married women, and the other the problem of children, are not in truth two problems; they are one. We could not separate them . . . [and] we would not if we could'.[71]

The Conference was happy to consider the nationality of children, but as a separate matter from any commitment to married women's citizenship equality. The United States had certainly repealed its conditional marital nationality laws, but many countries represented at the Conference still adhered to the foundational policy behind marital denaturalisation. Their overall position was guided by principles they considered deeper than citizenship equality: family unity in citizenship, and the avoidance of international conflicts. The fact that these were not mutually exclusive – indeed, they were mutually reinforcing – was to make the 'no distinction based on sex' principle all the harder to sell.

To the American resolution, the Conference added that the member states should consider whether it was possible, 'especially to decide that in principle the nationality of the wife shall henceforth not be affected without her consent, either by the mere fact of marriage or by any change in the nationality of her husband'. It could not, however, be persuaded to incorporate these resolutions into the Convention's Articles. All that could be agreed was that a married woman should not be stripped of her

[70] Hunter Miller, ibid, 681. [71] Hunter Miller, ibid.

citizenship if it would render her stateless. Chapter III of the Convention on the nationality of married women, incorporated this principle:

Article 8 – If the national law of the wife causes her to lose her nationality on marriage with a foreigner, this consequence shall be conditional on her acquiring the nationality of her husband.

Article 9 – If the national law of the wife causes her to lose her nationality upon a change in the nationality of her husband occurring during marriage, this consequence shall be conditional on her acquiring her husband's new nationality.

Article 10 – Naturalisation of the husband during marriage shall not involve a change in the nationality of the wife except with her consent.

Article 11 – The wife who, under the law of her country, lost her nationality on marriage shall not recover it after the dissolution of the marriage except on her own application and in accordance with the law of that country. If she does recover it, she shall lose the nationality which she acquired by reason of the marriage.

The Convention was adopted by the vote of forty states. The United States, objecting to several provisions, including Articles 8 and 9,[72] alone voted against it. The stance of the American delegation was well received in its own country. Indeed, the President of the American Society of International Law was 'filled with an exceeding joy'. As a result of the delegation's action, he proclaimed, the United States 'assume the moral leadership of the world, and with the refusal of the greatest and noblest and most progressive of countries to be a party to inequality in its dealing with the least respected of human beings, a new era begins in the history of humanity'.[73]

For married women, at least, this vision was wildly premature.[74] Commenting on the Convention, at the same meeting, the international lawyer and technical adviser to the American delegation, Edwin Borchard, added

[72] It also objected that Articles 1 to 4, and 7 were inconsistent with, and appeared to threaten, the American policy in favour of voluntary expatriation, as set forth in the Expatriation Act of 1868.

[73] James Brown Scott, 'The First Conference for the Codification of International Law', (1930) 24 *Proceedings of the American Society of International Law at its Annual Meeting* 213, 220–21.

[74] As it had been following the passage of the Cable Act. 'Perhaps the law makers of the world', speculated the contributor to the 'Current Legislation' column in the *American Bar Association Journal* in 1923, 'will follow the example of our Congress . . . and approve the triumph of the will of the individual over the unity of the family'. Chamberlain, 'Married Women's Naturalization Act', 58.

more soberly that he was surprised at just how many countries had agreed to modify their nationality laws, although he had expected many reservations to be recorded, 'and nobody knows to what extent there will be ratifications'.[75] Borchard noted the likelihood of a campaign by women against ratification of the Convention, and predicted its success.[76] His first prediction proved correct. Although ten of the forty nations that voted for the Convention did not sign it, and this change of mind was attributed by at least one equality campaigner to the United States' 'solitary stand' which, in turn had been prompted by the campaigners' decision 'to concentrate all our efforts on the United States delegation',[77] his second would prove less prescient.

The campaign against ratification

The American delegation's attitude was not applauded by others. The International Law Association noted the general support the Convention had received, and added that 'curiously enough and to the surprise of a great many of us the American delegation did not sign the Convention'. The Conference, it concluded, was rather disappointing; the result 'showed that there was a great disparity of opinion in regard to many matters within [the] three subjects' discussed.[78]

Profound differences had been expressed in the delegations' points of view about the nationality of married women. There were two extreme

75 Ultimately, twenty-seven of the forty countries that signed did not ratify the Convention. Those countries in which the Convention was put into force were: Australia, Belgium, Brazil, Burma, Canada, China, India, Monaco, Netherlands, Norway, Poland, Sweden, and the United Kingdom. Some of the non-ratifying countries had either already repealed their marital denaturalisation laws or did so independently of the Convention. Such laws also remained in operation in a significant number of other countries notwithstanding the international commitment to reduce statelessness among married women. Taking into account also the Hague Protocol on Statelessness, the International Law Commission concluded, nevertheless, that the Hague Convention was 'one of the most significant international instruments, because it . . . had been followed by a definite trend towards the amendment of national law': United Nations, Document A/CN.4/67, 6 April 1953, 'Nationality, including Statelessness – Analysis of Changes in Nationality Legislation of States since 1930'. Memorandum prepared by Ivan S. Kerno, Expert of the International Law Commission.

76 Borchard, 'The First Conference for the Codification of International Law', 220–21.

77 Stevens, 'America Takes Her Stand', 288.

78 Report of the Committee on Codification, International Law Association. (1930) 36 *International Law Association Representative Conference* 269, 273. (Report on Hague Conference, Mr Arthur Kuhn.)

views – the one favouring complete gender equality in nationality laws, and the other opposing any reduction of the policy of conditional marital nationality – with many gradations standing between. It was thus impossible to 'look forward to any development, even in the distant future, when all the nations of the earth will agree to regulate their family arrangements in accordance with one single ideal'. Borchard observed that '[t]here was a lot of ill-feeling created at the Hague', although, he added, 'the greatest amount of agreement was on a subject which is not, perhaps, strictly International Law at all, namely, the reconciliation of the conflicts of domestic law on nationality'.[79] Despite the agreement, and the adoption of the Nationality Convention by all delegations other than the United States, the Conference concluded without finality. The Cuban Delegation, leading the complete citizenship equality view, proposed that the Council of the League should examine 'whether it would be desirable to take up again, with a view to the next Conference for the Codification of International Law, the question of the nationality of women'.[80]

As predicted, citizenship equality campaigners rejected the Convention's Articles governing married women's nationality, as these only targeted maritally induced statelessness and did not question the policy that still made a woman's citizenship in most countries conditional upon that of her husband. Chrystal Macmillan, representing the 'Nationality of Married Women Pass the Bill Committee',[81] described the position of the opponents. The Hague Convention

> differentiates between men and women . . . It is objectionable since it gives recognition in an international convention to the old idea of the subordinate position of women in the matter of nationality and to the old custom by which a woman's nationality was made to depend on that of her husband.[82]

The Convention, Macmillan noted, was at variance with the Conference recommendation that had invited states to contemplate legislation

[79] Report of the Committee on Codification, International Law Association (1930) 36 *International Law Association Representative Conference* 269, 275–6. (Report on Hague Conference, Mr Borchard.)

[80] 'Progressive Codification of International Law, Observations on the Recommendations of the Hague Conference': Draft Resolution submitted by M. Orestes Ferrara (Cuba, 1930), (1931) 12 *League of Nations – Official Journal* 1586, 1587.

[81] A British Committee formed to promote the Private Members Bills for citizenship equality that were repeatedly, albeit unsuccessfully, introduced in the British Parliament in the 1920s (see Chapter 5).

[82] Macmillan, 'The Nationality of Married Women'.

reflecting the principle that the nationality of woman on marriage should not be changed without her consent.

A 'formidable protest' was staged by the International Alliance of Women 'to ensure that the Hague Convention would not be the final word on the subject', and to discourage their governments from ratifying the Convention.[83] Responding to continuing disagreement among the delegations and protest from outside, the Conference conceded that further investigation was desirable. The question of whether the Articles of the Convention would suffice remained open, indeed for the rest of the decade.

The campaign against the Convention continued, and during the League of Nations Council meeting in January 1931, in an orchestrated operation, protestors deluged members with telegrams. The Council responded by agreeing to place women's nationality on the Assembly agenda. It appointed a non-official Women's Consultative Committee on Nationality[84] and, in an unprecedented step, permitted the Committee to meet in the Secretariat and communicate directly to the Council and the Assembly.[85] Despite some divergence of views among the members of the Committee (some conceding that the Convention offered a degree of protection to married women[86]) the campaign continued. Further 'floods' of telegrams and petitions were directed at the Assembly meeting in Geneva in September 1931, and further deputations were organized.[87] The women's campaign, one historian has noted, 'ensured that the nationality of married women would be the first equal rights issue to be discussed in any detail by the League Assembly'.[88]

At its meeting in July 1931, the Women's Consultative Committee recommended the deletion of Articles 8–11 from the Convention. In

83 Miller, 'Geneva – The Key to Equality', 227.

84 With two representatives from each of: the International Council of Women; Women's International League for Peace and Freedom; Inter-American Commission of Women; Equal Rights International; World Union of Women for International Concord; All-Asian Conference of Women; International Alliance of Women for Suffrage and Equal Citizenship; International Federation of University Women. The different positions taken by these organisations on the details of what should be included in citizenship equality laws are set out by Bredbenner, *A Nationality of Her Own*, 219–20.

85 Arthur Henderson, President of the Council, received 210 telegrams in forty-eight hours. Miller, 'Geneva – The Key to Equality', 227.

86 Miller, ibid, 229. The Committee split in 1933 over the issue.

87 UK National Archives, HO 45/15147: 'Nationality of Married Women'. Oscar Dowson to F. A. Newsam, Home Office, London, 18 September 1931.

88 Miller, 'Geneva – The Key to Equality', 227.

doing so, it did not distinguish between statelessness and loss of birthright nationality in its account of the 'dangers' posed by ratification of the Convention. This was, of course, a necessary strategy, since admission that statelessness was the primary problem would have conceded the reasoning behind the Convention. But, more than this, their position highlighted the reality that many women who had been transformed into aliens in their former country experienced conditions similar to those of stateless women. Women, the Committee observed, were 'suffering to-day, as never before in recent times, from the disastrous consequences of unequal nationality laws'. In time of economic distress, large numbers of women, deprived of nationality, were denied employment because they were classified as aliens 'even in the land of their own birth'; some had had their professional licences taken away; others confronted new restrictions on trade or occupations; still others lost pensions or access to State hospitals: '[T]he woman who is destitute finds that she has no claim upon her own country for help'.[89]

In 'the light of the desiderata of the women's organisations', a proposal was circulated by the League of Nations to member states in early 1932 asking whether a conference to revise Articles 8–11 of the Convention should be convened, 'or whether . . . the results of the Hague Conference represented the maximum that can be secured by general international agreement at the present juncture'.[90] The latter view was to prevail. Eighteen responses were received by mid-1932: Australia indicated its willingness to accept the independence of married women's nationality but only so long as the United Kingdom and Dominions were 'agreeable to tak[ing] similar action'; Belgium indicated its preparedness to permit women at the time of marriage to opt for one nationality or another, but regarded the proposal to re-examine the Hague Convention to be inopportune at present; Brazil asserted that nationality law was not an international matter (and '[p]rogress in this sphere depends more on doctrine and intelligent propaganda than on an international agreement'). Its own law, it pointed out, had long been 'liberal' on women's nationality; Colombia indicated that it was possible to incorporate equality of nationality in its citizenship law, but recognised that a substantial number

[89] National Archives of Australia, A446 1964/46452. Memo, 29 March 1933, League of Nations, Nationality of Women. 'Observations by the Committee of Representatives of Women's International Organisations, 7 September 1932'.

[90] League of Nations, 'Nationality of Women: Observations submitted by Governments', Geneva, 23 July 1932.

of countries were not so prepared, and that the Hague Convention was the most that could be achieved; Czechoslovakia agreed that a new examination of the question of married women's nationality was desirable, and reported that nationality rules were currently on the agenda of the Czech National Assembly;[91] the Egyptian Government reported that it was 'unable to agree' to the Women's Organisations' proposals and that there was no need to modify the Hague agreement; Germany indicated that it was 'entirely favourable' to the Women's Organisations' 'endeavours', but believed that no international agreement on the 'complete assimilation' of women's and men's nationality was possible. Traditional and religious principles of family unity were, it observed, irreconcilable with principles of 'women's self-determination'; Great Britain and Northern Ireland indicated their willingness to support the Hague Convention, but noted that whether their government would be able to go further depended on the support of other countries, especially members of the British Commonwealth; Hungary reported that the proposals of the Women's Organisations were not 'in harmony' with Hungarian law, and that it was not desirable to reconsider the Hague principles; Japan reported that the equality of women with men in nationality was 'contrary to that family unity which forms the basis of the Japanese social system', and stated that it would not support a reconsideration of the Hague agreement; Monaco stated its support for the Hague principles without further explanation; Netherlands stated its desire to maintain the unity of nationality in marriage, governed by the husband. It was prepared to forego this principle in cases of the wife's statelessness, but would not accept a system where the wife and husband had different nationalities. Further discussion of the question, it concluded, would lead to no practical result; Norway reported that it had no objection to continuing the study of the question, and that it would give sympathetic consideration to any proposal for international agreement that marriage alone or its dissolution should not automatically lead to change in a woman's nationality; Rumania held that the Hague agreement represented the maximum achievable and that any further change would 'multiply the conflict of laws, compromise the unity of the family, and create difficulties as regards the nationality of children'; Siam stated that the unity of the family required that a husband and wife should be of the one nationality. It accepted the statelessness exception of the Hague Convention, but not the provision under which the husband's

[91] As Melissa Feinberg makes clear, nothing came of these developments at that time. Feinberg, *Elusive Equality.*

naturalisation did not automatically lead to his wife's naturalisation, as this was contrary to the law of Siam; Sweden reported that its own law already satisfied some of the 'desiderata' of the Women's Organisations, and if the majority of states agreed to take the question of women's nationality further, it would not oppose a new examination of the question; the United States recognised that the subject was 'highly controversial' and concluded that there was little likelihood of international agreement to any principles going beyond the Hague Convention. It pointed out that its own laws gave married women independence in nationality, and that the '"right of expatriation" . . . has been adhered to by [the US] Government for many years'.[92]

By late 1932, a total of thirty-three countries had responded. Several, including Chile, Turkey and Cuba, treated the Convention as merely a first step and stressed the importance of eliminating all the Articles that marked inequality in the legal status of men and women and that, in Chile's words, 'represented a condensation of the spirit of inequality underlying that Convention'. Sixteen countries concluded that it would be 'inexpedient at present' to convene a new conference on the question. Certain states, it was pointed out, had already begun to ratify the Convention as it stood, or were intending to do so, and for some the matter was urgent. Canada was among the latter, and there was general support for Canada's proposal that the Convention should 'shortly be put into practice'.[93]

Pressure from international organisations came from both sides, variously advocating retention or reconsideration of the draft Convention's provisions. On the 'reconsider' side, two mass petitions (one signed by women, the other by men) organised by the 'International Committee of Catholic Women for the Nationality of Married Women' were received by the League of Nations Secretary General. The Committee, described as 'a special ad hoc body of individual women in various countries interested in the cause advocated by the petitions', prayed that 'a woman, whether married or unmarried, should have the same right as a man to retain or change her nationality'.[94] Eight thousand signatures,

[92] League of Nations, 'Nationality of Women: Observations submitted by Governments', Geneva, 23 July 1932.

[93] National Archives of Australia, A446 1964/46452, 'Nationality of Women', 10 October 1932.

[94] Archives New Zealand, Ref no. IA1 2824, Record no 116/6, League of Nations, 26 September 1932. Nationality of Women. 'International Petition of Catholic Women', and 'International Petition of Catholic Men'.

from twenty-three countries, were attached. The attention of the League Secretariat was specially drawn to the signatures of eminent men: the Prime Minister of Australia (Joseph Lyons), a former Prime Minister of Newfoundland (Edward Morris), and many Australian, British, and French Members of Parliament, as well as an Archbishop and numerous Priests (including from Australia, France, Italy, Ireland, South Africa, Spain, USA and Japan). Tellingly, Canada's 'eminent' signatories were few (a King's Counsel, a medical doctor and one other individual). Many Canadians were committed to the principle of citizenship equality, but pragmatic and pressing interests supervened. Driven by its particular circumstances, Canada was, as we have noted, especially anxious to ratify the Convention and to amend its nationality law accordingly. On the other hand, many Catholic Canadians were troubled by the equality principle and concerned that it would erode family unity. The relative paucity of Canadian signatures may well reflect the conjunction of these perspectives.

On the 'retain' side, opponents were fearful that the League of Nations might yield to the pressure for reconsideration. A petition in August 1931 from the Union Internationale des Ligues féminines catholiques, which was communicated to the League Assembly, acknowledged that the current situation regarding the nationality of married women was unsatisfactory, and that reform of the laws was needed for cases of statelessness, dual nationality, and conflicts of laws. The petitioners

> venture[d], however, in the name of the twenty-five million Catholic women who belong to the Union, respectfully to call . . . attention to the danger involved in any infringement of the principle of the unity of the family. The Union is convinced that to defend the integrity of the family is entirely in the interest of the social and moral well-being, not merely of nations considered individually, but of humanity as a whole. Accordingly, the Union . . . [d]eclares its conviction that it is the principle of the unity of the family and not that of the emancipation of women which should predominate'.[95]

Pending the coming into force of such an international agreement, the petition continued, international rules for the settlement of conflicts should be established, in particular, for preventing marital statelessness, and 'for protecting women against any arbitrary change in their

[95] UK National Archives, HO 45/15147: 'Nationality of Married Women'. Geneva, 5 September 1931. League of Nations, 'Nationality of Women'.

nationality being effected by their husbands'.[96] Similar sentiments were expressed in a communication received by the President of the Hague Conference in early 1930 from women doctors of law in the Netherlands, calling for the uniform system of law governing the nationality of married persons to be governed by the unity of the family.[97]

In the event, the League of Nations did not go even as far as the family unity campaigners wanted. The Thirteenth Assembly of the League of Nations, meeting in 1932, rejected a proposal that the Convention should be revised to embody the principle that the nationality of the wife should not be affected, without her consent, by the fact of marriage or by any change in the nationality of her husband. While it reaffirmed the recommendation of the Hague Conference that governments should examine the possibility of the introduction of the principle of equality of women in nationality, it voted to endorse the ratification of the Hague Convention. It had been clear all along at The Hague that the Convention's anti-statelessness provisions were the most the international community would, at least at that time, concede. Nine member countries abstained on the 1932 vote to endorse the Convention, but it was carried. Although the shift in numbers may have been an indication that the equality campaign had had some impact, this was far from a victory.

A confidential memo from the High Commissioner (to the UK) of New Zealand, one of the countries most clearly committed to citizenship equality and open to going beyond the terms of the Hague Convention, summed up the impasse as it was perceived in 1936:

> There are few subjects coming before the Assembly which are more controversial. It is difficult to overcome national prejudices, nor are national customs sufficiently taken into account by those who, through the League, would internationalise much which is essentially national.

It was doubtful, the memo observed, that any progress would be made, and there was, 'of course, wide diversity as between the countries, the Anglo-Saxon and Nordic countries, with some others, having the most progressive legislation'. However,

96 UK National Archives, HO 45/15147: 'Nationality of Married Women'. Geneva, 5 September 1931. League of Nations, 'Nationality of Women'.

97 UK National Archives, HO 45/15147: 'Nationality of Married Women'. Geneva, 5 September 1931. League of Nations, 'Nationality of Women'.

> [e]ven in the countries in which there is equality as between the sexes [including Britain], the growth of freedom has been slow. We in New Zealand are proud of our enlightened outlook in the matter of the franchise and equality of the sexes. But it must be remembered that we are a new country, unhampered by certain customs and traditions which have a deep foundation elsewhere.[98]

In the event, despite voting for the Convention, New Zealand did not ratify. It incorporated the no-statelessness provisions in its enlarged and amended Nationality Act in 1934 (see Chapter 5).

Still, the campaigners did not give up, and they inched forward. The International Council of Women, meeting in Stockholm in mid-1933, passed a resolution 'expressing the hope that in 1936 the Hague Convention of 1930 would be amended in such a way as to make it possible for married women to have the right to choose their nationality'.[99] In 1935, women's organisations successfully petitioned the League for inclusion in the agenda of the Assembly of discussion of the Equal Nationality Treaty that had been adopted at the 7th Pan-American Conference, Montevideo (see below). Still, the Hague Convention entered into force in 1937, unamended, following ratification by the specified minimum of ten countries.

At the same time, a campaign was under way for the adoption of an international women's equal rights treaty and the Assembly was persuaded to turn its attention to this broader issue. The Twelfth Session of the League Assembly, having requested the governments of the state members of the League to examine whether it was possible to introduce into their law the 'principle that the nationality of the wife shall henceforth not be affected without her consent either by the fact of marriage or by any change of nationality of her husband',[100] the Sixteenth Assembly now asked member states to furnish details about the general political and civil status of women in their country, including with regard to

[98] Archives New Zealand, ref no. IA1 2825. C 421 252 Record no. 116/6, Item ID R19964 606, pt 4, Department of Internal Affair, 'Nationality of British women married to aliens – General file'. 'Confidential' Memo, Prime Minister's office, to Under-Secretary Department of Internal Affairs, 2 April 1936.

[99] UK National Archives, HO 45/15367, 'British Nationality and Status of Aliens Bill'. International Council of Women, Stockholm June–July 1933: Resolution re Nationality of Married Women.

[100] National Archives of Australia, A446 1964/46452. 'The replies received were inconclusive and despite the strong protests of the Women's Organisations represented at the Assembly or appearing before it, the Committee declined to go beyond the resolutions of the Hague Convention. The position is most unsatisfactory'.

nationality. A Committee for the Study of the Legal Status of Women was appointed to collect information on women's legal status from international law experts. Its focus was primarily upon the legal and political rights of women, but it also considered laws of divorce and domicile. The study was abandoned with the outbreak of war. Still, it offered a foundation for the subsequent work of the United Nations Commission on the Status of Women, following the Commission's establishment in 1946.[101] Out of that work, a commitment to citizenship equality would finally be secured.

The Montevideo Convention

The League of Nations was the major theatre for the international debate on policies of conditional marital nationality and on principles of citizenship equality, but it was not alone. The Pan American Union was also closely interested in the issue. By the 1920s, certain South American countries had joined the United States in repealing their marital denaturalisation laws. Several had long been ambivalent on the question of women's citizenship. Argentina's Civil Code had had no clear provision governing the effect of marriage on women's citizenship, and Argentina was consequently sometimes held up as an exception to the general practice of conditional marital nationality, although judicial decisions had tended to assume the latter. An amendment to the Code in 1926 granted civil rights to Argentinian women, with the effect of protecting married women's independent nationality.[102]

Brazil's legislature had introduced bills for conditional marital nationality in 1860 and 1899; these, however, were opposed as unconstitutional, a conclusion apparently confirmed by the Supreme Court of Brazil.[103] Naturalisation in a foreign country was, however, a ground for loss of

[101] Jaci Eisenberg, 'The Status of Women: A Bridge from the League of Nations to the United Nations' (2013) 4 *Journal of International Organizations Studies* 8.

[102] The Argentinian Ministry of Foreign Affairs issued circulars to consulates and legations in 1914 and 1918 declaring that the protection of Argentinian law was extended to the foreign-born wives (among other family members) of Argentinians, although not necessarily because these persons had acquired Argentinian nationality. Domicile in Argentina entitled them to receive Argentinian passports. As Kif Augustine-Adams has shown, the Supreme Court of Argentina systematically interpreted the law to require a married woman to take her husband's nationality, but only with regard to jurisdictional matters. Kif Augustine-Adams, 'She Consents Implicitly', 8.

[103] Lutz, 'Nationality of Married Women in the American Republics', 3.

Brazilian citizenship.[104] In the mid-1920s, the Brazilian legislature rejected a proposal from the Brazilian Federation for the Advancement of Women to extend Brazilian nationality and the protection of Brazilian laws to foreign wives, in cases where either they actively applied for nationality or where they had lost their own nationality through their marriage.

Chilean law had never adopted conditional marital nationality, whether for Chilean citizens married to foreigners or foreign women married to Chilean citizens (although naturalisation in a foreign country was a ground for loss of citizenship and may have resulted in denaturalisation for wives of foreign men). The law in Uruguay and Columbia at that time was similar. There were, however, several exceptions to the Latin American egalitarian trend; Bolivia, Cuba, Ecuador, Peru, and Mexico all retained marital denaturalisation laws. Still, despite differences, there was 'a greater tendency to uniformity in the American Continent than in the Old World' as regards married women's nationality.[105]

A 'remedy' of joint action among South American states was proposed.[106] It was not the first attempt to harmonise Latin American nationality law; among other initiatives, a conference on the topic, had taken place in 1877 at the instigation of Argentina and Uruguay, and a Congress in 1887. The Chilean delegation had taken the lead at The Hague in 1930, in pressing for a commitment to citizenship equality. A resolution favouring women's equal political rights had been passed at the Fifth Pan American Conference in Santiago, in 1923. The Sixth Conference, in Havana, in 1928, had unanimously adopted a resolution for the

104 The law governing naturalisation as a Brazilian citizen did not distinguish between men and women, and the residency requirements for naturalisation were dispensed with for 'foreigner[s]' married to Brazilian citizens. Regulations, Decree of May 1908. Flournoy and Hudson, *A Collection of Nationality Laws.*

105 Lutz, 'Nationality of Married Women in the American Republics', 5.

106 The law of nationality was identified as one of a small number of problems of international law which 'because of the special political economic or social conditions of the states of America, receive or are likely to receive a solution different from that which they receive in Europe'. Alejandro Alvarez, 'Latin America and International Law' (1909) 3 *American Journal of International Law* 269, 352. A principal distinction, according to Alvarez, was the desire of American countries for the descendants of foreigners to be 'incorporated' into the population, expressed in the *jus soli* rule, as opposed to the European preference for *jus sanguinis.* These, according to Alvarez, were 'antagonistic' principles. To the extent that an explanation can be proffered for the partial Latin American exceptionalism with regard to marital denaturalisation (and America's relatively late legislative provision for the practice), the reluctance to lose married women and their children from the 'incorporated' population may have played its part.

creation of an Inter-American Commission of Women, with its membership to consist ultimately of a woman from each of the twenty-one member countries.

The Commission selected the nationality of women as its first subject for research and it appointed a committee to draft a convention on women's nationality rights. In 1930, the committee recommended a draft which was unanimously adopted, and subsequently presented to the Hague Conference 1930, and then annually before the League of Nations Assembly.[107] In December 1933, the Seventh International Conference of American States meeting in Montevideo, Uruguay, unanimously adopted the Convention. Initial opposition from the United States was transformed into agreement, on the instruction of President Roosevelt, with the reservation that the agreement of the United States was to be subject to Congressional action.[108] The Senate unanimously consented to the Convention in December 1933.[109]

The 'Montevideo Convention on the Nationality of Women' contained a single substantive Article. The signatories agreed that '[t]here shall be no distinction based on sex as regards nationality, in their legislation or in their practice'. The provision, as Waltz noted, did not specify independent citizenship, as such, for women, but entailed a sexual equality principle.[110] Articles of a further Convention adopted at Montevideo dealing broadly with nationality declared that naturalisation and associated loss of nationality should affect only the relevant individual; and 'Neither matrimony nor its dissolution [should affect] the nationality of the husband, the wife, or of their children'. Together, these promoted both citizenship equality and independence with respect to marriage.

The Montevideo Convention was placed before the Sixteenth League of Nations Assembly in 1935, and the Secretariat then requested views on it from women's international organisations. The organisations were divided. The Women's Consultative Committee on Nationality endorsed the Convention; the International Alliance of Women for Suffrage and Equal Citizenship considered it a 'step in the wrong direction'; the World's Young Women's Christian Association, the International Co-operative Women's Guild, and the International Women's Committee of the Labour and Socialist International found it 'insufficient to meet

[107] Waltz, *The Nationality of Married Women*, 113–14. [108] Waltz, ibid, 114.
[109] Orfield, 'The Citizenship Act of 1934', 99.
[110] Waltz, *The Nationality of Married Women*, 116.

the desires of women';[111] such opponents believed that the 'equality' principle would mean that women would typically be the ones to lose their nationality.[112]

The First Committee of the Assembly was also divided. The meeting concluded, once again, that further steps could not yet be taken, but that League members should be informed that the Montevideo Convention was open to all states and at the same time reminded that ratifications by signatories of the 1930 Hague Convention were due. It resolved that national and international development of 'this important problem' should be monitored by the League Council 'in order to determine when such development has reached a point at which further concerted international action is justified'.[113] To accept stalemate on this issue, to undertake to monitor and transmit observations and reports to the League, to hope that conditions would somehow adjust themselves in the future, were the recurring outcomes of meeting after meeting in this interwar period.

As with many longstanding international issues, resolution finally became possible; the conditions for 'further concerted international action' on women's nationality did emerge. As had happened with the abolition of conditional martial nationality in individual countries over the years, by the end of the Second World War, the international community found itself capable of overcoming problems that it had previously considered intractable.

The conclusion to conditional marital nationality

The United Nations Convention on the Nationality of Married Women was adopted by the UN General Assembly in February 1957. It had grown from the initial work of the UN Commission on the Status of Women which had taken an interest in the question of married women's nationality since its first session in 1947, and was built on recommendations made by the Commission to the Economic and Social Council in 1948. The draft prepared in 1952 by Manley O. Hudson, Special Rapporteur to the International Law Commission on nationality and statelessness, included a first article modelled on the Montevideo Convention.[114] The Convention

[111] Waltz, *The Nationality of Married Women*, 117.

[112] Miller, 'Geneva – The Key to Equality', 229.

[113] National Archives of Australia, A981, Control symbol IMP 139 Part 2, 'Imperial Conference 1937 Nationality of Married Women Part 2'. 'Secret', Department of External Affairs, 27 January 1937. Notes re Nationality of Married Women.

[114] Manley O. Hudson, International Law Commission Yearbook, 1952, Vol II.

on the Nationality of Married Women, as we saw at the beginning, went beyond the avoidance of marital statelessness, and proclaimed the principle that a woman's nationality should not be altered or lost through marriage or the dissolution of marriage alone, or by the naturalisation of the woman's husband.

The ultimate success of the Convention remains remarkable, given the long and circuitous path that the issue of women's nationality had traversed, but its success should not distract from the obstacles that were faced. In 1949, noting that the Universal Declaration of Human Rights included the right to a nationality, the Economic and Social Council had proposed a Convention to assure gender equality in nationality, in particular to avoid statelessness. The International Law Commission was invited to draft a Convention, but declined, maintaining that the subject of women's nationality could not be treated separately from the whole question of nationality and statelessness, and stating that its volume of other work was too great at that time for it to undertake this task.[115] The Commission on the Status of Women had, itself, begun by drafting a convention on the status of married *persons*; its focus was refined after receiving responses from governments.

Addressing the UN Third Committee in November 1955 on the then draft Convention on the Nationality of Married Women, Hugh McClure-Smith, the Australian representative, summed up the alternative views, concluding, on balance, in the Convention's favour:

> The present item is a very important one. It concerns a question with which the Economic and Social Council and the Status of Women Commission have been concerned for some years. Undoubtedly the question of the nationality of married women is only one part of the general question of nationality and the related problem of the elimination of statelessness . . . [T]here are many problems which are not solved by this convention. . . . However, my delegation considers that the draft convention does provide certain guarantees which will prevent the more flagrant injustices and anomalies which arise from the present confusion of national laws on this question.[116]

This conclusion would prevail, despite deep divisions among member countries over women's rights priorities, as well as over the manner

[115] National Archives of Australia, A446/182, Control symbol: 1962/67117, Department of Immigration, 'UN Convention on Nationality of Married Women', Part 1.

[116] National Archives of Australia, A446/182, Control symbol: 1962/67117, Department of Immigration, 'UN Convention on Nationality of Married Women', Part 1. 17 November 1955.

in which women's nationality should be protected. Greece, China, Belgium, USSR, Egypt, Dominican Republic, the United Kingdom, Poland, Argentina, New Zealand, Yugoslavia, Mexico, Ethiopia, Iraq, Colombia, Denmark, Syria and Bolivia supported the draft Convention. The Netherlands opposed the Convention, proposing changes designed to preserve family unity rather than women's independent citizenship. Turkey objected that the Convention was less liberal than Turkish law and that it disregarded the unity of the family (and failed to make provision for children's nationality). Brazil's representative declared that his government was in sympathy with the principles, but would abstain on the vote because of discrepancies between its concepts and Brazilian law. Guatemala expressed support for the idea of a Convention on the nationality of married persons rather than married women. The United States found the draft unsatisfactory because it did not provide for the full equality of rights proclaimed in the Universal Declaration of Human Rights and the United Nations Charter. Others declared that their country was investigating the question further. Finally, after further debate and much turning in circles, the Convention was completed.[117]

The Convention, the outcome of so much deliberation and activity, and the legal resolution to the laws that had been progressively adopted around the world over a period of more than a century, has (in common with the history of women's nationality generally) attracted dismayingly little scholarly attention. A book devoted to women's rights and international organisations makes only a brief reference to it.[118] A chapter on the formation and work of the UN Commission on the Status of Women mentions it only briefly, in a manner suggestive of its having second-best status; the Commission, Laura Reanda writes, 'set aside its earlier goal of an instrument based on full equality between the sexes, for fear that it would not be widely ratified, and instead adopted a text which limited itself to protecting women against automatic loss of acquisition of nationality as a consequence of marriage'.[119]

[117] However, although many countries signed the Convention straight after its adoption in 1957, others delayed over concern with details, including over the fact that, unlike other international agreements, the Convention stipulated obligations to aliens.

[118] Nitza Berkovitch, *From Motherhood to Citizenship: Women's Rights and International Organizations* (Johns Hopkins University Press, 1999) 83, 107 fn2.

[119] Laura Reanda, 'The Commission on the Status of Women', in Philip Alston (ed), *The United Nations and Human Rights: A Critical Appraisal* (Clarendon Press, Oxford, 1992) 283.

The goal of full equality between the sexes would be declared twenty-two years later in the United Nations Convention on the Elimination of All Forms of Discrimination Against Women (CEDAW). Significantly, CEDAW expressly reaffirmed the independence of married women's nationality, as well as providing a comprehensive statement of the equality rights of women and gender non-discrimination. On marriage rights specifically, CEDAW went much further than the 1957 Convention, but it retained the core principle of citizenship equality, regardless of marriage. State parties, under section 9 commit to

> grant women equal rights with men to acquire, change or retain their nationality. They shall ensure in particular that neither marriage to an alien nor change of nationality by the husband during marriage shall automatically change the nationality of the wife, render her stateless or force upon her the nationality of the husband.

Importantly, what is protected here is specifically a woman's nationality. Marriage equality rights are treated separately, as a distinctive subject. This, in itself, marked a major historical shift. Under previous laws almost universally accepted by the international community, a woman's nationality, as we have seen, was conditioned by her choice of husband. Marriage and citizenship were conflated.

Now, nationality was recognised as a right, literally within its own right. The women from whom it had been taken, and those who had campaigned for its restoration, had long known it as such. They had, persistently and passionately, claimed it as a possession, not simply a stepping-stone to other rights or entitlements, but as an existential 'good' in itself. It was a good of particular value to women, precious, both functionally and existentially, and to be prized independently of its functional consequences, including political rights. Such rights remain of vital importance, of course, but they follow from, rather than define, citizenship. We explore this existential understanding of citizenship in the following, final chapter.

7

What is a citizen?

Conditional marital nationality was far more than simply a policy expressed in legal instruments. It was a human *experience* – something the women who were affected lived with, something that was internal to their existence, and that shaped both their identity in the community and their sense of self. The policy governed women's legal status, but went well beyond its legal and political consequences. The 'sentimental' side of nationality had long been recognised, even for women, but the personal stakes grew as the law continued to operate. 'It is not only in the field of international relations that the growing importance of nationality is seen', wrote one observer of citizenship's evolution in 1934; 'Today it is steadily acquiring a greater significance both for sentimental reasons and the rights which it gives'.[1] In the same year, Chrystal Macmillan described women's subordinate citizenship as 'a matter of the utmost gravity because of the psychological effect':

> [It is] founded upon the theory of the subjection of women. To recognise in practice this old idea is a refusal to treat a woman as a citizen in her own person. It is to deny her the status of an adult. Furthermore, it gives recognition to a system which has [not only negative practical effects, but] . . . spiritual consequences.[2]

All those who acquire a new citizenship by naturalisation must know something of this psychological experience: this change of identity, this shift of selfhood. But there was a critical difference between naturalisation and conditional marital nationality: the former was, and remains, voluntary, while the latter was not. The experience of marital denaturalisation was profoundly shaped by its involuntary character[3] and by the existential magnitude of the loss. What, then, was lost?

[1] Bicknell, 'The Nationality of Married Women', 106.

[2] Macmillan, 'The Nationality of Married Women'. Supplement, April 1932.

[3] The 'major grievance, in every case' of marital denaturalisation was, Macmillan wrote, 'that the loss of nationality and its consequential disadvantages are imposed without the

There is no single understanding or definition of citizenship. The literature on the subject is vast and multifarious. It covers multiple perspectives – historical, empirical, theoretical, normative, aspirational – sometimes converging or overlapping, at other times diverging to the point of incommensurability. Theorists have observed this multiplicity. In a survey of the extraordinary burgeoning of citizenship theory that began in the 1980s, Will Kymlicka and Wayne Norman distinguished 'citizenship-as-legal-status' (full membership of the political community) from 'citizenship-as-desirable-activity' ('cultural citizenship').[4] Linda Bosniak identified four different conceptualisations: citizenship as legal status; citizenship as rights; citizenship as political activity; and citizenship as collective identity and sentiment.[5] Audrey Macklin observed that 'citizenship describes status, rights, practices and performances' and it applies at different levels; it 'specifies relationships between the state and individual or group identities[,] . . . denotes various degrees of membership . . . and describes idealized subjects of governance . . . and that is only a partial list.[6] There are numerous other taxonomies.[7]

For all these theories, it is rare to find citizenship treated as both status and *experience*, as a quality of being that is, at the same time, grounded in the cold formalities of the law. Most conceptualisations are concerned with the consequences, with what follows from having or claiming the status of citizen. Certainly, the consequences – what one gets, what one is entitled to, how one is regarded and treated by others – are included, but the consequences are part of the larger experience. With a small number of powerful exceptions (discussed below), few theorists have considered this larger canvas: the quality of citizenship in itself, what it means to a person to *be* a citizen.

The history of women's conditional marital nationality offers this perspective. The contingency of citizenship, dependent on emotion and personal circumstances – the fact of love and marriage – which have nothing in themselves to do with one's status as a member of a jurisdictional or

consent of the woman, so that she is without the power to protect herself'. Macmillan, 'Nationality of Married Women', 144.

4 Will Kymlicka and Wayne Norman, 1994 'Return of the Citizen: A Survey of Recent Work on Citizenship Theory' *Ethics* 104 (2) 352–81.

5 Linda Bosniak, 'Citizenship Denationalized' (2000) *Indiana Journal of Global Legal Studies* 447, 455.

6 Audrey Macklin, 'Who is the Citizen's Other? Considering the Heft of Citizenship' (2007) 8 *Theoretical Inquiries in Law* 333: 334.

7 I bundle the above conceptualisations together, discussing citizenship as 'rights' and citizenship as 'participation'.

constitutional community, was revelatory of the experience. For women who lost their citizenship through foreign marriage, the loss revealed the character of the thing lost, even in cases where the functional consequences were favourable or neutral, and even as the practical problems and hardships caused by marital denaturalisation were, little by little, removed or alleviated by amendment to laws. But, the one effect that could not be altered, other than by repeal of the law altogether, was the loss of the right to be legally at home in their 'own' country.

Maritally denaturalised women experienced the withdrawal of the protection of their former state; they were literally *alienated*. This experience was both formal (reclassification as an alien with all the consequent disabilities; loss of entitlement to a particular passport, loss of legal protection abroad) and existential (the loss of 'home', the experience of alienage). At times, the loss was compensated by the gain – one home and one source of protection replaced another – but, even where this replacement automatically occurred, the exchange involved loss.

To approach citizenship from this perspective, to identify it as something dependent upon legal status, but more than its formal consequences, has significant implications. We are asked to think of citizenship as a primary value, not as against the citizens of other countries (that is, not nationalistically), but as a source of protection, a way of attaching persons to a territorial home, an important, indeed paramount, human need. This is not a new claim. The United Nations Declaration of Human Rights recognised the tragic dislocations and alienation of populations caused by persecution and war; it proclaimed, among others, the human right to a nationality. Subsequent international conventions – the 1951 UN Convention Relating to the Status of Refugees and the 1961 Convention on the Reduction of Statelessness – affirm both the human need for territorial security and the enormity of its loss. They do not disparage the political and legal rights that attach to citizenship and nor do they treat these as necessarily or even conceptually exclusive to citizens, but they acknowledge that nationality is a value in itself. They recognise that life is a condition of vulnerability, and that human thriving is impossible without protection. The territorial home offered by citizenship is a primary (if not always functional) barrier against vulnerability.

Citizenship as 'rights'

Citizenship laws, as we have noted throughout, govern the acquisition, retention and transmission of the legal status of citizens. They do not typically make reference to 'rights', political or otherwise. Rights are typically determined in other legal instruments; where citizenship is involved, it is a precondition or qualification for their enjoyment. It is assumed in such a precondition that a pre-existing law has already set down rules for the conferral of citizenship. Many citizenship theories (and, no doubt, widely held popular views), however, assert or assume that citizenship is defined by the holding of rights. They reason from the consequences, rather than the foundation.[8]

The primary 'right' associated with citizenship in, perhaps, most people's minds, is the right to participate in political decision-making, specifically through the right to vote, which is the principal means by which participation in a representative democracy is expressed. This right has been particularly important in the conceptualisation of women as citizens. The long historical struggle for the vote, we have noted, is the subject of many studies of women's citizenship, and its milestones are rightly recorded in public institutions, on democracy 'timelines', and in the commemorations of the lives and work of pioneering suffragists. We have also seen that, in some cases (the United States most notably), the repeal of conditional marital nationality was related to, or temporally coincident with, women's attainment of the franchise. But, we noted that, in other countries, these events were entirely unsynchronised (and, in the United States, in 1915, the Supreme Court rejected the argument that the protection of citizenship and the right to vote were conceptually interdependent[9]).

In the inter-war years, governments were repeatedly frustrated or bemused by the continuing campaign for the repeal of marital denaturalisation laws, even after (following the 1930 Hague Convention) statelessness as a result of marriage had been pre-empted, and even in cases where schemes for women's retention of political rights were adopted. In 1934, the New Zealand legal draftsman wrote to the Minister of Internal Affairs, regarding the proposal to amend the New Zealand law to permit maritally denaturalised women to reacquire the rights (but not the legal status) of British subjects: 'I think it may be assumed that the women's organisations . . . will not be satisfied, for they appear to be concerned

[8] Ann Dummett and Andrew Nicol, in a valuable history of British nationality law (that, unusually, takes account of marital denaturalisation) more subtly suggest that a discourse of citizenship is missing from British history and that Britain has not developed a culture of human rights or of popular sovereignty. British nationals (notwithstanding the change in legal terminology) are still, effectively, 'subjects'. Dummett and Nicol, *Subjects, Citizens, Aliens and Others: Nationality and Immigration Law.*

[9] *Mackenzie* v. *Hare* 239 U.S. 299 (1915).

with the retention of the status of British subject rather than with the actual rights incident to it'.[10]

The confusion between citizenship and the right to participate in choosing one's political representatives is neither accidental nor casual. Full membership of a constitutional community demands the opportunity, at least, for participation in the decision-making processes that give rise to the laws that bind members of that community. Such membership is legally signified by citizenship. But, while citizenship may be necessary, it is not sufficient. We know that not all citizens are permitted to vote,[11] and that in some countries, non-citizens can (or, historically, could) vote. We know that aliens live in the community's jurisdictional territory and are subject to its laws. But claims that they should, therefore, enjoy political rights do not presuppose them to be, or confuse them with, legal citizens. In countries where legal citizenship is a precondition for political rights (this is increasingly common), enjoyment of these rights rests upon a prior right: that of acquiring and retaining citizenship. The right to vote, that is, does not turn (alien) persons into citizens, and nor does it signify their citizenship if the class to which those persons belong is not legally entitled to citizenship in the first place (or, having held it, is subject to its involuntary loss).

Some theorists of citizenship acknowledge the historical centrality of the claim that citizenship is defined by rights, but challenge it, both normatively and factually. Alexander Bickel argued that citizenship was best treated as a relatively thin concept, carrying with it few, if any, special rights:

> Citizenship is a legal construct, an abstraction, a theory... Emphasis on citizenship as the tie that binds the individual to government and as the source of his rights leads to metaphysical thinking about politics and law, and more particularly to symmetrical thinking, to a search for reciprocity and symmetry and clarity of uncompromised rights and obligations, rationally ranged one next to and against the other... It is by

10 Archives New Zealand, R19964 605, pt 3, Ref no. IA1 2824, Record no. 116/6, Memo, 16 November 1934, to Minister of Internal Affairs, from J. Christie, Law Draftsman.

11 Children and persons with mental incapacity are (probably) universally ineligible to vote. In many countries, citizen prisoners are also ineligible, and in some, ex-prisoners remain ineligible. Some countries exclude citizens who live abroad from voting. Others exclude particular classes of citizen, such as dual citizens, from standing for public office. Certain of these disqualifications are controversial, but this does not alter the general acceptance that limitations on the right to vote are, in principle, legitimate.

> such thinking . . . that the claims of liberty may be readily translated into the postulates of oppression.[12]

This is an important statement. It recognises citizenship as something provided by law, detached from 'rights' and unrelated to conduct, and it foreshadows the dangers of conditioning citizenship upon tests of allegiance and reciprocity. Bickel's conclusion that little attaches to citizenship cannot, however, be correct. The 'concept' of citizenship may be thin in the sense that the rule of law and most constitutional protections (at least in the United States) are offered to all 'persons', and do not distinguish between citizens and aliens. However, regardless of how we approach a definition, the impact of holding citizenship (as we have seen, and as discussed below) cannot be dismissed as minor.

David Cole, in a similar vein to Bickel, argues for decoupling the concept of citizenship from claims about rights, specifically with respect to civil liberties: 'It is especially important for [those] . . . who advocate expanding concepts of citizenship as a way of expanding rights to be cognisant of the danger such claims may create for those who are not citizens'.[13] Cole's concern is that a discourse of citizenship rights (especially in times of crisis and heightened fears of foreigners) may encourage the withdrawal from, or denial of, legal protection to non-citizens. Cole illustrates this with examples of both the ill-treatment and the judicial vindication of individuals who were the subjects of anti-terrorist measures after the attacks in the United States on 11 September 2001.

Alexander Aleinikoff promotes a 'decentered' idea of citizenship, detaching formal citizenship from rights and liberties. He argues for the 'binary' distinction between legal citizens and immigrant aliens to be diminished, for a recognition of multiple sovereignties, and a 'thick', non-abstract, conception of citizenship.[14] Linda Bosniak also notes that a focus on the rights of citizens risks the conclusion that aliens deserve lesser protection; she observes that '[w]ithin the logic of constitutional citizenship theory itself, citizenship is not just for citizens'.[15] From this perspective, there should be no antinomy between the alien and the

12 Bickel, 'Citizen or Person?', 54.

13 David Cole, 'Against Citizenship as a Predicate for Basic Rights' (2007) 75 *Fordham Law Review* 2541, 2542.

14 Alexander Aleinikoff, *Semblances of Sovereignty: The Constitution, the State, and American Citizenship* (Harvard University Press, 2002).

15 Linda Bosniak, *The Citizen and the Alien: Dilemmas of Contemporary Membership* (Princeton University Press, 2002) 79.

citizen, no privileging of one over the other with regard to rights. Citizenship is not an all-or-nothing thing. In the past, Bosniak reminds us, women held 'nominal' citizenship but were denied many rights. Macklin also treats citizenship as a 'container that is seldom completely empty . . . or completely full'. She introduces the notion of the 'heft of citizenship' to describe the 'variability in the cumulative content of citizenship', and the spectrum of differentiation between the enjoyment of full citizenship at one end and statelessness at the other.[16]

A related body of citizenship rights literature is concerned with the conditions of equality among persons, either within the state or across states. If citizenship is a measure of full equality, this perspective suggests, formal citizenship and legal equality are insufficient, even derisory. This conclusion is the legacy of the theory of T.H. Marshall, who famously observed that full 'citizenship' goes beyond legal and political rights, and extends in 'equal partnership' to social rights, ranging from the state's responsibility to grant 'a modicum of economic welfare and security' to the rights of the person 'to share to the full in the social heritage and to live the life of a civilised being according to the standards prevailing in the society'.[17] Many subsequent theorists have extended this analysis to historically marginalised groups. Kenneth Karst, for example, writes of the historical struggle for the citizenship of women and racial minorities in the United States. The task of guaranteeing formal equality, he observes, is nearly completed, but 'a great many of the factors of social life that hurt women are beyond the direct reach of formal equality'.[18] Racial and gender stereotyping, Karst notes, still generate rights-denial and create inequalities in the national community.

Ayelet Shachar's *The Birthright Lottery* takes the equality argument further.[19] Shachar challenges both the focus on formal rights as a means of understanding citizenship and the normative claim that rights belong to citizens. Her argument, which offers an examination of the different life-chances and experiences that distinguish citizens from aliens and certain classes of citizen from others, stands as a major exception to the consequentialist theories of citizenship that overlook the experiential. Shachar is concerned centrally with the relationship between citizenship

[16] Macklin, 'Who is the Citizen's Other?', 337.

[17] T.H. Marshall, *Citizenship and Social Class: And Other Essays* (Cambridge University Press, 1950).

[18] Kenneth Karst, *Belonging to America: Equal Citizenship and the Constitution* (Yale University Press, 1989) 105.

[19] Shachar, *The Birthright Lottery*.

and the conditions of justice. She finds the arbitrary allocation of goods according to the accident – the 'lottery' – of citizenship to be undeserved and unjust. Some people in the world, Shachar writes, have the fortune of acquiring, by birth, the citizenship of a country of privilege; others are born to the citizenship of underprivileged countries. Citizenship, Shachar argues, is the equivalent of inherited property. For the fortunate – those whose parents were blessed with the citizenship of prosperous countries and permitted by law to transmit their blessing to their children – the inheritance brings vast benefits, including the opportunity to pass these on to future generations. For others, it brings nothing but deprivation and despair.

Shachar offers two ways of addressing this injustice, the second of which is relevant here.[20] It involves a redefinition of the test for allocating national 'goods' – what Shachar calls *jus nexi* – where 'citizenship' is measured by a close or 'genuine' connection between the person and the state, by 'actual membership and social attachment rather than mere birthright entitlement'.[21] As Shachar notes, this test resembles the reasoning in the Nottebohm case, in which (as we have seen) the International Court of Justice (ICJ) in 1955 held that a naturalised non-resident citizen of Liechtenstein did not have a sufficiently genuine connection with that country to be represented by it in an international dispute. The ICJ reasoned that citizenship involved 'a legal bond having as its basis the social fact of attachment, a genuine connection of existence, interests and sentiments, together with the existence of reciprocal rights and duties'.[22] Applying this reasoning positively, under the *jus nexi* approach, long-term residents with deep social connections to a country would be entitled to the rights and benefits that would normally be reserved for citizens. They would hold a type of alien citizenship.

Shachar's approach brings together the normative and the legal. It has the virtue of addressing citizenship as a both a legal reality and a lived experience, and it is aspirational without being romantic. Her conceptualisation recognises that citizenship has a profound effect on the life-histories and chances of its bearer, and importantly, it does not

[20] The first is a 'birthright privilege levy': a form of taxation obligation 'born by windfall recipients of membership entitlement in well-off polities to improve the life prospects of those alloted less under the birthright lottery'. Shachar, ibid, 15.

[21] Shachar, ibid, 188.

[22] *Liechtenstein* v. *Guatemala* 1955 I.C.J. 4, 23. As noted in Chapter 2, there is an argument that the ICJ's reasoning was not that Nottebohm was not a legal citizen, but that his claim amounted to an abuse of international law. Sloane, 'Breaking the Genuine Link'.

obscure the fact that there are emotional and interpersonal attachments associated with it. For that reason she does not advocate an unbounded cosmopolitanism:

> [T]ransferring the weight of political membership from a bounded community to the global scale risks washing away the entire collective identity aspect embedded in the various 'portals' of citizenship as we currently understand it. It may also lead to the disintegration of the social bonds and mutual responsibilities that, through joint action and decision making, help bind people together and motivate them to redistribute internally the benefits of membership in a relatively stable and self-ruling community.[23]

Shachar questions the focus on a 'demos' theory of citizenship, and argues that the 'focus on *formal equality of status* makes invisible the *inequality of actual life chances* attached to citizenship in specific political communities'.[24] She begins, therefore, with the task of questioning the formal political definition, not in itself, but because it obscures the actual impact of citizenship in the distribution of the good. In this, her primary concern remains citizenship's functional and consequential character: the 'rights', benefits, and goods to which it gives access. Although she writes of 'social bonds and mutual responsibilities', she relates these to action, engagement, decision-making and self-rule. Other theorists, Shachar notes, also promote the idea of 'making citizenship depend on functional and pragmatic rather than formal criteria', but again, the idea is 'that a generous and ascending scale of rights should be accorded to non-members as they extend and deepen their actual participation in a polity over time'.[25]

There are several observations to make here. First, the existential conceptualisation of citizenship that I offer is entirely compatible with the idea that 'rights' (including those of political participation) and 'goods' (resources, social benefits, housing, health care, education, and more) should be granted on an equal footing to citizens and to non-citizens alike, who, as fellow residents, are part of a state. It is also compatible with claims for 'open',[26] or at least relatively porous borders, and for enlarged and simplified opportunities for immigration and/or employment of non-citizens. It is also in principle compatible with the view that parents and children should have a common citizenship (albeit allowing for individual family members to hold other citizenships), and that

[23] Shachar, *The Birthright Lottery*, 47. [24] Shachar, ibid, 9. [25] Shachar, ibid, 169.

[26] Joseph Carens, 'Aliens and Citizens: The Case for Open Borders' (1987) 49 *The Review of Politics* 251.

law should facilitate this. It is compatible with – indeed, it logically suggests – a generous, expansive and proactive naturalisation program in every country. It is also neutral as to whether there might be circumstances that justify citizenship revocation (or in which this might be a rational or effective policy). It does not assume that denaturalisation can never be justified. That the Convention on the Reduction of Statelessness (Article 8) permits revocation for conduct 'seriously prejudicial to the vital interests of a state', at the same time as recognising the fundamental importance of territorial security, suggests serious consideration of such justification. But is also underlines what is the central theme of this work: that citizenship is existentially vital and that its loss is profound.

Secondly, although the criteria in Shachar's *jus nexi* test are functional and pragmatic, they may, as Shachar herself acknowledges, also extend to the affective. This assists with understanding that there is more to citizenship than political rights, or even more generally, membership of a political community. Applied narrowly, however, the genuine connection test creates problems, or at least rings alarm bells. It may have the effect of disqualifying those legal citizens who have a slight or thin 'connection' with the jurisdictional state, or of requiring the individual to demonstrate his or her attachment or participation, and even to have these tested, in order to be treated as a 'genuine' citizen, and thereby the recipient of citizenship rights.[27]

Logically, to contextualise this in our history, the approach that identifies citizenship with equal rights or benefits and goods would mean that the marital denaturalisation of women who automatically acquired their husband's citizenship by marriage (so long as the countries involved had equivalent regimes of comfort, security and opportunity) could not be treated as a loss. It would mean that the marital denaturalisation of women under the law of a country that offered relatively few opportunities for women's participation (and thereby for their genuine connection) was less harsh than marital denaturalisation under the law of a country

[27] Peter Nyers has also warned of the dangers in the discourse of 'accidental' citizens (those, for example, who happened, by the temporary circumstances of their parents, to be born in a *jus soli* jurisdiction, like the United States) as distinguished from 'essential' citizens. The distinction, he writes, has the potential to validate exclusions from protection of persons who belong to disfavoured groups (such as racial or ethnic sub-communities) or to categories that attract suspicion. Peter Nyers, 'The accidental citizen: acts of sovereignty and (un)making citizenship', (2006) 35 *Economy and Society*, 22. Nyers cites Juliet Stumpf, 'Citizens of an Enemy Land: Enemy Combatants, Aliens, and the Constitutional Rights of the Pseudo-Citizen' (2004).

that offered greater opportunities. Such a conclusion would be deeply problematic for a theory of justice. Those without access to the political process would be rendered doubly vulnerable. Theories of citizenship that start with membership of the *political* rights-conferring community (if only to enlarge it) push in this direction.

Citizenship as participation

Numerous studies have sought to explain citizenship as a particular type of conduct, distinguishing this perspective (related to the political rights definition) from both a focus on the formal legal status and from the conceptual approach found in the ideology of liberalism. These studies have, notably, approached citizenship as a 'republican' value, drawing inspiration from the history of classical republicanism and from the neo-classical republican ideas identified with the American Revolution. Republicanism, in this conceptualisation, entails two 'essential elements', as Richard Dagger writes: 'In a republic . . . the government of the state or society is a public matter, and the people rule themselves'.[28] For republicans, Dagger continues, the question is not whether these essentials are good things (they are assumed to be), 'it is how best to achieve them'. This question, then, draws attention to public conduct, to the degree to which individuals contribute to self-government and to 'fostering the public virtues that lead people to do their duties as citizens'.

Republican citizenship theorists argue that liberalism, which emphasizes individual autonomy, privacy, and self-interest, is antithetical to the promotion of public virtue, to participation in community and self-government. Dominated by the values of liberalism, they suggest, people have become less public spirited, less 'virtuous', and more interested in private pleasures and consumption. They are 'citizens' in name only. For the republicans, individuals are real citizens to the degree to which they display 'civic virtue'. Their legal status may be important, but it requires 'the supplement of the ethical dimension'.[29] This is more than an attitude; it demands active and selfless participation. Participation is educative; it engages and enlarges one's capacity to be a 'citizen'. In Michael Sandel's

[28] Richard Dagger, 'Republican Citizenship', in Engin F Isin and Bryan S Turner (eds) *Handbook of Citizenship Studies* (Sage Publications, 2002) 146.

[29] Dagger, ibid, 149.

words, republics must engage in 'a formative politics . . . that cultivates in citizens the qualities of character that self-government requires'.[30]

Alison Kesby, drawing on the theory of Jacques Rancière, offers a more complex version of the republican approach, bringing together rights and participation. Politics, Kesby explains, is not a sphere, but a process, and rights are held by 'those who, though lacking all qualification to do so, take them up, claim, and enact them'.[31] People show themselves to be citizens by their public act, the act of claiming their rights.[32] This perspective, Kesby writes, 'shifts our focus from the power of the state and its institutions to the agency of the excluded'.[33] The excluded emancipate themselves and thus demonstrate their equality and their citizenship. They claim citizenship as an act of self-assertion.

In common with other republican citizenship theories, this approach situates citizenship in the active, public sphere. It overlooks the question of whether or not the state will recognise what is asserted; that is, whether the claimant of citizenship and accompanying rights has any legally cognisable status. It leaves unconsidered the fact that nothing can come of self-asserted rights or self-constituted citizenship, without the willingness of the state to confer these upon the claimant. Aliens are not merely persons lacking the formal status of citizen but capable of becoming citizens through virtuous public conduct. They remain in a state of contingent recognition; any rights they enjoy (as permanent residents, for example) are dependent upon the patronage of the state. Nothing can come of claims for citizens' rights that are made by those who have no security in their right to take political action or to assert their 'citizenship' in the state against which they make these claims. Aliens may participate. This does not make them citizens.[34]

[30] Michael Sandel, *Democracy's Discontent: America in Search of a Public Policy* (Harvard University Press, 1996), quoted in Dagger, 'Republican Citizenship', 148.

[31] Alison Kesby, *The Right to Have Rights: Citizenship, Humanity, and International Law* (Oxford University Press, 2012) 121.

[32] Kesby, ibid, 126. Unusually for rights theorists, Rancière, as Kesby explains, illustrates this principle with a historical feminist claim, that of Olympe de Gouges, who protested during the French Revolution that 'if women are entitled to go to the scaffold, they are entitled to go to the Assembly'. Her protest, Rancière states, demonstrated political capacity, and thus citizenship.

[33] Kesby, *The Right to Have Rights*, 130.

[34] In Rogers Brubaker's words, 'There is a conceptually clear, legally consequential, and ideologically charged distinction between citizens and foreigners'. Brubaker, *Citizenship and Nationhood*, 21.

To tie citizenship to active conduct is also normatively to privilege the active and assertive, those who have the capacity to participate. To demand *action* as the core criterion of citizenship is to deprive 'actionless' persons of the status of citizen (although, notwithstanding republican claims, it makes no difference in fact to their legal status). It is to imagine citizenship as a reward for self-awakened rights, and to disparage those who, for whatever reason, do not have the capacity to engage in community life, or to show themselves to be civically 'virtuous'. It is a model of citizenship without compassion. Kesby recognises this problem, and acknowledges that Rancière's account is 'necessarily exclusionary',[35] that it risks excluding those who lack the capacity – either in their person or in their circumstances (such as in immigration detention centres) – to assert and campaign for their rights: 'Those least able to defend themselves, remain without a voice'.[36] She offers, as an alternative, passive forms of protest or self-assertion. She retains the participatory core.

Even in such a nuanced account, the historical precariousness of the legal citizenship of those who are not 'citizens' in the self-assertive or participatory sense appears logically to be justified. The stateless or denaturalised person who, having lost his or her citizenship, can have no citizenship rights, is logically conflated with the putative 'citizen' who has not yet achieved political rights. To conceptualise citizenship as a matter of active or potential participation in self-governance minimises the role of the state; it creates a barrier for recognising the relationship between the state and the individual as one of protection.

Protection and the subjective good

Rogers Smith writes that the idea of the 'connection of modern republican citizenship with active self-governance' was historically displaced in the (Westphalian) international order by a 'legalistic, protection-oriented, imperial version' of citizenship.[37] Smith's concept of 'protection' here is particular and narrow. In the post-revolutionary United States, he observes, the shift from self-government to formalism was accompanied by the denial of political rights to free African Americans and women,

[35] Kesby, *The Right to Have Rights*, 131. [36] Kesby, ibid, 132.

[37] Rogers Smith, 'Modern Citizenship', in Isin and Turner, *Citizenship Studies*, 108. Smith references David Held, *Democracy and the Global Order: From the Modern State to Cosmopolitan Governance* (Stanford University Press, 1995).

who, notwithstanding their legal citizenship, were guaranteed only 'limited rights to certain judicial and executive protections'.[38] Smith writes further that this post-Westphalian liberal ('Lockean') conception of citizenship presents civic membership 'basically as an instrument of a diverse range of self-interested personal life plans';[39] the guarantee of state protection (as 'contained in international law notions') is only to the minimum conditions of protection for property-owning, which is the core element in individual self-maximisation. These minimal guarantees of rights protection, in the liberal conception, are thought sufficient, 'so long as basic human rights are not violated'.[40]

This is a critical caveat. Nationality, we have noted, *is* a basic human right, not because it is a precondition for participation in self-government, but because it offers territorial identity, security, harbour, and, in the most fundamental sense, home: in other words *protection*. Smith's overview of modern citizenship is correct with respect to the emergence and development of formal jurisdictional citizenship, but it treats the protection of citizenship as primarily economic. Smith, however, is sceptical about predictions based on ideals of global or cosmopolitan citizenship as an alternative to liberalism, and he concludes: 'in some fundamental regards citizenship will probably remain what is has long been: a political status of profound importance for the well-being of those who fully and securely possess it, and of those who do not'.[41] This conclusion is significant, but, importantly, it leaves open the content of 'well-being'. Certainly, well-being includes economic security and, perhaps, property, but it cannot logically be confined to these (even if supplemented by the non-violation of basic human rights). If it were, the well-being of non-citizens who hold property and enjoy associated legal protections in foreign states would be equivalent to the well-being of property-owning legal citizens. It is not. What our history reveals, and what is profoundly important in legal citizenship, is that the 'protection' enjoyed by citizens has a deeper sense.

The association between citizenship and participation is not without critics, including those for whom *equality* is the essential characteristic of citizenship, and the circumstances of the vulnerable are a core consideration. Will Kymlicka conceptualises citizenship as relational, as describing a process; he begins with a rejection of 'a static list of the desired virtues or sites of responsible citizenship'. Instead, he writes, we should think about 'the dynamic and relational process' of what he calls *citizenisation*.

[38] Smith, 'Modern Citizenship', 108. [39] Smith, ibid, 109.
[40] Smith, ibid. [41] Smith, 114.

The process of citizenisation, Kymlicka argues, resembles the historical dynamic of replacing 'uncivil relations of domination, coercion, and intolerance, with newer relations of democratic citizenship'. Citizenisation 'is premised on values such as autonomy, agency, consent, trust, participation, authenticity and self-determination'. It assumes, Kymlicka writes, 'that citizens have a subjective good that they are able to express'. In Kymlicka's words, '[a] citizenship model presupposes that society exists to serve the interests of all its members', and 'social norms must be equally responsive to the good of all its members'.[42]

In this schema, even those whose capacity for active agency or engagement in public reason or political processes is weak, can be treated as part of the deliberative community of citizens, as those who are not incapacitated or disabled 'learn how to better understand [the] agency' of those who are, 'to identify their expressions of subjective good, and to create mechanisms that are more responsive to their good'. Citizenship is about 'recognising that we are members of bounded communities which shape the opportunities for us to flourish, supporting every member of the community to write their own life script'.[43]

Melissa Williams also considers the experiential dimension of citizenship.[44] She argues for a conception based on 'the idea that we are enmeshed in relationships of interdependence with other human beings that emerge from the past and extend into the future[,] . . . relationships of shared fate [transformed] into the boundaries of a moral community' by 'shared deliberation over a common good'.[45] Williams, importantly, recognises that structures of relationships among citizens need not be embraced or even valued by their members, and nor do they need to generate a strong sense of identity or loyalty or mutual affection; that is, she does not require a particular citizenship *affect* (as civic virtue theorists tend to do). But, the membership of the community of citizens – the community of 'shared fate' – is identified as united by a common commitment to the common good. Her approach, which appears to

42 Will Kymlicka, 'Responsible Citizenship' (2012) 4 *Trudeau Foundation Papers* 56.

43 Kymlicka, 'Responsible Citizenship'.

44 Melissa S. Williams, 'Nonterritorial boundaries of citizenship', in Seyla Benhabib, Ian Shapiro, and Danilo Petranovic (eds) *Identities, Affiliations, and Allegiances* (Cambridge University Press, 2007) 226, 228.

45 Williams, 'Nonterritorial boundaries of citizenship', 228. Williams wants to confront the realities of globalisation and replace the territorial aspect of historical citizenship with a conception of citizenship 'in functional or pragmatic terms – that is, in terms of the human ends it serves'. 229.

distinguish itself from accounts that dictate or weigh the moral quality of the affect of citizenship, thus also falls back on a metric of conduct.

Participatory theories that reason from the 'political' in the sense of individual activity or engagement make membership effectively a subset of the larger 'political community'. This, I suggest, makes it difficult to conceptualise citizenship from the starting point of the institutional, to recognise that a citizen is not self-constituted but is designated by law. It also makes it difficult, perhaps, to then contemplate the relationship from the other side, from the side of the citizen as an already designated person, and to ask what it means to *experience* citizenship, already conferred. It is the state that confers citizenship. The experience begins with this fact, with formal status, under law. Far from wanting to make this as bloodless as it may sound, my purpose is to fill the state with human persons, to contemplate their circumstances, their experience *as* citizens. In particular, I want to emphasise that human persons are vulnerable to the effect of the law that designates them as citizens of one or other state, but the boundaries of this relationship have limits.

Citizenship cannot be an empty concept, susceptible to any content the state chooses to give it, or capable of describing any type of relationship with the state. It must involve a relationship of protection, an obligation on the part of the state to protect those whom it designates as citizens. This claim is in one sense normative (not all states fulfil that obligation to all of their citizens[46]), but it is embedded, at least indirectly, in international law. As Alfred Boll writes, '[a]mong the most serious charges that can be levied against a state is that it has abandoned its nationals to their fate, rather than attempting to protect them against arbitrary or illegal treatment by other states'.[47] Protection is also embedded in domestic law and practice, and exemplified, in particular, by the fact that, historically, states wishing to withdraw their protection from individual persons or classes of person (in order to expel them or simply wash their hands of them), denaturalised them first, stripped them of their citizenship, and rendered them aliens or stateless persons under law. This, as we have

[46] As Audrey Macklin reminds us, citizenship of '"failed states" . . . delivers virtually none of the protection associated with membership in a functioning polity'. Macklin, 'Who is the Citizen's Other?', 348. States may, additionally persecute their own nationals. A well-founded fear of persecution in the country of one's nationality is, indeed, what defines the refugee under the 1951 United Nations Convention Relating to the Status of Refugees (and its 1967 Protocol). But such a country, the Convention recognises, has failed to offer the protection that is owed, under law, to its citizens.

[47] Boll, *Multiple Nationality and International Law*, 245.

seen, was the practice of virtually every state towards those of their women citizens who married foreign men.

The history of marital denaturalisation is a history of literal alienation, of withdrawal of protection and home, via a legal practice. It gives us the missing side of the story of modern citizenship – the women's side – that fills in the canvas and reveals the foundational character of citizenship.

Statelessness and home

An understanding of the existential conceptualisation of citizenship begins best with citizenship's antonym: statelessness. We approach what citizenship means, that is to say, by looking at what it means to be without it.[48] Hannah Arendt famously described statelessness as a condition of total 'rightlessness' and citizenship as 'the right to have rights'. This epigram has frequently been quoted (and sometimes misappropriated). Dissenting in a United States case, *Perez* v. *Brownell* (which upheld the denaturalisation of a citizen for asserting foreign nationality in order to avoid military conscription and for voting in a foreign country's election), Chief Justice Warren wrote that citizenship is a man's basic right. It is 'the right to have rights':

> Remove this priceless possession and there remains a stateless person, displaced and degraded in the eyes of his countryman. He has no lawful claim to protection from any nation, and no nation may assert rights on his behalf. His very existence is at the sufferance of the state within whose border he happens to be.[49]

Justice Frankfurter for the Court, however, was less anxious for the existential status of the denaturalised citizen. He acknowledged the history of denaturalisation, including of women, and described the 'essential significance' of the reasoning in *Mackenzie* v. *Hare* and *Savorgnan* v. *United States*[50] (which confirmed the denaturalisation of an American born

48 Audrey Macklin also poses the question; rather than asking 'who is the citizen?', she asks: '"who is the citizen's Other?," partly as a means of surfacing what we mean by citizenship through thinking about who we designate as its alterity'. Macklin describes statelessness 'as an antipodal reference point for citizenship'. Her approach, however, is not so much to understand the quality of citizenship itself, but to understand the 'emergent figure' of the possessor of citizenship without a state. Macklin, 'Who is the Citizen's Other?', 335.

49 *Perez* v. *Brownell*, 356 U.S. 44 (1958) 64.

50 *Savorgnan* v. *United States*, 338 U.S. 491 (1950). Rosette Savorgnan had undergone Italian naturalisation in order to marry an Italian diplomat in the United States, and without an awareness of the consequences for her American citizenship. She was unsuccessful in her

woman), as a 'rejection of the notion that the power of Congress to terminate citizenship depends upon the citizen's assent'.[51] What the cases established, the Court concluded, was that the citizens in question, like Mr Perez, had simply engaged in conduct that Congress had determined as grounds for citizenship deprivation.

Chief Justice Warren's dissent also acknowledged that his country had practised marital denaturalisation in the past. However, despite his impassioned plea for recognition of the existential nature of citizenship and the depiction of the tragic consequences of its loss, his treatment of that history was derisory. In his brief discussion of *Mackenzie* v. *Hare*, he described Ethel Mackenzie's loss of citizenship as no more than 'suspension'. In his words, the case 'simply acknowledges that United States citizenship can be abandoned, temporarily or permanently, by conduct showing a voluntary transfer of allegiance to another country'.[52] Marital denaturalisation was, Warren assumed, the consequence of a simple, consensual choice. The fact that restoration of citizenship was available, under the US law, after the marriage had terminated by divorce or the husband's death, was taken to mean that the loss of citizenship involved no 'degradation'.

It is impossible not to see in this opinion the view that a woman's citizenship was less valuable, and its loss less injurious than that experienced by a denaturalised man.[53] It was a view that persisted, and was not confined to cases where statelessness followed. The view expressed by Justice Frankfurter would, however, soon be overtaken by Justice Warren's perspective: citizenship, the Court would decide, could not be removed without the consent of the individual citizen (and not merely for conduct). It was, effectively, the property of the citizen, and not of Congress.

In *Trop* v. *Dulles*, a case concerning citizenship stripping for desertion in time of war, Chief Justice Warren for the Court described the resulting statelessness again in Arendtian terms, as amounting to 'the total

claim that she had not intended to renounce her allegiance to the United States and that her residence in Italy in the Second World War had arisen due to the expulsion of her husband from the United States during the period of hostilities.

[51] *Perez* v. *Brownell*, 356 U.S. 44 (1958) 61.

[52] *Perez* v. *Brownell*, 356 U.S. 44 (1958) 73.

[53] The view has, it seems, been laid to rest. In May 2014, the United States Senate passed a resolution expressing 'sincere regret' for the marital denaturalisation of American-born women. Ironically, despite noting that 'thousands of women' were affected, a news report of the resolution referred to the Expatriation Act as 'an obscure 1907 law'. (The report also noted a series of recent Senate apologies for past laws that were racially discriminatory or otherwise offensive.) *Los Angeles Times*, 16 May 2014.

destruction of the individual's status in organized society'.[54] This view prevailed. *Perez* was overruled. In *Afroyim* v. *Rusk*,[55] now the leading US case on citizenship deprivation, the Court proclaimed that Congress had no power to expatriate a citizen without his consent: 'The entire legislative history of the 1868 ["Expatriation"] Act makes it abundantly clear that there was a strong feeling in the Congress that the only way the citizenship it conferred could be lost was by the voluntary renunciation or abandonment by the citizen himself'.[56] Citizenship represents 'that which is his own, a constitutional right to remain a citizen' unless voluntarily relinquished.[57] The Court, this time, astonishingly, made no reference to the 1907 Expatriation Act or *Mackenzie* v. *Hare*.[58]

Stateless persons, as Arendt described them (and these cases confirmed) suffered losses far more fundamental and terrible than the loss of political or participatory rights, or even socio-economic rights (although they were often denied these). The stateless, Arendt wrote, suffered two losses: 'The first loss . . . was the loss of their homes, and this meant the loss of the entire social texture into which they were born and in which they established for themselves a distinct place in the world'.[59] The second was the loss of any government protection; the stateless person was 'out of legality altogether'. The calamity was that the stateless 'do not belong to any community whatsoever'. They are reduced to the abstract nakedness of being nothing but human.[60]

Arendt wrote that '[t]he world found nothing sacred in the abstract nakedness of being human'.[61] This is a powerful claim, and it has, perhaps, been overtaken by the advance of international human rights law, but even for its time, it was excessively binary. Between 'abstract nakedness' and secure legal citizenship, lay the citizen who held citizenship precariously:

54 *Trop* v. *Dulles*, 356 U.S. 86 (1958) 101.
55 *Afroyim* v. *Rusk* 387 U.S. 253 (1967).
56 *Afroyim* v. *Rusk* 387 U.S. 253 (1967) 266.
57 *Afroyim* v. *Rusk* 387 U.S. 253 (1967) 268.
58 However, in dissent, in order to make the argument that involuntary citizenship stripping had been accepted in previous cases, Justice Harlan did mention *Mackenzie* v. *Hare*. He rejected the view that Mackenzie had, in marrying a foreigner, voluntarily expatriated herself for the duration of her marriage: 'It is immaterial . . . that Mrs. Mackenzie's citizenship might, under the statute there, have been restored upon termination of the marital relationship; she did not consent to the loss, even temporarily, of her citizenship.' *Afroyim* v. *Rusk* 387 U.S. 253 (1967) fn 17.
59 Arendt, *The Origins of Totalitarianism*, 293.
60 Arendt, ibid, 295.
61 Arendt, ibid, 299.

in our case, the single woman for whom citizenship was conditional or contingent, for whom membership of a constitutional community could be lost or reassigned following the simple recitation of the marriage vow. As we have seen, in the international consensus that emerged in the early years of the modern constitutional state and lasted until the post-war era, the married woman was neither legally abstract nor legally 'concrete'. She was, in both a tangible and an existential sense, a legal enigma. She was the subject of the sovereign that might transform her in an instant and without process, into an alien, and in some cases (in the 1920s, in many cases), into a stateless person.

Even in conditions where a stateless person (or a refugee) is well cared for, the calamity and the misery remain. In recognising this condition, we recognise the value of being a citizen. Citizenship is a condition of 'statefulness' or 'homefulness'. It enables the protection that arises from having a legal right to a territorial home. The women who campaigned against marital denaturalisation understood this. As we saw, even where automatic naturalisation in their husband's citizenship followed their marriage, they described the stripping of their native citizenship as an injury. The association of home and protection was not merely functional; one citizenship home was not simply replaceable by another.

From the perspective of statelessness, a secure territorial home is, of course, the elemental need; the home of one's longing is secondary. As Macklin observes, 'one ought not to equate the declining importance of citizenship in a particular state with a diminution in the value of citizenship in *a* state'.[62] But, to repeat Arendt, the secondary loss is none the less profound; it is the loss of 'the entire social texture into which [the stateless] were born and in which they established for themselves a distinct place in the world'. Macklin also observes that 'citizenship is not fungible. The revocation of citizenship severs a unique relationship between the individual and a specific state', unique both in the specific opportunities and entitlements offered by that state and in the 'lived experience' of that relationship. She rightly eschews the establishment of a 'metric' to measure these experiences, and concomitantly, the impact of loss. If the task, indeed, was one of measuring the 'quantitative, qualitative, subjective, experiential, emotional, personal, familial, cultural, social, financial, linguistic and political impact'[63] of the loss it would suggest that citizenship

[62] Macklin, 'Who is the Citizen's Other?', 336.

[63] Audrey Macklin, 'Citizenship Revocation, the Privilege to Have Rights and the Production of the Alien' (2014) 40 *Queen's Law Journal* 2, 50.

is an entirely open-ended, fluid or contentless (at least immeasurable) quality. The history of the experience of citizenship deprivation tells us otherwise. However else the experience is quantified, citizenship is repeatedly articulated as an attachment to a particular territory, and with this, a sense of haven, a promise of 'return'.

This perspective does not suggest that the experience of citizenship as 'home' is necessarily sentimental. The citizen's enjoyment of a 'distinct place in the world' may be instrumental, even opportunistic. It may even be 'fungible'. For some, the place will have deep emotional resonance; but modern citizenship, as a legal construct, does not in itself carry the exclusionary or exclusive connotations of home as 'blood and soil'. It does not, in principle, preclude membership of non-native members by naturalisation, whatever their ethnicity. Modern citizenship, as it has developed, indeed, has the virtue of neutrality with regard to identity-markers such as ethnicity, race or gender.[64] Its application or acquisition in the past has differentiated on such grounds, but, formally, it is sui-generis and non-referential. It does not describe a closed class, and nor does it require patriotism or sentiment. For some people, to be a citizen is meaningful simply because it offers certainty against expulsion. This, however, is no small thing.[65]

The right not to be excluded

How well is the claim embedded in law that citizenship entails the right not to be excluded from the territorial state under which it is conferred? In a 'hard' sense, international law does not recognise the duty of a state to admit its citizens and harbour them, but 'state practice is almost without exception, to allow nationals entry and residence, so much so that the obligation on the state in international law might be conceived

64 Jürgen Habermas writes: 'It was the transformation of the units of organized power from communities of descent with inherited hierarchies into territorial-legal units in which power was organized impersonally and rationally that generated the new form of membership: citizenship'. Habermas, 'Citizenship and National Identity' (1990), Appendix II, in *Between Facts and Norms* (Polity Press, 1997) 494.

65 The impact of expulsion is not confined to the individual alien. Jacqueline Bhabha has drawn attention to the scale of forced removals from the United States; between 2001 and 2004, 'over 4.7 million people were compelled to leave the United States for immigration reasons. This has resulted in the destruction of family life for thousands of citizen children'. Bhabha, 'The "Mere Fortuity of Birth"? Children, Mothers, Borders, and the Meaning of Citizenship' in Seyla Benhabib and Judith Resnik (eds), *Migrations and Mobilities: Citizenship, Borders, and Gender* (New York University Press, 2009) 189.

as a right of the individual in international law'.[66] A state's duty, 'as between states, to admit its nationals into its territory ... is recognized in a number of international human rights instruments'.[67] Article 12 of the International Covenant on Civil and Political Rights provides that 'no one shall be arbitrarily deprived of the right to enter his own country'. Some countries' constitutions (for example, Canada's) expressly entrench the right of citizens to return; other countries affirm this in their legislation (for example, New Zealand's Bill of Rights Act, 1990) or in case law.[68] The rule of the United Nations Convention on the Reduction of Statelessness that a person cannot be stripped of citizenship if statelessness follows, indirectly affirms this. So, too, does the draft provision of the International Law Commission's 2000 review of the expulsion of aliens: 'A State shall not make its national an alien, by deprivation of nationality, for the sole purpose of expelling him or her'.[69]

The citizens' right to non-exclusion is also reflected, conversely, in laws governing the rights of non-citizens. Neither aliens nor stateless persons have a right of abode. As Macklin points out, the right of stateless persons or refugees to reside in any country is a 'revocable privilege'.[70] She cites a Canadian case concerning an application of a Palestinian man for refugee status, in which the court observed that the applicant did not have the requisite well-founded fear of persecution, but concluded: 'He needs a place to live'.[71] The observation is poignant and profound. Without a place to live, existence, let alone wellbeing, is precarious. Its denial may mirror persecution. It is guaranteed in law only to citizens.

Citizenship in countries with transnational agreements permitting unfettered residency for each other's citizens, such as in the Schengen

[66] Boll, *Multiple Nationality and International Law*, 286. While this has not always been accepted, such exceptions as are found today concern persons with multiple nationality.

[67] Knop and Chinkin, 'Remembering Chrystal Macmillan', 523, 540.

[68] Noting the European context, and case law confirming the prohibition on expulsion of citizens of member States to a third state, Dimitry Kochenov and Benedikt Pirker observe that 'residence security is at the core of ... the essential legal essence' of citizenship: 'Deporting Citizens within the European Union: A Counter-Intuitive Trend' (2013) 19 *Columbia Journal of European Law* 341, 374. Bridget Anderson, Matthew Gibney and Emunuela Paoletti also affirm that '[f]reedom from deportation power – the right to *genuinely* permanent residence – can be seen as one of the few remaining privileges which separates citizens from settled non-citizens in contemporary liberal states': 'Citizenship, Deportation and the Boundaries of Belonging' (2011) 15 *Citizenship Studies* 547.

[69] Discussed by Audrey Macklin, 'Citizenship Revocation, the Privilege to Have Rights and the Production of the Alien' (2014) 40 *Queen's Law Journal* 2, 12.

[70] Macklin, 'Who is the Citizen's Other?', 333.

[71] Macklin, ibid, 343.

area of Europe may appear to complicate this picture. In terms of rights to reside, to work, to enjoy benefits, the Schengen European is a 'citizen' of every member country. But, European citizenship remains conditional and territorial: one cannot be a European citizen without holding the citizenship of a member country. The relationship between the two citizenships is, furthermore, unidirectional. The European Court of Justice has affirmed that it is within the power of the member state to revoke the citizenship of a national of a European Union member state, although the revocation caused the loss of European citizenship (and, in a particular case, statelessness).[72] The exercise of the national law comes within the ambit of European Union law, but the European Union itself has no power to protect or confer EU 'citizenship'. The holding of national citizenship remains primary and necessary. In any case, the argument for citizenship as, fundamentally, a quality that engages the protection of the state of which a person is a citizen, is not an argument for exclusivity. It is compatible with multiple citizenships and with transnational rights of territorial residence and protection.

Several issues follow from the claim that citizens have a right not to be excluded from their territorial state, not merely because this is the customary practice and/or offered as a constitutional guarantee – although these are vital gauges – but because it describes the essential nature of citizenship, as such. The first issue concerns the justification, if there is one, for extending a protection to citizens that is denied to aliens. The second concerns reciprocity: whether citizens 'owe' duties or obligations to either their state or fellow citizens, in return for protection and the right to occupy the distinct place in the world to which their citizenship attaches them.

If citizenship provides a core safeguard against one of the most fundamental experiences of human vulnerability, what consequences does this protective conception have for aliens? Does it imply that only those who are legal citizens deserve this form of protection? The conclusion that it does is likely to be the strongest objection, one that finds expression in Shachar's argument against unearned privilege by virtue of the accident of birth. What case can be made that retains the protective, harbouring character of citizenship, but does not conclude with the neglect or ill-treatment or exclusion of non-citizens?

The first, and obvious, response is that there must be a right for all to a nationality, so that, in principle, all persons enjoy the particular type of

[72] Case C-135/08 *Janko Rottman* v. *Freistaat Bayern* (2010).

protection that citizenship offers. The international community's commitment to this principle is, as we have noted, reflected in the United Nations Declaration of Human Rights. This does not, of course, address the fact that citizenship of some countries offers meagre, if any benefits and, in some cases, is both inalienable and undesirable (bringing with it, for example, binding obligations to perform military service even on those who do not live in the country). The unequal distribution of goods attached to the holding of different citizenships is the source of the injustice identified in Shachar's 'birthright lottery'. But, to conclude that citizenship, as such, is adverse because of the distributional injustices it produces, is to mistake the consequences for the foundation. To detach the protective character from citizenship, or to neutralise or abolish citizenship as a qualification for residence, is to compound vulnerability, to make all persons effectively stateless, with the insecurity, both existential and material, this brings.

What, then, of the situation of aliens? Does the principle that citizenship entails a territorial home provide a justification for excluding or expelling aliens from the territory? John Finnis affirms that '[t]he power to admit, exclude and expel aliens' is one of 'the earliest and most widely recognised powers of the sovereign state' and argues that it should be recognised as a modern constitutional principle.[73] The power of exclusion, he writes, engages an underlying principle, as an element in the common good that a constitution promotes. The principle is reciprocity: 'protection within the realm entitles foreigners to the protection of subjects and with it the obligations of subjects'.[74] An alien's right to protection, Finnis suggests, rests conditionally upon the alien's conducting him or herself *as if* he or she were a citizen (or, in Finnis's terminology, 'subject'). The alien, in other words, must act like a citizen or risk expulsion from the community of real citizens.

But, here again, we confront the problem of describing citizenship in terms of conduct. The obligations Finnis would impose on aliens are not the obligations of citizenship. Citizens (at least birthright citizens) have few, if any, behavioural obligations specific to their status (compulsory voting, jury duty, and military service are among the exceptions, but only in some countries) but neither breach of these nor breach of general

[73] John Finnis, 'Nationality, Alienage and Constitutional Principle', University of Oxford Faculty of Law Legal Studies Research Paper Series, Working Paper No. 08/2008, 1. Finnis quotes from a House of Lords judicial opinion in 2005.

[74] Finnis, ibid, 2.

obligations (to pay taxes, obey the law, refrain from encouraging anti-social conduct, and so on) result in stripping of citizenship or expulsion from the state.

Finnis recognises, indeed, that legal citizens may not conform to the 'particular conceptions of common and public good that are embodied in our constitution and law', but the bargain with aliens, he contends, is that they do. 'Citizenly' conduct, his argument suggests, is required of the alien in practice, but of the citizen in theory. Bad birthright citizens, we may add – including criminals and those who are civilly disobedient – retain their legal citizenship. Citizens and aliens sharing a prison cell are legally indistinguishable, but Finnis would make them morally distinct: the alien (it seems) is more culpable, since his or her offence is not merely against the law but against the community of citizens that has offered (conditional) shelter.

Citizenship as allegiance

Finnis bases his conception of the distinction between citizens and aliens, and with it the power to expel the latter, on a historical 'contractual' relationship between citizen and state. The reciprocity he demands of aliens (as a condition of the privilege of living in a foreign state), he finds to be historically attached to the condition of citizenship. The condition of reciprocity rests upon allegiance.

The idea that protection is conditional for the citizen (no allegiance, no protection) is indeed historically long-standing and complex. As we have seen, before the nineteenth century, citizenship (in the sense of the status of 'subject') was treated as perpetual and inalienable. The idea that subjects owed allegiance to the sovereign and were granted protection 'in return' was an underlying or background, ascriptive assumption. It inhered, organically, in subjecthood. Concrete expressions of allegiance (taxes, tithes, military service) could be extracted from subjects, but disobedience or disallegiance did not entail the loss of subjecthood or 'citizenship'.

Once it was accepted that citizenship could be alienated (either voluntarily or compulsorily as a consequence of the transfer of allegiance) the relationship of reciprocity became more concrete. Once foreign naturalisation (entailing a transfer of allegiance) became possible, citizenship acquired by naturalisation could be revoked for disallegiant conduct performed subsequent to the grant of naturalisation (for example, residence in the country of former citizenship) or for naturalisation undertaken in bad faith (for example, to avoid military obligations in the country of former citizenship). Even birthright citizenship became conditional. Most countries stripped birthright citizenship from citizens who were naturalised in another country. Many countries stripped citizenship for conduct that was considered disallegiant, such as foreign military service or, in some cases, participation in foreign politics or in the service of a foreign power. And, of course, virtually all countries stripped birthright citizenship from women who married foreign men. Denaturalisation following foreign marriage, as we have seen, captured both the idea that the act of marriage was a type of disallegiance, and the idea that the act involved the transfer of allegiance, as in (real) foreign naturalisation.

In the complex landscape of citizenship law, the trend, following the Second World War, was to detach birthright citizenship from conduct, to diminish, even eliminate, the actual demands of reciprocity, and to elevate an idea of citizenship as a type of personal 'property', something that can only be lost by a positive, voluntary and willing act on the part of the citizen (and not on the ground of imputed or constructive consent). Conditional marital nationality laws were repealed in almost all countries. The international community came to accept, albeit reluctantly, that persons could hold more than one nationality – that allegiance was divisible – and that 'allegiance' was an abstract idea, even merely a manner of speaking about the character of citizenship. In many countries (although not all) foreign naturalisation ceased to lead to loss of prior citizenship.

To summarise the history, 'citizenship' once belonged, in the sense of adhering to, the subject as an inseparable part of his or her relationship with the sovereign; it could not be alienated, either by the subject's actions or by the sovereign's will.[75] As citizenship law developed and overtook the common or customary law, nationality was initially and principally conceptualised as an aspect of international relations, a tool of 'triage', determining whom to attribute to one state rather than another, a way of assigning the responsibilities of sovereignty. Consequences to, and consent of, the individual were secondary. With the concession in the mid-nineteenth century of the alienability of citizenship or subjecthood, came a small shift. The state still 'owned' the citizen, but the individual, under certain circumstances, could seek to change 'owner'. The end of the rule of perpetual allegiance meant that citizenship was now alienable and therefore insecure, subject to the will of the state, to changes in policy

[75] With the exception, irrelevant here, of the abandonment or concession of territory and its population to a new sovereign and, with it, a collective transfer of allegiance.

and law (even in countries, such as the United States, where citizenship appeared to attract constitutional protection[76]). Birthright citizenship could now be stripped by the state, including without the individual's consent. Women, indeed, were the majority of subjects of this practice (which, paradoxically, was based on the fiction of implied consent[77]). In the twentieth century, the recognition of citizenship as an element of personhood began to emerge. Among the claims made by women's citizenship equality campaigners, as we have seen, was that citizenship 'belonged' existentially (as I have described it) to the citizen, that it was an attribute of their personhood and a marker of their independent adult status.

The law, in some countries at least, was adjusted in the mid-twentieth century and the post-war era to meet this new conception. But no state has ever gone as far as to allow citizenship to rest on personal desire. No state permits an act or declaration of self-ascription to determine a person's national status. Where courts have been asked to rule on an individual's citizenship (in particular, determining susceptibility for deportation), subjective identification or self-description has never succeeded. But, in other ways, the individual 'ownership' conception inched ahead. In the United States, where the constitutional guarantees and limitations on citizenship have been at stake, the conception has succeeded. As we saw, in a series of cases following the Second World War, the Supreme Court progressively questioned the right of the state unilaterally to 'expatriate' citizens, even in cases of disallegiant conduct.[78] By the late 1960s, it had settled on the conclusion that loss of American citizenship could only occur through voluntary renunciation.[79]

76 Among the privileges of citizenship, identified in 1873 in the United States, was 'to demand the care and protection of the Federal government over [the citizen's] life, liberty, and property when on the high seas or within the jurisdiction of a foreign government. Of this', said the Supreme Court, 'there can be no doubt, nor that the right depends upon his character as a citizen of the United States'. *Slaughterhouse Cases* 83 U.S. 36 (1873).

77 As Kif Augustine-Adams explains, 'With Notice of the Consequences', 5.

78 Gordon, 'The Citizen and the State', 35.

79 Peter Shuck and Rogers Smith have defended this 'consensual' conception of citizenship – the idea that citizenship is based on free, individual choices and mutual consent between the national community and the individual. They have described the historical doctrine of ascriptive citizenship with its accompanying conception of perpetual allegiance as oppressive, and the *jus soli* acquisition of citizenship as inimical to historical and policy considerations. Peter H. Schuck and Rogers M. Smith, *Citizenship Without Consent: Illegal Aliens in the American Polity* (Yale University Press, 1985). Despite a lengthy examination of the history of the two conceptions of citizenship, including historical practices of expatriation, they make no mention of conditional marital nationality. Their argument

Other countries have tended to follow this approach, and the state, to a greater degree at least, has been restrained or has restrained itself in the extent to which it can deprive a person of citizenship acquired by birth. In some countries, birthright citizenship could (and can) still be lost when a person has voluntarily been naturalised in a foreign citizenship, but this rule, arising from an intolerance for dual nationality, has also progressively, albeit not entirely, fallen away.

Few of the commentaries that have observed this history have recognised citizenship stripping from women who married 'out' as expressing the outdated view that citizenship was 'owned' by the state. Charles Gordon, exceptionally, wrote of the Supreme Court's decision in *Mackenzie* v. *Hare* as capturing a 'new concept', that citizenship 'could be lost without regard to . . . desires'.[80] In reality the concept was not new. Involuntary denaturalisation, for various reasons, had been practised since at least the mid-nineteenth century in the United States and elsewhere. By 1907, the date of the Act at issue in the case, marital denaturalisation was already a long-familiar part of the law of other countries and had been affirmed in some common law cases in the United States. What was novel in its history, and what remained distinctive, was the idea that citizenship could be lost for reasons that had nothing to do with the qualities of citizenship itself, and even further, that it could be stripped for reasons of desire entirely unrelated to the 'desire' to give up citizenship itself, but rather the desire to be united in marriage with a particular person, an innocent action, historically encouraged, legally recognised, and otherwise rewarded by law.

Since the early years of the twenty-first century, there has been another shift, small, but discernible and growing, towards rethinking the relationship between citizen and state, revisiting the principle that citizenship is 'owned' by the state (in Catherine Dauvergne's term as an 'assertion of sovereignty'[81]). This has been expressed in the tightening of naturalisation tests and the proposed or actual expansion of grounds under which citizenship acquired by naturalisation may be lost, as well as in many new

that the conferral of citizenship should be confined to those 'subject to the jurisdiction' of the United States, in the sense of following from a consensual act, might, paradoxically, be construed as supporting marital denaturalisation (but not marital naturalisation). Similar arguments, indeed, were made in its era.

80 Gordon, 'The Citizen and the State', 324.

81 Catherine Dauvergne, *Making People Illegal: What Globalization Means for Migration and Law* (Cambridge University Press, 2008) 135.

initiatives regulating immigration.[82] The idea that otherwise lawfully resident aliens may legitimately be expelled for acting in a manner contrary to the public good, even short of committing a crime, is also strengthening. With this has come a recognition that citizens act in this manner too, that citizenship is not, in itself, enough to bind the individual to the community or secure allegiance.

Nevertheless, it remains the case that aliens may be expelled: citizens cannot. Proposals for stripping citizenship, even of birthright citizens, are for this reason also again in the air, and some countries have legislated to permit this for individuals, variously, on 'public good' grounds, or following convictions for certain types of crime.[83] Under international law, citizenship cannot be stripped if this leads to statelessness; only dual nationals, who have another citizenship to fall back on, may be denaturalised. But the sequence of the loss of one citizenship and the embrace of another is no longer symmetrical, at least in some countries. In 2014, both Canada and the United Kingdom amended their laws to permit deprivation of citizenship by executive decision in cases where the individual is eligible for an alternative citizenship. Critics, expressing outrage at this policy, have asserted that citizenship-stripping is new or at least was rare in the past, its historical novelty appearing to make it all the more abhorrent. It is not a cheap point to object that denaturalisation of birthright citizens is far from new, that it was practised extensively for many years until the relatively recent past, and that it affected probably millions of individuals over time. Marital denaturalisation, long forgotten or disregarded, cannot be treated as insignificant; it provides the key to an understanding of why modern citizenship-stripping is so harsh or punitive, even if relative security can be assured in an alternative state.

But it may, perversely, also offer an alternative perspective. It is very striking that a 2015 Canadian Federal Court case, upholding the application of Canada's new citizenship stripping legislation,[84] drew upon the

[82] Dauvergne also finds that the 'resurgence' of the authority of citizenship as a formal legal status is directly linked to the crackdown in many states on illegal migration. Dauvergne, *Making People Illegal*, 119.

[83] For an overview of these developments, see Audrey Macklin, 'Citizenship Revocation'.

[84] *Strengthening Citizenship Act* (2014), section 8 of which allows the Minister of Citizenship and Immigration to revoke the citizenship of both natural-born and naturalised Canadian citizens in cases of a conviction relating to national security, terrorism, treason and associated offences. Revocation may apply in cases where the citizen in question holds dual nationality or could hold a second nationality.

history of (among other things) marital denaturalisation. The case concerned a challenge to the Canadian parliament's constitutional power to pass such legislation (and focused on the Governor-General's authority to grant royal assent to the Act in question). The applicants argued that citizenship had become 'constitutionalized' in Canada, and was 'an immutable and inalienable right which cannot be revoked by legislation'.[85] Among the many instances in British and Canadian history that controverted this claim, marital denaturalisation received attention, with the judge pointing out that the Canadian Naturalization and Aliens Act of 1881, following the UK Act of 1870,

> provided that women who married aliens adopted the nationality of their spouses and were no longer British subjects. Further, the act had retroactive effect; women who had married aliens before the acts became law were automatically . . . deemed to be aliens.[86]

The denaturalisation of woman married to foreign men was, in many minds in its time, justified as a response to a type of disallegiance. The legislative rationale, I have argued, was only indirectly connected to this reasoning. Its primary purpose was to manage relations with other countries. It may be the case that the new wave of citizenship stripping for disallegiant conduct has a similar rationale, and the fact that the conduct is that of a citizen is, in itself, a secondary consideration (providing the opportunity, following its stripping, to expel the individual from the state).

If citizenship becomes conditional and therefore precarious, the essential protection that is conceptually attached to it becomes hollow. Protection cures vulnerability; protection upon which one cannot rely is not protection. The principle that the citizen cannot be excluded from his or her state is fragile if the citizen can be transformed into an alien, and thus excluded. To blur the distinction between the alien and the citizen (to punish the 'bad citizen' equivalently to the bad alien) is to render citizens doubly vulnerable; the knowledge that individual citizens are no less likely than individual aliens to behave in a threatening or undesirable way assumes that citizens are to be punished more severely because their conduct imports disallegiance. To be stripped of citizenship (as maritally denaturalised women experienced) is a form of banishment, either actual

[85] *Galati* v. *Canada (Governor-General)* 2015 FC 91.
[86] *Galati* v. *Canada (Governor-General)* 2015 FC 91 [84].

or psychological or both. If this penalty is additional to the penalty provided by law for the conduct in question, it imports a second punishment, one that is known to be, historically, especially severe.[87]

Aliens cannot be banished. Their expulsion does not entail the withdrawal of the protection they are offered in their own state where, once in that particular territory, they are transformed from aliens into citizens. The rule that foreigners can be deported and citizens cannot, is not discriminatory or arbitrary. It is a consequence of a deeper principle; citizenship entails an attachment to the jurisdictional territory that delineates the constitutional community. The citizen is not free from deportation because he or she is given preferential treatment, but because he or she is a citizen. None of this affects the obligation of states to give succour and protection to refugees, or to grant benefits and assistance to aliens, as well as extending to all the general and equal protection of the law, including due process in all decisions concerning their status as aliens. But freedom from exclusion belongs, categorically, to citizens.

Citizenship and residence

The claim for citizenship as foundationally existential is, our history reveals, associated with the fact that citizenship provides a person with a territorial home, a place in the world in which that person may live or to which he or she may return.[88] How much, then, does this argument imply that citizenship and residence are conceptually interdependent? Should the holding of citizenship be conditioned on the fact of having permanent residence – being domiciled – in the relevant country? Conversely, should all alien long-term residents of a particular country be treated *as* citizens because they have made their domicile in that country?

Does the idea that citizenship means a territorial home push us in the paradoxical direction, challenged above, of distinguishing between 'real' citizens and others who are citizens in name only, or, even further, of suggesting that citizenship should be conditioned upon the reality

87 Javier Bleichmar, 'Deportation as Punishment: A Historical Analysis of the British Practice of Banishment and its Impact on Modern Constitutional Law' (1999) 14 *Georgetown Immigration Law Journal* 144.

88 As Chief Justice Griffith of the High Court of Australia explained in 1908, in a case concerning an Australian-born (half Chinese) British subject's right to return to Australia, 'every human being . . . is a member of some community, and is entitled to regard that part of the earth occupied by that community as a place to which he may resort when he thinks fit'. *Potter* v. *Minahan* (1908) 7 CLR 277 at 289.

of residence? This latter idea is clearly reflected in naturalisation laws that require a period of continuous residence as the primary ground of eligibility, and historically, in many countries' laws (and the naturalisation treaties between countries) under which citizenship acquired by naturalisation was lost if the individual became domiciled in his or her former country. It was also indirectly reflected in United States law governing marital denaturalisation. The common law, prior to 1907, as we have seen, had assumed that a women's citizenship was lost upon foreign marriage, only if she had acquired her husband's citizenship and was permanently domiciled abroad.[89] The Expatriation Act of 1907, among other things, permitted a woman denaturalised upon marriage to resume her American citizenship if her marriage had terminated and she resided in the United States. The Cable Act of 1922 permitted the restoration of citizenship lost by marriage through re-naturalisation (with residency criteria), but a woman who had regained her citizenship could lose it again if she resided for more than two years in her husband's country or for more than five years otherwise abroad. However, in most countries, the principle of conditional marital nationality still overrode the test of residence. Women with alien husbands remained aliens, even if they lived permanently in their former state. Allegiance (or the imputation of allegiance), rather than residence, was the principal determinant.

If we set aside allegiance as an obsolete test of citizenship, are we left with residence? Is there a defence for 'opportunistic' birthright citizenship, the formal legal status held by many people in the world by virtue of descent (transmitted from one or more parent or acquired by the mere act of birth) that entitles them, if they choose, to reside in and enjoy the rights of a country in which some of them, perhaps many, have rarely or even never set foot? Should such persons – including those whom Christian Joppke calls 'mere transients and passers-by'[90] – be entitled to hold their citizenship forever, like an amulet or an insurance certificate, offering good fortune at will or somewhere to flee to if things go badly in their country of domicile? What of persons for whom their citizenship is enjoyed merely because it confers property or trading advantages in another country? Should we distinguish here between citizens of a country other than that in which they live (as aliens), always in the state of

[89] Hover, 'Citizenship of Women in the United States', 705. Hover, a US Naturalization Inspector, acknowledged that there were variations in practice and in judicial reasoning.

[90] Christian Joppke, 'Comparative Citizenship: A Restrictive Turn in Europe?' (2008) 2 *Journal of Law and Ethics of Human Rights* 128, 135.

insecurity that alienage brings, and citizens of the country in which they live who also hold the citizenship of a second (or subsequent) country? What do we make of individuals, like Nottebohm, who (as we have seen) acquired the citizenship of Liechtenstein, in order to lose his native German citizenship and avoid the wartime confiscation of his property in Guatemala where he had lived (but had never acquired citizenship)? His status as a Liechtenstein citizen would not have been in doubt had he acquired it by birth or descent. This, following the ICJ's reasoning, would have provided the 'genuine connection' sought by the court, and mitigated his lack of residence in Liechtenstein. Does such a conclusion mean that residence is only relevant for those who hold citizenship by naturalisation? Does it mean that naturalised citizens, as in the past, should lose their citizenship if they do not continue to reside in the country that granted their naturalisation?

Opportunistic citizenship has long been regarded with disapproval.[91] Even in an era when naturalisation was only available by special Act of parliament and was consequently very rare, Britain passed an Act to prevent 'Inconveniences that may happen by Bills of Naturalisation'. The Act's preamble observed that some persons had acquired naturalisation for the purpose of enjoying trading opportunities abroad without 'any design of fixing their Residence in Great Britain, or of becoming useful Subjects thereof'; such abuses of 'the true Intent of Naturalisation', it declared, were not to be permitted. No Bill of Naturalisation would subsequently be received without a

> Clause or Proviso inserted to declare that such Person shall not thereby obtain, or become intitled (sic) to claim, within any foreign Country, any of the Immunities or Indulgences in Trade which are or may be enjoyed or claimed therein by natural-born British Subjects by virtue of any Treaty or otherwise, unless such person shall have inhabited and resided within Great Britain, or the Dominions thereunto belonging, for the Space of Seven years.[92]

Logic ties eligibility for citizenship to residence (at least prior residence) in the case of naturalisation, and the view of citizenship as conceptually and constitutively associated with territorial home pushes in this direction.

[91] Opposing the proposed repeal of conditional marital nationality laws in Britain, one MP objected that 'women [want] to have the best of both worlds, to be able to dodge about between one country and another to see which they like best after marriage'. United Kingdom, House of Commons, *Debates*, 24 March 1943, 1714 (Commander Agnew).

[92] 14 Geo. III. c.84, 1774.

But to condition citizenship upon domicile would have adverse effects, undermining the security or promise of protection it offers. It would, to give one example, disqualify a person who, having grown up in his or her native country, but having married and established a marital home in a foreign country, from returning to the country of his or her youth, where family members may still live and where (to paint the picture further) elderly parents may be in need of care, or simply to resettle there. It would discourage persons from taking employment in another country, offering them the stark and unequal choice between their citizenship and their economic security. It would also, simply, require excessive executive oversight, and would generate unwieldy demands for administrative adjustment to deal with exceptional cases, associated legislative amendment and judicial review. These scenarios are neither hypothetical nor romanticised. They all correspond to the reality faced by women (and administrators) in the era of conditional marital nationality.

Macklin writes, further, that '[m]aking the intention to continue residing in [the country of naturalisation] a condition of citizenship' by naturalisation would 'produce a chilling effect on naturalized citizens' freedom to exercise their mobility rights'.[93] The extension of this observation is that 'opportunistic' or 'accidental' birthright citizens whose citizenship is questioned because they do not reside in the country of their citizenship would be similarly 'chilled'; there is no reasonable way of drawing a distinction between the mobility rights of naturalised citizens (the right post-naturalisation to live where they choose and are welcome) and the mobility rights of birthright or 'legacy' citizens who live in another country. The United States, as Macklin notes, ruled that revocation of a naturalised citizen's citizenship for residing in another country in the years immediately following naturalisation was contrary to the constitutional guarantee of equal protection under the laws.[94]

The long-standing international consensus against dual nationality presupposed intractable conflicts and embarrassments in international relations, specifically with regard to diplomatic protection. With the reality that dual nationality was unavoidable in a growing number of cases (as countries' rules for acquiring citizenship increasingly diverged) these conflicts were, eventually, pre-empted or accommodated with the adoption of protocols and conventions governing cases of 'divided loyalties' in which clashes would otherwise arise between the countries of a

[93] Audrey Macklin, 'Citizenship Revocation', 48.
[94] *Schneider* v. *Rusk* 377 U.S. 163 (1964).

person's citizenship, each in principle obliged to offer protection against the other. Such dilemmas indeed, were among the foremost reasons for international resistance to dual or multiple citizenship over a very long period of time. Notwithstanding the idea that more than one nationality was an 'aberration to be avoided at worst, and eliminated at best',[95] the international community was forced to recognise that it occurred. The international rules for its accommodation also ensured that a person would not be unprotected, that is to say, left without the protection of any of the states of which that person held citizenship.

To withdraw citizenship from persons who do not reside in the relevant state is also to run the risk of their losing protection, even becoming stateless, if they cease to live in a second state in which they have held or acquired citizenship. The experience of sequential losses and acquisitions of citizenship as a person moved to and resided in different countries would be a personal calamity as well as a legal quagmire.

The issue of citizenship acquisition is a different, albeit related, issue. Shachar's proposal that citizenship transmission should decline over generations (for those having no 'genuine connection' to the state in question) is already reflected in the law of many countries that do not permit citizenship transmission by descent beyond one generation. The transmissibility of nationality to second and subsequent generations was, to give one example, a significant policy issue for the British government before it settled on the first generation rule. Representations for, effectively, perpetual transmission made by British communities in foreign countries were heartfelt. In 1918, the President of the British Chamber of Commerce in Argentina explained that there were 30,000 British subjects in Argentina 'who remain entirely British in language and sympathy through several generations and whose connection with the Mother country it was very desirable to keep alive'. He sought the restoration of the law permitting the trans-generational registration of the children of British subjects.[96]

The argument for a generational limit on citizenship descent is better understood in such a context, than by treating it as a repeal of undeserved perpetual access to privileged citizenship (descent does not, in all cases, guarantee privilege. It may just as easily confer citizenship of a disfavoured

95 Boll, *Multiple Nationality and International Law*, 1.

96 UK National Archives, HO 45/11902: 'Nationality of Married Women', CO Minutes, 'Nationality of Children of British subjects born abroad. Observations on H.O. Memo'. Report of visit by Mr Gibson, 6 December 1918. The BNSA Act was amended in 1922, to permit (paternal) second generation registration of British subjects.

country). What the Argentinian example demonstrates is not that its British subjects wanted to retain their right to live in the United Kingdom, but that they wanted to retain their 'ethnic' distinctiveness. Ethnicity (and other identity markers that are considered indelible) is an exclusionary basis for citizenship, and indeed is antithetical to the neutral character of modern citizenship that remains one of the latter's principal virtues.

Recognition of the problems of citizenship maldistribution should not lead to the conclusion that one citizenship alone should be permitted for individuals or families. The idea that all immediate family members share a nationality has merit (allowing families to live securely together[97]), although it contributed importantly to the policy of conditional marital nationality in the past. Had a woman married to a foreigner been permitted to retain her native citizenship at the same time as acquiring her husband's, the experience of loss, the existential injury, would have been avoided. However, as we saw, this would not have satisfied many citizenship equality campaigners. For them, central to the experience of being a citizen, was the principle that its loss must only happen by a voluntary and deliberate act on the part of the citizen. In this argument, we saw the early expression of the principle that citizenship 'belongs' to the citizen, and not to the state. There are, of course, limits to this principle. But, if we were to apply a residency test or a no-transmission test to all, including birthright citizens, we would tilt the balance again towards citizenship as 'owned' by the state. Adverse consequences in individual cases would not be the only concern; the shift would facilitate the draconian policies of citizenship deprivation that were practised in the past and that governments are again contemplating or introducing today as a response to 'home-grown' terrorism.

Such policies are not incomprehensible. It is especially shocking that a citizen should terrorise the country that offers territorial security, the place that is, conceptually, jurisdictionally and often literally, his or her home. But, we are reminded that illegal conduct and its punishment do not differentiate between citizen and alien, that disloyalty is not exclusive to citizens, and even that treason can be committed by aliens

[97] Karen Knop, discussing the 'relational' character of nationality, makes this point, while also defending dual or multiple citizenship for individuals. Knop, 'Relational Nationality: On Gender and Nationality in International Law', in T. Alexander Aleinikoff and Douglas Klusmeyer (eds), *Citizenship Today: Global Perspectives and Practices* (Carnegie Endowment for International Peace, 2001).

(counterintuitive as this may seem). We may be morally outraged by citizens who turn against their own state, but outrage is an unsatisfactory basis for the law. It is also the thin-end-of the wedge. To tie citizenship to conduct or character is, again, to undermine the moral neutrality that, paradoxically, makes citizenship a less dangerous status than other forms of identity marker, and that makes opportunistic citizenship inoffensive. To tie citizenship to residence is, likewise, to condition citizenship upon conduct, to draw the dangerous line between 'real' citizens and others. Assumptions of disallegiant conduct and assumptions about conjugal residence provided the justification for conditional marital nationality in the past. We can recognise this injustice now.

Conclusion

It is meaningless to talk of a person as a citizen if he or she is not permitted to return or resort to, and seek the protection of his or her country of citizenship. Security of home and harbour does not require exclusivity. The extension of citizenship to others, or the fact that others hold citizenship, does not diminish a person's enjoyment or entitlement (just as an increase in family membership does not erode a person's status as a member, or diminish a family's 'family-ness'). In the words of Patrick Weil, 'there is no limit to the expansion of the number of citizens by transmission . . . [Citizenship] is both a club that limits entrance from outsiders and a public good which places no inherent limits on increases through transmission'.[98]

The language of allegiance (still commonly used in law and international relations) as entailing a type of contractual relationship with the state is better expressed as an 'equitable' relationship, engaging a duty of protection on the part of the state: a duty that is not contingent on personal conduct or the demonstration of virtue. To require citizenship to have no meaning in itself, apart from particular, valorised conduct, is to strip away the membership of the national community that constitutes modern identity. It is, to return to Arendt's conceptualisation, to render a person a non-person, a bare, apolitical person. But, it is, even more fundamentally, to strip a person of an essential means of meeting the core human need for a place in the world.

[98] Patrick Weil, 'From Conditional to Secured and Sovereign', 625.

In either case, citizenship is revealed as an existential quality. We throw the baby out with the bathwater if we dismiss this quality, paradoxically, in the quest for human equality and even compassion for non-citizens. We would render ourselves vulnerable in the name of combating vulnerability. It is this we learn from a gendered history of citizenship in the modern constitutional state.

BIBLIOGRAPHY

Secondary sources cited

Kerry Abrams, 'Citizen Spouse' (2013) 101 *California Law Review* 407.

Alexander Aleinikoff, *Semblances of Sovereignty: The Constitution, the State, and American Citizenship* (Harvard University Press, 2002).

Benedict Anderson, *Imagined Communities: Reflections on the Origin and Spread of Nationalism* (Verso, 1983).

Bridget Anderson, Matthew Gibney and Emunuela Paoletti, 'Citizenship, Deportation and the Boundaries of Belonging' 15 (2011) *Citizenship Studies* 547.

Hannah Arendt, *The Origins of Totalitarianism* [1951] (Harcourt, 1976).

Kif Augustine-Adams, '"She consents implicitly": Women's Citizenship, Marriage and Liberal Political Theory in Late-Nineteenth and Early-Twentieth Century Argentina' (2002) 13 *Journal of Women's History* 8.

'"With Notice of the Consequences": Liberal Political Theory, Marriage, and Women's Citizenship in the United States' (2002) 6 *Citizenship Studies* 5.

Suheir Azzouni, 'Palestine: Palestinian Authority and Israeli-Occupied Territories', in Sanja Kelly and Julia Breslin (eds) *Women's Rights in the Middle East and North Africa: Progress Amid Resistance* (Rowman & Littlefield, 2010).

Jacqueline Bhabha, 'The 'Mere Fortuity of Birth'? Children, Mothers, Borders, and the Meaning of Citizenship' in Seyla Benhabib and Judith Resnik (eds), *Migrations and Mobilities: Citizenship, Borders, and Gender* (New York University Press, 2009).

M. Page Baldwin, 'Subject to Empire: Married Women and the British Nationality and Status of Aliens Act' (2001) 40 *The Journal of British Studies* 522.

C. A. Bayly, *The Birth of the Modern World: 1780–1914* (Blackwell, 2004).

Nitza Berkovitch, *From Motherhood to Citizenship: Women's Rights and International Organizations* (Johns Hopkins University Press, 1999).

Christophe Bertossi, 'Country Report: France' (EUDO Citizenship Observatory, 2010).

Alexander M. Bickel, 'Citizen or Person? What is Not Granted Cannot be Taken Away', *The Morality of Consent* (Yale University Press, 1975).

'Citizenship in the American Constitution' (1973) 15 *Arizona Law Review* 369.

Beroë Bicknell, 'The Nationality of Married Women' (1934) 20 *Transactions of the Grotius Society* (published by the British Institute of International and Comparative Law) 106.

William Blackstone, *Commentaries on the Laws of England* [4 vols, 1765–1769] (University of Chicago Press, 1979).

Javier Bleichmar, 'Deportation as Punishment: A Historical Analysis of the British Practice of Banishment and its Impact on Modern Constitutional Law' (1999) 14 *Georgetown Immigration Law Journal* 144.

Alfred M. Boll, *Multiple Nationality and International Law* (Martinus Nijhoff, 2007) 245.

Edwin Borchard, 'The Diplomatic Protection of Citizens Abroad', 1913 (PhD dissertation, Columbia University; Nabu Public Domain Reprints) 497.

'Opinions of the Mixed Claims Commission, United States and Germany' (1926) 20 *American Journal of International Law* 69.

Linda Bosniak, 'Citizenship Denationalized' (2000) *Indiana Journal of Global Legal Studies* 447.

The Citizen and the Alien: Dilemmas of Contemporary Membership (Princeton University Press, 2002).

Candice Bredbenner, *A Nationality of Her Own: Women, Marriage, and the Law of Citizenship* (University of California Press, 1999).

Rogers Brubaker, *Citizenship and Nationhood in France and Germany* (Harvard University Press, 1992).

Kathleen Burke, *Old World, New World: Great Britain and America from the Beginning* (Atlantic Monthly Press, 2008).

Joseph Carens, 'Aliens and Citizens: The Case for Open Borders' (1987) 49 *The Review of Politics* 251.

J. P. Chamberlain, 'Married Women's Naturalization Act' (1923) 9 *American Bar Association Journal* 57.

David Cole, 'Against Citizenship as a Predicate for Basic Rights' (2007) 75 *Fordham Law Review* 2541.

Nancy F. Cott, 'Marriage and Women's Citizenship in the United States, 1830–1934' (1998) 103 *American Historical Review* 1443.

Nancy Cott, *Public Vows: A History of Marriage and the Nation* (Harvard University Press, 2000).

Lucas Crane, 'The Nationality of Married Women' (1925) 7 *Journal of Comparative Legislation and International Law* 53.

Richard Dagger, 'Republican Citizenship', in Engin F Isin and Bryan S Turner (eds) *Handbook of Citizenship Studies* (Sage Publications, 2002) 146.

Catherine Dauvergne, *Making People Illegal: What Globalization Means for Migration and Law* (Cambridge University Press, 2008).

Francis Déak, 'Research in International Law, Draft Conventions on Nationality, Responsibility of States, Territorial Waters; League of Nations, Conference for the Codification of International Law' (Review) (1930) 30 *Columbia Law Review* 142.

A. V. Dicey, 'A Common Citizenship for the English Race' (1897) 71 *Contemporary Review* 457.

Lawrence Distasi, 'Derived Aliens: Derivative Citizenship and Italian-American Women During World War II' (2011) 9 *Italian Americana* 23.

Ann Dummett and Andrew Nicol, *Subjects, Citizens, Aliens and Others* (Weidenfeldand Nicolson, 1990).

Jaci Eisenberg, 'The Status of Women: A Bridge from the League of Nations to the United Nations' (2013) 4 *Journal of International Organizations Studies* 8.

Melissa Feinberg, *Elusive Equality: Gender, Citizenship, and the Limits of Democracy in Czechoslovakia, 1918–1950* (University of Pittsburgh Press, 2006).

John Finnis, 'Nationality, Alienage and Constitutional Principle', University of Oxford Faculty of Law Legal Studies Research Paper Series, Working Paper No. 08/2008.

Peter Flora (ed), *State Formation, Nation Building, and Mass Politics in Europe: The Theory of Stein Rokkan* (Oxford University Press, 1999).

Richard W. Flournoy, 'The New British Imperial Law of Nationality' (1915) 9 *The American Journal of International Law* 870.

'The New Married Women's Citizenship Law' (1924) 33 *Yale Law Journal* 159.

'Nationality Convention, Protocols and Recommendations Adopted by the First Conference on the Codification of International Law' (1930) 24 *American Journal of International Law* 467.

Richard W. Flournoy and Manley O. Hudson (eds) *A Collection of Nationality Laws of Various Countries as Contained in Constitutions, Statutes, and Treaties* (Oxford University Press, New York, 1929).

Martha Gardner, *The Qualities of a Citizen: Women, Immigration and Citizenship, 1870–1965* (Princeton University Press, 2005).

J. W. Garner, Editorial Comment, 'Uniformity of Law in Respect to Nationality' (1925) 19 *American Journal of International Law* 530.

Matthew Gibney, '"A Very Transcendental Power": Denaturalisation and the Liberalisation of Citizenship in the United Kingdom' (2013) 61 *Political Studies* 637.

Philip Girard, '"If two ride a horse, one must ride in front": Married Women's Nationality and the Law in Canada 1880–1950' (2013) 94 *The Canadian Historical Review* 28.

Evelyn Nakano Glenn, *Unequal Freedom: How Race and Gender Shaped American Citizenship and Labor* (Harvard University Press, 2002).

Warren H. Goodman, 'The Origins of the War of 1812: A Survey of Changing Interpretations' (1941) 28 *The Mississippi Valley Historical Record* 171.

Charles Gordon, 'The Citizen and the State: Power of Congress to Expatriate American Citizens' (1964–5) 53 *Georgetown Law Journal* 315.

Daniel Gorman, *Imperial Citizenship: Empire and the Question of Belonging* (Manchester University Press, 2006).

Radha Govil and Alice Edwards, 'Women, Nationality and Statelessness' in Alice Edwards and Laura van Waas (eds) *Nationality and Statelessness under International Law* (Cambridge University Press, 2014).

Jürgen Habermas, 'Citizenship and National Identity' (1990), Appendix II, *Between Facts and Norms* (Polity Press, 1997).

Jennifer Ngaire Heuer, *The Family and the Nation: Gender and Citizenship in Revolutionary France, 1789–1830* (Cornell University Press, 2007).

Ernest Hover, 'Citizenship of Women in the United States' (1932) 26 *American Journal of International Law* 700.

Manley O. Hudson, *Report on Nationality, Including Statelessness* (International Law Commission, Yearbook, 1952, Vol II).

Helen Irving, 'Still Call Australia Home: Citizenship and the Right of Abode' (2008) 30 *Sydney Law Review* 133.

J. Mervyn Jones, *British Nationality Law* (Clarendon Press, Oxford, 1956).

Christian Joppke, 'Comparative Citizenship: A Restrictive Turn in Europe?' (2008) 2 *Journal of Law and Ethics of Human Rights* 128.

Kenneth Karst, *Belonging to America: Equal Citizenship and the Constitution* (Yale University Press, 1989).

Linda Kerber, *No Constitutional Right to be Ladies: Women and the Obligations of Citizenship* (Hill & Wang, 1998).

'The Paradox of Women's Citizenship in the Early Republic: The Case of Martin vs. Massachusetts, 1805' (1992) 97 *American Historical Review* 351.

'Toward a History of Statelessness in America' (2005) 57 *American Quarterly* 735.

Alison Kesby, *The Right to Have Rights: Citizenship, Humanity, and International Law* (Oxford University Press, 2012).

James H. Kettner, *The Development of American Citizenship, 1608–1870* (University of North Carolina Press, 1978).

Karen Knop and Christine Chinkin, 'Remembering Chrystal Macmillan: Women's Equality and Nationality in International Law' (2001) 22 *Michigan Journal of International Law* 523.

Karen Knop, 'Relational Nationality: On Gender and Nationality in International Law', in T. Alexander Aleinikoff and Douglas Klusmeyer (eds) *Citizenship Today: Global Perspectives and Practices* (Carnegie Endowment for International Peace, 2001).

Dimitry Kochenov and Benedikt Pirker, 'Deporting Citizens within the European Union: A Counter-Intuitive Trend' (2013) 19 *Columbia Journal of European Law* 341.

Will Kymlicka, 'Responsible Citizenship' (2012) 4 *Trudeau Foundation Papers* 56.

Will Kymlicka and Wayne Norman 'Return of the Citizen: A Survey of Recent Work on Citizenship Theory' (1994) *Ethics* 104(2) 352.

Margaret Lambie, 'Presumption of Cessation of Citizenship: Its Effect on International Claims' (1930) 24 *American Journal of International Law* 264.

Bertha Lutz, 'Nationality of Married Women in the American Republics' (1926) *Bulletin of the Pan American Union*, April.

Heather MacClintock, 'Sexism, Surnames, and Social Progress: The Conflict of Individual Autonomy and Government Preferences in Laws Regarding Name Changes at Marriage' (2010) 24 *Temple International Law and Comparative Law Journal* 277.

Audrey Macklin, 'Citizenship Revocation, the Privilege to Have Rights and the Production of the Alien' (2014) 40 *Queen's Law Journal* 2.

'Who is the Citizen's Other? Considering the Heft of Citizenship' (2007) 8 *Theoretical Inquiries in Law* 333.

Chrystal Macmillan, 'Nationality of Married Women: Present Tendencies' (1925) *Journal of Comparative Legislation and International Law* 142.

F. W. Maitland, *The Constitutional History of England* [1908] (Cambridge University Press, 1963).

T. H. Marshall, *Citizenship and Social Class: And Other Essays* (Cambridge University Press, 1950).

David A. Martin and T. Alexander Aleinikoff, 'Double Ties' *Foreign Policy* (133) (November–December 2002) 80.

Sidney Eve Matrix, 'Mediated Citizenship and Contested Belongings: Canadian War Brides and the Fictions of Naturalization' (2007) *Topia* (17) 68.

Carol Miller, '"Geneva – The Key to Equality": Inter-war Feminists and the League of Nations' (1994) 3 *Women's History Review* 219.

David Hunter Miller, 'The Hague Codification Conference' (1930) 24 *American Journal of International Law* 674.

Robert S. Miller, 'Recent Developments in the Law Controlling Nationality of Married Women' (1932–33) 1 *George Washington Law Review* 330.

Peter Nyers, 'The Accidental Citizen: Acts of Sovereignty and (Un)Making Citizenship', (2006) 35 *Economy and Society* 22.

Lester B. Orfield, 'The Citizenship Act of 1934' (1934–5) 99 *Chicago Law Review*.

Jürgen Osterhammel, *The Transformation of the World: A Global History of the Nineteenth Century* (Princeton University Press, 2014).

Dorothy Page, '"A Married Woman, or a Minor, Lunatic, or Idiot": The Struggle of British Women Against Disability in Nationality, 1914–1933', 1984 (PhD thesis, University of Otago).

Lennart Palsson, *Marriage in Comparative Conflict of Laws: Substantive Conditions* (Springer, 1981).

Cynthia Patterson, 'Citizenship and Gender in the Ancient World: The Experience of Athens and Rome' in Seyla Benhabib and Judith Resnik (eds) *Migrations and Mobilities: Citizenship, Borders, and Gender* (New York University Press, 2009).

G. G. Phillimore, 'Nationality of Married Women' (1917) *Journal of the Society of Comparative Legislation* 165.

Laura Reanda, 'The Commission on the Status of Women', in Philip Alston (ed), *The United Nations and Human Rights: A Critical Appraisal* (Clarendon Press, Oxford, 1992).

J. S. Reeves, 'Nationality of Married Women' (1923) 17 *American Journal of International Law* 97.

Ruth Rubio Marin, 'The Achievement of Female Suffrage in Europe: On Women's Citizenship' (2013) 12 *International Journal of Constitutional Law* 4.

Saskia Sassen, *Territory, Authority, Rights: From Medieval to Global Assemblages* (Princeton University Press, 2006).

Peter H. Schuck and Rogers M. Smith, *Citizenship Without Consent: Illegal Aliens in the American Polity* (Yale University Press, 1985).

James Brown Scott, 'Nationality, Jus Soli or Jus Sanguinis' (1930) 24 *American Journal of International Law* 58.

Catheryn Seckler-Hudson, *Statelessness: With Special Reference to the United States* (Digest Press, 1934).

Ayelet Shachar, *The Birthright Lottery: Citizenship and Global Inequality* (Harvard University Press, 2009).

Ernest J. Schuster, 'The Peace Treaty in its Effects on Private Property' (1920–1) *British Year Book of International Law* 167.

Gerry Simpson, 'International Law in Diplomatic History', in James Crawford and Martti Koskenniemi (eds) *The Cambridge Companion to International Law* (Cambridge University Press, 2012).

Robert D. Sloane, 'Breaking the Genuine Link: The Contemporary International Legal Regulation of Nationality' (2009) 50 *Harvard International Law Review* 1.

G. Addison Smith, 'British Nationality and Naturalization' (1906–7) 18 *The Juridical Review* 273.

Peter J. Spiro, *Beyond Citizenship: American Identity After Globalization* (Oxford University Press, 2008).

Brigitte Studer, 'Citizenship as Contingent National Belonging' (2001) 13 *Gender and History* 622.

Laura Tabili, 'Outsiders in the Land of Their Birth: Exogamy, Citizenship, Identity in War and Peace' (2005) 44 *Journal of British Studies* 796.

George T. Tamaki, 'The Canadian Citizenship Act, 1946' (1947) 7 *The University of Toronto Law Journal* 68.

Charles Tilly, 'The Emergence of Citizenship in France and Elsewhere' (1995) 40 *International Review of Social History* 223.

Barbara J. Todd, 'Written in Her Heart: Married Women's Separate Allegiance in English Law' in Tim Stretton and Krista J. Kesselring (eds) *Married Women and the Law: Coverture in England and the Common Law World* (McGill-Queen's University Press, 2013).

John Torpey, *The Invention of the Passport: Surveillance, Citizenship and the State* (Cambridge University Press, 2000).

E. J. Trevelyan, 'Marriages between English Women and Natives of British India' (1917) 17 *Journal of the Society of Comparative Legislation* 223.

Waldo Emerson Waltz, *The Nationality of Married Women: A Study of Domestic Policies and International Legislation* (The University of Illinois Press, Urbana, 1937).

Patrick Weil, 'From Conditional to Secured and Sovereign: The New Strategic Link between the Citizen and the Nation-State in a Globalized World' (2011) 9 *International Journal of Constitutional Law* 615.

How to be French: Nationality in the Making Since 1789 (Duke University Press, 2008).

The Sovereign Citizen: Denaturalization and the Origins of the American Republic (University of Pennsylvania Press, 2013).

Hattie Plum Williams, 'The Road to Citizenship' (1912) 27 *Political Science Quarterly* 399.

Melissa S. Williams, 'Nonterritorial Boundaries of Citizenship' in Seyla Benhabib, Ian Shapiro, and Danilo Petranovic (eds) *Identities, Affiliations, and Allegiances* (Cambridge University Press, 2007).

Aristide R. Zolberg, *A Nation by Design: Immigration Policy in the Fashioning of America* (Harvard University Press, 2006).

INDEX

African Charter on Human and People's Rights, 27
Afroyim v. *Rusk*, 255
Aleinikoff, Alexander, 242
Alien Property Custodian, United States, 140
Alienage, consequences, 87, 88
Alienage, declaration, 59, 109, 122, 129, 166, 167, 200, 216
Aliens Act 1905, UK, 92
Aliens Acts, 87
Aliens Restriction Act 1919, UK, 92
Allegiance
  historical, 40
  perpetual, 20, 38, 39, 40, 41, 44, 45, 64, 66, 67, 73, 97, 261, 262
American marriage to German, 139
American marriages to titled foreigners, 154
American Revolution, 33, 34, 52, 247
American Society of International Law, 198, 199, 220
American soldiers
  marriage to German women, 209
Arendt, Hannah, 21, 22, 26, 253, 255, 256, 273
Argentina, 10, 100, 151, 230, 231, 235, 275
  British community, 271
Asian
  racial citizenship disqualifications, 14, 152, 159, 223
Astor, Nancy, 181
Auden, W.H., 84
Augustine-Adams, Augustine, 15
Australia, 179
  'White Australia', 159
  debates on marital denaturalization, 90
  House of Representatives resolution against marital denaturalisation, 1926, 167
  implementation of Hague Nationality Convention, 1936, 176
  marital denaturalisation. *See* Nationality Act, 1920
  Parliamentary Committee on marital nationality, 147
  restoration of political rights to denaturalised women, 25, 179
  women's franchise, 16
Australian marriage to German, 112

Baldwin, M. Page, 11
Bancroft Treaties, 64
Banishment, 50, 266
Bayly, C.A., 32, 36
Bedford, Sybille, 84
Belgium, 9, 109, 113, 150, 151, 224, 235
Bennett, Richard, 101
Bentham, Ethel, 113, 167
Bickel, Alexander, 88, 89, 241, 242
Bigler-Eggenberger, Margrith, 142
Birthright lottery, 28, 243
Blackstone, William, 19, 38, 51
BNSA Act. *See* British Nationality and Status of Aliens Act, 1914 (UK)
Bolivia, 9, 231, 235
Boll, Alfred, 216, 252, 258, 271
Booth, Frederick, 106, 107
Borchard, Edwin, 220, 221, 222
Bosniak, Linda, 238, 242, 243

Brazil, 4, 10, 224, 230, 235
Constitution, 10
Federation for the Advancement of Women, 231
Bredbenner, Candice, 14, 18, 21, 63, 92, 98, 103, 118, 119, 159
Brennan, William, 123, 254
Britain
women's franchise, 16
British marriage to American, 111, 210
British marriage to Austrian, 130, 142
British marriage to German, 127, 133, 137
British marriage to Italian, 138, 143, 144
British marriage to Russian, 109
British marriage to Spaniard, 112
British marriages to Japanese, 131
British Nationality and Status of Aliens (in New Zealand) Act 1923, 177
British Nationality and Status of Aliens Act 1914, 58, 75, 86, 100, 125, 160, 212
British naturalisation laws. *See* Naturalization Act 1870
Burnyeat, Hildegarde, 125
Butcher, John, 126, 127, 166, 167, 177

Cable Act, 1922, 14, 17, 70, 91, 119, 139, 151, 152, 154, 159, 160, 161, 164, 165, 184, 200, 206, 209, 210, 268
Cable, John, 54, 71, 91, 139, 155, 158
California, women's franchise, 95
Canada, 11, 80
'White Canada', 12, 159
Canadian marriages to Americans, 94, 101, 104, 175. *See also* war brides
concerns over marital naturalisation, 163
debates on marital denaturalisation, 90
implementation of Hague Nationality Convention, 1931, 175
naturalisation law. *See* Naturalization Act
prostitution and marital naturalisation, 83
women's franchise, 16
Canterbury Women's Institution, New Zealand, 140
Catholicism and marital citizenship, 226
Cazalet, Victor, 2, 91, 167
Cecil, Robert, 198
CEDAW. *See* Convention on the Elimination of All Forms of Discrimination Against Women
Chile, 9, 219, 226, 231
Constitution, 9
Delegation at the League of Nations Conference on the Codification of International Law, The Hague, 218
China, 9, 109, 235
Chinese. *See* racial disqualifications
citizenship
revocation laws, 21st century, 265
citizenship and right not to be excluded, 257
citizenship resumption, 110
Citizenship, Expatriation, and Protection Abroad, Congressional Report 1906, 67
Civil Code, French, 64
Civil Code, French, 1804
'Napoleonic Code', 5
Cockburn, Alexander, 65
Colombia, 139, 224, 235
Comitis v. *Parkerson*, 97
Committee of Representatives of Women's International Organisations, 89
Common code, British nationality, 106, 159, 168, 169, 181, 186
Commonwealth Conference on Nationality and Citizenship 1947, 190
Commonwealth Expert Committee on Nationality, 1947, 162
Conference on the Operation of Dominion Legislation, 1929 UK, 164

Conflicts of marriage law, 85, 86
Congress of Vienna, 1815, 35
Congress, United States, 17, 33, 53, 69, 95, 96, 140, 154, 195, 231, 263, 277
Convention on the Elimination of All Forms of Discrimination Against Women, 1, 236
Convention on the Nationality of Married Women, 1, 2, 6, 21, 22, 27, 29, 107, 191, 234
Cosmopolitan citizenship, 29, 250
Cott, Nancy, 13
Coverture, 12, 19, 20, 42, 67, 68, 71, 97
Cuba, 9, 151, 226, 231
  Delegation at the League of Nations Conference on the Codification of International Law, The Hague, 222
Czechoslovak Republic, 9, 12
Czechoslovakia, 9, 12, 13, 90, 225

Dagger, Richard, 247
Dauvergne, Catherine, 264
de Gouges, Olympe, 248
de Haven-Alten, Augusta, 140, 155
Declaration of Independence, 1776, 33, 52
Denizen status, 50
Denmark, 114, 235
Desertion by husband, 111
Dicey, A.V., 117, 120, 121
Dickinson, Willoughby, 105, 127, 138
Dillingham Commission, 82
Dominican Republic, 235
Dominions
  response to Hague Nationality Convention, 175
Dominions, British, 75, 125, 162, 164, 169, 172, 176, 179, 182, 183, 184, 190
Dual nationality, xiii, 4, 7, 39, 43, 56, 57, 59, 66, 71, 85, 93, 106, 107, 115, 158, 163, 164, 169, 174, 176, 191, 194, 204, 212, 213, 215, 216, 218, 265, 270
Dummett, Ann, 11
Duncan-Hughes, John, 90, 129, 167

Ecuador, 231
Egypt, 235
Enemy Aliens Tribunals, 130, 132, 145, 146
Equalisation Act 1934, United States, 156
Ethiopia, 235
European Convention on Nationality, 27, 216
European Court of Justice, 259
Expatriation Act 1868, United States, 57, 61, 63, 97
Expatriation Act 1907, United States, 13, 14, 17, 21, 55, 67, 74, 97, 110, 117, 137, 152, 156, 159, 197, 214, 254, 255, 268

Feinberg, Melissa, 12, 13, 89, 90
Feudalism, 38, 39, 52
Finnis, John, 260, 261
Fitzroy Case, 97, 98
Forbes, George, 102
Fourteenth Amendment
  United States Constitution 1868, 8, 13, 34, 44, 57, 69, 96, 97, 153, 160
France, 3, 8, 10, 11, 16, 24, 32, 34, 37, 43, 64, 81, 87, 101, 108, 111, 116, 132, 150, 227, 278
  revolutionary citizenship, 43, 63, 88
Frankfurter, Felix, 253, 254
French
  concept of citizenship, 11
  Civil Code. *See* Napoleonic Code
French Revolution, 34
Gardner, Martha, 13
Garran, Robert, 163
Gual, Florence, 92
German
  Nuremberg Citizenship Law, 141
German-American Mixed Claims Commission, 214

Germany, 8, 26, 37, 84, 112, 125, 127, 134, 141, 142, 146, 178, 214, 225
  Nazi citizenship law, 141
Girard, Philip, 12
Girouard v. *United States*, 118
Glyn-Jones, William, 105
Goldman, Emma, 84
Gordon, Charles, 264
Gorman, Daniel, 12
Greece, 235
Guatemala, 109, 235
Habermas, Jürgen, 33, 257
Hague Nationality Convention, viii, 86, 104, 107, 108, 141, 142, 144, 172, 173, 174, 175, 176, 184, 186, 196, 198, 199, 204, 209, 213, 217, 222, 223, 224, 225, 226, 228, 229, 233, 240
Harcourt, Lewis, 8, 106, 107, 190, 275
Harvard Law School
  Draft Convention on Nationality, 201, 202, 203, 204, 213
Harvey, Thomas, 105
Hearne, John, 185, 186, 189
Herrick, Manuel, 155
Heuer, Jennifer Ngaire, 10, 87
Holmes, Oliver Wendell, 119
Holt, Richard, 128
Honduras, 109
Hudson, Manley O., 233
Hungary, 9, 111, 181, 225

Imperial Conference, 112, 113, 161, 164, 168, 169, 170, 175, 176, 181, 182, 183, 187
Institut de Droit International, 194, 195, 202
Inter-American Commission of Women, 209, 223, 232
International Alliance of Women, 223
International Alliance of Women for Suffrage and Equal Citizenship, 232
International Committee of Catholic Women for the Nationality of Married Women, 226
International Co-operative Women's Guild, 232
International Council of Women, 76, 150, 156, 223, 229
International Court of Justice, 48, 244
International Covenant on Civil and Political Rights, 258
International Institute of Law, 67
International Law Association, 200, 202, 221
International Law Commission, 221, 233, 234, 235, 258
International Woman Suffrage Alliance, 200
International Women's Committee of the Labour and Socialist International, 232
Internment of enemy aliens, 123, 124, 132, 135, 138, 145, 146
Iraq, 235
Ireland
  Citizenship Act 1956, 189
  Constitution 1922, 183
  Constitution 1937, 189
  Nationality and Citizenship Act 1935, 108, 176, 184, 188
Italy, 109, 111, 141, 144, 227
  Fascist citizenship law, 142, 144

Japan, 3, 8, 37, 111, 225, 227
Japanese Citizenship Law 1899, 109
Jewish women, 84, 141
Joppke, Christian, 268
jus sanguinis rule, 36, 37, 44, 171, 196, 231
jus soli rule, 36, 37, 44, 50, 76, 147, 171, 188, 196, 231
  exceptions, 37

Karst, Kenneth, 243
Kelly v. *Owen*, 62
Kennedy v. *Mendoza-Martinez*, 123, 254
Kerber, Linda, 20
Kesby, Alison, 248, 249
Kymlicka, Will, 238, 250, 251

Lambie, Margaret, 160
League of Nations, 2, 87, 89, 107, 151, 161, 167, 175, 185, 186, 189, 198, 199, 201, 205, 211, 223, 224, 226, 227, 228, 230, 232, 279

League of Nations (*cont.*)
Committee for the Study of the Legal Status of Women, 230
Committee of Experts on the Progressive Codification of International Law, 199, 201, 203
Conference on the Codification of International Law, The Hague, 18, 205, 212, 217, 221, 224, 228, 232
London, Meyer, 155
Lyons, Joseph, 183, 227
Lyttelton, Edith, 167

MacDonald, Ramsay, 181
Mackenzie v. *Hare*, 69, 253, 254, 264
Mackenzie, Ethel, 69, 95, 96, 97, 98, 254, 255
Macklin, Audrey, 238, 243, 256, 258, 270
Macmillan, Chrystal, 111, 112, 113, 137, 172, 173, 222, 237
Macphail, Agnes, 90
Maitland, F.W., 120
Man Without a Country, 94
Mann, Edward, 168
Mann, Erika, 84
Marriage termination, 68, 70, 110, 111, 153, 207, 214, 215
Married women and husband's name, 3
Married Women's Independent Nationality Act. *See* Cable Act
Married Women's Property Acts, 20, 78
Marshall, T.H., 243
Matrix, Sidney Eve, 81
McClure-Smith, Hugh, 234
McDonald, John, 101
Mexico, 9, 134, 231, 235
Mills, Ogden, 156
Monaco, 225
Montevideo Convention 1933, 108, 230, 232, 233
Montevideo Treaty, 1933, 108, 157, 229, 230, 232, 233
Morris, Edward, 227

Nansen certificates, 211
Napoleonic Code
French Civil Code 1804, 5, 7, 10, 11, 34, 35, 44, 64, 74, 77, 116, 197
National Association of Women Lawyers, 204
National Council for Women, 166, 172
National Insurance Act, 1911 UK, 105
Nationalism, 36
Nationality Act 1948, United Kingdom, 147
Nationality Act 1920, Australia, 112
Nationality of Married Women Bill, United Kingdom, 156, 166
Nationality of Married Women Pass the Bill Committee, 222
Naturalization Act 1870, United Kingdom, 7, 12, 58, 66, 74, 76, 93, 109, 166, 197
Naturalization Act 1903, Australia, 14
Naturalization Act 1790, United States, 53
Naturalization Act 1795, United States, 53
Naturalization Act 1844, United Kingdom, 62
Naturalization Act 1855, United States, 6, 55
Naturalization Act 1914, Canada, 101
Naturalization Act 1881, Canada, 266
Naturalization treaties, 64
Netherlands, 109, 225, 228, 234, 235
New Zealand
implementation of Hague Nationality Convention, 1934, 176
marital denaturalisation law. *See* British Nationality and Status of Aliens (in New Zealand) Act, 1923
nationality law and franchise, 163
restoration of political rights to denaturalised women, 177
women's franchise, 16
New Zealand marriage to American, 102
Nicol, Andrew, 11
Nineteenth Amendment, United States Constitution, 17, 119

Norman, Wayne, 238
Norway, 109, 114, 148, 225
Nottebohm case, 48, 244, 269
Numbers affected by marital denaturalisation laws, 24

O'Higgins, Kevin, 185, 187, 212
Oath of allegiance, 27, 38, 50, 51, 53, 65, 69, 116, 117, 118, 119, 120, 153
Oglivie Gordon, Maria, 172
Opportunistic citizenship, 82, 83, 269

Palestine, 27, 86, 258
Pan American Conference, 231
Pan American Union, 10, 157, 209, 230
Paraguay, 151
Parliament
  Canada, 24
  United Kingdom, 25, 45, 61, 91
Parliamentary Committee on the Nationality of Married Women, 1923 UK, 138
Parr, James, 102
Passports, 29, 30, 49, 82, 83, 91, 100, 102, 104, 109, 133, 140, 142, 143, 165, 187, 200, 209, 211
  League of Nations Passport Conference, 87
Pedder, John, 163
Pension Acts, 91
Pensions, 87, 93, 105
Pensions Act 1910, UK, 105
Perez v. *Brownell*, 70, 253
Perley, George, 163
Persia, 109
Peru, 231
Philippines, 27
Poland, 235
Politis, Nikolaos, 217
Portugal, 9, 109
Property rights and citizenship, 12, 16, 19, 20, 38, 43, 50, 52, 57, 58, 78, 79, 88, 90, 121, 138, 140, 208, 209, 250
Prostitutes, 83
Prostitution, 82, 85

Rancière, Jacques, 248, 249
Reanda, Laura, 235
Re-naturalisation, 70, 119, 125, 131, 135, 152, 174
Re-naturalisation in war, 125
Residence and citizenship, 39, 43, 44, 52, 53, 55, 63, 65, 70, 71, 82, 92, 101, 104, 111, 151, 152, 160, 161, 202, 203, 207, 209, 210, 213, 258, 267
Restoration of citizenship, United Kingdom, 135
  wives of enemy aliens, 129, 130
Restoration of citizenship, United States, 68
Right to vote, women's, 16, 17
Roberts, Charles, 128
Rogers, Edith, 158
Rogers, John, 17
Roosevelt, Franklin D., 232
Royal Commission into Naturalization, 1869 United Kingdom, 57, 61, 88, 166
Rubio Marin, Ruth, 16
Ruckgaber v. *Moore*, 68
Rumania, 93, 150, 225
Russia, 26, 83, 103, 104, 109
  1917 Revolution, 151

Salvador, 109
Samuel, Herbert, 126
Sandel, Michael, 247
Sandeman Allen, John, 167
Savorgnan v. *United States*, 253
School Teachers Superannuation Act, 1910 UK, 93
Schwimmer, Rosika, 118, 119
Seckler-Hudson, Catheryn, 207
Select Committee on The Nationality of Married Women, 1923, United Kingdom, 164, 165
Sex Disqualification (Removal) Act 1919, UK, 20, 93, 168
Shachar, Ayelet, 28, 243, 244, 245, 246, 259, 260, 271
Shanks v. *Du Pont*, 67, 97
Shelley v. *United States*, 119
Shelley, Rebecca, 119

Sherwell, Arthur, 128
Shipley, Ruth, 219
Shuck, Peter, 263
Siam, 109, 225
Smith, Rogers, 263
South Africa, 159
Soviet Union, 9, 84, 90, 104, 109, 151, 205, 235
Spain, 112, 143, 227
  Constitution, 1931, 143
  Fascist citizenship law, 143
Special Conference on Nationality and Naturalization, 1918 UK, 76, 162
Spivakovsky, Leonore, 103, 211
State formation, 31
Statelessness, marital, 205
  in the United States, 24, 207
Story, Joseph, 67
Sweden, 9, 114, 151, 226
Swiss marriages to Germans, 142
Switzerland, 3, 9, 37, 111, 142
Syria, 235

Tabili, Laura, 12, 137
Tangney, Dorothy, 147
Todd, Barbara, 12
Treaty of Versailles, 138
Trop v. *Dulles*, 254
Turkey, 226, 235

Undesirable women, 83, 110
Union Internationale des Ligues féminines catholiques, 227
United Kingdom. *See also* Naturalization Act 1870
  House of Commons resolution against marital denaturalisation, 1925, 167
  House of Lords, 59, 60, 61
  implementation of Hague Nationality Convention, 1933, 174
  marital naturalisation law 1844, 44, 51, 55, 58, 76, 177
  nationality law. *See* British Nationality and Status of Aliens Act
  naturalisation. *See* Naturalization Acts
  naturalisation by Act of Parliament, 50
  repeal of marital denaturalisation, 148
  Royal Commission into Naturalization 1869, 57, 61, 88, 166
United Nations
  Report on Statelessness, 206, 208
United Nations Commission on the Status of Women, 39, 230, 233, 234, 235, 280
United Nations Convention on the Nationality of Married Women, 1, 2, 6, 21, 22, 27, 29, 107, 191, 233, 234
United Nations Convention on the Reduction of Statelessness, 239, 246
United Nations Convention Relating to the Status of Refugees, 258
United Nations Declaration of Human Rights, 2, 239, 260
United Nations Economic and Social Council, 233, 234
United States, 151. *See also* Congress, Expatriation Act 1907
  Alien Act 1918, 84
  American marriages to Canadians, 24
  Delegation at the League of Nations Conference on the Codification of International Law, The Hague, 219, 221
  marital denaturalisation. *See* Expatriation Act 1907
  marital naturalisation law, 1855, 45, 54, 97
  Nationality Act 1940, 154
  naturalisation. *See* Naturalization Acts
  naturalisation power, 53
  repeal of marital denaturalisation. *See* Cable Act, 1922
  repeal of marital naturalisation, 159

women's franchise, 17. *See also* Nineteenth Amendment
United States Act of March 2 1907. *See* Expatriation Act 1907, United States
United States Supreme Court, 62, 67, 69, 70, 89, 95, 97, 118, 123, 255
Universal Declaration of Human Rights, 1948 United Nations, 21, 234, 235
Uruguay, 151, 231, 232

Venezuela, 5, 109

Waltz, Waldo Emerson, 196, 213, 232
War brides, Canadian, 24, 80, 81
War of 1812, Britain and United States, 60, 116, 277
Ward, Irene, 144
Ward, Joseph, 163
Warren, Earl, 70, 253, 254
Weil, Patrick, 22, 42, 44, 273
Westphalia, Treaties, 31, 35
Westphalian order, 31, 32, 249, 250
Widowhood, 66, 70, 93, 110, 111, 127, 200
Widowhood and citizenship, 54, 59, 64, 77, 81, 188, 214, 215
Wilkinson, Ellen, 73, 167
Williams, Melissa, 251
Wold, Emma, 195
Women's Consultative Committee on Nationality
League of Nations Conference on the Codification of International Law, The Hague, 223, 232
Women's International League for Peace and Freedom, 76, 223
Women's International Organisations, 186
Wong Kim Ark Case, 96
World's Young Women's Christian Association, 232

Young, Alexander, 103
Yugoslavia, 93, 235

For EU product safety concerns, contact us at Calle de José Abascal, 56–1°, 28003 Madrid, Spain or eugpsr@cambridge.org.

www.ingramcontent.com/pod-product-compliance
Lightning Source LLC
LaVergne TN
LVHW011525200926
848484LV00001B/152